AMERICAN ENERGY CINEMA

Energy and Society
Brian Black, Series Editor

AMERICAN ENERGY CINEMA

Edited by
Robert Lifset,
Raechel Lutz,
and
Sarah Stanford-McIntyre

WEST VIRGINIA UNIVERSITY PRESS / MORGANTOWN

ISBN 978-1-952271-76-2 (paperback) / 978-1-952271-77-9 (ebook)

Library of Congress Control Number: 2022049987

Cover design by Than Saffel
Cover image: Film still from *There Will Be Blood*. United Archives GmbH / Alamy Stock Photo

Contents

Part 1: When Disaster Strikes

Part 2: Energy and Nature

Part 5: Energy and the State

List of Illustrations

Figures

Tables

Introduction

*A*merican Energy Cinema investigates how Hollywood films have represented America's energy history from the beginning of the twentieth century through the early twenty-first.[1] The authors in this volume collectively argue that film is a prime medium through which we can understand how Americans wrestled with the promise and perils of energy consumption, production, and diffusion. They foreground the fact that no film is created in a vacuum. A film's artistic and narrative content cannot be separated from broader historical context and the industrialized and globalized American film industry is inextricable from interconnected energy systems. In this book, we understand energy systems to include a range of mineral and renewable sources from fossil fuels to nuclear energy, from the electricity grid to hydroelectric dams. In turn, we see energy and energy systems as shapers of human history that impact both daily life and the trajectory of large-scale social change. The search for energy has dramatically shaped geopolitical rivalries. Energy infrastructures have regulated the relationships between corporations, governments, and consumers. Energy security has been the catalyst for wars. The consequences of energy consumption have ongoing global environmental ramifications. As a result, the essays in this volume place energy's cinematic representations within a broader narrative of energy production, consumption, and transport.

Energy in America

The histories laid out in this book are inextricable from American efforts to harness and use an ever-increasing amount of energy. Energy is the foundation of all life on Earth. Solar energy drives photosynthesis, which feeds plant life, which in turn sustains an array of interconnected lifeforms. Though these cycles of energy remained mostly immutable for much of Earth's history, the past three centuries have seen a dramatic increase in human energy use. The United States has been at the forefront of energy production and consumption since the nineteenth century.

American commercial agriculture was a catalyst for increased energy use and early industrialization was powered by direct waterpower from dams and mills built on rivers. However, in the first half of the nineteenth century this was replaced by coal-fired steam engines. Factories grew in size and moved from the countryside to cities, propelling a wave of urbanization that lasted well into the twentieth century. Coal made possible the manufacturing of iron and steel. Coal also served as an energy source for new modes of transportation, such as railroads and steamships. Together, this increased the amount of energy consumed far beyond anything possible in a world powered by muscle, waterpower, and wood. Most importantly, the shift to coal also initiated human dependence on fossil fuels.

American reliance on mineral energy sources deepened in the second half of the nineteenth century due to the rise of the American oil industry and the widespread adoption of electrification. Oil was first used as an artificial illuminant, replacing whale oil for use in lamps, and then in transportation—cars, trucks, ships, and railroads—and more broadly as a fuel source across the industrial sector. As early as the mid-nineteenth century, such American energy dependence helped drive the nation to become a leading producer of oil. And over the next one hundred years, oil, coal, and natural gas helped fuel a national push for electrification. Electricity was developed as a form of artificial illumination in the 1890s and quickly replaced coal-fired steam engines in machines and motors. While electricity still mostly relied on fossil fuels, especially coal, hydroelectricity (turbines moved by running water) emerged as a highly publicized means of producing electricity in the early twentieth century. Whatever the fuel source, electrification did more to construct the modern world than anything since the transition to coal, transforming industrial and domestic life. For example, easy access to electricity jump-started the early film industry. By the middle of the twentieth century, oil, natural gas, coal, and newly developed nuclear energy were the most common sources of American electricity despite the continued presence of hydroelectric power. In the early twenty-first century, wind and solar power made important advances, reflecting a growing movement to eventually end reliance on fossil fuels.

Our Argument

Since the mid-nineteenth century, the United States has been the world's largest energy producer and consumer, and its sprawling energy industries helped shape the form and content of American media. Access to energy shaped the material reality of American culture, from the layouts of cities to the rise and fall of fashion trends. Such cultural touchstones were introduced and reinforced by the film industry, which, like many other American industries, was financially dependent upon access to cheap energy and the fossil fuel industry's deep pockets. For this reason, exploring energy cinema is one way to follow the linkages between American cultural production and changes in American politics, diplomacy, business, labor, and the environment.

Collectively, we see the essays in this volume as making a two-part argument. First, analysis of film production and funding highlights the connections between Hollywood, Washington, and Wall Street. As a result, top-down analysis of energy cinema reveals how elites and policymakers represented both key moments and long-term trends in the history of twentieth-century American energy policy and politics. Second, energy cinema provides a window into American popular understandings of energy. Bottom-up analysis of energy culture uncovers how audiences interpreted specific energy films and how energy was used as a metaphor for battles over race, class, and gender in the twentieth century. Such a mix of top-down and bottom-up—material and cultural—analysis is crucial to understanding the fossil fuel industry's grip on the American cultural imaginary and must frame any effort to imagine a post-petroleum future.

Energy, Film, and Culture

American Energy Cinema builds on a rich body of existing scholarship in energy history, environmental history, and the environmental humanities. Energy history as a field has grown dramatically, aligning itself with environmental history.[2] There is a growing interest among environmental historians in cultural, visual, and film studies.[3] Indicatively, edited volumes such as *Petrocultures* and *Energy Humanities* include essays on the portrayal of energy in individual films. However, *American Energy Cinema* is the first edited volume to exclusively and extensively address how filmmakers have portrayed energy and the energy industries across the twentieth and into the twenty-first century.[4]

Scholars of literature, especially those working in ecocriticism, have also provided analysis of select energy films, addressing energy cinema in the context of environmental film or ecocinema. They have completed groundbreaking analysis of cinematic visual aesthetics.[5] Similarly, the field of energy humanities, led by scholars such as Stephanie LeMenager and Imre Szeman, has strengthened the scholarly conversation about the representation of energy on screen and the resulting social and environmental entanglements. However, such scholarship could benefit from more thorough attention to the historically contingent, material connections between energy technologies, labor practices, financial systems, and cinematic representations of energy infrastructures. For this reason, this work seeks to bridge disciplinary divides, representing as much an effort to encourage more historians of energy, capitalism, and technology to take culture seriously as it is a call for scholars of film and culture to pay attention to the long historical trajectory of energy production and consumption. This volume collectively foregrounds that no energy system or work of cultural production exists in a vacuum, adding needed breadth and scope to existing analyses.

This volume situates individual films in their historical contexts, collectively asserting that the historian's methods and foci are crucial to the scholarly conversation in energy culture, energy humanities, and ecocinema. Our authors articulate the fundamental agency of filmmakers, producers, and actors and underscore the intentionality of their cinematic choices. Our contributors draw from a variety of analytical styles and theoretical traditions. Some take a materialist approach, emphasizing the flows of money between Hollywood and the fossil fuel industries and the ways in which Hollywood either became a mouthpiece for US foreign policy goals or dared to critique dominant narratives. Others focus on the symbolic or visual style of specific films, drawing on visual studies scholarship to consider shot composition, the gaze, and other filmic elements. Still others highlight plot analysis and critique the underlying or unremarked cultural norms reflected on screen. All provide key historical context that will help readers use individual films to better understand how cinema has echoed popular American anxieties, hopes, and tensions.

In making these arguments, the editors intentionally concentrated on films produced by and for Americans. We did this for two reasons. First, a global study of energy cinema, which has incredible potential, would have necessitated scholarly networks, literature awareness, and a cultural fluency that we, the editors, do not possess. Second, Hollywood is an international industry and American energy cinema has long been a part of the twentieth-century American imperial project—both as a tacit instrument of American soft power and as a vehicle to alternatively critique or enforce US foreign policy. We feel that such context helps to bind films made in the United States or made for the American public in a way that enables a collective analysis that would not be possible if our scale accounted for multiple national contexts of production and consumption. Though select films in these collections were made outside of the US, the perspectives of American audiences influenced marketing and, at times, the filmmaking process. All this said, we hope that future scholars will take up the challenge of analyzing energy cinema in international contexts.[6]

When Disaster Strikes

While we do not propose that energy cinema represents an artistically coherent genre, our authors do identify several broad and recurring themes that have shaped American films about energy throughout the twentieth and early twenty-first centuries. We view these themes as indicative of a cultural feedback loop in which popular anxieties and elite desires worked in mutually reinforcing tandem to build a dominant cultural understanding about appropriate energy production, consumption, and policy.

First, catastrophe drives the narrative in many energy films. In "Part 1: When Disaster Strikes," we see different ways in which energy disasters have been portrayed over time. In these films, energy system failures are sites of narrative tension and conflict. Julie Cohn's essay on *Where Were You When the Lights Went Out* (1968) analyses the film's uniquely comedic presentation of energy optimism in the face of a large-scale power outage. The film's upbeat tone stands in marked contrast to the later films in this section, which display the late-twentieth-century waning of faith in energy abundance and infrastructural safety.

Caroline Peyton analyzes two films, *The China Syndrome* (1979) and *Silkwood* (1983), pointing out that both were released at the peak of American antinuclear protest. Peyton argues that these films defy easy categorization and demonstrate America's ambivalence toward nuclear power and the existential threat it posed. Chris Dietrich's essay on *The Road Warrior* (1981) asserts that the film's dystopian future—in which health and safety are inextricably tied to the possession of gasoline—represents a remarkably stark juxtaposition to contemporary society's fragile dependence on oil.

In his essay on *Deepwater Horizon* (2016), Tyler Priest examines the decision to focus on offshore rig workers' heroic struggle against fire and explosion, rather than the resulting environmental disaster. Priest argues that environmental messaging was considered less compelling for audiences and sees this decision as mirroring the resurgence of conservative populism. Kate Brown's analysis of the dramatic HBO television series *Chernobyl* (2019) shows how even the most horrible environmental disasters can be a powerful tool for state propaganda, even decades later. In addition to the films in this section, disasters play a major role in Dan Macfarlane, Ila Tyagi, and Robert Lifset's essays.

Collectively, these essays assess how an array of directors at a number of historical moments have imagined human responses to energy-based cataclysm and social disruption. Such narratives identify an existential fear that contemporary society depends upon large-scale energy systems that are beyond individual understanding or control. Such realizations call into question assumptions of individual self-sufficiency and autonomous personal safety that are central to American identity. Like other examples of disaster or apocalyptic fiction, these films pit individuals against far-reaching systematic forces, to varying degrees of success. As our authors demonstrate, these works of energy cinema focus on sudden and spectacular moments of infrastructure failure and provide only limited context for the long-term development, maintenance, and decline of failed or flawed energy systems.[7]

Energy and Nature

The environmental movement has waxed, waned, and reinvented itself many times throughout American history. Accordingly, the environmental narratives presented in energy films have also changed dramatically over time.[8] Depictions of nature are strongly represented in many if not all of the films in this collection. Energy consumption is predicated on the use of natural resources and most works of energy cinema highlight the sacrifice of the land in the name of human ideological or monetary gain. Dichotomies inherent to the genre of environmental film—such as the constructed distinction between humanity and nature, civilization and wilderness—are also common.

The five essays that comprise "Part 2: Energy and Nature" problematize or expand upon standard understandings of environmentalism and environmental film. In Conevery Bolton Valencius's essay on *Wings* (1927), oil enables the aerial triumph over the boundaries of nature and gravity that infuse this depiction of World War I aerial warfare. Valencius points out that this technological feat was important to the way Americans renegotiated their relationship with the natural world in the wake of the second industrial revolution.

Natural phenomena become evocative symbols in energy cinema. Michaela Rife's essay "Derrick and Skull" highlights the importance of landscape to energy films' visual backgrounds. For Rife, extraction landscapes and the derricks that cover them are symbolic of America itself. In the third essay in this section, Emily Roehl's piece on petro-documentaries in the 1940s reveals that Standard Oil co-opted natural imagery to promote a vision of oil extraction as harmonious with the natural environment. Roehl points out that oil companies like Standard Oil worked to present themselves as stewards, rather than exploiters, of nature. Donald Jackson's essay argues that *Wild River* (1960) critiques the big government of Franklin D. Roosevelt's New Deal in order to highlight the social costs of TVA dam construction. Here, the valley and the river are central symbols in director Elia Kazan's criticism of New Deal hydropower infrastructure. Jackson shows that nostalgia for certain landscapes makes the imagery of the film powerful.

By the 1970s, energy became the source of widespread social anxiety and the subject of a new generation of cinematic representation. This anxiety can be traced to two factors. First, during the energy crises of the 1970s the United States experienced real energy shortages, which also significantly increased the price of all forms of energy. This was shocking to a nation accustomed to oversupply, low prices, and the comfortable postwar cultural perception of abundance. Second, a growing environmental movement fostered awareness of the environmental consequences of energy consumption and production. Such context shaped subsequent representations of nature in energy cinema. Teresa Spezio's essay analyzing *On Deadly Ground* (1994) illustrates this long shift in perspective. Spezio questions whether post-1970s action films can successfully carry an environmental message, analyzing a Steven Seagal film that tried, but failed, to marry big-budget action with environmentalist values.

Energy and the Western

The Hollywood Western is a genre born out of American imperialist fantasies, and its popularity has been driven by nostalgia for a fictional version of the American past. Westerns are named for their geographic coherence, and most take place in the preindustrial western United States of the mid- to late nineteenth century. A generation of scholars have argued that the Western is fundamentally violent, inextricable from the American push for territorial domination and the genocide of Native Americans.[9] While the Western's origins begin in the eighteenth century, the genre exploded in popularity at the end of the nineteenth century, due to the arrival of film and anxieties about the rapidly industrializing nation. The very first narrative film, *The Great Train Robbery* (1903), was the first cinematic Western, and over the course of the next century the genre developed a distinct range of visual, narrative, and stylistic elements.[10] However, as the genre aged, it fell out of favor with moviegoers and film critics alike, and filmmakers have struggled to adapt it for new audiences.

The five essays in "Part 3: Critiquing the Western" assess how a variety of filmmakers have represented resource extraction using the trappings of this storied genre. These essays demonstrate that the Western's tradition of spectacular, individualistic violence and the racially charged juxtaposition between "civilization" and "savagery" have been convenient narrative tools to promote particular resource agendas. These essays also show that the same set of Western tropes have resonated with filmmakers looking to critique unequal relationships of power and environmental degradation inherent to extractive economies.

Westerns reached the height of their popularity in the decades between the end of World War II and 1975. During this period, the Western was a cultural touchstone that helped to assuage various domestic anxieties.[11] Sarah Stanford-McIntyre's essay focuses on two Westerns from this era: *Tulsa* (1949) and the iconic film *Giant* (1956). She argues that while these films are set in the American West and steeped in Western tropes, they are driven by anxieties antithetical to the genre—the growing American dependence on foreign resources. Ila Tyagi identifies *Hellfighters* (1968) and *Fires of Kuwait* (1992) as two films that utilize the well-known tropes of the rugged Western hero to valorize American extractive expansion in the Middle East.

The other three authors in this section address efforts to expand the thematic scope of the Western. The "revisionist Western" or "post-Western" has its roots in the late 1960s and was the product of a new trend toward cinematic realism and moral ambiguity, which continued into the twenty-first century.[12] Revisionist Westerns challenge race and gender stereotypes and critique the genre's implicit bias toward American continental expansion. Such films find new antagonists, including the energy industries, to be combated in old ways. Ryan Driskell Tate assesses two B movie efforts, *Montana* (1990) and *Powwow Highway* (1989). Tate sees these films as interjecting a new villain into the genre, even as they engage in the kind of moral didacticism and nostalgia for a preindustrial West common to its earliest examples. In contrast, James R. Allison III discusses *Matewan* (1987) as a film explicitly working to circumvent genre assumptions in its depiction of the Battle of Matewan. Finally, Mark Boxell characterizes *Hell or High Water* (2016) as a traditional outlaw Western set among the economic apocalypse facing the rural Southern Plains in the early twenty-first century.

Taken together, these films demonstrate how far myth has drifted from reality. The Western is a genre that has historically mythologized westward expansion by obscuring the centrality of exploitative extractivism in constructing the West. From British and French fur trappers to agriculture to mineral resources, the West has been a long-standing source of American wealth and the cornerstone of the American industrial economy.[13] These essays push the boundaries of the Western as they highlight attempts to use the genre to interject class-based concerns and critique economic inequality. Historically, these themes are at the heart of daily conflict in the West but have not made their way into the collective imaginary. Through this reasoning, it is not a stretch to say that energy films are the truest Westerns.

Energy and Morality

Governments, reformers, and religious leaders have long understood films to be acutely dangerous agents of moral suasion and have thus sought to shape their content and themes. For a time, this led to explicit censorship in the form of the Production Code, while the commercial pressure to make money has pushed the film industry to reflect dominant moral values.[14] In addition, the 1970s energy and environmental crises recast the relationship between society and oil, creating what Stephanie LeMenager describes as "petromelancholia," or grief for a world now lost.[15] "Part 4: Energy and Morality" discusses how such forces have shaped how energy cinema portrays right and wrong.

The moral anger in Raechel Lutz's essay examining *The Formula* (1980) is directed toward the oil industry. A palpable sadness flows beneath the surface of the film, grounded in the fantasy of a pollution-free formula for converting coal to oil. As Lutz argues, desire for the formula reflects Americans' longing for a time when their energy consumption seemingly produced no environmental, diplomatic, or economic problems. Likewise, Caleb Wellum's essay on *Convoy* (1978) reveals a yearning for the past, as fossil-fueled mobility is challenged not by the oil industry but by an oppressive dystopian state dictating how fast people can drive.

Shifting the moral focus to oil itself, Brian Black's examination of *There Will Be Blood* (2007) argues that the film seeks to recast our understanding of oil by revising its origin story, exposing an inherent immorality that corrupts every relationship, individual, and community it touches. Finally, in Alexander Finkelstein's essay on the New Deal-era film *High, Wide and Handsome* (1937), it is the lack of access to oil that is morally problematic, rather than oil itself. Juxtaposed with unscrupulous businessmen who foster vice and drive families apart, the story's hero is an oilman determined to fight for fair competition, arguing in true New Deal fashion that the United States could create a form of capitalism that was not devoid of morality.

The essays in this section of the book highlight how energy is a consistent moral issue in the American consciousness. We have never been able to separate the use of energy from the consequences of its use. This tension, of accepting the use of energy while challenging the unequal relationships and negative consequences of its use, reflects ongoing and persistent moral concerns.

Energy and the State

The state has always intentionally and unintentionally subsidized and disincentivized energy production and consumption through a range of energy, environmental, land, and labor policies. A truly free market is a myth.[16] "Part 5: Energy and the State" considers this relationship, starting with Yuxun Willy Tan's investigation of how tax policy connected Hollywood and the oil industry through a web of business contacts and tax shelters. The only essay in this volume that does not focus on films themselves, Tan reveals that by the middle decades of the twentieth century, Hollywood became an important and effective defender of the oil industry's special tax breaks.

Examining *A Is for Atom* (1953), a film sponsored by General Electric (GE), Sarah Robey's essay considers an energy industry created entirely by the state: nuclear power. Designed to disassociate nuclear power from the atomic bomb, Robey argues that with this film, GE sought to launch its nuclear power business by paving the way for the public acceptance and subsidies necessary for a nuclear future. While GE never interrogates the costs associated with that future, Robert Lifset's essay on *Syriana* (2005) explores a film entirely focused on the foreign policy consequences of contemporary oil dependence. The film contends that the US sacrificed its values in the service of pursuing Middle Eastern foreign and military policy. In this context, Lifset argues that *Syriana* suffers from a failure of imagination in assuming that capitalism and democracy can solve the region's problems, and that it overlooks the extent to which those problems are caused by a reliance on fossil fuel exports.

While the first three essays in this section highlight Hollywood's depiction of the state as a subsidizer of energy production, the final essay considers how filmmakers have rendered state-built infrastructures. Dan Macfarlane compares three films' portrayals of an iconic piece of energy infrastructure: Hoover Dam. If representations of large-scale energy infrastructure tend to be triumphalist in the mid-twentieth century, Macfarlane finds that by century's end, cultural depictions of the dam become shrouded in anxiety and conspiracy.

It is possible to see these films as the products of larger processes of American state-making over the course of the twentieth century. In times of war or national emergency, the state and state actors are made extremely visible, while they recede from view during times of peace and economic prosperity. It is a long-standing trope in American popular culture that a strong or highly visible state is a sign of weakness or sudden emergency. The essays in this section reveal just how contradictory and inaccurate such assumptions can be.

The Limits of Energy Cinema

Energy cinema easily imagines the species-level consequences of climate change and the conflicts that arise due to wealth stratification, industry corruption, and resource poverty. However, such films have simultaneously been much slower to visualize how American energy consumption and production have been influenced by other social categories—especially those of race and gender. Such failure reflects American society's own reluctance to adequately reckon with how racial and gendered oppression shape both daily life and popular culture. For this reason, we want to highlight some ways in which race and gender are powerful lenses of critique through which we can further analyze these films.

Energy cinema mirrors the rigid gender politics of the American energy industries. Just as these industries are historically masculine, so too have energy films often solely focused on male characters. Doing so hides the powerful role that women play not only in energy systems, but also in broader society and culture. Sometimes the smallness of women's roles in these films echoes the male-dominated culture of Hollywood and film production as well as the perception that the energy industry is a man's world. Though Raechel Lutz's essay only briefly mentions femme fatale Lisa Spangler—a role that is overly complex, unnecessarily sexualized, and ultimately made unimportant to the film's plot—her character epitomizes the misogynist perception that women's roles were inconsequential if not actively destructive to the world of politics, power, and petroleum. Challenging this perspective is Caroline Peyton's essay, which compares two unique films about energy featuring female leads. Peyton makes clear that women can be complicated, flawed, and righteous actors in energy films. In addition, Sarah Stanford-McIntyre and Ryan Tate's essays both grapple with what gender can tell us about energy history. Collectively, we have found that the films that highlight women can often reveal sometimes subtle and often overt social tensions inherent in energy regimes.

Energy cinema often reinforces racial stereotypes and reflects the whiteness of the American film industry throughout much of the twentieth century. Many of the films analyzed in this book are the products of almost entirely white filmmakers and casts. Representations of Indigenous peoples, as several *American Energy Cinema* authors show, is shallow at best and outright offensive and racist at worst. Likewise, although the sole Asian figure in *The Formula*,

Detective Caine's partner, constantly attempts to assert his autonomy and agency, his role is ultimately reduced to that of another victim that Caine has to save. And yet in films such as *Tulsa* (1949) and *Giant* (1956), a critique of racism serves as a central plot device. *Giant*, for example, shows characters consistently challenging the white protagonist's assumption that his son, who wants no part of his father's lifestyle, is the best heir for the family cattle ranch. In contrast, he plainly overlooks a local Mexican American boy with all the necessary skills because of his class and racial heritage.

The decades between World War II and the 1970s enjoyed both high rates of economic growth and increased income and wealth equality. The films in this period often reflect a working-class perspective and an optimism about the efficacy of capitalism. However, many also reveal anxiety about the ability to make fast money through natural resource extraction. Protagonists often struggle against corporate and sometimes government actors who have forgotten their roots or are abusing their power. Class is thus a central theme in many of these films, and authors in this volume found characters struggling against the consequences of their own success. *High, Wide and Handsome*, *Boom Town*, *Tulsa*, and *Giant* all feature protagonists who achieve fantastic wealth only to lose their true friends and moral centers.

Beginning in the 1970s, US economic growth and increased income and economic inequality reached levels unseen since the early twentieth century.[17] The films produced during this era are more likely to follow middle-class protagonists or working-class characters unhappily stuck in their economic circumstances.[18] Indeed, between *Boom Town* and *Hell or High Water*, there is a growing and distinct disenchantment with the idea of capitalism as a vehicle for the honest and fair creation of wealth.

Conclusion

How the American public perceives and understands energy matters. *American Energy Cinema* argues that energy films constitute a thematically interlinked body of work that provides a glimpse into the different ways that Americans have understood energy creation and use over time. Analysis of important themes within energy cinema—disasters and catastrophes, energy and nature, energy and Westerns, energy and morality, and energy and the state—demonstrates that the development and maintenance of energy systems are inextricable from changes in American society, politics, and culture. Analysis of the financial and political links between Hollywood and the energy industries demonstrate that energy cinema was understood to be an important shaper of public consensus. Like all films, energy cinema presents evolving depictions of race, gender, and class that poignantly reflect changing social relationships and the limits inherent in these social categories.

Although our authors cover significant cinematic terrain in this book, there is plenty more work to do. We invite future scholars to continue this analytical work.[19] Such an effort is deeply urgent. How we produce and consume energy is among the most environmentally intensive activities we engage in as a society. The burning of fossil fuels to produce energy has caused a rapid and catastrophic increase in global atmospheric temperatures. If our energy history and energy culture play a role in initiating and sustaining the policies that result in the energy production and consumption at any given time, then understanding this energy culture begins the process by which we might imagine the cultural requirements of a post-petroleum future.

Notes

1. Historians have written about films in numerous ways and contexts. In addition to the scholarly study of films, historians have created an online community on Twitter to group watch and critique Hollywood films. Historians at the Movies (#HATM), organized by historian Jason Herbert, also exemplifies that film analysis is not only useful but can also be fun. For a prime example of film history scholarship, see Matthew Frye Jacobson and Gaspar González, *What Have They Built You to Do? The Manchurian Candidate and Cold War America* (Minneapolis: University of Minnesota Press, 2006). For more about #HATM, see Jason Herbert, "Historians at the Movies and Bridging Gaps between the Academic Community," *American Historian*, December 2019, https://www.oah.org/tah/issues/2019 /history-and-the-movies/historians-at-the-movies-and-bridging-gaps-between -the-academic-community.

2. The academic journal *Environmental History* has become a prominent home for energy history scholarship. Between January 2010 and January 2020, *Environmental History* published twenty articles on energy and the environment. Though this might not seem like a lot, it demonstrates the continued and overlapping nature of the two topics. In addition, the frequency of energy-themed articles has increased since 2013.

3. Some examples include Finis Dunaway, *Natural Visions: The Power of Images in American Environmental Reform* (Chicago: University of Chicago Press, 2005); Finis Dunaway, *Seeing Green: The Use and Abuse of American Environmental Images* (Chicago: University of Chicago Press, 2015); Amy R. W. Meyers and Lisa L. Ford, *Knowing Nature: Art and Science in Philadelphia, 1740–1840* (New Haven, CT: Yale University Press, 2011); David Schuyler, *Sanctified Landscape: Writers, Artists, and the Hudson River Valley, 1820–1909* (Ithaca, NY: Cornell University Press, 2012). One might also include the emergence of ecocritical studies in art history as evidence. See Alan C. Braddock and Christoph Irmscher, eds., *A Keener Perception: Ecocritical Studies in American Art History* (Tuscaloosa: University of Alabama Press, 2009); Karl Kusserow and Alan C. Braddock, *Nature's Nation: American Art and Environment* (Princeton, NJ: Princeton University Art Museum, 2018).

4. For books exploring the energy humanities, see Dominic Boyer and Imre Szeman,

eds., *Energy Humanities: An Anthology* (Baltimore: Johns Hopkins University Press, 2017); Imre Szeman, *On Petrocultures: Globalization, Culture, and Energy* (Morgantown: West Virginia University Press, 2015); Jeff Diamante and Imre Szeman, eds., *Energy Culture: Art and Theory on Oil and Beyond* (Morgantown: West Virginia University Press, 2019); Adam Carlson, Imre Szeman, and Sheena Wilson, eds., *Petrocultures: Oil, Energy, and Culture* (Kingston, ON: McGill-Queens University Press, 2017); Karen Pinkus, *Fuel: A Speculative Dictionary* (Minneapolis: University of Minnesota Press, 2016). For scholarship exploring the overlap between energy, environment, and film scholarship, see Elena Past, *Italian EcoCinema: Beyond the Human* (Bloomington: University of Indiana Press, 2019); Hiroki Shin, "Translation, Conversion, and Domestication in UK Energy-Themed Films in the Twentieth Century" (paper presented at the Annual Meeting for the Society for the History of Technology, Milan, Italy, October 2019); "Film Forum," *Environmental History* 24, no. 2 (April 2019): 370–82; "Film Forum," *Environmental History* 22, no. 2 (April 2017): 331–54. For books exploring energy and culture, see Ross Barrett and Daniel Worden, *Oil Culture* (Minneapolis: University of Minnesota Press, 2014); Robert Johnson, *Carbon Nation: Fossil Fuels in the Making of American Culture* (Lawrence: University Press of Kansas, 2014); Amitav Ghosh, *The Great Derangement: Climate Change and the Unthinkable* (Chicago: University of Chicago Press, 2016); Matthew T. Huber, *Lifeblood: Oil, Freedom, and the Forces of Capital* (Minneapolis: University of Minnesota Press, 2013). Stephanie LeMenager, *Living Oil: Petroleum Culture in the American Century* (New York: Oxford University Press, 2014); Roger M. Olien and Diana Davids Olien, *Oil and Ideology: The Cultural Creation of the American Petroleum Industry* (Chapel Hill: University of North Carolina Press, 2000).

5.   Stephen Rust, Salma Monani, Sean Cubitt, *Ecocinema Theory and Practice* (New York: Routledge, 2012); Paula Willoquet-Maricondi, *Framing the World: Explorations in Ecocriticism and Film* (Charlottesville: University of Virginia Press, 2010); Joseph K. Heumann and Robin L. Murray, *Ecology and Popular Film* (New York: SUNY Press, 2009); Greg Mitman, Reel Nature: America's Romance with Wildlife on Film (Seattle: University of Washington Press, 1999); Maria Dahlquist and Patrick Vondreau, eds., *Petrocinema: Sponsored Film and the Oil Industry* (New York: Bloomsbury, 2021).

6.   In this effort, we suggest two films as a potential starting point: *Siberiade* (1979), a Russian film about the discovery of oil in a small Siberian village, and *The Mattei Affair* (1972), an Italian film about Enrico Mattei, a Nazi-fighting Italian nationalist who goes on to direct state-run oil corporation ENI.

7.   For scholarship on the politics of disaster and risk, see Ted Steinberg, *Acts of God: The Unnatural History of Natural Disaster in America* (New York: Oxford University Press, 2006); Ulrich Beck, *Risk Society: Towards a New Modernity* (New York: Sage, 1992).

8.   Here, *American Energy Cinema* responds to Ellen E. Moore's call for more scholarship on how entertainment media has characterized the environment. Ellen E. Moore, *Landscape and the Environment in Hollywood Film: The Green Machine* (Cham, Switzerland: Palgrave McMillan, 2017), 3. We also recognize that the creation of films in and of themselves can be an environmentally destructive act. See Hunter Vaughan, *Hollywood's Dirtiest Secret: The Hidden Environmental Costs of the Movies* (New York: Columbia University Press, 2019).

9.   Richard Slotkin, *Gunfighter Nation: Myth of the Frontier in Twentieth-Century America* (Norman: University of Oklahoma Press, 1998); Patricia Nelson Limerick,

The Legacy of Conquest: The Unbroken Past of the American West (New York: W. W. Norton, 1987); Phil Deloria, *Indians in Unexpected Places* (Lawrence: University Press of Kansas, 2004).

10. To give an often-parodied example, Westerns of the 1920s and 1930s took on the trappings of the morality tale with the "white hat" defeating the "black hat" in single combat.

11. Stanley Corkin, *Cowboys as Cold Warriors: The Western and US History* (Philadelphia: Temple University Press, 2004).

12. Exemplified by the Dollars Trilogy of Italian "spaghetti Westerns," these Westerns were more violent and more sexually charged.

13. Richard White, *It's Your Misfortune and None of My Own: A New History of the American West* (Norman: University of Oklahoma Press, 1991).

14. Films only began to challenge that moral code after the decline of the Production Code in the 1960s. See Leonard J. Leff and Jerold L. Simmons, *The Dame in the Kimono: Hollywood, Censorship, and the Production Code from the 1920s to the 1960s* (Lexington: University of Kentucky Press, 2001), and Gregory D. Black, *Hollywood Censored: Morality Codes, Catholics and the Movies* (Cambridge, UK: Cambridge University Press, 1994).

15. See LeMenager, *Living Oil.*

16. Paul Sabin, *Crude Politics: The California Oil Market, 1900–1940* (Berkeley: University of California Press, 2005), 1–15.

17. On the decline of economic inequality in the postwar decades and then its increase beginning in the 1970s, see Judith Stein, *Pivotal Decade: How the United States Traded Factories for Finance in the 1970s* (New Haven, CT: Yale University Press, 2011).

18. This reflects a general decline in depictions of working-class characters. On the disappearance of the working class from American culture, see Jefferson Cowie, *Stayin' Alive: The 1970s and the Last Days of the Working Class* (New York: New Press, 2010).

19. Many films that utilize depictions of energy did not make it into this volume, and there are plenty left for scholars to analyze. Key among those are films from the *Marvel Cinematic Universe* for its use of alien energy sources, and films about cars like the *Fast and Furious* franchise, *Grand Theft Auto* (1977), *Gone in 60 Seconds* (1974 and 2000), or the Disney film *Cars* (2006). In addition, cultural histories of depictions of energy in science fiction and movies, such as *Star Trek* and *Star Wars*, about space could be informative as limitless energy is often a key imaginary component to human expansion in space. For more analysis of energy in films see also: Jose Sebastian Terneus, "'Y'all Sitting Up Here Comfortable': Extracting the Afrofuturist Myth from Ryan Coogler's *Black Panther*," conference paper presented at "Energy Cultures in Crisis," at "Humanities on the Brink: Energy, Environment, and Emergency," July 10–30, 2020, an ASLE-sponsored NCN symposium hosted by the University of California, Santa Barbara; and Robin L. Murray and Joseph K. Heumann, "Fast, Furious, and Out of Control: The Erasure of Natural Landscapes in Car Culture Films," in *Explorations in Ecocriticism and Film*, ed. Paula Willoquet-Maricondi (Charlottesville: University of Virginia Press, 2010), 154–69.

PART 1

When Disaster Strikes

Blackouts, Bad Guys, and Belly Laughs: Exploring America's First Cascading Power Failure in *Where Were You When the Lights Went Out?* (1968)

Julie A. Cohn

O n November 9, 1965, a minor maintenance oversight resulted in a major power failure that interrupted the daily activities of 30 million people in eight US states and Ontario, Canada. This was the first major cascading power failure experienced in North America. It prompted a multitude of technical reports, congressional hearings, political naysaying about utility companies, and editorials across the news spectrum. Congress considered groundbreaking legislation that would introduce government oversight of power systems reliability—an intrusion into what had been decidedly private and voluntary system coordination. Americans confronted the very real fragility of the world's largest power network, the Eastern Interconnection, while the president, utility executives, and others made pronouncements both denouncing and supporting the value of interconnected power systems. And then, after two years of study and much public attention, the reliability of the nation's transmission network faded from public view and returned in the form of a comedy film.

Where Were You When the Lights Went Out? (hereafter *Lights*) appeared on cinema screens in the summer of 1968.[1] Starring Doris Day, this was the first film to use a cascading power failure as a plot device and in doing so illustrates how filmmakers reinterpret energy events and complex technologies for the American public. The specific ways in which veteran screenwriters Everett Freeman and Karl Turnberg depict the blackout and use it as a frame for a silly comedy reflect a moment in American history when the country shifted from energy optimism to energy anxiety. This was not a sudden change but a trending change, reflected in the longer history of blackout movies. While *Lights* offers the optimistic view, other films released at the same time highlight the darker perspective on America's energy economies. Environmental humanities scholar Kerstin Oloff, for example, argues that *Night of the Living Dead* (1968) marks a shift in the aesthetics of the zombie movie genre from a labor critique to an oil critique.[2] By examining the origins of *Lights*, how the plotting and representation of the blackout developed, and how the final film paradoxically pairs disaster and humor, we can trace the evolution of American theatergoers' familiarity with their power networks and its fragility, and their allegiance to myths rather than detailed technical realities.

From the moment Americans turned on electric lamps in the late nineteenth century, the lights also went off. Generator failures, stormy weather, squirrels chewing through power lines, operator errors, and inadequate technology all left customers in the dark from time to time. Filmmakers began turning out the lights, as well. In 1930, for example, the Marx Brothers used a power failure to perform a hilarious painting swap.[3] Beginning in the 1950s, unknowable alien forces, monsters, and ghostly spirits caused lights and motors to stop. In most of these later films, bad things happened when the lights went out. Historian David Nye explains that blackouts can be understood "as a disruption of the social order, as a military tactic, as a crisis in the networked city, as the failure of engineering systems, as the outcome of inconsistent political and economic decisions, as a sudden encounter with sublimity, and as memory, aestheticized in photographs." Nye asserts that the "the arrested moment of each blackout provides a snapshot of the electrical system and of social relationships."[4] Movies like *Lights* reflect those social experiences.

In *Lights*, the screenwriters offer up a fluffy love triangle triggered by a power failure that is never explained, rife with misunderstandings, and resolved with the mythology of a blackout-induced baby boom. Unlike other movies in which stormy weather, aliens, bad guys, and war volunteers turn out the lights, in this film the blackout itself is never menacing. Metro-Goldwyn-Mayer (MGM) released *Lights,* a vehicle for the popular Doris Day, just as the country reached an energy turning point. Intense energy expansion and use characterized the years from World War II to the early 1970s, while energy crises, concerns about scarcity, and technological pessimism marked the years afterward.[5] Electricity usage climbed steadily from 1900 to 1973, while per-kilowatt-hour prices dropped.[6] Americans in general enjoyed cheap and abundant energy and optimistically anticipated the same in the future.

These trends changed, however, after 1970 as a result of OPEC-imposed oil embargos, inflation, technical and managerial challenges to power system expansion, and environmental opposition to energy projects.[7] In addition, a second major cascading power failure hit New York in the summer of 1977, accompanied by widespread looting and related crimes. By the end of the 1970s, energy optimism had tamped down.[8] Freeman and Turnberg's comedic treatment of a major national disaster provides important insights into how filmmakers chose to present power networks and complex technical challenges, and also how the American public consumed information about energy systems.

A Split-Second Difference between Comedy and Tragedy

When imagining the opening of this blackout movie, Freeman and Turnberg first made an effort to capture the technical story:

> Page 1. Scene 1. OPENING: We see a stylized drawing of the great power grid which supplies electricity to [all of] New York, [all of] New England, part of Canada. A voice [explains what this is], stress[ing]es that the grid is a [most] perfect example of the automated, mechanized computer age in which we live. [It is] Foolproof. Nothing possibly could go wrong with it, but something did.[9]

But multiple versions of the screenplay reveal that the writing team quickly abandoned this approach. Instead, in the final MGM release, a jaunty, jazzy, musical introduction precedes scenes of the noise and bustle of Times Square at night. While pausing to check his watch against the giant Accutron clock, central character Waldo Zane (Robert Morse) narrates the film's theme—a "split second one way or another" can be the difference between comedy and tragedy. The tone of the opening already indicates that laughs are coming. As Waldo navigates the busy streets, barely missing numerous disasters, he lays out the story. He is a rising young executive at the fictive Megatronics Corporation, anticipating promotion to company president. When his hopes are dashed, he instead steals the company's cash profits and prepares for an escape to South America. Waldo introduces the other key characters, all of whom are strangers to him: Maggie Garrison (Doris Day), a popular actress starring in a Broadway show titled—not without tongue in cheek—*The Constant Virgin*; her husband, Peter Garrison (Patrick O'Neal), a successful architect; and Ladislaus Walichek (Terry-Thomas), Maggie's conniving and money-grubbing director. Maggie and Peter are having marital difficulties, and Maggie plans to leave theater to take on more domestic pursuits. Peter is on the verge of committing adultery with an attractive reporter. Ladislaus is plotting to sign Maggie to a multiyear Hollywood contract. And then the lights go out.

A reprise of the catastrophic 1965 Northeast blackout precipitates the hijinks in *Lights*. Maggie discovers her husband's philandering ways and heads for the couple's Connecticut cottage. Airplanes are grounded, so Waldo cannot fly to South America. He instead drives toward Boston, but his car breaks down near Maggie's cottage. She lets him in, and within a short period of time, Maggie and Waldo, separately and unbeknownst to one another, consume a heavy-duty sleeping draught and fall asleep entangled on the sofa. Peter arrives to make amends and discovers the two "lovers." In the film's funniest and best-acted sequence, Peter attempts to rouse Maggie and Waldo while accusing them of having an affair, but neither of the two can stay awake long enough to follow what he is saying. Ladislaus arrives and complicates matters. And then the lights are on again. Following a lengthy series of misunderstandings and purposeful misdirections, the Garrisons are reconciled, the funds are restored—briefly—to Megatronics, Waldo is president of the company, and Ladislaus disappears. The film ends with the Garrisons arriving at a hospital while Waldo explains in voice-over that they have joined myriad couples in welcoming new babies exactly nine months after the blackout.

Lights draws attention to the 1965 Northeast blackout in multiple ways, and the film's origins reflects how a major energy event can trigger responses from the entertainment industry. The night scenes in New York City offer a fond, and in many ways accurate, depiction of the real blackout. The lack of detail about how and why it occurred parallels waning public interest in this disruptive event. The blackout itself causes confusion, changes in normal routines, and extraordinary behavior, suggesting that a world without electricity operates differently than a world with it.[10] The film's closing scene also demonstrates how myths become enshrined in public discourse. As a comedy, *Lights* perpetuates the general sentiment in media reports of good nature and patience among those affected by the actual blackout. And within a long series of science fiction films, thrillers, dramas, and horror movies that preceded and followed it, *Lights* also suggests that the real blackout gave filmmakers a different imaginary about how power systems work—and fail.

Turning on *Lights*

Before it was a movie, *Lights* was a play. Throughout the early 1960s, Academy Award–winning screenwriter Julius Epstein worked to adapt a French stage play, *Monsieur Masure*, for MGM.[11] This three-person sex farce features a witty exchange between a married couple and a stranger.[12] The wife, who is an adulteress, takes a sleeping draught at her country cottage while awaiting the arrival of both her husband and her paramour, the latter of whom is never seen. The stranger's car has broken down, and he wanders into the cottage and also drinks the sleeping draught. The husband arrives to find his wife and the stranger asleep together on a divan and attempts to awaken them. The ensuing banter appears in all the adaptations for Epstein's screenplay, titled *A Likely Story*, as well as in *Lights*. Over the course of numerous revisions, Epstein introduced additional characters, relocated the country home to Italy, and, notably, added a power failure at a gym club. In his final version, the wife, who is now Italian but not an adulteress, fails to believe the husband's tale of the power failure and leaves him for their country home, where the central comedic mix-up unfolds.[13] Although the Production Code Administration determined that several sequences were "unacceptable by reason of their length and overly suggestive dialogue," MGM included *A Likely Story*, starring Sophia Loren and produced by Carlo Ponti, in its list of prospective films for 1964–1965.[14] In addition, the pending film appeared in a profile of Sophia Loren in September 1966.[15] Yet the studio never produced *A Likely Story*.[16]

Between November 9, 1965, and September 1966, MGM had already begun work on *Lights*. In the early summer of 1966, the studio signed Everett Freeman to write the screenplay, announcing that the story would be "based on the east coast electrical blackout of a few months ago."[17] By October, Freeman and Karl Turnberg were working on the script. In the earliest available version, the writers had already integrated the misconstrued ménage à trois scene from *Monsieur Masure*.[18] Evidently, the MGM filmmakers decided to wrap the events of the blackout around the hilarity of the unwitting lovers on the couch, and abandoned the Loren/Ponti project.

In its first incarnations, the *Lights* script opens with dramatic views of New York City at night and with narration that evokes the technological sublime.[19] Suggestions for the visuals include "An air shot of New York blazing with lights," "A spectacular view of the city blazing with light," and "A SPECTACULAR *Night* SHOT of the New York sky line."[20] The proposed narration continues with "[*power systems are*] marvels of the scientific age," "hundreds of miles of grids . . . criss cross . . . the country," and "domestic life is totally dependent on this intricate pattern of power lines & turbines."[21] Vignettes of the city during the blackout accompany the film titles; for example, "People stranded in elevators, subways, in traffic jams at corners no longer controlled by lights," and a view of Times Square "blacked out, choked with stalled cars and traffic and mobs."[22] These experiments with the opening sequences suggest that the writers very much wanted to conjure a city they loved, a country in awe of its technological prowess, and the gritty reality of negotiating Manhattan in the dark.

In the end, however, Freeman and Turnberg resorted to a framework Epstein had employed for *A Likely Story*—narration by the stranger. In the film, Waldo introduces the key characters and provides plot teasers as he walks through the busy streets of Manhattan at night. The camera cuts back and forth between Waldo, other street scenes "ablaze" with lights, and interior scenes featuring Maggie, Peter, Ladislaus, and Megatronics executives. Following a cacophony of images of nightlife in the big city, blocks of light—akin to windows—spell out the name of the movie against a blacked-out Manhattan skyline.[23] In this way, the filmmakers give the blackout a role in the film without making it the highlight. They further signal that the audience should expect humor, not drama or a physics lesson.

Reliving the Blackout

The filmmakers go to some length to emulate New York's blackout experiences. Throughout the film, for example, the camera periodically visits a group of forlorn citizens gathered on an interior stairway in Grand Central Terminal, much like a photo published in *Life* magazine soon after the event.[24] At first, they sit looking weary and worried while a priest hands out candles (17:55). Next, we see them still sitting and holding the lit candles, as Waldo pushes his way through (23:42). In the third such scene, an older man is offering whiskey to his fellow travelers, and Waldo drinks it as he passes by (24:30). Much later in the film, the group on the steps is singing "Row, Row, Row Your Boat" in hearty fellowship (38:12). The last time we see the stepsitters they are waking up, cheering, and embracing as the lights come on (51:06). The priest with the candles, the whiskey, and the camaraderie all appeared in actual news reports of the blackout.[25] Other scenes, such as passengers stuck on a stalled subway car, civilians directing traffic with flashlights, and black outlines of skyscrapers against the night sky, likewise drew from news reportage and printed images.

The filmmakers shot the Grand Central Terminal scenes on site on August 4 and 5, 1967.[26] This event precipitated excited news coverage. *Film Daily* deployed a reporter to work as an extra, and he described the efforts of many of his cohort to replicate their own experiences from sixteen months earlier.[27] Actor Robert Morse recalls that with "lots of complicated shots in Grand Central" involving "a million extras . . . with the lights out," it wasn't an easy picture to direct.[28] These scenes required a seventy-person crew, 396 extras, six production assistants, and eight policemen, as well as the main cast members.[29]

Radio communications played a significant role in the public response to the actual blackout, and the filmmakers took note. A fictional radio newscaster, Morgan Klein (Steve Allen), appears throughout the film, describing the blackout as the central plot unfolds. While Klein attempts to provide straight reporting, he has a number of comic pratfalls involving candles, flames, water glasses, and microphones. In this way, the comedy belies the importance of radio during the disaster. Because stations within the blackout area had little or no backup power, companion stations in neighboring states carried broadcasts, even after their normal hours of operation, while citizens listened on transistor and car radios. Media and government officials alike reported that radio broadcasters kept the public informed, calm, and entertained.[30]

In addition, *Lights* perpetuated one of the longest-standing myths of the blackout. The film ends as Maggie and Peter head into a hospital, lively adults descending the steps holding new babies and pushing carriages. Waldo, in voice-over, explains, "A biological phenomenon . . . happened to thousands upon thousands of New Yorkers who, nine months to the day after the blackout were still asking each other . . ." And then the movie's theme song plays (1:25:23). In August 1966, the *New York Times* did actually report an apparent bump in births at certain hospitals in Manhattan.[31] Within just a few years, demographers and public health researchers questioned the validity of this report and handily debunked it.[32] The mythology, however, continues. Actor Robert Morse, like many others, raised this as one of his first remarks about working on *Lights*.[33] Thus, the film reflects what the public knew in the short term and also sustains a long-running misperception of a link between power failures and romance.

The screenwriters attempted to introduce the technology story, as well. Early scripts included lengthy and detailed explanations of the blackout that later disappeared. In one version, Waldo expounds:

How was I to know that at *precisely* 5:15 pm [on November 9, 1965], up state somewhere, a small boy would drop an electric toothbrush in the toilet— . . . causing a short circuit which would blow a fuse, which would back up the local power line which ordinarily cuts off a [local] conduit leading to the [Adrian] *Adam* Beck Power Plant, which in turn would overload the other lines and cause circuits to back up and other safety cutoffs to shut down other power lines in an amazing demonstration of electronic efficiency. As power line after power line was cut off a [general] *chain* reaction was set [up] *in motion, and this ??? system failed.* The circuits [backed up] counter-clockwise, moving from Niagara Falls [across New England down into New York

and plunging the entire city into darkness. XXXXXXXXXX [sic] eastward—knocking out at exactly 5:28 PM all the lights in New York, New
England, and parts of Canada![34]

Despite the creative interpretation, this passage somewhat accurately reflects the Federal Power Commission (FPC) report on the blackout, issued
on December 6, 1965.[35] The FPC detailed the start of the blackout at precisely 5:16:11 p.m. at the Sir Adam Beck Hydroelectric Generating Station in
Ontario and the ensuing failures that spread across the electrical grid to New
York, New England, and Ontario within twelve minutes. The press shared the
FPC's findings widely.[36] Freeman and Turnberg had no doubt read or heard
these descriptions. While their grasp of the technical details falls short, in the
early scripts they do convey the key concept of a cascading failure in which
one small action or error leads to a series of additional actions that ultimately
result in a widespread outage. The nature of the cascading power failure and
its scale distinguished it from the more familiar blackouts the public had
experienced previously. In fact, utility executives reported that they could
not have imagined something like the 1965 Northeast blackout until it happened.[37] By the spring of 1967, however, Freeman and Turnberg abandoned
this attempt to capture both the astonishment and technical complexity of
the power failure.[38]

Although *Lights* presents a cascading power failure as an inconvenience
that resulted in many happy endings, the blackout itself was much more
disturbing for Americans in general and the power industry in particular.[39]
Industry experts had long advocated for increased interconnection of power
networks to improve reliability, but the blackout gave them pause. Speaking
before congressional committees, they argued both for and against interconnection.[40] Yet just months after the blackout, an industry-government task
force began work to link the eastern and western systems.[41] Rather than engaging the shifting public and private debates about power systems, the filmmakers chose to maintain an ironic perspective on the grid and technological
modernity. Toward the end of *Lights*, a newscaster describes the experience of
the outage: "Man obviously relished his release from dependence on the machine . . . and became an individual again. There were no plane crashes, no train
wrecks, no crime waves or looting sprees, and no panic" (1:14:58).[42] The film
reinforces a sense that twentieth-century technology is both magnificent and
controlling, but even if it fails, engineering ingenuity can protect Americans
against true disaster.

The filmmakers also banked on waning public interest in the hows and
whys of the grid, and by the time MGM released *Lights*, focus had indeed

shifted away from technical and regulatory reviews. For many months after the event, though, reports and press releases kept the story in the news, covering the hubris of some utility executives and the ambivalence of others.[43] Industry journals also probed public understanding of power systems. One survey, for example, showed that most North Americans had never heard of the grid before the blackout, and afterward believed their electrical fate should not be linked to other states and countries.[44] Throughout the following two years during which MGM developed *Lights*, the blackout reappeared periodically in the press and in public discourse. In late 1965 and throughout 1966 and 1967, Congress held hearings on the blackout, proposed bills, and discussed related matters.[45] The FPC suggested that the commission undertake more authority over utilities and later released its final report in 1967, with extensive recommendations for preventing future power failures.[46] But Congress dropped consideration of legislation to increase the FPC's authority, and the utility industry announced a plan to improve self-regulation through the creation of the National Electric Reliability Council.[47] And although the blackout did not entirely disappear from the public imagination, by 1968 widespread attention to it had ceased, leaving *Lights'* filmmakers to construct their own narrative.

Other Lights Go Out

Framing the blackout as safe and comedic, the filmmakers diverged from the approach of most movies in which the lights go out. Of a sample set of 129 feature films, shorts, and episodes of television shows released between 1930 and 2018, only twenty-nine are comedic; of those, ten also fall into the thematic categories of thriller, science fiction, horror, and crime.[48] Figure 1.1 illustrates the number of "blackout" movies by decade. Noticeably, the total number spikes in the early 2000s. There are comedies throughout, but science fiction films appear only after 1950, while dramas all but disappear between the war years and the late 1980s. Also of importance, very few filmmakers used the blackout as a plot device during the 1950s and 1960s. In the majority of blackout films, bad weather, bad science, sabotage, and alien powers variously cause the lights to go out, and bad things happen in the aftermath.

Over time, movie themes reflected contemporaneous imaginaries about electrification. During the 1930s and 1940s, for example, several dramas featured linesman who heroically restore the power during severe thunderstorms.[49] This was the era of big federal dam projects and rural electrification.[50] The 1937 film *Slim* opens with views of the newly completed Hoover Dam and scenes of linesmen on transmission poles stretching across vacant Western

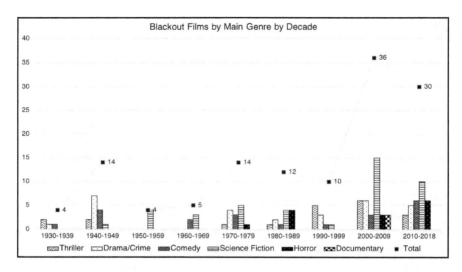

Fig. 1.1. Films in which the lights go out, by main genre, by decade. *Sources*: IMDb, TCM Movie Database, Google.

lands. The drama surrounds the repair of downed power lines during a blizzard, but does not dwell on the effects of the blackout. By this time, Americans were sufficiently familiar with both electric lights and short-lived power failures to take them in stride. The linesmen films, instead, focused on human derring-do in the face of the competing forces of technological and natural wonders. By contrast, in the 1951 movie *The Day the Earth Stood Still*, an alien force causes all machinery and lighting to stop.[51] A visiting space traveler uses a brief and planned power outage to impress upon humans the need to rein in nuclear weapons. For the earthlings in the movie, and presumably audiences as well, this scene introduces the possibility that forces beyond human understanding could wreak havoc upon our essential technologies. Notably, this film followed the first Russian nuclear weapons tests by only two years. As historian Martin Melosi argues, films like this from the early 1950s reflected growing anxiety about the Cold War and the atomic age in the United States.[52] In the succeeding years, space aliens, monsters, ghostly spirits, and other unknowable elements knock out the power in thirty films, the roots of outages are unknown in more than a dozen others, and storms and sabotage are to blame in thirty more (see figure 1.2).

Following *Lights*, another dozen films and TV episodes featured or referenced cascading power failures between 1977 and 2007. At least seven took the July 13–14, 1977, New York blackout as the signal event, all of them referring

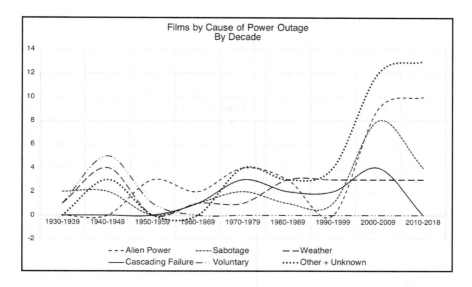

Fig. 1.2. Movies in which the lights go out, by cause, by decade. *Sources*: IMDb, TCM Movie Database, Google, Wikipedia.

to the dark side of how New Yorkers experienced the power failure. This was the country's second cascading failure on a scale similar to the 1965 outage. Unlike the first one, however, this event occurred during a hot summer characterized by social unrest in the city. Widespread looting and related crimes took place in the darkened metropolis. As David Nye notes, in 1965 a blackout was an anomaly, "a violation of the expected order of things." By 1977, New Yorkers expected annoying summer power problems, but blackouts had become "less potential carnivals than opportunities for criminality."[53] During the 1970s, Americans also faced multiple energy crises affecting both the cost and availability of gasoline, natural gas, and electricity. While energy optimism had prevailed earlier, anxiety about energy resources, technology, and pollution took hold after the 1970s. This might explain the very small number of power failures in films that appeared between World War II and the 1977 New York blackout, and the sudden rise in productions after that date.

Beginning in the early 2000s, filmmakers began to tackle serious and scientific concerns about America's energy future. California experienced its own energy crises in 2000 and 2001, punctuated by the demise of Enron Corporation at the end of 2001. Between 2001 and 2018, a number of documentaries took on the crucial questions of energy security, corporate overreach, and climate change.[54] Studios released more than sixty blackout movies during those same years, and the vast majority address concern about energy resources. Even the 2015 comedy *Christmas Eve*, which features a Manhattan blackout triggered by a minor but fraught traffic accident, grapples with trepidation about the energy future. The sudden darkness throws a number of strangers into close quarters where they make personal discoveries and forge new friendships. Interestingly, two of the characters invent a new approach to energy delivery that they believe will avert the pending disaster posed by climate change. The actors draw charts and calculations, intended to persuade movie watchers that they have the technical know-how to achieve this innovation, but the film is woefully short on details about what this new energy form might be.[55] *Christmas Eve*, like *Lights*, employs the device of the blackout to allow the audience to laugh in the face of technological failure and to leave the theater with some optimism. But unlike *Lights*, *Christmas Eve* takes on contemporary energy challenges.

Conclusion

Lights failed to achieve cinematic greatness but performed fairly well for MGM. The film earned over $7.9 million in domestic box office receipts and ranked number twenty of the one hundred top grossing films of 1968.[56] Reviewers generally criticized the film as "predictable," "mediocre," "ordinary," and "disappointing."[57] Some applauded the idea of using the blackout as a plot device, but most felt that the movie failed to fully exploit its comedic potential.[58] Several offered sarcastic critiques of the send-up of Doris Day as the "constant virgin," as her chastity in the face of male pursuers was legend by 1968.[59] Day herself had no fondness for this film.[60] Her recent obituary makes no mention of *Lights,* and it is difficult to find a copy of the film to view in any format.[61] But despite this lackluster cinematic legacy, *Lights* offers surprising insight into America's energy story in 1968.

Lights stands out in a longer history of power failures in the movies for its comedic bent, its effort to accurately portray the street scenes of the country's first major cascading power failure, and its embrace of energy optimism. The movie reached theaters shortly before the 1969 Santa Barbara oil spill, the passage of the National Environmental Policy Act (1970), and the first Earth Day (1970). Though minor in the catalogue of great hits of the twentieth century and even in the canon of popular Doris Day films, *Lights* defines an important moment in America's energy history. The movie helps us understand that even in the face of a catastrophic power outage in 1965, Americans were willing to sustain an optimistic view of technological systems, human ingenuity, and a future of energy abundance. It reminds us that public memory of a major disaster can be relatively short-lived, particularly when the precipitating technical failure is complex and virtually invisible except during the event itself. *Lights* illustrates the cross-pollination of media reporting and popular culture, underscoring the enduring mythologies that frame national events of any type. In this case, Americans recall the 1965 Northeast blackout with some fondness for the camaraderie reported by the media and reflected by the movie, and continue to repeat the notion that blackouts cause baby booms. Further, the film obscures the complexity of the blackout's causes, the ensuing political fights over control of power systems, and the industry's ability to wrest the discourse away from Congress and recommit to the path of expansion, integration, and self-regulation they had pursued for many decades. Finally, some scenes in *Lights* are really funny, and for that reason alone it is worth revisiting the film to see where we have been and how we might face our energy future with an occasional laugh, even as we attempt to resolve serious and intractable challenges.

Notes

1. Hy Averback, dir., *Where Were You When the Lights Went Out?* (Hollywood, CA: Metro-Goldwyn-Mayer, 1968).
2. Kerstin Oloff, "From Sugar to Oil: The Ecology of George A. Romero's *Night of the Living Dead* (1968)," *Journal of Postcolonial Writing* 53, no. 3 (2016): 312–28.
3. Victor Heerman, dir., *Animal Crackers* (Hollywood, CA: Paramount Pictures, 1930).
4. David E. Nye, *When the Lights Went Out: A History of Blackouts in America* (Cambridge, MA: MIT Press, 2010), 2–3.
5. Robert Lifset, ed., *American Energy Policy in the 1970s* (Norman: University of Oklahoma Press, 2014); Martin V. Melosi, *Coping with Abundance: Energy and Environment in Industrial America* (Philadelphia: Temple University Press, 1985); David E. Nye, *Consuming Power: A Social History of American Energies* (Cambridge, MA: MIT Press, 1998); Benjamin K. Sovacool and Roman Sidortsov, "Energy Governance in the United States," in *The Handbook of Global Energy Policy*, ed. Andreas Goldthau (Malden, MA: Wiley, 2013), 443.
6. Julie A. Cohn, *The Grid: Biography of an American Technology* (Cambridge, MA: MIT Press, 2017), 182–85.
7. Cohn, *The Grid*, 182–87; Richard F. Hirsh, *Technology and Transformation in the American Electric Utility Industry* (Cambridge, UK: Cambridge University Press, 1989).
8. Philip H. Abelson, "A Modest Basis for Energy Optimism," *Science* 207, no. 4428 (1980): 26.
9. Everett Freeman and Karl Turnberg, script outline, October 13–19, 1966, 3342.f–W-552, WHERE WERE YOU WHEN THE LIGHTS WENT OUT? Turner/MGM Scripts, Margaret Herrick Library, Los Angeles (hereafter *Lights* Collection). For material quoted from draft scripts, brackets and italics appear as they do in the original.
10. Nye, *Lights Went Out*; David E. Nye, personal communication with the author, September 27, 2019.

11. Jack Palmer White, reader's report, July 10, 1956, MONSIEUR MASURE, by Claude Magnier, 3339.f–W-538, *Lights* Collection; Bill Cole, reader's report, November 12, 1962, ODD MAN IN, adapted from the French (*Monsieur Masure*) by Robert Maugham, 3339.f–W-538, *Lights* Collection; Julius Epstein, untitled treatment, April 16, 1962, 3340.f–W-540, *Lights* Collection.

12. Robert Maugham, *Odd Man In: A Comedy in Three Acts* (London: Samuel French, 1958), adapted from Claude Magnier, *Monsieur Masure* (Paris: Gerard Billaudot, 1958).

13. Julius Epstein, temporary complete screenplay, August 7–20, 1962, 3340.f–W-551, *Lights* Collection.

14. "MGM Has 26 Major Story Properties in Active Preparation for 1964–65," *BoxOffice*, November 18, 1963, 4; Letter from Geoffrey M. Shurlock to Robert M. Vogel, June 25, 1962, and letter from Geoffrey M. Shurlock to Robert M. Vogel, August 15, 1965, 3343.f–W-564, A LIKELY STORY, Motion Picture Association of America, Production Code Administration Records, Margaret Herrick Library, Los Angeles.

15. "NATO's Star Award to Sophia Loren," *BoxOffice*, September 5, 1966, 7.

16. Folder marked "unproduced," 3343.f–W-564, A LIKELY STORY, Motion Picture Association of America, Production Code Administration Records, Margaret Herrick Library, Los Angeles.

17. "Freeman Doing Original," Hollywood Reporter, July 5, 1966, 2; "Freeman Also Producing 'Lights' for Metro," Variety, July 5, 1966, 2.

18. Freeman and Turnberg, outline, October 13–19, 1966.

19. David E. Nye, *American Technological Sublime* (Cambridge, MA: MIT Press, 1994).

20. Freeman and Turnberg, outline, October 10, 1966, sc. 1, p. 1; October 12, 1966, script notes; October 13, 1966, sc. 1, p. 1.

21. Freeman and Turnberg, outline, October 11, 1966, sc. 1, p. 1.

22. Freeman and Turnberg, outline, October 12–13, 1966, p. 2.

23. "MGM Intros New Title Technique in 'Lights Out,'" *Hollywood Reporter*, December 22, 1967.

24. Louden Wainwright, "The View from Here: A Dark Night to Remember," *Life*, November 19, 1965, 42.

25. Homer Bigart, "A Night of Confusion, Frustration and Adventure," *New York Times*, November 11, 1965; David Wilson, "Where Were You When the Lights Went Out," *Boston Globe*, November 11, 1965; "Blackout Blues of 1965, or Where Were You When the Lights Went Out?" *Variety*, November 17, 1965, 2, 60.

26. Vincent Canby, "The Lights Go Out Again at Grand Central Station—But Only for a Movie: Cameras Rolling Where Trains Could Not, as Blackout Is Rerun," *New York Times*, August 5, 1967.

27. Si Seadler, "'Quiet,' Cried the Director, and, Perhaps for the First Time, Grand Central Was," *Film Daily*, August 10, 1967.

28. Robert Morse, telephone interview with the author, March 6, 2019.

29. Canby, "Lights Go Out Again."

30. "Editorial: Mighty Mite," *Broadcasting*, December 29, 1965, 86; "Transistors to the Rescue," *Variety*, November 10, 1965, 33, 52; Julius Bleiweis, Walter D. Brown, and Leonard M. Olmsted, "The Blackout: It All Happened in 12 Minutes," *Electrical World* 165, no. 4 (1965): 67–72; "Blackout Aftermath: Unending Kudos for Radio," *Broadcasting*, November 22, 1965, 72; "Radio's Role in Blackout: Survey Shows It Relieved Listener's Fears and Helped Avert Panic," *Broadcasting*, January 10, 1966,

49; "Lessons Learned from the Blackout: More Broadcasters Should Prepare Themselves for Emergency Operations," *Broadcasting*, January 17, 1966, 52; Federal Communications Commission, *A Report by the Federal Communications Commission on the Northeast Power Failure of November 9–10, 1965 and Its Effect on Communications* (Washington, DC: US Government Printing Office, 1966).

31. Martin Tolchin, "Hospitals Report Birth Rates Gradually Returning to Normal," *New York Times*, August 12, 1966; "Theories Abound on Birth Increase: Possible Link with Blackout Will Not Be Determined for Two More Weeks," *New York Times*, August 11, 1966; "Births Up 9 Months after the Blackout: Hospitals Report Rise in Births 9 Months after Power Failure," *New York Times*, August 10, 1966.

32. Alan J. Izenman and Sandy L. Zabell, "Babies and the Blackout: The Genesis of a Misconception," *Social Science Research* 10, no. 3 (1981): 282–99; J. Richard Udry, "The Effect of the Great Blackout of 1965 on Births in New York City," *Demography* 7, no. 3 (1970): 325–27.

33. Morse, interview with author.

34. Freeman and Turnberg, WALDO'S VOICE, outline, October 2, 1966, p. 7.

35. Federal Power Commission, *Report to the President by the Federal Power Commission on the Power Failure in the Northeastern United States, and the Province of Ontario on November 9–10, 1965* (Washington, DC: US Government Printing Office, 1965).

36. Eileen Shanahan, "F. P. C. Criticizes Power Systems in Nov. 9 Failure," *New York Times*, December 7, 1965; "FPC Blames Inattention: Blackout Remedies Offered," *Boston Globe*, December 7, 1965; "Portions of F. P. C. Report on Northeastern Blackout Nov. 9," *New York Times*, December 7, 1965; "The Blackout," *The Sun*, December 8, 1965; Neal Stanford, "Power Blackout: Causes, Cures," *Christian Science Monitor*, December 8, 1965; Ted Sell, "Blackout Can Reoccur, Official Report States," *Los Angeles Times*, December 7, 1965.

37. Gene Smith, "Utilities Failed Major Test for Grid," *New York Times*, November 14, 1965.

38. Everett Freeman and Karl Turnberg, temporary complete screenplay, December 12–14, 1966, 3342.f–W-557, *Lights* Collection.

39. Smith, "Utilities Failed."

40. *Northeast Power Failure, November 9, 10, 1965: Hearings before the Special Subcommittee to Investigate Power Failures of the Committee on Interstate and Foreign Commerce*, 89th Cong. (1965–1966); *Hearing before the Committee on Commerce on S. 1934: Amending the Federal Power Act and Related Bills*, 90th Cong. (1967).

41. Julie Cohn, "When the Grid Was the Grid: The History of North America's Brief Coast-to-Coast Interconnected Machine [Scanning Our Past]," *Proceedings of the IEEE* 107, no. 1 (January 2019): 232–43.

42. Dialogue cutting continuity, scene of cab arriving at cottage, reel 5, p. 11, 13343.f–W-563, *Lights* Collection. The dialogue continuity is more clearly understandable than the on-screen voice.

43. "Power Row Stirred Up: Vast Line Interconnections Across Nation at Issue," *The Sun*, November 16, 1965; John M. Lee, "Ontario Accepts Blame for Blackout in Northeast," *New York Times*, November 16, 1965; Shanahan, "F. P. C. Criticizes Power Systems in Nov. 9 Failure"; Gene Smith, "A Nationwide Grid Termed Solution," *New York Times*, November 10 1965; Smith, "Utilities Failed."

44. "Did Blackout Tarnish Utility Image?" *Electrical World* 164, no. 21 (1965): 31–34; Joseph A. Pratt, *A Managerial History of Consolidated Edison, 1936–1981* (New York: Consolidated Edison Company of New York, 1988), 148; McCandlish Phillips,

"Behind the Light Switch Lies Complex Power Network Covering Entire Northeast," *New York Times*, November 15, 1965.

45. *Northeast Power Failure, November 9, 10, 1965: Hearings*; Committee on Commerce, *Responses to Inquiries about the Northeast Power Failure November 9 and 10, 1965: Interim Report of the Committee on Commerce, United States Senate on the Northeast Power Failure* (Washington, DC: Government Printing Office, 1966); *Annual Report of the Public Service Commission* (Albany: State of New York, 1966); *Hearing before the Committee on Commerce on S. 1934.*

46. "Chairman Urges More Authority for FPC," *St. Petersburg Times*, December 16, 1965; "Laws Called Answer to Power Losses," *Toledo Blade*, December 16, 1965; "Legislation Held Need in Power Problem," *The Dispatch*, December 16, 1965; Eileen Shanahan, "F. P. C. Asks Right to Set Electric Power Standards," *New York Times*, December 16, 1965; Federal Power Commission, *Prevention of Power Failures: An Analysis and Recommendations Pertaining to the Northeast Failure and the Reliability of U.S. Power Systems, a Report to the President by the Federal Power Commission* (Washington, DC: Government Printing Office, 1967); Gordon D. Friedlander, "Prevention of Power Failures: The FPC Report of 1967," *Spectrum, IEEE* 5, no. 2 (1968): 53–61.

47. Gene Smith, "Electric Utilities Form Group," *New York Times*, June 12, 1968.

48. IMDb, search variables "blackout," "power failure," "power outage," accessed February 2019, https://www.imdb.com; TCM Movie Database, search variables "blackout," "power failure," "power outage," accessed February 2019, http://www.tcm.com/tcmdb; Google, search variables "blackout movie," "power failure movie," "power outage movie," accessed February 2019, https://www.google.com.

49. Ray Enright, dir., *Slim* (Burbank, CA: Warner Bros., 1937); Raoul Walsh, dir., *Manpower* (Burbank, CA: Warner Bros., 1941); William Berke, dir., *High-Powered* (Hollywood, CA: Pine-Thomas Productions, 1945).

50. Anthony F. Arrigo, *Imaging Hoover Dam: The Making of a Cultural Icon* (Reno: University of Nevada Press, 2014); David P. Billington and Donald C. Jackson, *Big Dams of the New Deal Era: A Confluence of Engineering and Politics* (Norman: University of Oklahoma Press, 2006).

51. Robert Wise, dir., *The Day the Earth Stood Still* (Los Angeles: 20th Century Fox, 1951).

52. Martin V. Melosi, *Atomic Age America* (Boston: Pearson Education, 2013), 107.

53. Nye, *Lights Went Out*, 132–33.

54. Michael Chandler, dir., *Blackout* (Berkeley, CA: Cam Bay Productions, 2001); Alex Gibney, dir., *Enron: The Smartest Guys in the Room* (New York: Jigsaw Productions, 2005); Davis Guggenheim, dir., *An Inconvenient Truth* (Los Angeles: Lawrence Bender Productions, 2006).

55. Mitch Davis, dir., *Christmas Eve* (New York: Amplify/Go Digital, 2015).

56. "Top Grossing Movies of 1968," The Numbers (website), accessed May 3, 2019, https://www.the-numbers.com/market/1968/top-grossing-movies.

57. "MGM's 'Lights Went Out' Wacky Screen Comedy," review of *Lights*, *Hollywood Reporter*, June 6, 1968; Review of *Lights*, *Cue*, August 17, 1968; Charles Champlin, "Doris Day Stars in 'Lights' Comedy," review of *Lights*, *Los Angeles Times*, August 2, 1968.

58. "MGM's 'Lights Went Out,'" review of *Lights*, *MP Herald*, June 12, 1968; Review of *Lights*, *Time*, August 9, 1968; Champlin, "Doris Day Stars"; Murf. [Arthur D.

Murphy], review of *Lights*, *Variety Weekly*, June 12, 1968; Review of *Lights*, *Independent Film Journal*, June 11, 1968.

59. Renata Adler, "From Euphemism to Innuendo: Doris Day Starred in Tale of '65 Blackout," review of *Lights*, *New York Times*, August 9, 1968; Roger Ebert, review of *Lights*, *Chicago Sun Times*, July 3, 1968, https://www.rogerebert.com/reviews /where-were-you-when-the-lights-went-out-1968; Dennis Bingham, "'Before She Was a Virgin . . .': Doris Day and the Decline of Female Film Comedy in the 1950's and 1960's," *Cinema Journal* 45, no. 3 (2006): 3.

60. A. E. Hotchner, *Doris Day: Her Own Story* (New York: William Morrow and Company, 1976), 221.

61. Aljean Harmetz, "Doris Day, Movie Star Who Charmed America, Dies at 97," *New York Times*, May 13, 2019.

Chapter 2

Meltdown: Nuclear Cinema and the Martha Mitchell Effect in *The China Syndrome* (1979) and *Silkwood* (1983)

Caroline Peyton

During the opening sequence of *The China Syndrome*, television reporter Kimberly Wells, played by Jane Fonda, asks a simple question as she waves into the camera: "Hey, fellas, [is] anybody listening to me?"[1] It was a question worth asking in 1979. More than a straightforward conspiracy thriller about nuclear power, *The China Syndrome* transforms the energy politics of the 1970s into a smart, commercially oriented film that reflects much broader themes characterizing American society during this period: the erosion of faith in institutions, skepticism toward protest-based movements and whistleblowers, and a generalized sense of frustration prompted by the era's energy troubles. Despite the film's success at the box office, nuclear power and radioactive waste have typically served as B-movie subjects, while explorations of nuclear weapons have dominated atomic cinema.[2] In this essay, I examine two notable exceptions: *The China Syndrome* and *Silkwood*, both of which offer representations of the nation's nuclear complex at the very moment that criticisms of the industry peaked in the late 1970s and early 1980s.

Directed by James Bridges, *The China Syndrome* depicts a near catastrophe at the fictional Ventana nuclear plant set in Southern California. Coincidentally, Kimberly Wells and her team witness the accident. When she digs deeper into a possible cover-up, Wells manages to nudge the plant supervisor, Jack Godell (Jack Lemmon), into analyzing the snafu further. Troubled by what he discovers, Godell becomes a whistleblower with a tragic but heroic end. Similarly, *Silkwood*, directed by Mike Nichols and written by Nora Ephron and Alice Arlen, examines the true story of Karen Silkwood, who worked at energy conglomerate Kerr-McGee's Cimarron plutonium processing plant near Cimarron City, Oklahoma. The film traces Silkwood's conversion from a flighty woman with a troubled life into a labor activist, whose concern about safety violations prompts her whistleblowing efforts. Mysteriously contaminated by plutonium, Karen Silkwood died in a car accident in 1974, allegedly carrying documents to a *New York Times* reporter. Although antinuclear, environmental, and feminist movements subsequently adopted her as a martyr, Silkwood was a labor activist, as historian Jefferson Cowie has rightly emphasized. Her activism was primarily driven by concerns about worker safety and corporate accountability.[3] Both films portray a nuclear industry crippled by greed and financial pressures, but more importantly, by an organizational culture that contributed to lax safety measures and limited avenues for addressing serious technical issues and a punishing atmosphere for whistleblowers.

Fittingly, whistleblowers, both real and fictive, play essential roles in *The China Syndrome* and *Silkwood*, allowing the films to examine both the problems inherent in the nuclear industry and a corporate culture that values profits over the public interest. Through the presence of whistleblowers, I argue that these films underline the importance of insider access rather than routinized protest to make credible claims. Still, in *The China Syndrome* and *Silkwood*, whistleblowers' claims are dismissed, their sanity questioned, and their personal lives scrutinized. During an era that spawned the "Martha Mitchell effect"—a phenomenon in which a patient is misdiagnosed but whose delusions are, in fact, real—it's not surprising that films examining an industry shrouded in secrecy would wrestle with notions of believable claims and acceptable risk, and hint at conspiracy while avoiding neat resolutions.[4] When does an allegation move from the realm of the implausible to a verifiable truth? Like Martha Mitchell, who gave the press the first indications of the Watergate scandal and whom Richard Nixon's administration quickly maligned as a mentally ill drunk, the whistleblowers in both films, but especially in *Silkwood*, do not escape the audience's critical eye.[5]

Because of this critical eye, particularly toward female characters, viewers must grapple with the nearly claustrophobic dilemma whistleblowers face from all parties—the government, the industry, and their fellow workers. In their lack of resolution, *The China Syndrome* and *Silkwood* build suspense by undercutting industry claims, while also casting doubt on whistleblower protagonists. Bypassing neat solutions to America's energy problems, *The China Syndrome* and *Silkwood* cleverly offer their audiences cinematic representations of an era defined by public skepticism toward institutions *and* those who sought to challenge them.[6] Thus, *The China Syndrome* elevates whistleblowers to heroic status by the film's end, but both Wells and Godell endure a process of intense scrutiny. While historian Finis Dunaway has lamented the uninspiring portrait of antinuclear activists in *The China Syndrome*, the film's portrayal arguably reflects the pervasive skepticism that Americans harbored toward protest movements in the 1970s.[7]

Despite their commercial and critical success, some critics have faulted *The China Syndrome* and *Silkwood* for not providing a more definitive stance on nuclear power and Karen Silkwood's story.[8] Commenting upon *Silkwood*, critic David Sterritt claimed the film is "fogged in by ambiguity," speculating that the filmmakers either sought to avoid legal liability from Kerr-McGee, who were in the midst of a legal battle with Karen Silkwood's estate when the film was produced, or were "paying token service to objectivity."[9] I argue that such critiques miss the deliberate quality of that ambiguity; a central part of the drama in both films comes from *not knowing* if the Ventana plant depicted in *The China Syndrome* is unsafe, or if Karen Silkwood has been contaminated by Kerr-McGee, through her own carelessness, or by a concerted attempt to harm the company. These films indisputably sow seeds of doubt about the nuclear industry. However, as public opinion polls indicated after the accident at Three Mile Island, they simultaneously mirror the reluctance that many Americans felt about removing nuclear power as a possible option for their energy future.[10] Thus, the films successfully transcend simplistic, antinuclear messaging and instead offer apt representations of Americans' lack of clarity about the safety and necessity of commercial nuclear power.

In each film, the audience confronts a nuclear industry conducting their business in the backwoods—rural, concealed locations populated by blue-collar operators and technicians.[11] I argue that this emphasis on blue-collar labor and the plants' rural locations serve as critical components of both films. This is not a tightly orchestrated, centralized system; the distance between the Nuclear Regulatory Commission (NRC), owners, and management on the one hand and the workers and day-to-day industry operations on the other is vast. Engineers struggle to weigh technical and safety concerns against the demands of corporate management, while ordinary operators—the films' hard hats—must sort through their suspicions about the antinuclear movement, mounting financial pressures, and their desire for personal safety alongside acceptable levels of risk. As a result, each film evokes sympathy toward both the whistleblowers and the ordinary workers who populate the industry. In addition, they each explore broader questions about the nuclear industry, corporate power, and the capacity for regulating the nation's vast energy complex.

Finally, with their female leads, *The China Syndrome* and *Silkwood* offer two iterations of women-in-the-workplace dramas. Thus, in addition to questions about industry malfeasance and whistleblowing, the films depict the challenges faced by women in this context. Notably, Kimberly Wells's and Karen Silkwood's stories do not resemble the "career-girl comedies" of the 1930s and 1940s, nor do they embrace the subsequent paradigms of triumphant career women in late-1980s popular cinema.[12] Even when they seem to vindicate their female leads, *The China Syndrome* and *Silkwood* resist the breeziness of 1980s and 1990s postfeminist films. Instead, the filmmakers portray women whose working lives take on new significance as they become whistleblowers, but neither film gives viewers any indication that substantive changes will result from their actions. Without a triumphal vision of women conquering the industry and remaking it from within, the audience is left, again, with a sense of unease about nuclear energy.

The China Syndrome

Scholars have devoted more far attention to *The China Syndrome* than to *Silkwood*. Among other reasons, the film was commercially successful, generating the "highest income of any film" released during a "nonholiday period" at that time, and generally received favorable reviews.[13] The eerie timing of the movie's release on March 16, 1979, and the accident at the Three Mile Island nuclear plant in Harrisburg, Pennsylvania, on March 28, 1979, generated further attention. As many writers have observed, this intersection between fiction and reality augmented the movie's impact. Incredibly, a film exploring a potentially catastrophic accident at a nuclear power plant hit movie theaters at virtually the same time as the accident at Three Mile Island; this coincidence has prompted scholarly considerations of public responses to the film, particularly about how it shaped public opinion about nuclear power and how the accident influenced the film's reception. Scholars have also explored the film's genesis and the filmmakers' intentions, specifically whether or not *The China Syndrome* intended to create an antinuclear or political film.[14] Based upon interviews, the filmmakers—especially Jane Fonda, whose production company IPC helped back the project (along with Columbia Pictures), and producer Michael Douglas—sought commercial success while hoping to provoke debate about nuclear power without shrill messaging. For Fonda, to win audiences over, "you can't propagandize."[15]

The China Syndrome and Three Mile Island did not introduce the American public to nuclear issues, however. As one film critic noted in his review of *The China Syndrome*, only a week before the movie's release, the trial investigating Karen Silkwood's death was ongoing in Oklahoma, and several days later the NRC shut down "five nuclear power plants as unsafe in the event of an earthquake."[16] Although the accident at Three Mile Island became the biggest news story, steady coverage of nuclear issues, including plant construction and delays, saturated news media in the 1970s.[17] And yet, *The China Syndrome* dramatized the inner workings of a nuclear plant in a way no other film or news story had done before.

The audience first encounters the fictional Ventana nuclear power plant as television reporter Kimberly Wells and two cameramen, Richard (Michael Douglas) and his assistant Hector (Daniel Valdez), go onsite to film a spot for an "energy special." The special is styled as informative but not investigative, no doubt a commentary upon the industry's promotional materials that offer superficial engagement with nuclear power.[18] It is unsurprising that a film featuring twin stories about a nuclear plant and a news station emphasizes *seeing*, as both news media and the nuclear industry are quite literally mediated through visual and print media, promotional materials, and, for the latter, routinized public hearings. Like the era's other conspiracy thrillers, *The China Syndrome* depicts the difficult process of navigating such cloistered enterprises and the herculean effort required to pierce that veil. Fredric Jameson aptly describes such disorientation: "[The] figuration of conspiracy as an [unconscious] attempt . . . to think a system so vast that it cannot be encompassed by the natural and historically developed categories of perception with which human beings normally orient themselves."[19] *The China Syndrome*, like Sidney Lumet's *Network* (1976), draws attention to mediation and the difficulties of accurate perception through the repeated use of monitors.[20]

This self-referentiality calls into question not only the transparency of the news media but also nuclear power production; utility companies, regulatory agencies, and television news continuously filtered information about the inner workings of nuclear plants before it reached the public. Obtaining meaningful insight into plant operations, or potential cover-ups, necessitated insider access. Somewhat ironically, even the film production team had to rely upon one furtive tour of the Trojan nuclear power plant in Oregon and materials in the public domain to reproduce an accurate rendering of a plant. In order to create the visual illusion of the fictional plant's exteriors, the audience sees composite shots instead of an actual power plant, while other scenes featuring a jostling reactor relied upon miniature effects to replicate a working nuclear reactor.

Set in the hinterlands, the Ventana plant operates far beyond lush LA proper; it's a parched landscape, so much so that one writer described the film as "ugly . . . in a way that no Bridges film was before or after."[21] The plant's exterior hints at its labyrinthian, claustrophobic character. Concrete, a lack of windows, and the inability to view inside or outside (again, the theme of seeing), the plant possesses a foreboding quality. After Kimberly Wells and her news crew finish filming Ventana's exterior, California Gas & Electric (CG&E) public relations representative Bill Gibson (James Hampton) gives the trio an obligatory explanation of how the plant produces power. Before moving on to the tour, though, they quickly reshoot several close-ups of Wells "listening" to the spiel (after Gibson's exit), reminding the audience of the medium's arti-fice. Tonally, the filmmakers draw our attention to the mundane; the audience, like Wells, must listen to a rehearsed speech from a PR representative before embarking upon a canned tour. The colossal character of the plant, its maze of pipes and equipment, and the deafening noise hint at the plant's enormity and the risk associated with nuclear power production—a stark contrast to Gibson's assurances that plant operations are simple. Not yet cognizant of the danger ahead, Wells's primary concern is the plant's poor lighting, which prompts a detour to the viewing gallery above the plant's control room. The television studio and the control room are parallel spaces; Jean Baudrillard has described them as "the homology of the nuclear and of television." [22]

Through the viewing gallery, the drama of nuclear power production sud-denly becomes visible to Wells, her cameramen, and the audience. A near di-saster occurs after the reactor automatically shuts down (commonly known as a SCRAM incident). Jack Godell and others desperately try to fix the problem, which nearly causes a catastrophic meltdown of the reactor core. Even before this incident, Wells starts to have misgivings about the plant's operation. She notices that the workers in the control room, clad in jeans, denim jackets, and hard hats, appear not as brilliant nuclear engineers but as operators in any industrial setting; a distinction that arguably shapes viewer perceptions of nuclear safety. Sonja Schmid has demonstrated that the Soviet system dif-ferentiated "atomshchiki (reactor designers) from the civilian, and therefore supposedly less diligent, somewhat less qualified, and less disciplined non-nuclear energetiki." [23] Similarly, *The China Syndrome* highlights the working-class character of plant construction and operation, making it clear that the day-to-day operations of nuclear power plants are far removed from the "magi-cal transformation" of theoretical physics and thus require faith not merely in engineers but also in blue-collar expertise. This sector maintains its own hierarchy, as well, in which former US Navy nuclear trainees like Jack Godell retain greater privileges than "company men," like his best friend, Ted Spindler (Wilford Brimley). While Godell escapes scrutiny, Spindler endures a seven-hour interrogation from the US Nuclear Regulatory Commission and fears the company will cast him as the scapegoat for the near accident that Wells and others witnessed during the tour.

Early in the film, Godell defends the plant by noting that its quality con-trol system is equal to NASA's, yet the control room has an exceedingly casual feel, reflected in the operators' wardrobes. It's more Bakersfield than Berkeley. The company's organizational culture has enabled a climate in which falsified weld X-rays are dismissed as minor issues, as the plant manager admonishes Godell that the company can't produce "every stupid document the government calls for." This reproach comes even as the physical act of the faulty welds rupturing illustrates the technological complexity and material vulnerability of nuclear plants. In addition, including a depiction of contractors is important not simply for its realism. The construction of plants required contractors, which meant that quality control was, in fact, a piecemeal process and not easily audited. Moreover, it's the construction company's "security men" who pursue both Godell and Hector the cameraman as they attempt to submit the falsified weld X-rays into the NRC's public hearing for another CG&E power plant, suggesting that the industry also relies on more nefarious means to escape regulatory oversight.

Inspired and concerned by the near accident she witnessed, Kimberly Wells seeks to air her crew's illegally captured footage of the action inside the control room. However, the "energy-media complex" rebuffs her initial efforts; the station manager cites legal obstacles but also has a cozy relationship with CG&E. When Wells continues to pursue the story, she is reminded of her role as a "performer" rather than a serious reporter. As she continues her fact-finding mission and visits the lone, country music-playing tavern near the plant—another allusion to the rural, hard-hat mentality of plant workers—Jack Godell stonewalls Wells by emphasizing her inability to understand the plant's complex operations with a blunt response: "Well, you wouldn't understand." Similarly, the plant workers refer to antinuclear activists as "bozos," who from their perspective cannot understand the importance of the plant's power production to their daily lives. This organizational tendency to shield Ventana from external criticism provides yet another subtle indictment of nuclear power and further reinforces the heroic role of whistleblowers to expose safety violations.

Beyond its smart examination of nuclear power, *The China Syndrome* employs Wells's and Godell's career-minded single lives as metaphors for the erosion of institutional integrity and adherence to traditional values in the 1970s. As others have noted, Godell is wedded to his job; when he begins his downward spiral, he admits that he "lives" for work and even confesses to loving the plant.[24] For workaholics, corporations replace families and in the process demand a type of loyalty that fundamentally undermines public safety. Tellingly, once Godell becomes entirely unmoored and tragically intervenes to stop the plant's operation, the company officials who order the SWAT team that kills him claim that they "kept it in the family" for as long as possible. In Kimberly Wells's case, misplaced corporate priorities have shaped television news into innocuous content about faulty hot air balloon landings instead of hard-hitting journalism. To achieve her professional aspirations, Wells endures humiliating situations and neglects her personal life. After a night of navigating objectifying comments from the station manager, Wells retreats to her apartment alone, with only her pet tortoise for company. Profit motives and regulatory capture have eroded the trustworthiness of government and corporations peddling high-risk energy technology, and larger changes have upended the traditional structure of family and work in American lives. Despite the ascendancy of corporate power and fears of derailing their careers through whistleblowing, Kimberly Wells's and Jack Godell's heroism derives from their willingness to use their professional expertise for public good.

At the film's climax, the audience experiences the culmination of the Martha Mitchell effect; suddenly emboldened by his commitment to the truth, Jack Godell behaves in a manner that appears erratic and unstable. Fearing a serious nuclear accident, Godell has turned over the falsified documents, thereby fulfilling his whistleblower status. After cameraman Hector is run off the road by the construction company's security men (in a reference to Silkwood's fate), Godell makes the decision to testify at the Point Conception power plant hearings, only to find himself being chased by the security men, as well. Seeking safe haven in the Ventana plant, Godell once again urges the plant operators not to bring the reactor online. He then seizes the security guard's gun and attempts to hold the reactor control room hostage. A SWAT team storms in and fatally shoots Godell. As reporters swarm outside, the company describes Godell as emotionally disturbed and intoxicated, but company man Ted Spindler breaks free of corporate secrecy, telling reporters "he was the sanest man I ever knew." Stunned by Godell's death and the events more generally, Wells goes on air, emotionally shaken, but delivers a commanding performance. Despite this small victory, Godell's martyrdom, the company's denial, and the film's lack of resolution offer the audience little reassurance about the ever-growing number of nuclear plants in their own communities.

Silkwood

The nuclear industry carved out its own niche in nuclear fuel production and missile silos in America's heartland. As critic Vincent Canby puts it, energy production transformed the "vast plains" into a "petrochemical-nuclear" landscape with "huge, sophisticated industrial facilities." [25] The critically acclaimed film *Silkwood* examines the controversial real-life and mysterious death of Karen Silkwood (played by Meryl Streep), a technician turned labor activist at one of these facilities, the Kerr-McGee Cimarron fuel fabrication plant near Cimarron City, Oklahoma. The plant fabricated plutonium pellets for an experimental breeder reactor in Hanford, Washington. Allegations of Kerr-McGee's corporate negligence and worker contamination, including of Karen Silkwood, prompted widespread investigative reports on Silkwood and the plant, along with a major civil lawsuit against the company brought by Silkwood's estate, in which her estate ultimately won a major settlement.[26]

As in *The China Syndrome,* viewers are presented with a whistleblower figure who represents the fragmentation in American society during the 1970s, the "complexity of speaking out," and wresting oneself from "capitalist Stockholm Syndrome," as Kyle Stevens has argued.[27] Loosely reflecting Silkwood's life, she has a distant relationship with her three children in the film, one of whom questions, "Momma?" during their one encounter; when she contemplates simply taking her kids and hitting the road, her roommate Dolly (played by Cher) asks what she would even do with them. Silkwood has an on-again, off-again relationship with Drew Stephens (played by Kurt Russell), who desires a greater commitment than she's willing to give. The film depicts Karen Silkwood as a woman who is not particularly punctual or concerned with societal conventions, as evidenced by her propensity to flash others in the workplace and chew gum in the fuel fabrication room, and through neglecting her health. The audience rarely sees her eat; she's usually pictured smoking a cigarette, and the film hints at her regular use and possibly abuse of prescription medicine. And yet, according to screenwriter Nora Ephron, the writers intended not to make Silkwood a saint, but rather a complicated character.[28] That process of presenting her as a complex but flawed woman reflects more than Karen Silkwood's attributes in real life; it is central to the film's broader message about the dislocation of people's lives in the 1970s, the declining autonomy of workers in industry, and the way that whistleblowers are scrutinized professionally and personally.

Beyond its representation of Karen Silkwood's strengths and shortcomings, the film casts doubt upon the safety of the nuclear industry. The audience encounters a fuel fabrication plant in the backwoods of America, rural Oklahoma. Rather than a high-tech operation populated by skilled, credentialed employees, it appears to be a mostly local endeavor that employs blue-collar workers who might work in any factory. Upon the film's release, at least one former Kerr-McGee worker disagreed with the film's portrayal of the employees, stating that *Silkwood* "made it look like only Farm-Belt types worked there—I worked with college educated people."[29] The film offers a different perspective. Karen Silkwood only belatedly discovers the risk involved in her job. As Karen and Dolly sit on their front porch, Karen reads from a pamphlet with information about nuclear radiation: "This says all that stuff about acceptable levels and all—it's bullshit . . . It says here, 'Plutonium gives you cancer.' It says it flat out." [30] The workers are monitored for radiation exposure, but any major contamination incidents are addressed by a doctor, possibly a vet, instead of someone trained in health physics. This process of radiation monitoring appears arbitrary and inexact, which is more disturbing when one considers that "there were 574 reported exposures to plutonium" at the Cimarron facility between 1970 and 1975.[31]

When Silkwood and her boyfriend, Drew Stephens, visit Los Alamos to determine the nature of her contamination, the scientists first assure her that she is well within the maximum permissible limit, only to volunteer a caveat—measures could be plus or minus 300 percent. Not only does the US Atomic Energy Commission feel entirely removed from the regulatory process, but the employees are constrained by their own economic pressures and face decertification from the Oil, Chemical, and Atomic Workers International Union (OCAW). Silkwood's whistleblowing threatens their livelihoods, while the desire to retain those livelihoods, even if it means ignoring dangerous practices, undermines plant safety. It's a subtle portrait, intended to cast doubt even as it avoids overt messaging. Viewers are presented with an industry populated by blue-collar Americans whose short-term economic interests encourage safety violations.

Kerr-McGee repeatedly highlighted its global imprint in promotional literature during this period, but in the film the action is mostly contained to the Cimarron facility.[32] A viewer ignorant of Kerr-McGee's scope might even think it's a local company. At the Cimarron plant, plutonium pellets are produced in a setting one critic described as resembling a "lethal nursery for preemies." [33] The audience learns that the fuel pellets are intended for an experimental breeder reactor in Hanford, Washington; sees Karen Silkwood and her fellow union representatives visit DC; and gets brief aerial shots of the petrochemical complex in Texas when Karen visits her children. The connections between all of these places are loose ones; the energy apparatus appears disconnected—too vast to comprehend and certainly to regulate.

Both in the film and in reality, Kerr-McGee accused Karen Silkwood of deliberately contaminating herself with plutonium to hurt the company— something that only a person driven to near-suicidal commitment would do. Kerr-McGee's lawyers no doubt intended for jurors to question Silkwood's sanity and her claims. Ultimately, the filmmakers do not take a definitive stance on this issue, which some critics found disappointing. Sheila Benson, writing for the *Los Angeles Times*, offered a simpler and fair assessment: "The film cannot supply the truth because no one really knows the truth." [34] Over four decades later, the contamination of Karen Silkwood's home and her tragic death remain a mystery, but Kerr-McGee's safety violations and disregard for the environment and its workers' health, particularly in its nuclear division, are well documented.[35]

Echoing Silkwood's own life, legal battles defined the early stages of making the film. Jane Fonda sought the rights to the story but was rebuffed, and two persistent film students, Buzz Hirsch and Larry Cano, managed to secure the rights from the Silkwood estate, only to be threatened with legal action by Kerr-McGee.[36] The company's lawyers, who were engaged in a legal battle with Karen Silkwood's estate, issued a massive subpoena in the discovery process, requesting any and all information the filmmakers might have had about Silkwood, including correspondence and documents pertaining to activists involved in and journalists who had reported on the Silkwood case. The subpoena also demanded any documentation of her personal habits, specifically "relating to the use, abuse, or possession . . . after August, 3, 1972 of marijuana, LSD, methaqualone, or any other dangerous or controlled substances or any other drugs."[37] As in the film, where Silkwood's body is violated by the plutonium embedded in her lungs, and the bodily horror experienced by contaminated employees who underwent the "Silkwood shower" (most horrifically portrayed by a wigless, screaming worker), Kerr-McGee's legal tactics unsurprisingly pursued every possible avenue to discredit her, posthumously violating her privacy in a far-reaching and public manner. By arguing that Karen Silkwood purposely contaminated herself with plutonium, the company cast her as more than a disgruntled employee; Karen Silkwood was mentally unstable enough to condemn herself to terribly painful and potentially fatal plutonium exposure.

Ironically, the company that devoted enormous energy to discrediting its chief whistleblower has avoided meaningful revelations about its own practices. For a global energy conglomerate with a long history, Kerr-McGee's donated papers, housed at the University of Oklahoma's Western history collection, amount to two paltry boxes. Those boxes are almost entirely filled with promotional pamphlets, brochures, and drafts of company histories, with one folder of clippings related to Karen Silkwood. Virtually nothing is revealed, and yet at the time of *Silkwood*'s release, press coverage indicated that Kerr-McGee had requested a copy of the script during production to offer input outlining the "facts in the case."[38] Director Mike Nichols, along with screenwriters Nora Ephron and Alice Arlen, faced enough criticism for weaving fact and fiction together that Nichols wrote a scathing letter to the *New York Times* defending the film. He concluded that "the manner of her life . . . marked her out, for history as well as for journalism," and argued that a "film with actors and dialogue" provides another way to think critically about what

Karen Silkwood's life, or what "an unheroic woman driven to heroism," reveals about the nuclear industry, Kerr-McGee's power to shape that story, and the politics of whistleblowing.[39]

Conclusion

Until the 2019 HBO miniseries *Chernobyl*, the commercial nuclear industry rarely made an appearance in American popular culture after the 1980s, during which the debate over the nuclear industry still raged. The most notable exception is the long-running animated series *The Simpsons*, in which Homer Simpson, family patriarch and blue-collar everyman, works at the Springfield Nuclear Power Plant as a safety inspector. Given his chief attributes—"lifelong stupidity" and "general boorishness"—Homer Simpson hardly possesses the characteristics of a qualified safety inspector.[40] Of course, the discord between Homer's ineptitude and the high-stakes operations of a nuclear power plant is a joke that keeps on giving. Only in the twelfth season—after Homer has a crayon removed from his brain, which markedly raises his IQ and creates a sudden propensity for high achievement—does Homer report a safety violation to the Nuclear Regulatory Commission, causing the plant to shut down and lay off Homer and his friends. After deciding that intelligence seems to create more problems than it solves, Homer has the "debilitating crayon reinserted."[41] For a moment, Homer Simpson was a whistleblower, but soon determines that neither intelligence nor the act of interfering in the plant's operations produced desirable results.

There is plenty of connective tissue between *The Simpsons*, *Silkwood*, and *The China Syndrome*. While *Silkwood* and *The China Syndrome* adopt a serious posture—no doubt products of an era shaped by the energy crisis and intense concern about the safety of the nuclear industry—the creators of *The Simpsons*, in gallows-humor fashion, arguably could not have found a more fitting workplace for Homer Simpson in a corporate-dominated, post-Chernobyl world. Homer Simpson, Karen Silkwood, and the ordinary workers in *The China Syndrome* populate a vast and sprawling nuclear industry, far from the watchful eyes of regulatory agencies, and harboring an organizational culture geared more toward following orders than asking questions. Kimberly Wells and Jack Godell, as part of the professional class, experience different constraints; they are burdened with the desire to excel in their careers and perplexed by defining what exactly success is—climbing the corporate ladder or adhering to a professional code that exceeds corporate values.

The China Syndrome and *Silkwood* reflect a much broader crisis of confidence in the nation's energy future, mirrored in the fractured lives of their protagonists and their depictions of the nuclear industry and its workers. To oppose a corrupt organizational culture and puncture a web of corporate-government power is to imperil one's sanity and physical safety, and open one's life to outside scrutiny. By challenging the nuclear industry with its inherently risky, complex technologies and searching for a clear resolution, whistleblowers are driven to despair—emotional meltdowns in order to prevent nuclear ones. And yet these films avoid the trap of heavy-handed antinuclear messaging. Taking decisively ambiguous stances, both films successfully capture the immense insecurity and bewilderment Americans felt about the best path forward in terms of energy production. Even as "soft power" options, like wind and solar, offered new possibilities, many Americans were not ready to scrap nuclear power plants. As *The China Syndrome* and *Silkwood* prominently feature, they harbored doubts about institutions *and* the people who challenged them. Navigating the murky territory of delusion versus reality, these films deftly render the minefield and inescapable ambiguity of 1970s energy politics.

Notes

1. James Bridges, dir., *The China Syndrome* (Culver City, CA: Columbia Pictures, 1979).
2. Paul Boyer, *By the Bomb's Early Light: American Thought and Culture at the Dawn of the Atomic Age* (Chapel Hill: University of North Carolina Press, 1994); Mick Broderick, *Nuclear Movies: Critical Analysis and Filmography of International Feature Length Films Dealing with Experimentation, Aliens, Terrorism, Holocaust, and Other Disaster Scenarios, 1914–1990* (Jefferson, NC: McFarland and Co., 1991); Joyce A. Evans, *Celluloid Mushroom Clouds: Hollywood and the Atomic Bomb* (Boulder, CO: Boulder Westview Press, 1998); Cyndy Hendershot, *Paranoia, the Bomb and 1950s Science Fiction Films* (Bowling Green, OH: Bowling Green State University Popular Press, 1999); Margot A. Henriksen, *Dr. Strangelove's America: Society and Culture in the Atomic Age* (Berkeley: University of California Press, 1997); Toni A. Perrine, *Film and the Nuclear Age: Representing Cultural Anxiety*, 2nd ed. (New York: Routledge, 2018); Jerome F. Shapiro, *Atomic Bomb Cinema: The Apocalyptic Imagination on Film* (New York: Routledge, 2011).
3. Jefferson Cowie, *Stayin' Alive: The 1970s and the Last Days of the Working Class* (New York: New Press, 2012), 67.
4. Andrew Colman, *A Dictionary of Psychology* (Oxford, UK: Oxford University Press, 2015), 441.
5. At the time of the Watergate break-in, Martha Mitchell was married to John Mitchell, former US attorney general and director of Richard Nixon's reelection campaign.
6. For this argument, see Finis Dunaway, *Seeing Green: The Use and Abuse of American Environmental Images* (Chicago: University of Chicago Press, 2015), 133–35.
7. Sociologist Penny Lewis has argued that even as a growing number of Americans opposed the Vietnam War, polling data shows that an even greater number of Americans disliked antiwar protestors. Penny Lewis, *Hardhats, Hippies, and Hawks:*

The Vietnam Antiwar Movement as Myth and Memory (Ithaca, NY: Cornell University Press, 2013), especially chapters 1 and 7.

8.   James Bridges, Mike Gray, and T. S. Cook wrote the screenplay for *The China Syndrome*.

9.   David Sterritt, "'Silkwood': Good Intentions are Fogged in by Ambiguity," *Christian Science Monitor*, January 5, 1984, https://www.csmonitor.com/1984/0105/010506 .html.

10. For example, in one 1980 poll, 32 percent of those surveyed favored building more plants, 42 percent favored operating only those already built, 16 percent thought all nuclear plants should be closed down, and 9 percent were undecided. See survey conducted by Center for Political Studies, University of Michigan. American National Election Study, November 1980, USCPS.80POST.QT05, Roper Center for Public Opinion Research, iPOLL [distributor], accessed November 21, 2015. In another poll conducted in May 1979, 52 percent of those surveyed supported building more nuclear power plants, while 42 percent opposed it. See survey conducted by ABC News/Louis Harris and Associates, May 18–May 22, 1979, USABCHS.062179.R1, Roper Center for Public Opinion Research, iPOLL [distributor], accessed November 21, 2015. Sixty percent of those surveyed in an October 1979 poll stated that nuclear power must be part of America's energy future. See survey conducted by Cambridge Report/Research International, October 1979, USCAMREP.79OCT.R090, Roper Center for Public Opinion Research, iPOLL [distributor], accessed November 21, 2015. Thus, even in the wake of Three Mile Island, Americans often expressed support for continuing the operation of nuclear plants, while expressing doubt about the industry's honesty. In one survey, only 20 percent of participants thought the nuclear industry had honestly described the dangers associated with nuclear power plants.

11. This portrayal in *The China Syndrome* and *Silkwood* reflects the fascination with blue-collar Americans in popular culture during this period. See Cowie, *Stayin' Alive*. Capitalizing on this interest, James Bridges followed *The China Syndrome* with *Urban Cowboy (1980)*, which chronicles a blue-collar couple (played by John Travolta and Debra Winger) in Houston, Texas, during the energy boom of the 1980s. James Bridges, dir., *Urban Cowboy* (Hollywood, CA: Paramount Pictures, 1980).

12. Rosie White, "*Working Girl* and Second Wave Feminism: Re-viewing the 1980s," *Film International* 14, no. 3/4 (2016): 331–32.

13. J. Samuel Walker, *Three Mile Island: A Nuclear Crisis in Historical Perspective* (Berkeley: University of California Press, 2004), 2.

14. For scholarly discussions of *The China Syndrome*, see Walker, *Three Mile Island*, 1–3; Dunaway, *Seeing Green*, 121–37; Tony Shaw, "'Rotten to the Core': Exposing America's Energy-Media Complex in *The China Syndrome*," *Cinema Journal* 52, no. 2 (December 2013): 93–113; Marsha Weisiger, "When Life Imitates Art," *Environmental History* 12, no. 2 (April 2007): 383–85; Charles Derry, *The Suspense Thriller: Films in the Shadow of Alfred Hitchcock* (Jefferson, NC: McFarland and Co., 1998), 167–71; Peter Tonguette, *The Films of James Bridges* (Jefferson, NC: McFarland and Co., 2014), 104–25; Jean Baudrillard, "The Evil Demon of Images," in *Film Theory: Critical Concepts in Media and Cultural Studies*, vol. 4, eds. Philip Simpson, Andrew Utterson, and K. J. Shepherdson (New York: Routledge, 2004), 181–91; Robert F. Wilson Jr., "On the Air/On the Line: Parallel Structure and Contemporary History in *The China Syndrome*," *Film & History: An Interdisciplinary*

Journal of Film and Television Studies 9, no. 3 (September 1979): 49–53; Brian Rose, "Mass Mediated Images: The Force of Television in *The China Syndrome*," *Journal of Popular Film and Television* 8, no. 3 (Fall 1980): 2–9; Peter Krämer, "The Politics of Independence: *The China Syndrome* (1979), Hollywood Liberals, and Antinuclear campaigning," *Alphavilla: Journal of Film and Screen Media* 6 (Winter 2013), http://www.alphavillejournal.com/Issue6/HTML/ArticleKramer.html; John Wills, "Celluloid Chain Reactions: *The China Syndrome* and Three Mile Island," *European Journal of American Culture* 25, no. 2 (August 2006): 109–22.

15. Gary Crowdus, review of *The China Syndrome*, *Cinéaste* 9, no. 3 (Spring 1979): 45–47.
16. David Denby, "More Heat Than Light," *New York Magazine*, April 2, 1979, 79.
17. For a general overview of nuclear power in the United States during this period, see J. Samuel Walker, "The Nuclear Power Debates of the 1970s," in *American Energy Policy in the 1970s*, ed. Robert Lifset (Norman: University of Oklahoma Press, 2014), 221–56.
18. For an in-depth analysis of this topic, see Rose, "Mass Mediated Images."
19. Fredric Jameson, *The Geopolitical Aesthetic: Cinema and Space in the World System* (Bloomington: Indiana University Press, 1992), 2.
20. As in *The China Syndrome*, *Network* interrogates the ruthless transformation of news media into corporatized, entertainment-driven television programming. Sidney Lumet, dir., *Network* (Beverly Hills: Metro-Goldwyn-Mayer Studios, 1976).
21. Tonguette, *Films of James Bridges*, 111.
22. Baudrillard, "Evil Demon of Images," 184.
23. Sonja D. Schmid, "Organizational Culture and Professional Identities in the Soviet Nuclear Power Industry," *Osiris* 23, no. 1 (2008): 82–111.
24. Wayne J. McMullen, "'The China Syndrome': Corruption to the Core," *Literature/Film Quarterly* 23, no. 1 (1995): 55–62.
25. Vincent Canby, "Karen Silkwood's Story," *New York Times*, December 14, 1983.
26. For a popular overview of Karen Silkwood's story, see Richard Rashke, *The Killing of Karen Silkwood: The Story Behind the Kerr-McGee Plutonium Case* (New York: Open Road Media, 2014).
27. Kyle Stevens, *Mike Nichols: Sex, Language, and the Reinvention of Psychological Realism* (New York: Oxford University Press, 2015), 153.
28. Patrick McGilligan, "Nora Ephron: Feminist with a Funny Bone," in *Backstory 5: Interviews with Screenwriters of the 1990s*, ed. Patrick McGilligan (Berkeley: University of California Press, 2009), 41.
29. Deborah Caulfield, "'Silkwood': Reaction in Oklahoma," *Los Angeles Times*, December 17, 1983.
30. Mike Nichols, dir., *Silkwood* (Hollywood, CA: ABC Motion Pictures, 1983).
31. William J. Broad, "Fact and Legend Clash in 'Silkwood,'" *New York Times*, December 11, 1983; Hans Baer, "Kerr-McGee and the NRC: From Indian Country to Silkwood to Gore," *Social Science and Medicine* 30, no. 2 (1990): 237–48.
32. See Kerr-McGee Corporation Collection, Western History Collection, University of Oklahoma Libraries, Norman, Oklahoma.
33. Sheila Benson, "Nuclear-Age Horror Story in *Silkwood*," *Los Angeles Times*, December 14, 1983.
34. Benson, "Nuclear-Age Horror Story."
35. Baer, "Kerr-McGee and the NRC"; David Burnham, "A.E.C. Finds Evidence Supporting Charges of Health Hazards at Plutonium Processing Plant in

Oklahoma," *New York Times*, January 8, 1975; Comptroller General of the United States, "Federal Investigations into Certain Health, Safety, Quality Control, Criminal Allegations at Kerr-McGee Nuclear Corporation," report to the Subcommittee on Reports, Accounting, and Management Committee on Government Operations, May 30, 1975, US Government Accounting Office, Washington, DC, https://www.gao.gov/assets/120/113110.pdf.

36. Stephen F. Rohde, "Reel to Reel: The Hirsch Case and First Amendment Protection for Filmmakers' Confidential Sources of Information," *Pepperdine Law Review* 5, no. 2 (1978): 351–402; Gene Triplett, "Plans Made for Silkwood Movie," *Oklahoman*, May 23, 1982; Deirdre Carmody, "Court Extends Right of Press to Filming: Federal Panel Rules Documentary Maker is Entitled to Protect Sources under Constitution," *New York Times*, October 2, 1977; Michael Blowen, "The Bizarre Filming of a Real Life Thriller: A Ten Year Struggle to Tell How One Woman Waged War against the Nuclear Industry," *Boston Globe*, December 11, 1983.

37. United States District Court deposition subpoena for *Karen G. Silkwood v. Kerr-McGee Corporation*, February 26, 1977, box 1, folder 22, case materials, Karen Silkwood, February 1977, Roberta Ann Paris Funnell Collection, Western History Collection, University of Oklahoma, Norman, Oklahoma.

38. Michael London, "Silkwood Still Stirring: ABC Pictures and Kerr-McGee Are Posed for a Battle over Facts Surrounding the Life and Death of Karen Silkwood," *Los Angeles Times*, November 18, 1983.

39. Mike Nichols, letter to the editor, *New York Times*, January 8, 1984; London, "Silkwood Still Stirring."

40. Chris Turner, *Planet Simpson: How a Cartoon Masterpiece Documented an Era and Defined a Generation* (New York: Random House, 2010), 117.

41. Turner, *Planet Simpson*, 117–18.

Chapter 3

"The Juice": *The Road Warrior* (1981) and the Cultural Logic of Energy Denial in the Early Days of Modern Globalization

Christopher R. W. Dietrich

When the dystopian action film *The Road Warrior* arrived in the United States from Australia in May 1982, the national economy felt more bullish than it had in over a decade, and it was clear in ticket sales. More than 2.5 million moviegoers across the nation shelled out $2.75 or $3.00 on opening weekend for the higher-budget, slicker sequel to *Mad Max*. Other sectors of the national economy also seemed to be faring well. Massive public and private spending in science and technology, the rise of commercial television and air-conditioning, the reinvigoration of the auto and electronics industries, and the growing fields of telecommunications and computing all pointed to a glowing future of economic expansion. At the global level, American banks and investment companies capitalized on the opening of foreign markets, standardized container shipping tripled, and the dollar remained the world currency. If these economic indicators and public rhetoric were to be believed, the nation had begun to rise above the economic crises of the 1970s, characterized by the US trade deficit, the end of Bretton Woods, stagflation, deindustrialization, and the energy crisis.[1]

In the political arena, many Americans attributed the economic recovery to the free market. Allowing business to act with minimal government intervention, they believed, would pull the United States out of the worst downturn since the Great Depression. "Some say the future is looking impossible, filled with danger and uncertainty and scarcity," Ronald Reagan told a group of business leaders in 1981 when pitching his administration's Economic Recovery Program. But such cynicism was ill-founded, he said, when the US government was enacting lower taxes and throwing out regulations in order to "make the 1980's the most exciting, successful decade our nation has ever known—years of renaissance for American entrepreneurs, years when millions of free men and women went out and found the energy to make us secure."[2] Such rhetoric linking capitalism with democracy through individualist values of freedom and choice—or, as celebrity economist Milton Friedman put it, economic freedom as "an indispensable means toward the achievement of political freedom"— was widespread.[3] At the time and ever since, economists and other experts have consistently pointed to the rise of American-led capitalist globalization as the bell rope that wound this view of the world together. They have created a triumphalist vision of the 1980s, one that links the spread of markets with the expansion of human liberty and depicts US-led globalization as a natural and benevolent process.[4]

But it was an imperfect recovery in the United States and globally. Massive deficit spending combined with pro-business policies gave the lie to the notion that small government and a pure free market were as much practice as ideology.[5] Scholars also have identified the gross wealth and power disparities that came afterward and uncovered the connection between calls for open markets, policies supporting the concentration of wealth, and hawkish militarism.[6] At the deepest level, these studies remind us that neoliberalism and neoconservatism are two sides of the same coin.

It is beyond the scope of this essay to examine the debates, benefits, and drawbacks of US policy in the era of contemporary globalization. But it is fair to say that within that context, energy supply was among the weightiest concerns for policymakers and the public. The Australian-made *The Road Warrior*, the second movie in the original *Mad Max* trilogy, captured the more dystopian preoccupations of the era. Through an examination of the film's content and reception in the context of US politics and culture, this essay holds that the film's themes of energy deprivation and justified violence reflect a fearful logic of denial that was widespread in the United States in the early 1980s.

The logic of denial can be considered ideological production along the lines of what Judith Butler has described as the creation of "obviousness." By this, Butler means to track the creation of certain ideological tenets, in culture or politics or both, that became so strong that they not only enveloped mainstream society but soon became entrenched to the point that they were resistant to well-reasoned counterarguments.[7] Building on Butler, it is important to note that obviousness often develops through opaque processes, and contemporary actors often do not understand exactly how various beliefs come to be regarded as the "natural" truth. One of the jobs of historians is to make more transparent the different practices and actions that come together to form ideological principles and interpretations. In the context of the energy crisis of the 1970s and the promised market recovery of the 1980s, *The Road Warrior* provides one means of understanding the depth of the fear of energy denial that penetrated Western society and popular culture, as well as some of its consequences.

Without Fuel They Were Nothing

Context is crucial to understand the commercial success of *The Road Warrior* in the United States. Portraying the postapocalyptic future as one in which control over oil meant mobility and power, the movie embodied the alarm over energy denial that engulfed US society in the 1970s and after. Several scenes stand out for the way they capture the essence of energy denial, and they remind us that contemporary actors understood the ways in which "natural" processes of globalization had a cultural basis in widely shared—obvious—ideological assumptions.

The first scene of the movie exposes the difference between its fictional civilization before and after the apocalypse. A deep-throated narrator speaks over a montage of Mel Gibson—"The Road Warrior, the man we called Max"—staring into a void. As the void transforms into black-and-white stock footage of oil derricks and refineries, the narrator continues:

> To understand who he was, you have to go back to another time, when the world was powered by the black fuel and the deserts spouted great cities of pipe and steel. Gone now, swept away. For reasons long forgotten, two mighty warrior tribes went to war and touched off a blaze which engulfed them all. Without fuel, they were nothing. They built a house of straw. The thundering machine sputtered and stopped.

The twin allusion to oil consumption and nuclear war was clear to all who had eyes to watch. The black-and-white montage turns to a whirlwind of historical scenes of looting, riot, and war. Society crumbled, cities collapsed, and dreams were ruined, and gangs began to take over the highways. "Only those mobile enough to scavenge, brutal enough to pillage, would survive," the narrator says.[8] The struggle for fuel and mobility is the central premise of postapocalyptic life in the Wasteland. In the first of many action scenes, Max outmaneuvers an attacking gang and returns to an accident on the highway to scavenge for fuel. He even uses his gloves to soak up gasoline on the ground, squeezing them into a spare container. Every last drop of the precious liquid counts, for it is the source of survival.

Shortly after, Max learns of a settlement that has tapped oil and begun to refine it. He sets out for the settlement, but finds it under siege. A gang led by a psychotic goliath aptly called the Humungus or Lord Humungus surrounds the colony. Humungus has discovered that the settlers plan to take their gas out of the Wasteland to their imagined paradise, the Coast. Indicting them as "selfish because you hoard gasoline," he avows, "Humungus will not be denied." He offers the settlers a compromise. In return for "walking away from your pump, your oil, your gasoline, your whole compound," he will spare their lives. The settlers decide that even if they did trust the promise of safe passage, they cannot leave their gasoline. "Remember one thing: that is more than just a tanker of gas," the wisest among them, Pappagallo, says. "It is our lifeline to a place beyond that vermin on machines." Threatening to take their oil jeopardizes the settlers' vision of leaving the Wasteland for a peaceful and prosperous world. Those who would deprive themselves or others of gasoline are depicted as illogical or ruthless, and their pursuits are irreconcilable with humankind's wellbeing.

Many settlers are not convinced by Pappagallo's logic, however. "You can't expect to compete against that," one woman says, indicating the roaring circle of motorcycles and dune buggies outside the compound. Her point is well taken. The settlers might have oil, but they do not have the ability to move it safely. They live in an anguish that can only become deeper with the passage of time: "Every day we get weaker and they get stronger."

Here, *The Road Warrior* makes another direct allusion to contemporary oil politics: the sense that the loss of control over oil reflected the relative decline of Western society. Instability in the Middle East caused by the 1979 Iranian Revolution, and the subsequent increase in oil prices was understood as the greatest threat to US economic recovery in the 1980s. The tyrannical Humungus is even known as "the Ayatollah of Rock 'n' Rollah"—a clear nod to the Iranian Revolution and Western industrial societies' growing concerns about the political and economic implications of Islamic fundamentalism. Arguments that connected oil, "political Islam," and regional instability revealed another aspect of the logic of energy denial: oil was too important to leave under Middle Eastern control. This too was a hallmark of post–energy crisis American culture. Like professional wrestling's Iron Sheikh and Marvel Comics' Roxxon Energy Corporation, the Ayatollah of Rock 'n' Rollah is a stereotypical enemy to be defeated.

The literary scholar Paul Williams has analyzed the cultural stereotypes in *The Road Warrior*—what he eloquently describes as the movie's "visual codes of savagery and civilization." The settlers are all white, "Aryan in appearance" and dress, whereas Humungus and his gang are swarthier, dressed in fur and feathers, wear mohawks, and unleash guttural war cries.[9] Oil's role within those themes of race, barbarism, and civilization is interesting, too. By dint of owning the technology to refine oil, the white settlers and their gasoline embody civilization. Civilization and power, in turn, are defined by the potential for mobility. Without oil, there is no mobility; without mobility, no sustenance.[10] In its absence, then, oil represents the loss of these assets. Deprivation leads to isolation and savagery.

The Logic of Oil and Insecurity

"The great question for those still alive is the supply of energy," syndicated film critic Stanley Kauffmann wrote in his 1982 review of *The Road Warrior*.[11] He understood what most other politically aware commentators did: the 1970s was marked by rocketing oil prices, regional gas shortages across the world, and a deep sense of insecurity in the United States. Many politicians in the US and elsewhere attacked the Organization of Petroleum Exporting Countries (OPEC), often lumping that group together with the "Arab oil producers," for that new insecurity, and in the process they often mislabeled the 1973 Arab oil embargo as "the OPEC embargo." [12] US senators also called hearings on oil companies' "windfall taxes" from high oil prices, echoing economist M. A. Adelman's charge that the companies were the OPEC members' "tax collectors." [13] Magazines across the United States advertised energy-saving techniques for the home and road, and President Jimmy Carter famously declared "a moral equivalent of war" on energy waste.[14]

Concerns about energy supply impacted different levels of US society. In April 1980, to cite one example, Energy Secretary Charles Duncan Jr. announced that the United States would resume filling its Strategic Petroleum Reserve (SPR), inciting a minor conflict in US-Saudi relations. "Events in the Middle East are a clear reminder of our need for a substantial SPR," Duncan wrote to Carter, referring to the Iranian Revolution and the Soviet invasion of Afghanistan. But when Saudi Arabia threatened to cut production if the United States continued its emergency stockpiling, Duncan reversed his decision. For many, Duncan's about-face revealed how vulnerable the United States had become to Saudi oil power. Senator Bill Bradley and others argued in special hearings that it was essential to redefine "national security" to include maintaining the SPR and other nonmilitary threats to the national economy. Duncan agreed privately and told Carter that "uncertainties exist on the supply side which could make for a tight market, particularly if there are significant production cutbacks or supply interruptions."[15] Bradley publicly inserted a four-part *Chicago Sun-Times* exposé into the *Congressional Record*, asserting that Duncan's turnaround meant that the United States could "easily be blackmailed or stampeded in a crisis situation."[16] Other influential voices joined the senator's. "The retreat from the Strategic Petroleum Reserve is a national embarrassment, and a dangerous confession of failure," read a staff editorial in the *Washington Post*. "Instead of providing protection against future disruptions in this country's oil supply, the reserve has become a prominent symbol of American vulnerability."[17]

That *The Road Warrior* echoed this logic shouldn't be surprising. Oil denial loomed large among politicians, officials, and corporate executives, as well as the general public. Many agreed with Bradley's complaint that Arab producers were "able to push us around and dictate our policy."[18] Melvin Conant, a high-ranking federal energy official and former Exxon political advisor for the Far East, worried that the Carter administration was playing with "a very slim margin."[19] In the even more immediate context of the Iranian Revolution, the Iran hostage crisis, the beginning of the Iran-Iraq War, and the doubling of oil prices in 1980, many believed Carter to be the weakest president in memory. In 1980 and 1981, the same time that *The Road Warrior* was in production, Ronald Reagan's presidential campaign again and again connected economic malaise in the United States with Carter's indecision on energy and foreign policy. "It is well known that we are in an energy mess," Reagan campaign advisor John McKetta told campaign chair William Casey a week before Bradley's Senate hearings began. The United States' "sickening dependence" on Arab oil, McKetta argued, had led to Carter's broader "intimidation in the conduct of foreign policy."[20]

Reagan attacked Carter for allowing the United States to fall victim to foreign control of strategic resources. He also criticized the oil-producing countries for threatening global economic health before and after he assumed the presidency, picking up on arguments made popular by Henry Kissinger and others since the late 1960s. Once in office, Reagan made the Strategic Petroleum Reserve the cornerstone of his "free market" energy strategy. In his statement upon signing the Energy Emergency Preparedness Act of 1982, Reagan emphasized that his government had added oil to the reserve "at an impressive rate"—about three hundred thousand barrels per day, or "as fast as permanent storage can be made available." The president also celebrated that due to these efforts, the reserve contained around 265 million barrels— "an amount equal to more than 6 months of our imports from Arab OPEC countries." The government-mandated surplus was crucial for Reagan's plan for price deregulation. Those and other policies, he said, greatly reduced "the vulnerability of the United States and our allies to possible shocks from oil supply interruptions."[21] In an astute political sleight-of-hand, the president used government control to make an argument that the oil producers acted against the free market.

The Strategic Petroleum Reserve thus served as a foreign policy tool, meant to protect the United States should any instability in the Middle East or US intervention lead to reprisal from oil producers. To preclude that possibility, the Reagan administration also cultivated important regional clients. To cite one example, as its first major military initiative, it pressed for arms sales to regional allies Pakistan and Saudi Arabia. Supporters also linked hawkish calls for military strength abroad with domestic calls for deregulation and, at the extreme end, denounced environmentalists as unpatriotic. James Watt, who as Reagan's secretary of the interior consistently attacked "environmental extremism" for limiting domestic production and causing insecurity, captured this sentiment in an October 1973 speech to students at the University of Wyoming:

> This unhappy sketch of the international energy climate clearly establishes the risks involved in depending on imports for essential energy supplies. In order to guarantee a secure America, and live up to our responsibilities in the community of Nations, the United States must develop the capacity to meet its energy needs through the conservation, development, and employment of our abundant domestic energy reserves. . . . We must strive to regain our national self-sufficiency.

For Watt, the American West "had been blessed with an abundant fossil fuel supply, capable of meeting our energy needs for generations."[22] And according to McKetta, it was not too far-fetched to say that environmentalists and their supporters in Washington were "linked together in a plot to bring America to eventual disaster by making domestic energy expansion impossible."[23] To *not* harness that energy, to *not* open up the drilling market in the face of the threat of OPEC or the "Arab oil producers," was criminally illogical.

The Road Warrior encapsulates this fear of energy denial and some of its consequences in its basic premise and plot. The film unfolds in the aftermath of total war and environmental apocalypse and imagines the resulting social dystopia. The setting is one of a classic conflict between refined civilization and immoral savagery. In this way, the movie joined a long lineage of cinematic dystopia.[24] Like many genre movies, it served as a window into the present, not least by reminding audiences of the potential repercussions of environmental destruction or nuclear war.[25] The film was produced and released at a specific moment in the Cold War, to be sure, but its narrative arc and celebration of heroism against remarkable odds was representative of the genre.

For Kauffmann the film critic, Mel Gibson's character was "a posthistoric man . . . trying to preserve the last of fuel and energy in order to preserve the remnants of humanity."[26] When he announced his presidential candidacy in 1979, Reagan told the nation that "the only way to free ourselves from the monopoly pricing power of OPEC is to be less dependent on outside sources of fuel."[27] Such arguments connected the many specters that endangered energy security together in a logic that emphasized scarcity, and energy insecurity loomed as a credible threat to economic recovery.[28] The perils posed by OPEC, Arab oil producers, oil companies, Carter, and environmentalists all converged to form an ethos of impending denial in the United States in the early 1980s. Many feared that deprivation exposed a crucial weakness of the United States.

Precious Juice and Permanent Vulnerability

Yet, in its presence, oil granted life. For many in the United States in the 1980s, oil stability meant the recovery of American power, the celebration of American strength, and the spread of capitalist thinking and practices. But recovery was not foreordained, and in today's age, still conditioned by Cold War and neoliberal triumphalism, it is easy to forget how fragile the late 1970s and the early 1980s felt. The beginning of the new decade was characterized less by self-confidence and more by what oil expert Walter Levy called "the inherent dangers for the non-communist world of dependence on insecure sources of oil supplies."[29]

The threat of energy denial thus also meant potentially embracing violence to protect not only oil but also the ethos it represented. The film likewise explores this problem. In return for five gallons of diesel "juice" and some high-octane gasoline, Max offers to help the settlers secure a Mack truck so they can escape to the Coast with their oil tanker. When they outwit and outrun Lord Humungus and his horde in the movie's climax, Max and the settlers brutally kill their enemies. Many of the settlers also heroically sacrifice their own lives. Such is the cost of security. The movie ends when Max, aided by a feral child, crushes Humungus with the tanker, which is revealed to have been filled with sand rather than oil. The diversion, hidden from the audience and Humungus alike, is successful, and the settlers escape with "their precious juice." As the film studies scholar J. Emmett Winn has written, *The Road Warrior* depicts the settlers' violence as defensive and therefore justified.[30]

But many critics, including Stanley Kauffmann, criticized the violence of the film as gratuitous. For him, *The Road Warrior* was filled with "moralistic simplicities"—not so different from how some viewed Reagan's renewed Cold War foreign and economic policies—that dramatized the "threat of fuel exhaustion" in order to embrace grisly scenes of car-crazed bloodletting.[31] (Indeed, over three-quarters of the film takes place on wheels, and the amount of gasoline burned is certainly more than the settlers had in their tanker.) Another US reviewer lamented how the film reveled in the frailty of the human body through "the infinitude of ways" it could be squashed, dismembered, exploded, crushed, or burned. Humungus's gory death was enough to turn the stomach of even the least squeamish (as was the scene in which Gibson wolfs down a can of wet dog food. The movie was so revolting, the reviewer quipped, that it shouldn't carry an X or R rating, but a warning from the surgeon general).[32]

Some viewers disagreed. The violence of the film was the whole point, one moviegoer from upstate New York wrote; its relentlessness reflected a society in which "violence has become so common that the populus [sic] is desensitized to it."[33] Richard Corliss, the critic for *Time* magazine, also believed that the violence did not detract from but rather complemented *The Road Warrior*'s theme of protecting "precious petrol."[34] Likewise, a student reviewer at the University of North Carolina shrewdly noted that, after all, it was oil that people fought for. Oil meant survival in the dog-eat-dog (or dogfood-eating) world of the postapocalyptic Wasteland. "The survivors are all behaving pretty much like people did in New York City's last big power failure," she wrote, with no dearth of regional snark.[35]

These and other discussions about the film's violence emphasized its link to energy deprivation and the loss of mobility. Such a connection reflected serious concerns in US foreign relations, as well. In fact, justified violence was perhaps the most important feature of the United States' official trepidation about energy denial. In the wake of the end of the Vietnam War and the energy crisis, many believed that the United States had allowed itself to become too much of a victim. Just as the settlers needed Max to deliver their gas and their freedom, so too did the United States need a more muscular foreign policy. In his January 1980 State of the Union address, President Carter discussed this problem, reminding the nation that the Persian Gulf held two-thirds of global oil. With the Soviet invasion of Afghanistan, the Red Army was now within striking distance of the Straits of Hormuz, the world's most important "choke-point." It was the Kremlin's objective "to consolidate a strategic position, therefore, that poses a grave threat to the free flow of Middle East oil," Carter charged. "Let me be absolutely clear. Any attempt by any outside force to gain control of the Persian Gulf region will be regarded as an assault on the vital interests of the United States of America, and such an assault will be repelled by any means necessary, including military force."[36]

Ronald Reagan's electoral campaign nonetheless attacked Carter for bungling both Middle East and energy policy. Campaign surrogate Henry Kissinger gave testimony to a Senate committee on the geopolitics of oil that campaign director William Casey later distilled into a radio advertisement. Only the nation's military defense was more important to national security than stability in oil supply and prices, Kissinger said; "We cannot tolerate being forced into a state of permanent vulnerability."[37] Once in office, the Reagan administration continued to espouse this rhetoric. National Security Decision Directive 114 again called for expanded military power in the Gulf with energy security as its main justification: "Because of the real and psychological impact of a curtailment in the flow of oil from the Persian Gulf on the international economic system, we must assure our readiness to deal promptly with actions aimed at disrupting that traffic."[38]

This reaction to energy denial—oil insecurity as a justification for force—was enduring. By the 1990s, influential actors in the George H. W. Bush administration had begun to argue that regime change, supported by US occupation if necessary, was the best solution to the national security threats the United States faced in the Middle East. "We recognize that a collective effort will not always be timely and, in the absence of US leadership, may not gel. Where the stakes so merit, we must have forces ready to protect our critical interests," Defense Secretary Dick Cheney wrote in an influential paper. Non-American control over critical resources remained a significant threat in the Persian Gulf. According to Cheney, the United States needed to actively discourage the rise of hostile challenges to "our access to international air and seaways and to the region's important sources of oil." He continued, "We must remain prepared to act decisively . . . if our vital interests there are threatened anew." More importantly in terms of the logic of impending denial, Cheney, Paul Wolfowitz, Lewis "Scooter" Libby, and the paper's other authors proposed "Planning for Uncertainty" as the primary underlying strategy of their argument. The United States could not squander the security that allowed "our domestic life to flourish."[39]

The Cultural Politics of Oil Denial

Susan Sontag once argued that even seemingly impartial forms of art could not be essentially objective: "There is no neutral surface, no neutral discourse, no neutral theme, no neutral form."[40] It is important to appreciate that such an argument complements and transcends Butler's call for scholars to pull back the curtain on obviousness. For Sontag, identifying the obvious was a step toward moving audiences away from disinterest and toward action—action that would carry them beyond what she considered outmoded ways of thinking and being. *The Road Warrior* captures the cultural politics of oil denial that dominated public discussion in the 1980s. Those without gasoline are immobile, marginalized, doomed. At the same time, the movie and other cultural artifacts posit a broader understanding of denial as a terrifying prospect, not only in postapocalyptic imaginaries but also in a post–energy crisis society.

Obviousness is not neutral. The concern with denial continues today. National Security Advisor John Bolton accused Iran of attacking United Arab Emirates oil tankers in May 2019, arguing that it was part of a longer pattern of destabilizing Iranian aggression in the region. At the same time, families who take long road trips during summer vacation still refer to themselves as "road warriors." The trope of energy denial and vanquishing it runs deep in national politics and culture. If we hope to understand how fear of deprivation continues to shape the concerns that face us in the twenty-first century, we should continue analyzing how it was reflected in energy culture in the twentieth. Better put, channeling Butler and Sontag, we should work to understand both how this fear became obvious and why it is not neutral. Only then can we understand it as a perspective built during a specific moment in history, discard it as an outmoded way of thinking, and move toward more rational insights on how "the juice" impacts our society—now and in the future.

Notes

1. Daniel J. Sargent, *A Superpower Transformed: The Remaking of American Foreign Relations in the 1970s* (New York: Oxford University Press, 2014); Judith Stein, *Pivotal Decade: How the United States Traded Factories for Finance in the Seventies* (New Haven, CT: Yale University Press, 2010); Daniel Rodgers, *Age of Fracture* (Cambridge MA: Harvard University Press, 2011).

2. Ronald Reagan, "Remarks on the Program for Economic Recovery at a White House Reception for Business and Government Leaders," June 11, 1981, American Presidency Project (hereafter APP), University of California Santa Barbara, Santa Barbara, California, https://www.presidency.ucsb.edu/node/246911.

3. Milton Friedman, *Capitalism and Freedom* (Chicago: University of Chicago Press, 1962), 8–9. On economists and other scholars as celebrities, see Nicholas Cullather, "That Touch of Mink," in *The Familiar Made Strange: American Icons and Artifacts after the Transnational Turn*, ed. Brooke L. Blower and Mark Bradley (Ithaca, NY: Cornell University Press, 2015), 116–24.

4. Hal Brands, *Making the Unipolar Moment: U.S. Foreign Policy and the Rise of the Post-Cold War Order* (Ithaca, NY: Cornell University Press, 2016); Thomas Friedman, *The Lexus and the Olive Tree: Understanding Globalization* (New York:

Farrar, Straus and Giroux, 2000); Francis Fukuyama, "The End of History?" *National Interest* 16 (1989): 3–18.

5.   Monica Prasad, "The Popular Origins of Neoliberalism in the Reagan Tax Cut of 1981," *Journal of Policy History* 24, no. 3 (July 2012): 351–83; Tony Smith, *A Pact with the Devil: Washington's Bid for World Supremacy and the Betrayal of the American Promise* (New York: Routledge, 2007); Kim Phillips-Fein, *Fear City: New York's Fiscal Crisis and the Rise of Austerity Politics* (New York: Henry Holt, 2017).

6.   Thomas Piketty, *Capital in the Twenty-First Century* (Cambridge, MA: Harvard University Press, 2017); Gretta R. Krippner, *Capitalizing on Crisis: The Political Origins of the Rise of Finance* (Cambridge, MA: Harvard University Press, 2011); Marion Fourcade, *Economists and Societies: Discipline and Profession in the United States, Britain, and France, 1890s–1990s* (Princeton, NJ: Princeton University Press, 2009). Further study is needed on the place of defense spending within this vision of American economic power, rather than as an aberration from the anti–federal spending rhetoric of early neoliberals and neoconservatives. For an important start, see the recent book by Michael Brenes, *For Might and Right: Cold War Defense Spending and the Remaking of American Democracy* (Amherst: University of Massachusetts Press, 2020).

7.   Judith Butler, "Ordinary, Incredulous," in *The Humanities and Public Life*, ed. Peter Brooks and Hilary Jewett (New York: Fordham University Press, 2014), 20–23. Butler cites Louis Althusser, who dedicates a shorter discussion to obviousness as part of his analysis of the Marxist state apparatus: Louis Althusser, *Lenin and Philosophy and Other Essays* (New York: New York University Press, 2001).

8.   George Miller, dir., *The Road Warrior* (Sydney: Kennedy Miller, 1981).

9.   Paul Williams, "Beyond '*Mad Max III*': Race, Empire, and Heroism on Post-Apocalyptic Terrain," *Science Fiction Studies* 32, no. 2 (July 2005): 309.

10. It is interesting to note here that in *Mad Max beyond Thunderdome*, the oasis of Bartertown has built its own sustainable energy infrastructure on methane produced by Underworld pig farmers, controlled by the totem duo of Master Blaster. "It's where Bartertown gets its energy," Aunty Entity (played by Tina Turner) tells Max when first showing him the Underworld through a reversed periscope. "What, oil? Natural gas?" he asks. "Pigs," she says. "Bullshit," he answers. "No, pigshit." At one point in the movie, Master Blaster uses an embargo to force Aunty to admit on intercom that "Master Blaster runs Bartertown." George Miller and George Ogilvie, dirs., *Mad Max beyond Thunderdome* (Sydney: Kennedy Miller, 1985). Jerome Shapiro has compared the Master Blaster plot to the Arab oil embargo and the OPEC price increases. Jerome Shapiro, *Atomic Bomb Cinema: Apocalyptic Imagination on Film* (New York: Routledge, 2002), 175–80.

11. Stanley Kauffmann, "Australian Graffiti; French Pastry," *New Republic*, October 11, 1982, 24.

12. See David S. Painter, "Oil and Geopolitics: The Oil Crises of the 1970s and the Cold War," *Historical Social Research / Historische Sozialforschung* 39, no. 4 (2014): 186–208.

13. M. A. Adelman, "Is the Oil Shortage Real? Oil Companies as OPEC Tax Collectors," *Foreign Policy* 9 (Winter 1972): 69–107; Jay E. Hakes, "Conflict or Consensus? The Roots of Jimmy Carter's Energy Policies," in *American Energy Policy in the 1970s*, ed. Robert Lifset (Norman: University of Oklahoma Press, 2014), 52–53.

14. Daniel Horowitz, *The Anxieties of Affluence: Critiques of American Consumer Culture, 1939–1979* (Amherst: University of Massachusetts Press, 2004), 203–44.

15. Memorandum from Secretary of Energy Duncan to President Carter, February 7, 1980, doc. 258, *Foreign Relations of the United States, 1969–1976, vol. XXXVII: Energy Crisis, 1974–1980*, ed. Steven G. Galpern (Washington, DC: United States Government Printing Office, 2012), https://history.state.gov/historicaldocuments/frus1969-76v37/d258.

16. Thomas J. Moore, "Saudis Veto Filling of Oil Reserve," *Chicago Sun-Times*, April 10, 1980.

17. "To Fill the Oil Reserve," *Washington Post*, April 16, 1980.

18. *Hearing before the Subcommittee on Energy Resources and Materials Production of the Committee on Energy and National Resources*, US Senate, 96th Congress, 2nd Session (April 18, 1980), 37.

19. Thomas J. Moore, "Oil Pinch May Push U.S. to War," *Chicago Sun-Times*, April 13, 1980.

20. John McKetta, "The U.S. Energy Problem Grows Worse and Worse and . . ." (paper, National Petroleum Refiners Association Annual Meeting, New Orleans, LA, March 23–25, 1980), box 292, William J. Casey Papers, Hoover Institution Archives, Stanford, California.

21. Ronald Reagan, "Statement on Signing the Energy Emergency Preparedness Act of 1982," August 3, 1982, APP, https://www.presidency.ucsb.edu/node/246296.

22. Remarks by James G. Watt at the University of Wyoming, October 25, 1973, box 13, James G. Watt Papers, American Heritage Center, University of Wyoming, Laramie, Wyoming.

23. McKetta, "U.S. Energy Problem."

24. Mick Broderick, "Surviving Armageddon: Beyond the Imagination of Disaster," *Science Fiction Studies* 20, no. 3 (November 1993): 362–82.

25. Fredric Jameson, *Archaeologies of the Future: The Desire Called Utopia and Other Science Fictions* (New York: Verso, 2005).

26. Kauffman, "Australian Graffiti; French Pastry," 24.

27. Ronald Reagan, "Remarks Announcing Candidacy for the Republican Presidential Nomination," November 13, 1979, APP, https://www.presidency.ucsb.edu/node/255827.

28. Roger J. Stern, "Oil Scarcity Ideology in US Foreign Policy, 1908–97," *Security Studies* 25, no. 2 (2016): 214–57.

29. Walter J. Levy, "Oil: An Agenda for the 1980s," *Foreign Affairs* 59, no. 5 (Summer 1981): 1079–101.

30. J. Emmett Winn, "*Mad Max*, Reaganism, and *The Road Warrior*," *Kinema* (Fall 1997).

31. Kauffman, "Australian Graffiti; French Pastry," 25.

32. Robert Harch, "Films," *Nation*, February 19, 1983, 219.

33. Letter to the editor, *Oswegian*, February 14, 1983, 9.

34. Richard Corliss, "Apocalypse . . . Pow!" *Time*, May 10, 1982, 119.

35. Mimi Peel, "Costumes, Cinematography Make 'Road Warrior,'" *Daily Tar Heel*, June 8, 1982, 8.

36. Jimmy Carter, "The State of the Union Address Delivered before a Joint Session of the Congress," January 23, 1980, APP, https://www.presidency.ucsb.edu/node/249681.

37. Henry Kissinger, "Statement of the Honorable Henry Kissinger on the Geopolitics of Oil before the Committee on Energy and Natural Resources of the United States Senate," July 31, 1980, box 291, folder 6, William Casey Papers, Hoover Institution Archives, Stanford, California.

38. Ronald Reagan, "U.S. Policy toward the Iran-Iraq War," National Security Decision Directive 114, November 26, 1983, Electronic Briefing Book no. 82, doc. 26, National Security Archive, George Washington University, Washington, DC, https://nsarchive2.gwu.edu/NSAEBB/NSAEBB82/iraq26.pdf.

39. Secretary of Defense Dick Cheney, "Defense Strategy for the 1990s: The Regional Defense Strategy," January 1993, 1–2, 5, 23–24, National Security Archive, George Washington University, Washington, DC, https://nsarchive2.gwu.edu/nukevault /ebb245/doc15.pdf.

40. Susan Sontag, *Styles of Radical Will* (New York: Farrar, Straus and Giroux, 1969), 910.

Chapter 4

Built for Pyro: A Perfect Inferno on the *Deepwater Horizon* (2016)

Tyler Priest

O n April 20, 2010, a deepwater oil well in the Gulf of Mexico blew out. As those alive at the time are unlikely to forget, the explosion aboard the *Deepwater Horizon*, a Transocean semi-submersible drilling vessel under contract with oil giant BP, killed eleven workers and injured many more among the 126-member crew, before propelling the flaming rig five thousand feet down to the ocean floor. The uncontrolled well—ironically named Macondo, after the fictional town destroyed by four years of rain in Gabriel García Márquez's *One Hundred Years of Solitude*—eventually spilled nearly five million barrels of oil into the Gulf before it was finally capped in September. For many Americans who watched plumes of oil churn from the busted seafloor wellhead via live video feed, this was the first they had heard that the oil industry was drilling wells off the US coast, let alone a mile or more beneath the surface of the ocean.[1]

Oil drilling, however, had been steadily moving deeper into the Gulf since the first freestanding platform was erected in ten feet of water in 1938. By the end of the 1970s, companies had reached the edge of the continental shelf in one thousand feet of water. In 1995, Shell Oil brought in prolific oil production from its tension leg platform known as Auger, positioned in 2,860 feet of water, setting off a race for companies to acquire federal leases to access even deeper water, leapfrogging each other to eight thousand to ten thousand feet by the mid-2000s. BP raced ahead of the rest, cutting corners as it drilled a large inventory of ten-year exploratory leases set to expire in 2010–2011. The Macondo well was located in a mere five thousand feet of water in the Mississippi Canyon, off the mouth of the great Mississippi River, but it turned out to be a particularly obstreperous one—the "well from hell," as Transocean rig hands referred to it.[2] The disaster on the *Deepwater Horizon* fostered serious soul-searching about society's seemingly sudden dependence on high-risk forms of extraction and the awful vulnerability of people and nature when something goes wrong.[3]

In September 2016, the story of the *Deepwater Horizon* oil disaster came to the big screen. The eponymous Summit/Lionsgate production, directed by action-feature specialist Peter Berg, strives to live up to its subject's billing by depicting the final, harrowing hours of April 20, 2010. The film carefully eschews the multifaceted controversies that attended what President Barack Obama called "the worst environmental disaster America has ever faced."[4] Instead, *Deepwater Horizon* focuses on the fateful, last-minute decisions made on the vessel and workers' acts of valor in escaping its exploding machinery.[5]

Of the many ways the story of the *Deepwater Horizon* disaster could have been told, it is unsurprising that a big-budget Hollywood production chose a "cross between *The Perfect Storm* and *Towering Inferno*," as the film was marketed to foreign distributors.[6] The filmmakers defended their choice as a commitment to honoring the dead and survivors of the tragedy, which they claimed had been overshadowed by the public obsession with the environmental aftermath. Although this effort to humanize oil workers and place them at the center of the drama is a necessary corrective to the way Hollywood has traditionally portrayed the oil industry, it also avoids drawing larger meaning from the incident in favor of making the film palatable to a larger audience. What starts as a meticulously accurate rendering of life and technology on a deepwater rig ultimately transforms into a dazzling, pyrotechnical, computer-enhanced disaster flick. If there is a message, it is a simplistic one about how greed compelled BP to put profits before people. One could say the same about the filmmakers' determination to maximize *Deepwater Horizon*'s box-office potential.

Staging

The film project initially appeared to be headed in a different direction. The original director was J. C. Chandor, who had earned a reputation "for making sharp, slow-burn dramas imbued with a certain intelligence as well as a desire to explore various aspects of human nature."[7] In early 2015, citing "creative differences," Lionsgate replaced Chandor with Peter Berg, who had recently directed the big-budget flop *Battleship* (2012) and the more successful *Lone Survivor* (2013) about a Navy SEAL counterinsurgency mission in Afghanistan. Mark Wahlberg, who had starred in the latter and had been secured as headliner and producer for *Deepwater Horizon*, recruited Berg for the position. This put the film on a course of more action and less contemplation.[8]

Berg and lead producer Lorenzo di Bonaventura insisted that they were not interested in assigning blame for what went wrong or chronicling the environmental aftermath of the spill, both of which were ongoing subjects of multi-billion-dollar litigation. They stressed that the script—written by Matthew Michael Carnahan and Matthew Sand, based on a December 2010 *New York Times* front-page feature, "Deepwater Horizon's Final Hours"—would be a "human story," focused on "salt-of-the-earth, working-class American heroes who got caught in a very dangerous and violent situation, and tried to get out of it."[9] The filmmakers invited the families of the deceased onto the set, met with survivors to "assure them that their suffering wasn't being exploited," and hired two of them, chief electronics technician Mike Williams and drilling floorhand Caleb Holloway, as consultants. Other oil-field workers, idled by a downturn in the offshore business, were hired as extras or welders in constructing the sets. Trace Adkins, a former offshore roughneck turned country music star, makes a cameo at the end of the movie as a panicked father in search of his son, presumably among the dead. His 2003 song, "Missing You," about a lovesick offshore driller, was played as a tribute to the eleven killed in the disaster at a Jackson, Mississippi, memorial service in May 2010.[10]

More than the workers, however, the real star of the film is the main set, an enormous façade replica of the semi-submersible's base structure, drilling deck, and helipad. Berg sought permission to film on an offshore rig but was rebuffed by BP and other firms associated with the oil giant. He claimed that BP even sent threatening radio messages to him as he tried to take an aerial helicopter tour of the *Deepwater Horizon*'s sister ship, the *Deepwater Nautilus*.[11] "You know, BP's not real keen to give an oil rig to film on right now," Berg noted at the time. So, the studio built its own. Heralded as "the biggest practical set ever constructed," the mock rig stood 85 percent to scale at 75 feet tall and 150 feet wide, and incorporated 1,600 tons of steel, all immersed in a gigantic tank filled with 2 million gallons of water to simulate the surrounding sea.[12] It took 150 workers eight months to create the set at an abandoned Six Flags amusement park in New Orleans East.[13] "This is not a set," observed Chris Seagers, the film's production designer. "This is a major piece of construction. . . . Then you're setting the whole thing on fire."[14]

The imitation semi-submersible conjured the scale, complexity, and sublimity of the actual vessel. To remember those who died or escaped the *Deepwater Horizon*, the filmmakers and stars repeatedly emphasized the movie's dedication to "realism," "accuracy," "authenticity," and "truth."[15] Berg and Lionsgate staked their claim to realism on getting the visual details right. "Directors think mostly in visual terms," writes film historian Mark C. Carnes, "hence a movie that *looks* like the past *is* like the past."[16] The director, cast, and crew spent time at Shell's Deepwater Training Facility in Robert, Louisiana, to see how equipment on a deepwater drilling rig worked. The producers acquired an iron roughneck, a hulking piece of hydraulic machinery that feeds and removes pipe from the well bore, and built a lightweight replica of a top drive, a mechanical device mounted on the derrick's traveling block that applies massive torque to the drill string. They procured genuine lifeboats. They salvaged pieces of old rigs. They contacted manufacturers to determine what ten-year-old bridge instrumentation equipment looked like in order to recreate the rotary drilling deck and control room. The simulated drilling vessel included a functioning helicopter pad perched seventy feet in the air that handled a nineteen-passenger Sikorsky helicopter.[17] For all these efforts, the film won two awards: one for Outstanding Model in a Photoreal or Animated Project and the other for Outstanding Supporting Visual Effects in a Photoreal Feature, both presented by the Visual Effects Society Awards in 2017.

Making the film approximated the *Deepwater Horizon* incident in other ways, as well. The challenges of creating a $156 million reenactment of the disaster were analogous to those of drilling the slightly less expensive well (before factoring in the costs of the blowout). Falling behind schedule and going over budget preoccupied executives at both BP and Lionsgate. Revenue streams from deepwater oil wells and major motion pictures follow a similar trajectory, rising steeply at the beginning of a well's productive life and a picture's opening weekend, before sharply tapering off.[18] The presence of fire, fumes, and heavy machinery around people working at great heights on the set necessitated frequent safety meetings, just like in an offshore drilling operation. Such risks subjected both the real and fake platforms to government safety inspections and permits. Major government financial incentives also assisted both projects. The federal Deepwater Royalty Relief Act (1995) had spurred on deepwater oil drilling in the Gulf of Mexico, while Lionsgate benefitted from $38 million in tax credits from the State of Louisiana to produce the most expensive movie ever made in that state.[19] Furthermore, just as Louisianans agitated to capture the billions of dollars in federal fines that BP paid for the spill, local activists petitioned the producers to dedicate a percentage of the film's proceeds to ongoing cleanup efforts in the Gulf.[20]

Verisimilitude

The first fifty minutes of *Deepwater Horizon* achieves a certain verisimilitude recognizable to anyone who has ever helicoptered out to a deepwater platform. "There's a strong documentary quality to Berg's films," writes Rich Cohen. "They're laced with footage of real events, towns, and faces."[21] We follow two central characters, Transocean employees Mike Williams (Mark Wahlberg), the chief electronics technician, and Andrea Fleytas (Gina Rodriguez), a twenty-three-year-old dynamic positioning operator, as they make their journey to the rig. There is some effort to develop these characters through Williams's devotion to his loving wife Felicia (Kate Hudson) and daughter Sydney (Stella Allen), and Fleytas's troubles with her Ford Mustang, which becomes a motif that cements her friendship with Williams. But these attempts are secondary to the staging, which begins with an aerial view of the industrial facilities at Port Fourchon, Louisiana—the major departure point for workers heading offshore in the Gulf of Mexico and where Fleytas and Williams join Transocean offshore installation manager "Mr. Jimmy" Harrell (Kurt Russell).[22] We travel with these three and two BP managers, David Sims (Joe Chrest) and Pat O'Bryan (James DuMont)—who, ironically, are there to present Transocean with a safety award for seven years without a lost time accident—as they helicopter across the Louisiana coastal marsh and arrive at the awe-inspiring *Deepwater Horizon*. There, Williams takes us on a handheld-camera tour of the vessel as he makes the rounds to check in with various workmates.

Although many viewers found these scenes "boring" or were put off by "technical jargon," those with experience in the industry were pleasantly surprised to see a Hollywood blockbuster portraying the subject of oil in a familiar and accurate way.[23] In addition to the faithful recreation of the rotary deck, control room, and living quarters, many of the small details are spot-on, down to the Transocean, BP, and M-I SWACO logos on the workers' overalls and their personalized hardhat decorations. Early in the film, the camera accompanies a lifelike remotely operated vehicle (ROV) exhibiting an LSU Tigers sticker as it travels down the drilling riser to inspect the blowout preventer. Steve Jablonsky's mesmerizing musical score mimics engine revs, sonar pings, and muffled underwater sounds with eerie foreboding. Moreover, the banter between the characters is strikingly true to offshore "Gulf Coast Cowboy" culture.[24] When Williams inquires about the French oil services firm, Schlumberger, using the French pronunciation *Schlum-ber-jay*, toolpusher Jason Anderson (Ethan Suplee) corrects him: "It's *Slum-burger*, you Democrat!" Williams then stops by the rotary deck to ask Caleb Holloway (Dylan O'Brien) and Shane Rosto (Henry Frost) why the Schlumberger team did not run the downhole cement bond log (CBL) test to ensure the integrity of the cement job. "Is that stupid, not running a CBL?" Williams asks. Holloway and Rosto reply, almost in unison, "I don't know if it's stupid, but it ain't smart!"

Confusion about the canceled CBL fills much of the drama prior to the blowout. In this way, director Berg attempts to condense and encapsulate the onboard drama and risky decisions that led to the blowout. As tension builds toward the inevitable catastrophe, factual errors start to pile up and the script veers from the established record of events. Some of this is unavoidable in order to package the story within an entertaining 107 minutes. But Berg's emphasis on a "high degree of realism" opens the film up to fact checkers' criticism, informed with details reconstructed down to the minute by official investigations, court testimony, and forensic evidence. Deviations from the historical record are excusable if they are in service to illuminating larger issues or truths. In this case, however, they tend to obscure those truths and narrow the context. The visual and audio verisimilitude of the first half of the film is not enough to compensate for the simplified morality play and pyromania that preoccupy the latter half.

Misrepresentations

Critics and audiences alike found many errors in the film. In the opening scene, for example, Williams's daughter, Sydney, demonstrates a school project simulating her father's work. Intending to show how her father "tames the dinosaurs"—a popular but incorrect reference to crude oil's origins—she sticks a capped straw into a Coke can, the pressure building until the carbonated soda blasts through the straw toward the ceiling in an unsubtle foreshadowing of the blowout. Later, right after arriving on the rig, Williams tosses a lucky nickel into the moon pool. It floats down the riser to the seafloor, where we see gas start to bubble from the mud. This, along with a later scene in which large plumes of gas escape from the bed around the well, are contrived. The hydrocarbons, formed millions of years ago by decayed marine organisms, exploded up through the well, not outside of it.[25]

Further inaccuracies surface in the film's depiction of Donald Vidrine, BP's acting night rig supervisor, who was charged but not convicted of involuntary manslaughter for his role in the tragedy. Vidrine is played with "dastardly" panache by John Malkovich, who acts as a stand-in for all of BP's sins.[26] Critics made much of Malkovich's strange Louisiana accent, one "that's either Cajun or Transylvanian," or "[Democratic political operative] James Carville crossed with Hannibal Lecter."[27] Indeed, Malkovich seems to have watched too many clips of Carville, whose exaggerated River Parishes accent is actually quite different from that of Vidrine's Evangeline Parish accent from southwestern Louisiana.[28] Malkovich's Vidrine chastises the Transocean men for being "nervous as cats" and is cavalier about safety as he drives the crew to rush the completion of the well, which, at forty-three days behind schedule, is costing BP more than $1 million a day. In the film, it is Vidrine who is responsible for accepting the result of the negative pressure test—an assessment to determine if the well had been safely sealed before temporarily abandoning it—and attributing the test's faulty result to a spurious "bladder effect" caused by mud in the well. Post-accident investigations, however, identified Transocean employee Jason Anderson as the source of the bladder effect theory.[29]

According to those who knew him, the real Don Vidrine was very different from Malkovich's. Lillian Espinoza-Gala, an industry veteran and safety consultant, described him as "the most safety-conscious, risk-averse man, extremely conservative."[30] Vidrine did not appear at federal hearings due to ongoing health problems resulting from the disaster, but he did testify against his day rig supervising partner, Bob Kaluza, in exchange for pleading guilty to a misdemeanor pollution charge and evading one for manslaughter. Vidrine claimed that Kaluza, who was eventually acquitted, had neglected to provide crucial information about the negative pressure test.[31] In addition, in his interview with BP, Vidrine reported that he questioned Transocean employees at length about the negative pressure test result, but that they had an explanation for it (the bladder effect) and "even seemed to make fun of him for worrying about it."[32] Vidrine battled heart problems in the aftermath of the disaster and died of cancer seven months after the film debuted.

The larger problem with attributing so much responsibility for the blowout to Vidrine is that it exonerates BP "town" management and engineers in Houston. These included wells team leader John Guide, who was principally in charge of Macondo, engineering team leader Gregory Walz, and drilling engineers Brian Morel and Mark Hafle, all of whom were in constant communication with their onboard subordinates and directed the decision making on the rig. In their rush to complete the "well from hell," BP's Houston supervisors made repeated last-minute modifications to the temporary abandonment procedure, such as foregoing the cement bond log. They made many of these changes to save money and time, but in doing so also magnified the safety risks. "It's a new deal every time we get up," the real Jason Anderson complained to his father.[33] According to the National Oil Spill Commission's final report, "There is no evidence that these changes went through *any* sort of formal risk assessment or management of change process."[34]

All official investigations found BP's safety culture and organization seriously deficient as well as unresponsive to a preceding series of refinery accidents, pipeline ruptures, and excessive cost-cutting measures across its vast worldwide operations. Compounding safety problems at Macondo, BP had just reorganized its exploration business. This change created separate managers and channels of communication for the rig's planning and workflow, thus generating confusion about accountability.[35] In an evocative scene, Vidrine even

lectures Williams about the challenges of overseeing a major industrial operation like drilling a deepwater well:

> We a big company, BP. Very big for a reason. Complex organization.
> Lotta movin' parts. Millions of movin' parts. Thousands upon thou-
> sands of people. We all work very hard to ensure that those people
> and all those movin' parts are functioning as a means to an end, a
> very profitable end for all of us. So, they the big picture, and they
> the little picture, like you and the malfunctioning shit. But you see,
> in point of fact, they all kind of interconnected. They a flow at work
> here Mike. So, if you off, it's off. Then, I'm off. We off. Then the whole
> damn train is off.

If only BP had paid closer attention to the "little picture" at Macondo.
Williams responds to Vidrine's reprimand with a folksy tale about precau-
tions he and his buddy take when "noodlin'" for catfish: "I don't stick my
hand in that hole with that monster and hope for the best. Uh-uh. Hope ain't
a tactic, Don."

The film never follows up on this suggestive piece of dialogue and ultimately dodges the "big picture." The credits note that the court dismissed the
manslaughter charges against Vidrine and acquitted Kaluza (Brad Leland), who
is barely present in the movie. They curiously fail to point out, however, that
BP pled guilty to multiple felonies, including gross negligence and willful misconduct under the Clean Water Act. There is also no mention of BP accepting
a record $4 billion criminal fine and tens of billions of dollars more in cleanup
costs, civil penalties, and settlements.

Not only does the film let BP as an organization off the hook, but it also
absolves the other firms involved. Halliburton, the company that performed
the botched cement job, is fully absent. The name is never even spoken aloud
(perhaps for legal reasons), even though the oil services company later pled
guilty to destroying evidence and paid $1.1 billion to compensate businesses,
individuals, and local governments for incurred losses. Transocean and its employees also appear as innocent victims of Vidrine's steely resolve, as dramatized in a heated discussion over the failure of the first negative pressure test:

"Mr. Jimmy" Harrell: BP's well?
Don Vidrine: It is.
Harrell: BP's oil.
Vidrine: Indeed.
Harrell: We just the help y'all hired to drill a hole.

VIDRINE: You are correct, Mr. Jimmy. But we fifty days late, and the
hole ain't drilled.

MIKE WILLIAMS: It's forty-three days, not fifty. Yup, think you money-
hungry sons a bitches at least be good at math.

The reality is that both BP and Transocean had become overconfident and
complacent about the risks that had accumulated at Macondo. The National
Commission concluded that "the Macondo blowout was the product of several
individual missteps and oversights by BP, Halliburton, and Transocean, which
government regulators lacked the authority, the necessary resources, and the
technical expertise to prevent." [36] In 2013, Transocean pled guilty to violating
the Clean Water Act and paid $1.4 billion in civil and criminal fines and penal-
ties—the second-largest environmental penalty in US history (after BP). [37] This
piece of information is also missing from the film's credits.

In other words, there was plenty of blame to go around. But such ambiguity and complexity do not work in a Hollywood film bent on pleasing the
masses. Director Peter Berg needed a hero to serve as a counterpart to Vidrine's
villain. Transocean's offshore installation manager, Mr. Jimmy—played with
endearing gruffness by Kurt Russell—is the guy. Russell's Mr. Jimmy, like the
man himself, is "revered by his crew, regarded as approachable, competent and
to the point." [38] He is a father figure, looking after his Transocean employees'
well-being, and the film's moral conscience, urging BP to take a cautious approach to finishing the well.

Although somewhat truer-to-life than Vidrine, the film's characterization
of Mr. Jimmy as a pawn of BP's ruthlessness is exaggerated. He appears frus-
trated and helpless about the vessel's "three hundred ninety items" of deferred
maintenance as a result of BP's refusal to let the rig have any downtime to
take care of them. But Harrell and Transocean management were ultimately
responsible for these issues, especially the lack of maintenance on the blowout preventer. [39] In his testimony during the joint US Coast Guard–Minerals
Management Service hearings, Harrell denied that BP had pressured his
Transocean crew to complete work faster. He also countered earlier reports of
a "heated debate" with BP officials on April 20. Harrell testified that the day
before the blowout, he had expressed concern to Kaluza about the original
abandonment plan omitting a negative pressure test (which the film basically
gets right), but that he had been satisfied with the results of the two tests that
were ultimately performed. [40]

In subtle ways, however, the film does hint at Harrell's culpability. After
the second negative pressure test on the "kill line" comes back as Vidrine predicted ("No mud, no flow, we gots to go"), Harrell accepts the findings and

orders the drill shack to begin displacing mud in the well with seawater. In a climactic scene, Harrell and Vidrine run into each other on the bridge after the blowout, amid ongoing carnage. Harrell, his right eye swollen shut with bits of fiberglass insulation after getting blown out of the shower, thrusts his face forward, inches away from Vidrine's. He is clearly livid with rage, but rather than exclaiming "You did this!" remains silent for five seconds. Then Harrell calmly says, "Get your ass to a lifeboat." The scene poignantly conveys that, yes, BP as the operator is ultimately to blame, but Harrell knows that he and Transocean are not faultless.

The Fury of the Rig

The last hour of *Deepwater Horizon* focuses on the star of the film: the rig. After the well fails to hold, oil and gas blow through the drilling floor and ignite, plunging viewers into the chaos with pulse-racing and ear-pounding special effects. The unending explosions, hellacious fireballs, and hurtling bodies animate the breathtaking still images of the doomed vessel that saturated the media in May 2010. The producers take Hollywood's fetish for spectacular pyrotechnics to another level, integrating the gas-fueled fires on set with computer graphic (CG) effects.[41] Giant LED screens, the size of those found in football stadiums, intensify the illumination. Producer Lorenzo di Bonaventura bragged that the "sets were built for pryo," giving credence to charges that the film comes perilously close to a cinematic celebration of the disaster.[42] Unlike most Hollywood disaster films, which have grown in popularity and ostentation since the 1970s, this one reenacted a true story, and soon after the actual event.[43] Even so, as Benjamin Lee of *The Guardian* writes, Berg "stages the action horribly well, capturing the panic and gruesome mayhem without the film ever feeling exploitative."[44]

The rescue and escape scenes largely conform to tales told by the survivors, but the heroics are compressed into the characters of Williams and Harrell. As one reviewer wrote, "Wahlberg is the main focus, grunting and grimacing around the platform as it burns, rescuing survivors and generally acting like a captain going down with his ship (even though his role appears to be something more like middle management)."[45] Wahlberg's Williams performs rescues that were actually the result of brave actions by real life colleagues, such as Chad Murray, the chief electrician, who is not a character in the film.[46] The big finale is Williams's dramatic ten-story leap from the helipad into the flaming waters, which he first recounted in a *60 Minutes* interview with Scott Pelley in May 2010. In the film, Williams saves a frightened Fleytas by pushing her off the helipad before him, but the real Fleytas told the Coast Guard that she fell out of a descending life raft.[47] Meanwhile, Jimmy Harrell, bloodied and hobbled, directs the evacuation and assists the severely injured, but his actions incorporate those actually performed by Transocean chief engineer Steve Bertone and senior toolpusher Miles "Randy" Ezell. After mustering on the *Damon Bankston* mud supply vessel, lit up by the fires of the *Deepwater Horizon* burning behind them, Harrell solemnly calls out the names of the eleven dead men and then leads the kneeling group in the Lord's Prayer.

The fury of the rig paid off for the film. It received generally positive reviews from critics and viewers. CinemaScore, which polls audiences, gave the film an A–, and it reached "certified fresh" status on Rotten Tomatoes.[48] BP, not surprisingly, gave it a thumbs-down, saying that the film "ignores the conclusions reached by every official investigation: that the accident was the result of multiple errors made by a number of companies."[49] It was hard for other reviewers, however, to weigh in with heavy criticism of a film with such brilliant technical effects, quality acting from an A-list cast, and a simple plot that honored survivors and the departed—mostly God-fearing white working-class men, the kind who would flock to the polls weeks after the film's opening to elect Donald Trump president. The decision to play it safe by limiting the film's focus was a profitable one. *Deepwater Horizon* grossed $179 million (in the US and worldwide) by December 2016 on an estimated budget of $110 million (after factoring in the Louisiana tax credit).[50]

Still, for many people, the film was ultimately unsatisfying. While *Deepwater Horizon*'s world premiere at the Toronto International Film Festival received a standing ovation, about one hundred activists picketed the film outside the theater and stopped traffic to protest the construction of the Dakota Access Pipeline.[51] This protest seemed to highlight the film's tone-deaf refusal to address how the *Deepwater Horizon* blowout and oil spill—the biggest news story of 2010—had changed the public discussion about our relationship to oil.[52] Near the end of the film, as survivors straggle into the Crowne Plaza hotel in Kenner, Louisiana, to the music of Gary Clark Jr.'s "Take Me Down" ("Gotta one-way ticket / I'm going home / back where I started from"), many viewers were left wondering: Is that it?

The only sign in the movie of the disaster's environmental impact is a single, oiled seabird—in a nevertheless Oscar-worthy performance—that flops around on the *Damon Bankston*. Most striking is that the story's end, in which the survivors are reunited in elated relief with their families, is just the beginning of a long nightmare for the human and animal inhabitants of the Gulf Coast region. The slow, attritional environmental damage from the spill was not captured on live video feed, and it eventually receded from the gaze of corporate media.[53] It is also absent from the film, in favor of the visceral special effects and action heroes that generate ticket sales on opening weekend.

Notes

1. Brian Black, "On BP's Deepwater Horizon Live Video Feed," *Environmental History* 15, no. 4 (October 2010): 741–45.
2. David Barstow, David Rohde, and Stephanie Saul, "Deepwater Horizon's Final Hours," *New York Times*, December 26, 2010, 26.
3. For a historical overview of offshore oil development in the Gulf of Mexico, see National Commission on the BP Deepwater Horizon Oil Spill and Offshore Drilling, *Deep Water: The Gulf Oil Disaster and the Future of Offshore Drilling; Report to the President* (Washington, DC: US Government Publishing Office, 2011), chap. 2, https://www.govinfo.gov/content/pkg/GPO-OILCOMMISSION/pdf/GPO-OIL COMMISSION.pdf, written by the author, who served as senior policy analyst on the commission.
4. "*Deepwater Horizon*," Bomb Report, accessed June 7, 2019, https://bombreport .com/yearly-breakdowns/2016–2/deepwater-horizon; Alan Silverleib, "The Gulf Spill: America's Worst Environmental Disaster?" *CNN*, August 11, 2010, http:// www.cnn.com/2010/US/08/05/gulf.worst.disaster/index.html.
5. Peter Berg, dir., *Deepwater Horizon* (Santa Monica, CA: Summit Entertainment, 2016). Summit is a subsidiary of Lionsgate and ultimately distributed the film.
6. Mike Scott, "'Deepwater Horizon' Movie Review: Honor or Exploitation?" *Times-Picayune*, September 26, 2016, https://www.nola.com/entertainment_life/movies _tv/article_d799587d-9082-5f34-963c-130bc01c52dc.html.
7. Mike Scott, "'Deepwater Horizon': What Does the Change in Directors Mean for the Oil-Spill Drama?" *Times-Picayune*, February 2, 2015, https://www.nola.com /movies/2015/02/deepwater_horizon_what_does_th.html.
8. Scott, "Change in Directors."
9. Barstow, Rohde, and Saul, "Deepwater Horizon's Final Hours," 1, 26–28; Mike Scott, "'Deepwater Horizon' Director Peter Berg Aims for Authenticity in What He Describes as a Tale of Heroism," *Times-Picayune*, March 27, 2015, https://www .nola.com/movies/2015/03/deepwater_horizon_movie.html.
10. Gordon Russell, "Amid Louisiana Film Downturn, 'Deepwater Horizon' Sets New Mark for State Subsidies," *New Orleans Advocate*, September 29, 2016, https:// www.theadvocate.com/new_orleans/news/politics/article_aac54cee-869a-11e6 -9a4e-9f8be0194fba.html; "Victims of Deepwater Horizon Explosion Honored at Somber Memorial," *AL.com*, May 25, 2010, https://www.al.com/live/2010/05 /victims_of_deepwater_horizon_e.html.
11. Peter Berg, "The 'Well from Hell'—My Fight with BP to Film Deepwater Horizon," *The Guardian*, October 4, 2016, https://www.theguardian.com/film/2016/oct/04 /the-well-from-hell-my-fight-with-bp-to-film-deepwater-horizon.
12. K. Austin Collins, "'Deepwater Horizon' Is Just a Disaster Movie," *The Ringer*, October 3, 2016, https://www.theringer.com/2016/10/3/16040504/deepwater -horizon-mark-wahlberg-disaster-movie-be3e1b2004b5.
13. Katie Macdonald, "How'd They Get That Shot? *Deepwater Horizon*," *Popular Mechanics*, October 2016, 24.

14. Mike Scott, "The Real Star of 'Deepwater Horizon'? Its Insane Oil Rig Set," *Times-Picayune*, August 19, 2016, https://www.nola.com/movies/2016/08/deep water_horizon_oil_rig_set.html. A second, smaller set was also built at the Ranch Studios in Chalmette, Louisiana.

15. Scott, "Director Peter Berg"; "The Fury of the Rig," special feature, *Deepwater Horizon*, directed by Peter Berg (2016; Santa Monica, CA: Summit Entertainment 2017), Blu-Ray.

16. Mark C. Carnes, "Shooting (Down) the Past: Historians vs. Hollywood," *Cinéaste* 29, no. 2 (Spring 2004): 47; Rich Cohen, "Master of Disaster," *Esquire*, October 2016, https://classic.esquire.com/article/2016/10/1/master-of-disaster.

17. "Fury of the Rig."

18. For an insightful analysis of the many economic affinities between the film and oil businesses, see Yuxun Willy Tan's essay in this volume, "There's No Business Like Oil Business: The Allure of Tax-Sheltered Oil Income to Hollywood's Wealthy."

19. The Deepwater Royalty Relief Act, signed into law by President Bill Clinton in 1995, exempted companies from paying federal royalties on a portion of production from deepwater wells. Had BP's Macondo well been completed safely and turned into a production well, BP would have been exempt from paying federal royalties on the first nine million barrels of oil and natural-gas equivalent.

20. Russell, "Amid Louisiana Film Downturn"; Mike Scott, "Petition Urges 'Deepwater Horizon' Filmmakers to Put Their Money Where Their Mouths Are," *Times-Picayune*, August 18, 2016, https://www.nola.com/movies/2016/08 /deepwater_horizon_movie_petition_123172.html.

21. Cohen, "Master of Disaster."

22. This was filmed at the Bristow Heliport in Galliano, Louisiana, north of Fourchon.

23. See, for example, some of the user reviews at "Deepwater Horizon," IMDb, accessed June 15, 2019, https://www.imdb.com/title/tt1860357/reviews.

24. "Gulf Coast Cowboy" originally referred to local nineteenth-century cattlemen, but in recent years came to describe rough-and-tough white working-class men who took risks riding oil rigs rather than horses. Frank Foster's 2011 eponymous song gave popular expression to the term. See Frank Foster, "Gulf Coast Cowboy," SongLyrics.com, accessed November 1, 2019, http://www.songlyrics.com/frank -foster/gulf-coast-cowboy-lyrics.

25. For a detailed narrative of the blowout and sinking of the *Deepwater Horizon*, with extensive background on its entire cast of characters, see John Konrad and Tom Shroder, *Fire on the Horizon: The Untold Story of the Gulf Oil Disaster* (New York: HarperCollins, 2011).

26. David Hammer, "'Deepwater Horizon' Movie: Fact vs. Fiction," *Milwaukee Journal Sentinel*, September 21, 2016, https://www.jsonline.com/story/life/nation -now/2016/09/21/deepwater-horizon-movie-fact-vs-fiction/90813762.

27. David Sims, "*Deepwater Horizon* Stays Too Close to Surface," *The Atlantic*, September 30, 2016, https://www.theatlantic.com/entertainment/archive/2016 /09/deepwater-horizon-review/502376; Joel Achenbach, "'Deepwater Horizon' Movie Gets the Facts Mostly Right, but Simplifies the Blame," *Washington Post*, September 29, 2016, https://www.washingtonpost.com/news/achenblog /wp/2016/09/29/deepwater-horizon-movie-gets-the-facts-mostly-right-but -simplifies-the-blame.

28. This observation comes courtesy of Don Boesch, professor of marine science at the

University of Maryland and commissioner on the National Commission on the BP Deepwater Horizon Oil Spill and Offshore Drilling.

29. National Commission, *Deep Water*, 107.

30. Kenneth Stickney, "Donald Vidrine, Deepwater Horizon Rig Supervisor, Dies at 69," *Daily Advertiser*, June 5, 2017, https://www.theadvertiser.com/story /news/2017/06/05/donald-vidrine-deepwater-horizon-rig-supervisor-dies-69 /370528001.

31. Clifford Krauss, "Donald J. Vidrine, Supervisor on Ill-Fated Deepwater Horizon Rig, Dies at 69," *New York Times*, June 6, 2017, https://www.nytimes.com/2017/06/06 /business/energy-environment/donald-vidrine-died-deepwater-horizon-supervisor .html.

32. Tom Fowler, "BP Official's Recollections at Odds with Transocean Workers'," *Houston Chronicle*, August 19, 2010, https://www.chron.com/business/energy /article/BP-official-s-recollections-at-odds-with-1593304.php.

33. Barstow, Rohde, and Saul, "Deepwater Horizon's Final Hours," 26.

34. National Commission, *Deep Water*, 104.

35. Tom Fowler, "BP Emails Indicate Strain before Gulf Oil Spill," *Houston Chronicle*, April 5, 2011, https://www.chron.com/business/energy/article/BP-emails-indicate -strain-before-Gulf-oil-spill-1615641.php.

36. National Commission, *Deep Water*, 115. For an academic critique of the film for neglecting to address the "regulatory environment of the oil drilling industry," see Shane Dixon and Tim Gawley, "Crude Exploration: Portraying Industrial Disaster in *Deepwater Horizon*, a Film Directed by Peter Berg, 2016," *New Solutions* 27, no. 2 (2017): 264–72. Dixon and Gawley argue that this omission "serves to potentially reproduce messages that privilege individualistic, isolated, views of industrial disaster and prioritize immediate over distal causes" (p. 264).

37. Michael Martinez, "Transocean Pleads Guilty, Fined 2nd-Biggest Penalty for Gulf Spill," *CNN*, February 14, 2013, https://www.cnn.com/2013/02/14/justice/trans ocean-deepwater-fine/index.html.

38. Barstow, Rohde, and Saul, "Deepwater Horizon's Final Hours," 26.

39. In the film, the blowout preventer's (BOP) blind shear ram (BSR) is shown activating when Harrell hits the emergency disconnect system button from the bridge, perhaps fifteen minutes after the explosions start. On the contrary, both the Det Norske Veritas Joint Investigation Team's forensic examination of the BOP stack and Judge Carl Barbier's civil ruling held that the BSR did not activate until the morning of April 22, when it was finally triggered by an ROV.

40. Pam Fessler, "Hearing: Rig Manager Contradicts Chief Mechanic," *NPR*, May 28, 2010, https://www.npr.org/templates/story/story.php?storyId=127230250; David Hammer, "Hearings: Transocean Official Untroubled about Various Red-Flag Issues," *Times-Picayune*, May 27, 2010, https://www.nola.com/news/gulf-oil-spill /2010/05/hearings_transocean_official_u.html.

41. The renowned special effects company Industrial Light & Magic, founded in 1975 by George Lucas, did the CG work for the film. For a history of the environmental effects and pyromania of Hollywood films, see Hunter Vaughn, *Hollywood's Dirtiest Secret: The Hidden Environmental Costs of the Movies* (New York: Columbia University Press, 2019).

42. "Fury of the Rig"; Mark Meszoros, "Movie Review: 'Deepwater Horizon' a Disaster Film with Excellent Technical Work," *News-Herald*, September 29, 2016, https:// www.news-herald.com/entertainment/

movie-review-deepwater-horizon-a-disaster-film-with-excellent-technical/article
_c465913d-c700–5fed-a52a-29934af9e739.html.

43. On disaster films in American culture, see Matthew Schneider-Mayerson, "Disaster Movies and the 'Peak Oil' Movement: Does Popular Culture Encourage Eco-Apocalyptic Beliefs in the United States?" *Journal for the Study of Religion, Nature, and Culture* 7, no. 3 (2013): 289–314.

44. Benjamin Lee, "Deepwater Horizon Review: Mark Wahlberg v. BP in Angry Disaster Movie," *The Guardian*, September 13, 2016, https://www.theguardian.com/film /2016/sep/14/deepwater-horzion-review-mark-wahlberg-toronto-film-festival.

45. Sims, "Too Close to the Surface."

46. Loren Steffy, "Truth and Fiction on the Horizon," *Texas Monthly*, September 29, 2016, https://www.texasmonthly.com/the-daily-post/truth-fiction-horizon.

47. Dan Jackson, "How Accurate Was the Crazy Climax of 'Deepwater Horizon'?" *ThrillList*, October 3, 2016, https://www.thrillist.com/entertainment/nation /deepwater-horizon-real-story-mark-wahlberg-oil-rig-jump.

48. Jack Doyle, "Deepwater Horizon: Film & Spill; 2010–2016," *Pop History Dig*, July 14, 2018, https://www.pophistorydig.com/topics/deepwater-horizon-film-and -spill; "Deepwater Horizon," Rotten Tomatoes, accessed June 15, 2019, https:// www.rottentomatoes.com/m/deepwater_horizon.

49. Quoted in Doyle, "Film & Spill."

50. "Deepwater Horizon," IMDb.

51. Andrew Pulver, "Deepwater Horizon Premiere in Toronto Hit by Dakota Pipeline Protest," *The Guardian*, September 14, 2016, https://www.theguardian.com/film /2016/sep/14/deepwater-horizon-premiere-hit-by-dakota-pipeline-protest-toronto -film-festival.

52. Ishaan Tharoor, "The BP Oil Spill: The Top 10 of Everything of 2010," *Time*, December 10, 2010, http://content.time.com/time/specials/packages/article /0,28804,2035319_2035315_2035680,00.html.

53. On "slow" environmental damage or "slow violence," see Rob Nixon, *Slow Violence and the Environmentalism of the Poor* (Cambridge, MA: Harvard University Press, 2013).

Chapter 5

Chernobyl (2019): A Soviet Propaganda Win—Delivered Thirty-Three Years Late

Kate Brown

Craig Mazin's *Chernobyl* miniseries is a hit—the highest-rated TV series of all time, according to crowd-sourced reviews on IMDb. Radio, TV and print journalists, podcasters, and bloggers have formed a global chorus to comment on the show. The tiny city of Pripyat, built to house fifty thousand nuclear operators and their families in the remote Ukrainian Pripyat Marshes, has become the center of global attention with a 30 percent uptick in tourism. Why? What is it about the show that surpasses the riveting cliffhangers of *Game of Thrones*?

The magnetic attraction of the show originates in part from its political plasticity. Commentators and viewers can devise any number of contradictory parables from the fictionalized drama (that confusingly also purports to be a work of historical nonfiction). Sonia Soraiya writes in *Vanity Fair* that the show produced for her an "addictive dread," as she obsessively googled facts about the accident, while her father mapped the nearest power reactors. The hospital scenes show how acute radiation exposure is, as *The Guardian* put it, "a horrible way to die."[1] The Union of Concerned Scientists points to *Chernobyl* to underline the message that politicians should not dismiss scientists for fear of public relations problems.[2] Masha Gessen in the *New Yorker* uses the show to drill down the message that the Soviet Union was a "psychotic regime" unable to tell the truth or even recognize it.[3] Certainly, as Gessen demonstrates, the show has revived Cold War tropes about the mendacity and fatal flaws of Soviet communism. The 1950s-sounding stage directions in Mazin's script show that Gessen's interpretation is no mistake. A neo–Cold War narrative makes it easy for commentators to avow with calm assurance that, though terrifying, such an accident could never happen here, wherever "here" is.[4]

I find most strange that the show has produced an obsession with asserting that the fictional drama is true. BuzzFeed calls it a "truth offensive." [5] Jim Geraghty of the *National Review* reports that "Chernobyl" is . . . way more terrifying than most offerings in the horror genre because it's all true (or as accurate as the brilliant creator-writer Craig Mazin could determine, given contrasting historical accounts)." [6] Indeed, Mazin paid close attention to material culture. His characters dress Soviet, walk through Soviet interiors, drive in Soviet vehicles, and converse in the wooden tones of Soviet-speak. Mazin also lavishly downloads into the drama technical facts about nuclear reactors and how the RBMK blew up that are surprisingly detailed for popular entertainment. The insistence on getting the optics and technology correct helps the fictional drama blur into nonfiction; the details serve as truth legitimizers.

Mazin has helped this process along by repeating that his show is foremost "anti-Soviet and anti-lie." That is an astounding statement because so much of Mazin's narrative outline falls in step with the plot lines Soviet propagandists sketched out in the weeks following the accident. Communist Party leaders sent trusted journalists to the accident site to report on the mass mobilization of technology and the heroic efforts of patriotic Soviets who pitched in to contain the disaster. [7] Just two months after the accident, Soviet leaders were planning a monument to these "liquidators." [8] Mazin features the grim, determined miners, stripped to their underwear and impervious to their exposure, tunneling under the blown plant. He spotlights young soldiers, outfitted as "bio robots," who had ninety seconds to shovel radioactive graphite from the roof of reactor 3. Those images come straight from Soviet newspaper and TV reports, stories cultivated to project an image of calm, masculine heroism. Mazin in an interview asserted that only Soviets could mobilize so many citizens and resources to battle the radioactive foe. [9] Yegor Ligachev, a member of Mikhail Gorbachev's Politburo, sounded out a similar sentiment: "It is important in this awkward time that we show the entire world that we are capable of righting this disaster ourselves; that we did not tolerate panic." [10]

A Normal Accident

Mazin's control room scenes would also have made Soviet propagandists happy. *Chernobyl* shows an impatient and domineering deputy chief engineer, Anatoly Dyatlov, berating and threatening his staff to violate one safety regulation after another until they drove the reactor to overheat and blow up. Once the plant exploded, Dyatlov could not believe it, and for confirmation he sent two operators to the reactor face and to their deaths. Dyatlov's orders to override the safety system and pull out control rods (to slow and control the reactor)—his confusion, incompetence, and irascibility—made up the basis of the indictment against him and his colleagues, a narrative Politburo members devised two months after the accident and pursued at the trial in July 1987.[11]

In the final episode's court room scene, Mazin points to the second causal factor for the accident. The RBMK reactor had a fatal design flaw, which caused the reactor to momentarily speed up on shut down when too many control rods were removed from the reactor. On the night of April 26, plant operators violated regulations and removed nearly all the control rods, which left the reactor in an extremely unstable state. After the 1979 Three Mile Island accident in 1979, Charles Perrow, a sociologist, wrote a book in which he argued that for complex systems such as nuclear power plants, accidents are "normal events" because there are so many regulations; some, as Perrow points out and Mazin shows, are crossed out and superseded by later stipulations. With multiple, confusing directions and beeping, flashing indicators, operators have no capacity or time in an emergency to process what is happening and react appropriately. So when these "normal" operating errors occur, Perrow showed, employees experience them as unexpected and incomprehensible, much like Dyatlov refused to accept the fact that reactor 4 had blown—similar to how Japanese officials dissimulated for not three days but a two full months before admitting to the meltdown of three reactors at the Fukushima Daichi nuclear power plant, and like officials at Metropolitan Edison who issued statements after the meltdown of the Three Mile Island reactor that "conditions are stable" on the same morning when they were venting radioactive gas and pressure to save the reactor's containment structure.[12]

Mazin makes out that the discovery of major design flaws came from a dissident scientist, the fictionalized Belarusian physicist Ulana Khomyuk, while Valery Legasov, the chief scientist appointed to the cleanup, took it upon himself to publicize the problem. In reality, KGB chief Filipp Bobkov led the commission that determined that the reactor's positive void coefficient contributed to the accident. He also reported a host of other problems with radioactive waste and a sluggardly alarm system.[13] Behind the closed doors of the Kremlin situation room, Mikhail Gorbachev was more than happy to use the catastrophe to unseat powerful longtime leaders of the Soviet nuclear weapons industry, which had become an impervious, impenetrable fiefdom.[14] Gorbachev also immediately saw the value in divulging to the West the technical specifics of the accident. As he told his Politburo members on July 3, 1986: "We need to define what information to give the IAEA [International Atomic Energy Agency] and other countries and to do so without classifying that which needs to be disclosed. We need to reveal the maximum possible. That will give us a big win."[15]

A big win indeed. Gorbachev deputized Legasov to speak to the IAEA in late August 1986 in Vienna. Legasov truthfully told IAEA delegates that Chernobyl operators violated regulations maintaining that at least fifteen control rods be left in the reactor.[16] He provided a lot of technical detail about the RBMK. It would have been easy from Legasov's speech to grasp the primary design flaw of the RBMK reactors. American engineers knew it well because their first reactors created to produce plutonium for nuclear weapons also had a positive void co-efficient.[17] Legasov's speech was extremely unusual. Western commentators were accustomed to Soviet secrecy, especially in regard to nuclear topics. Legasov did not tell all, but he said a lot as part of Gorbachev's new propaganda strategy of "openness." Gorbachev won from Legasov's spectacle of transparency a soft-ening of Cold War rhetoric. After initially doubting Soviets accounts of accident damage, American and other commentators ceased to second-guess Soviet press reports, and eventually, as I show in my book *Manual for Survival*, collaborated with Soviet leaders in minimizing the reported effects of the disaster.[18]

Soviet Propaganda in 2019

Mazin's faithfulness to Soviet plotlines is arguably the most historically ac-curate aspect of the miniseries. Soviet propagandists created the narrative of operator incompetence, selfless mass mobilization, and masculine heroism while spatially containing the accident narrative to the depopulated thirty-kilometer Chernobyl Zone and temporally to just the months following the disaster. Soviet leaders, eager to pronounce the accident over as quickly as possible, used these narrative strategies to obscure a much greater drama that was occurring in fully populated, contaminated territories around the blown plant in the years following the catastrophe. In *Manual for Survival*, I examine archival documents that show an unfolding public health disaster in the years after the accident, one that continues to this day.[19] The sociologist Olga Kuchinskaya notes how Chernobyl oscillated over two decades between existing under the glare of a sharp media focus and fading from view entirely. Periods of invisibility, she concludes, turned into ignorance about the health effects caused by the accident.[20] Mazin's *Chernobyl* shows how intense visibil-ity can also lead to a lack of knowledge; a truth-telling spectacle that serves as a projection of contemporary politics. Mazin is appalled that people come away from his show feeling an "addictive dread." "For a million reasons," he told reporters, "this was not an anti-nuclear polemic. It's anti-Soviet govern-ment, and it is anti-lie, and it is pro-human being. But anyone who thinks the point of this is that nuclear power is bad, is just, they've just missed it."[21]

So why have so many viewers missed Mazin's message and come away frightened by nuclear power? Mazin's commentary helps solve that riddle. In the show's podcast, Mazin says "It is impossible to watch this miniseries with tales of government malfeasance and lies without thinking of what is going on in America and across the world today."[22] Some viewers might be thinking of the less than truthfulness of leaders in the Democratic Party. Others might recall the precarious relationship with President Donald Trump. Major media outlets regularly fact check the president and find that he deals as liberally with the truth as any Soviet party hack. Meanwhile, the Trump administration backs nuclear power with the single-minded optimism that Soviet leaders embraced their reactors. Trump's administration recently bailed out the construction of two bankrupt nuclear power plant construction sites in Georgia to the tune of $3.7 billion.[23] The same government in 2019 resolved to work out the intractable problem of high-level waste at the country's largest superfund site, the Hanford nuclear reservation, by recategorizing extremely hazardous toxins as medium level waste.[24] The Environmental Protection Agency and the Department of Energy have in the past few years cleansed damning words like *climate change* from official state documents much like Soviet leaders banned the words *radiation* and *plutonium*. President Trump's mantra—"Everything is great. Everything is getting even better"—reminds one of Stalin's pronouncements in the grim 1930s that "life is getting better and happier every day."

Many viewers follow the logic of Mazin's horror genre. They are left feeling not comforted, but scared. What frightens them? On Twitter seven people posted that the Chernobyl accident occurred as an outgrowth of totalitarianism. In contrast, several hundred expressed fears that a similar accident could happen where they live: "As I finish watching *Chernobyl* on HBO, I'm frightened by how Democrats and big government leftists are similar to Soviet officials"; "The parallels between Chernobyl and our current political state in the US is scary"; and "It happened, it's still happening."[25] Bret Stephens in the *New York Times* concurred: "What happens when we have our own Chernobyl, or another 9/11, or something worse, and the credibility of government becomes essential to the survival of the state?"[26] It appears many viewers are not taking away the intended message: that Russians, socialism, or totalitarianism caused the disaster. Instead audiences want to distill the "truth" from the *Chernobyl* drama because a recent centralization of power and money has been accompanied by a concentration of technical knowledge. As in the Soviet period, the truths delivered from podiums or TV screens have become suspect. As Soviet history shows, the first casualty of a disintegrating empire is believability.

Notes

A version of this essay was previously published as Kate Brown, "Johan Rench, director. Chernobyl. Written and created by Craig Mazin," *American Historical Review* 124, no. 4 (2019): 1373–76. Reprinted by permission of Oxford University Press.

1. Julie McDowell, "A Horrible Way to Die:" How Chernobyl Created a Nuclear Meltdown," *The Guardian*, June 4, 2019.
2. Anita Desikan, "HBO's Chernobyl: A Fictionalized Representation of the True Horrors of Sidelining Science," *Union of Concerned Scientists*, https://blog.ucsusa .org/anita-desikan/hbo-chernobyl-horrors-of-sidelining-science.
3. "What HBO's 'Chernobyl' Got Right and What It Got Terribly Wrong," *New Yorker*, June 4, 2019.
4. Henry Fountain, "Plenty of Fantasy in HBO's 'Chernobyl,' but the Truth Is Real," *New York Times*, June 2, 2019, https://www.nytimes.com/2019/06/02/arts /television/chernobyl-hbo.html; Michael Shellenberger, "Why HBO's 'Chernobyl' Gets Nuclear So Wrong," *Forbes*, June 6, 2019, https://www.forbes.com/sites /michaelshellenberger/2019/06/06/why-hbos-chernobyl-gets-nuclear-so-wrong /#4aeb80ff632f.
5. Georgy Birger, "'Chernobyl' Shows How Modern Russia's Propaganda Machine Is Falling Apart," *BuzzFeed*, June 19, 2019, https://www.buzzfeednews.com/article /georgybirger/chernobyl-modern-russia-propaganda-collapse.
6. Geraghty, "Conservatives Ought to Watch Chernobyl," *National Review*, May 29, 2019.
7. "Direktiv: Dlia osveshcheniia na press-konferentsii osnovnykh voprosov," K Protocol no. 21, June 4, 1986, Alla Yaroshinskaya, *Chernobyl: Sovershenno sekretno*, (Moscow: Drugie Beriga, 1992): 347.
8. "KPSS Central Committee Politburo Meeting," July 3, 1986, classified, single draft copy, Alla Yaroshinskaya, personal collection.
9. Mazin: "What we did not get on our side of the news is that this could have only happened in the USSR but also that only the Soviets could have solved this problem."
10. "KPSS Central Committee Politburo Meeting," July 3, 1986, classified, single draft copy, Alla Yaroshinskaya, personal collection.
11. At this meeting, Politburo members discussed the KGB investigation and fault for the accident. "KPSS Central Committee Politburo Meeting," July 3, 1986, classified, single draft copy, Alla Yaroshinskaya, personal collection.
12. Charles Perrow, *Normal Accidents: Living with High-Risk Technologies* (Princeton, NJ: Princeton University Press, 1999), 9; "TMI Truth," Beyond Nuclear, accessed June 14, 2019, http://www.beyondnuclear.org/tmi-truth; "Fukushima Meltdown Alert 'Was Delayed,'" February 24, 2016, sec. Asia, https://www.bbc.com/news/world -asia-35650625.
13. "KPSS Central Committee Politburo Meeting," 31.
14. "KPSS Central Committee Politburo Meeting," 43.
15. "KPSS Central Committee Politburo Meeting," 44.
16. "Информация об аварии на Чернобыльской АЭС и её последствиях, подготовленная для МАГАТЭ, Доклад №1," (INSAG-1), accessed June 12, 2019, http://magate-1.narod.ru/4.html.

17. Alvin M. Weinberg, *The First Nuclear Era: The Life and Times of a Technological Fixer* (New York: American Institute of Physics, 1994), 188.
18. Alex S. Jones, "Press Sifts through a Mound of Fact and Rumor," *New York Times*, May 1, 1986; Stuart Diamond, "Long-Term Chernobyl Fallout: Comparison to Bombs Altered," *New York Times*, November 4, 1986, C3.
19. See, for example, Nuclear Consulting Group, "Chernobyl Cancer Rates Revised Upwards," May 2, 2019, https://www.nuclearconsult.com/blog/chernobyl-cancer -rates-revised-upwards.
20. Olga Kuchinskaya, *The Politics of Invisibility: Public Knowledge about Radiation Health Effects after Chernobyl* (Boston: MIT Press, 2014), Kindle location 3586.
21. "The Drama of Chernobyl," World Nuclear News, June 5, 2019, http://www .world-nuclear-news.org/Articles/The-drama-and-the-facts-about-Chernobyl.
22. *Chernobyl*, HBO, podcast for episode 1, May 6, 2019, https://www.hbo.com /chernobyl/podcast.
23. Ari Natter, "Trump to Finalize $3.7 Billion in Aid for Troubled Nuclear Plant, *Bloomberg*, March 19, 2019.
24. Kashimira Gander, "Trump Wants to Reclassify Radioactive Waste from Nuclear Weapons to 'Low Level' so Disposal Is Cheaper," *Newsweek*, December 11, 2018.
25. Informed Electorate (@Informedelect), June 6, 2019; BojankReviews (@BojankReviews), June 6, 2019; Lori Coletti Campbell (@loricolly), June 12, 2019.
26. "What 'Chernobyl' Teaches about Trump," *New York Times*, June 20, 2019, https:// www.nytimes.com/2019/06/20/opinion/chernobyl-hbo-lies-trump.html.

PART 2

Energy and Nature

Chapter 6

Wings (1927): Aviation, War, and Energy

Conevery Bolton Valencius

Beginning in 1927, Americans packed theaters for a thrilling $2 million epic of the Great War, the first major aviation war film and a worldwide sensation. *Wings* was directed by William Wellman and starred Richard Arlen, Charles "Buddy" Rogers, and Clara Bow. Earlier that year Bow had starred as the plucky saleswoman hero of the film *It* and become known as the era's "It Girl," embodying energetic wit, youthful athleticism, and unaffected sex appeal. *Wings* dramatized military air power in similar ways. The high-stakes heroism and deathly glamour of air-to-air combat symbolized the new realities of war remade through human ascent to the skies. The film sweeps viewers along as fossil fuels lift human beings high in the air and into a new interaction with the natural world, while also engaging them in the most brutal of conflicts and poignant relationships of friendship and love.[1]

Filmgoers loved *Wings*. The stars were appealing, the drama was compelling, the funny scenes made everyone laugh. *Wings* ran at New York's Criterion Theater for sixty-three consecutive weeks and captured two inaugural Academy Awards in 1929: Engineering Effects and Best Production (which would later become Best Picture). Its depiction of fighter pilots as skyborne knights was lastingly influential, familiar to anyone who has watched World War II cinema, savored the films of Hayao Miyazaki, or thrilled to the drama of *Star Wars*.[2] The film has been lauded as an artistic success and a triumph of technologically innovative photography. *Wings* likewise marks a revolution in American energy history. Use of fossil fuels transformed combat not only on the ground but also in the skies, making possible the gladiatorial aviation at the heart of this drama. Yet even as *Wings* shows how newly utilized energy sources allowed humans to ascend into the heavens and wage new forms of war, the film demonstrates a larger truth of American energy: a central element of the transformation wrought by fossil fuels is to obscure and downplay their central role. A film that beautifully bears witness to the impact of petroleum portrays fuel only as a joke. Soaring flight, not the oil that enables it, is what thrills viewers. The film effaces the energy source whose transformative power it so beautifully demonstrates.

Cars, Planes, War

It is 1917 in a mid-American town of square streets and large lawns. Viewers meet fresh-faced Mary Preston (Bow) as she scrambles over a fence to see her neighbor Jack Powell (Rogers). She climbs under the engine alongside him to tinker with his racecar, which she names the *Shooting Star*, but Jack—heedless of her interest in him as well as his car—dashes off to visit town beauty Sylvia Lewis (Jobyna Ralston). In the first shot of the next pair, lovely Sylvia and wealthy David Armstrong (Arlen) sway back and forth on an oversize tree swing as the camera travels with them high up into the air and then back down. Jack interrupts this whimsical ride, tugging Sylvia away to show off his car. This scene establishes the theme of ascent into the air, introduces the film's impressive camerawork, and sets up a triangle: unassertive Sylvia, serious and brooding David, and cheerfully oblivious Jack.

With the coming of war, David and Jack both report to a recruiting station. Reading the German name of one would-be recruit, Herman Schwimpf (El Brendel), the sergeant doubts his patriotism. In response, Herman tears off his jacket. The sergeant punches him flat on his back, but Herman points to the tattoo of an American flag that waves as he flexes his bicep. Mollified, the sergeant accepts the recruit, and the film's central comedic character is established. So too is its central drama: before leaving town, Jack rushes in to say goodbye to Sylvia. He seizes a photo of her, jubilant in his belief that he has won her heart. Yet once he is gone, Sylvia embraces David, for whom she had intended the photo. In his own stately home, David bids goodbye to his formal mother, his older father in a wooden wheelchair, and his beloved dog, taking a toy bear with him for luck.

Jack and David, along with the ebullient Herman, enlist as pilots. During hand-to-hand training, Herman is knocked over by another great bull-faced sergeant, and the sergeant's face fills the screen over him in a manner familiar to any viewer of subsequent twentieth-century cinema: this is how bullies loom. Jealous of Sylvia's affection, Jack picks a fight with David, but his animosity changes to admiration at David's willingness to keep fighting even after being knocked woozy to the ground. The two become friends.

Back home, Mary, the automobile enthusiast, reads that the Women's Motor Corps is recruiting those who drive what the placards call "Ford cars"—still too new for the shorthand "Fords." All three main characters are now off to war. As Jack and David are called up for active duty overseas, large-scale mobilization plays out across the screen. A broad valley stretches to the horizon, filled with converging lines of marching infantry and men on horse-back, flanked by rows of tanks and trucks. The sky above fills with images: soldiers rush across a battlefield, artillery battalions entrench and fire, horses gallop with heavy wagons, tanks plow forward into enemy fire, infantry advance and are cut down. This dramatic sequence shows the machinery of war: human and animal bodies propelled by metabolic energy, and literal machines now propelled by fossil fuels.[3]

Hydrocarbons and War

Wings swept viewers along in the power and romance of a profound techno-logical change. Scenes throughout emphasize the organic energy necessary for war: alongside soldiers' bodies, the film is full of shots of horses as well as dogs accompanying troops and pulling carts. Yet a new source of energy defined this conflict: World War I was the first major war fought with petroleum. Campaigns were shaped by supplies of fossil fuel, just as in earlier wars they had been constrained by available fodder for draft animals. In celebrating the human flight made possible by this new source of energy, *Wings* marked a momentous transition in energy use.[4]

By the early twentieth century, inventors and tinkerers had long been frus-trated in the quest for directed flight. Innovators starting in the seventeenth century experimented with kites and balloons capable of carrying a person's weight. By the 1790s, French reconnaissance employed hydrogen-filled bal-loons to observe enemy positions, and such observation balloons continued in use through the US Civil War. Stationary balloons continued to provide obser-vations in the Great War: in a dramatic scene in *Wings*, Jack and David shoot one down. Yet in at least three steam-powered attempts at winged flight, the engines and fuel proved too heavy.[5]

A new fuel made the difference. Starting in the late 1850s, entrepreneurs in Eurasia and the American Eastern Seaboard began pulling oil out of the ground in commercial quantities to refine into an illuminant as well as a lu-bricant. Business innovators swiftly began to develop systems of refining and transporting ever-larger amounts of oil and finding new ways to put it to use. Oil's energy density meant that it held the capacity for much more power than a similar weight of other sources of combustion (straw, wood, dried dung, charcoal, and even coal). Engineers developed a new form of engine using this energy-dense fuel, one in which combustion took place within the central chamber rather than outside it, as in a steam engine. The explosion of gases powered cam-linked cylinders with what eventually become standardized as a four-stroke pattern of intake and exhaust. Internal combustion allowed ground vehicles to move independently with a new product: gasoline. Beginning in the mid-1880s, automobiles were a rich person's novelty, but after 1910 they became a pervasive consumer product in the United States, once Henry Ford's standardized and mass produced cars made them affordable.[6]

Inventors quickly transferred that power to liftoff. The development of small, reliable, and efficient high-speed gasoline engines in the 1880s and 1890s enabled the production of the gas-powered dirigible (a rigid-frame airship) in France and, soon after, the American-born airplane. Late in 1903, Orville Wright and Wilbur Wright—at the vanguard of many similar innovators—demonstrated successful flight in a winged airplane with a gasoline-powered engine. By 1910, many models were made in small workshops across the country.[7]

Over the course of the Great War, airplanes went from small-scale products of uncertain performance to mass-produced commodities playing a crucial role in battle. Aviators like Jack and David were key to the Allied war effort, but most of the developments were European; Americans did not lead in air power design until the next great war. Still, industrial innovation in the American automobile industry led to the mass production of the lightweight, air-cooled Liberty engine, much as similar transformation would later enable bombers to roll off Detroit assembly lines in World War II. Operations, logistics, and various crucial but mundane aspects of aircraft design, delivery, and supply likewise gained efficiency, specialization, and scale as the US Armed Forces took to the skies.[8] Moreover, the development of Allied air power was made possible by American aviation fuel—mostly flowing from Pennsylvania oilfields—needed to replace European supplies once drawn from Sumatra and Borneo. US aviation fuel was less reliable and powerful, however, with a tendency to "knock" (produce ignition too soon in the engine chamber), and thus posed a significant problem solved only after the war. Still, just as the organic energy of straining muscles remained important, organic sources of oil were critical to the new hydrocarbon regime. The US planted 100,000 acres of castor beans for Liberty Aero Oil to lubricate the new Liberty engine. In all, the American war effort required 4,825,697 gallons of aviation gasoline (as well as 617,815 gallons of castor oil).[9] The motive power provided by hydrocarbons propels the action of *Wings*—as it did the mechanization of the Great War itself. Fossil fuels were fundamental to the Great War and to the graceful, deadly sky ballet that makes this war movie so compelling.

Soaring Flight

In *Wings*, flight is a triumph from the moment viewers first experience it with Jack and David. From inside the long rectangular opening of the American hangar, the audience sees planes lining up as music lifts and swells. Today, such music is a soundtrack, but in the original screenings, musicians—a pipe organ player in small theaters but a whole orchestra in larger venues—improvised at each showing based on the film's scoring notes, aided by standard compilations of mood music with short scores conveying love, dramatic tension, horror, and the like. In *Wings*, sound along with sight establishes the drama of liftoff. The audience watches as the planes move faster and faster along the ground, small against the backdrop of trees and open space (South Texas, representing France). Then, in a slightly receded shot, viewers witness the planes leave the ground and start to gain altitude just above a group of marching soldiers and a parked truck. The planes climb up and away, much faster than the earthbound troops. Once in the air, the vista expands, the view relaxes, and planes swim smoothly through the sky, the music rising to new heights along with them.[10] In later films smooth takeoffs often give way to rough flights, but the fundamentally optimistic drama of *Wings* follows the pilots' view, looking out across an ever-widening landscape as the little planes gain altitude. Crescendos of music underscore the visual glory. Scarves whipping in the wind, the pilots soar and audiences soar along with them.[11]

The heroes' first mission is a triumph of filmmaking. Cameras accompany the pilots as they engage a German air patrol. The astounding, gut-wrenching death spiral of one German plane was filmed by stunt pilot Frank Clarke with a camera mounted in front of his cockpit. He collapses, seemingly dead, as he releases lampblack to simulate a flaming engine billowing smoke, and puts his plane into a real-life out-of-control spin from six thousand feet. The only special effects were the hand-painted flames, added later, frame by frame. Clarke's ability to act dead while plummeting toward possible death impressed professional colleagues and audiences alike.[12]

Weeks of battle pass before viewers see Mary again, jauntily whistling behind the wheel of a supply truck in the French countryside, feet up on the dashboard as she confidently drives along. Her "puddle-hopper" brings medical supplies to a small village hit by what placards identify simply as "flu"—the 1918 influenza outbreak that ultimately killed more people worldwide than even this terrible war. The village of Mervale has been targeted by a dreaded Gotha, a huge German bomber. Viewers see the Gotha from above as crews

Fig. 6.1. The young heroes of *Wings* take flight, soaring above and outpacing the earthbound vehicles beneath them. Today, the planes seem small, and liftoff is unremarkable. But in 1927, few viewers had themselves been in the air: being able to see the world from a pilot's point of view was exciting and revelatory.

roll it out of its hangar, its sinister bulk and sinuous painted lines making it, as the intertitle reads, a "great dragon" roaring out to "seek its prey." The Gotha bombs Mary and the village of Mervale, but Jack and David's squadron—called in from another little village—roars to the rescue. Jack and David dash to their planes, pulling on their coats and leather helmets, and creating a visual trope of pilots rushing to their battle stations that would become recognizable across aviation cinema, including in the first *Star Wars*. The GIs in Mervale cheer their rescuers, one recognizes Jack's *Shooting Star*, and Mary blows a kiss. By intermission, the film's narrative is clear: heroism in the skies helps carry the war. But beneath the surface lies a subtler narrative: that energy-dense petroleum powers the lorries, tanks, and sky fighters filling the screen.[13]

Airplanes and Energy

In the mid-1910s, aircraft were small and rickety, and could be blown backward by a strong wind. When the United States declared war in April 1917, the Aviation Section of the US Signal Corps had fewer than 1,200 officers and men. In 1918, American aeronautics was organized as the Army Air Service (and then reorganized as the Air Corps in 1926; the US Air Force was established as a separate military branch in 1947). Of the two hundred training airplanes available in 1917, none were battle ready, and no warplanes of any kind were being manufactured within the US. Even so, by war's end, Americans had learned to fight in the air. US air forces had taken part in over 150 bombing raids, which dropped over 275,000 pounds of explosives, and had taken more than eighteen thousand aerial photographs of enemy positions.[14]

The initial and enduring military use of aircraft was reconnaissance, but these missions soon led to plane-mounted weaponry, and then to what became known as "dogfights" between rival fighters. Pursuit planes—those engaging in battle midair—took on an increasingly important role in the war, and sky fights captured popular imagination. Other countries followed the French in celebrating "ace" pilots—those who had downed at least five enemy fighters. So did American popular culture: Flying Ace Snoopy battled the Red Baron throughout Charles M. Schulz's long-running *Peanuts* comic series. In *Wings*, after Jack and David down the Gotha that menaced the village of Mervale, a French commander awards Jack and David with medals to recognize them—as the intertitle reads—with "the name of ace."[15]

Public imagination soared alongside the fighters of the air. In 1927, the year *Wings* premiered, Charles Lindbergh flew solo across the Atlantic. Amelia Earhart became a media darling for feats of daring and valor. Young men and women practiced takeoffs and landings in small airfields across the country, dreaming of being the next Lindbergh or Earhart. Within a generation after the Great War, innovation leapt past streamlined airliners to jet propulsion and soon past the sound barrier. But *Wings* captured the exciting period of both technological and imaginative liftoff.[16]

Invisible Oil

Early in the film, while Jack and David are at aviation school, two events take place: one central to the narrative and one whose importance may pass by almost unnoticed. The two young aviators are in awe upon arriving in camp. Their older, self-assured tentmate (Gary Cooper, whose international stardom was launched by this magnetic performance) enjoys part of a chocolate bar before being summoned for a training run, during which his plane fatally crashes.[17] When an officer orders the new arrivals to wrap up his belongings, they stare in horrified fascination at the partly eaten chocolate bar.[18] The audience experiences through their reactions the terrible risks of flight. The

Fig. 6.2. Pursuit pilot Jack Powell and the American unit engage a German air patrol. Innovative camera design and daring stunts carried audiences high into the skies: the flying sequences were shot largely by pilot-actors who had fought in the war they were now fictionalizing. The energy bestowed by fossil fuels underlies every key action of the film but remains unremarked.

second scene involves Herman Schwimpf, who failed pilot school but whose irrepressible patriotism kept him in the war as a mechanic. Viewers see Herman filling a jerrycan with fuel from a large truck as a motorcycle speeds past in the background. An officer approaches, and Herman salutes with the hand holding the fuel nozzle. Petroleum sprays as the officer yells and stomps and knocks Herman down. This played-for-laughs sequence is the first of only two depictions of hydrocarbons in the film. Later, viewers catch a glimpse of mechanics working in the distance, small figures tending the planes, but this is the only part of the film that actually depicts the motive power for the internal combustion operating the trucks, cars, and motorcycles on the ground and the airplanes lifting up into the skies. Otherwise, the message is clear: speed and flight are for heroes; fuel that makes that speed and flight possible is for buffoons.

The small, comedic nod to refueling hints at a larger truth that emerges in following scenes. At a crucial moment in the film's first half, two Fokker aircraft chase Jack and machine-gun the fuselage of his plane. The cameras close in on a ruptured oil line and gauge falling toward zero. As Jack's plane flips in a thrilling high-speed crash landing, the action underscores pursuit pilots' skills and the danger they face, and diverts viewers' attention away from the fuel making their reach for the air possible.

Yet energy sources shape subtleties of action throughout the film. When Jack and David are called for their first dawn patrol, they are told to look out for the German Captain Kellerman and his "flying circus." Americans watching the film at its release would have understood the dead-serious German strategy underlying this playful label. A flying circus was a group of pursuit planes that could be partly disassembled, loaded onto trucks or trains, and then taken to a different site to be reassembled. The procession resembled a circus, with planes painted in similarly bright colors to aid visual tracking. Transporting the planes by ground between actions allowed German forces to conserve their increasingly scarce aviation fuel for the crucial elements of reconnaissance and pursuit.[19] Present-day audiences likely do not recognize the ways that energy sources—and fear of their scarcity—shaped matter-of-fact elements of war, but *Wings* subtly conveys significant energy concerns of the early twentieth century.

Throughout the second half of the film, Jack—the cheerfully energetic everyman—continually fails to recognize important elements of what is going on around him, just as the film allows viewers to touch only lightly on the hydrocarbon power facilitating the ravages of mechanized warfare. On leave, Jack gets happily drunk in a marvelously shot scene in a Paris club. He does not realize that leaves are canceled. Loyal Mary comes looking for him, but he is heedless. In an early demonstration of female bathroom solidarity, the French restroom attendant gives her a dancer's dress to get his attention. Mary hustles Jack up to his room so he can return to his post, but MPs burst in to discover her changing back into uniform behind a modest screen and send her back stateside in disgrace (a strategically placed mirror captured a partly naked Clara Bow, to the delight of many theatergoers).[20] Jack and David fall into conflict over Sylvia amid the Battle of Saint-Mihiel, the first US-led offensive of the war. Called up to fly support, Jack chases down a German general in an open motorcar: in a dramatic pursuit quoted by Alfred Hitchcock's 1959 thriller *North by Northwest*, the plane runs the car off the road. David is shot down, and Jack realizes as he packs David's things and finds letters from Sylvia that David has been protecting him by not telling him of Sylvia's true feelings. David daringly seizes a German plane to escape back to American lines, but Jack does not recognize him—just as he did not recognize Mary in the Paris bar. Determined to avenge his friend, Jack shoots down the German plane. In an iconic framing, Jack climbs over the ruined wall of the farmhouse, rows of white crosses in the background, and is struck still with shock realizing that the pilot he shot down was his beloved friend. Jack embraces David as he dies: the camera cuts to a plane rotor that slowly stops turning. A chastened Jack returns home, greeted by crowds with a parade and festive warplane made of flowers, and he brings David's toy bear back to his heartbroken parents. Jack begins to appreciate Mary. Sitting on the *Shooting Star*, they see a shooting star, and finally kiss. The bittersweet ending underscores *Wings* as a story of friendship and of love, but also as an allegory of seeing and not seeing, as audiences share through Jack's eyes a growing recognition of the circumstances and costs of war.

Realism, Technology, and the Making of *Wings*

In its triumphalism and romance, and in the cheerful heedlessness of the pilot hero Jack, *Wings* expresses certain realities of its moment in American history. The film succeeded through technologies of realism, drawing on the wartime experiences of many in the cast and crew. Paramount Studios chose relatively inexperienced director William A. Wellman in part because he had served with the Lafayette Flying Corps, Americans who volunteered before US entry into the war. Screenwriter John Monk Saunders had flown against German forces as a teenager and star Richard Arlen (David) had been a combat flier in the Canadian RFC. Many of the camera operators were also combat veterans or pilots. Buddy Rogers (Jack) learned to fly for his role.[21]

Participation and support from the US Armed Forces created a convincing war drama. The US military eagerly supported a film that glamorized air strength, much as the 1986 blockbuster *Top Gun* would several generations later. Air Service pilots flew in many of the scenes, and much of the picture was filmed at Camp Stanley, near San Antonio, Texas, with aerial sequences shot above Kelly Field. The US War Department enabled the film's massive reenactment of the Battle of Saint-Mihiel, with field guns bombarding Camp Stanley into an image of the devastated French countryside, while signal and ordnance companies laid communication networks and supervised an enormous number of explosions. Authentic trenches were created by the 2nd Engineer Battalion, which had served in the actual, noncinematic battle. Real bombs, tanks, trucks, field gear, eighteen airplanes, and over five thousand extras—$16 million of government equipment in all—made the ground sequences compelling and convincing.[22]

Moreover, to film new technology, the crew used new technology. Paramount hired Harry Perry, an early Akeley camera specialist. Akeley cameras captured fast motion in a fluid shot that communicated the excitement of action sequences. This "pancake camera" was soon used for many kinds of work, including news photography, Westerns, and natural history films. The Akeley camera was partly modeled on a turret-mounted machine gun. In *Wings*, such technological innovation came full circle, as the crew redesigned machine gun ring mounts to enable a camera to swing all the way around a pilot. Perry and his team of visual operators mounted cameras in ways never attempted before, jury-rigging power sources and adapting cameras to battery power for aerial action sequences. A massive structure resembling an oil derrick allowed for multilevel shots of ground action. To film the bombing run on Mervale, crews even wedged cinematographer E. Burton Steene into a bombing compartment inches from a dozen hundred-pound TNT bombs, to film each one as they dropped.[23] These masterful innovations created stunning, authentic sequences throughout the film.

At times, the realism of *Wings* became all too real. Stunt pilot Dick Grace crash-landed too hard and was hospitalized for what was supposed to be a year (after six weeks, he broke his cast with a hammer and climbed out the hospital window to go to a dance in downtown San Antonio). Actors also recalled witnessing and hearing about multiple deaths of Air Force pilots during filming.[24] Such consequences were invisible to audiences but underscored the depth and costs of the verisimilitude created through technology and craft.

New technology played a dominant role in presenting the film, as well. Many theaters, including the New York cinema where the film premiered, used Magnascope, a process that employed multiple projectors and huge screens. During the aerial sequences, viewers saw the action broaden out, encompassing them in the takeoffs, landings, and dogfights. As what one recent film critic called "a high work of craft," *Wings* was on the cusp of cinematic change. The first "talkie"—Al Jolson's *The Jazz Singer*—also premiered in 1927, yet with its vision and technologies, *Wings* represented what black-and-white silent features could convey when given huge budgets and enormous technical assistance.[25] The result was a production that showcased the significant changes wrought by powered air flight to the war it chronicled.

Energy, War, Air

Wings dramatized the power of newly harnessed energy to allow human beings to soar to new heights, capturing both the glamour and lethality of the skies. It also showed how swiftly and completely the fossil fuels powering that revolution would be rendered unseen, relegated to the background. The film depended upon decades of energy innovation and technological change, but it depicted an early moment in which fuels from beneath the earth gave human beings the ability to transcend gravity and make war among the clouds, and take for granted the hydrocarbons that enabled them to do so.

Notes

Grateful thanks to Boston College Undergraduate Research Fellow Andrew T. Ritter and BC colleagues Charles R. Gallagher, SJ, Stacie Kent, Jonathan S. Krones, María de los Ángeles Picone, and Ling Zhang, who improved this essay, and students in the Boston College Core class "Powering America," who inspired it.

1.   *Wings* previewed early in 1927 but was not widely released until January 1929. William A. Wellman, dir., *Wings* (Los Angeles: Paramount, 1927); AFI Catalog of Feature Films, "Wings (1927)," American Film Institute, Los Angeles, accessed July 20, 2020, https://catalog.afi.com/Catalog/moviedetails/13362; Rob Byrne, "Wings (1927) (review)," *Moving Image* 13, no. 1 (Spring 2013): 236–40; James Ross Moore, "Bow, Clara (1905–1965), film actress," *American National Biography*, February 1, 2000, https://www.anb.org/view/10.1093/anb/9780198606697 .001.0001/anb-9780198606697-e-1800137; Kevin L. Ferguson, "Aviation Cinema," *Criticism* 57, no. 2 (Spring 2015): 310, 320; Michael Paris, "Wings," *History Today* 45, no. 7 (1995): 44–50; George Turner, "Wings: Epic of the Air," *American Cinematographer* 66, no. 4 (April 1985): 36; Robert Eberwein, "Wings," *Quarterly Review of Film and Video* 27, no. 5 (2010): 438.
2.   Turner, "Epic of the Air," 36; Byrne, "Wings (1927)"; Eberwein, "Wings," 438; Turner, "Epic of the Air," 41; Ferguson, "Aviation Cinema," 320; Paris, "Wings," 49. The only other (mostly) silent film to win the Academy Award for Best Picture is *The Artist* (2011). Tara Patel, "'The Artist' Wins Top Oscar Honors in Bow to Silent Films," *Bloomberg News*, February 27, 2012, https://www.bloomberg.com/news /articles/2012-02-27/five-oscars-awarded-to-the-artist-mark-a-record-haul-for-a -french-movie.
3.   Twentieth-century film criticism portrays *Wings* as having two male main characters, but that characterization reflects more about twentieth-century film criticism than the film itself or its cultural reception at the time. Dino Everett, "Wings," n.d., Index of Film Essays, National Film Preservation Board, Library of Congress, accessed June 30, 2019, https://www.loc.gov/static/programs/national -film-preservation-board/documents/wings.pdf.
4.   Feeding mules and horses remained an enormous logistical focus during the Great War as well—typically of energy transitions, oil augmented but did not replace bodily labor. Mark Fiege, *The Republic of Nature: An Environmental History of the United States* (Seattle: University of Washington Press, 2012), chap. 5; Daniel Yergin, *The Prize: The Epic Quest for Oil, Money, and Power* (New York: Simon and Schuster, 1991), chap. 9; Christopher F. Jones, *Routes of Power: Energy and Modern American* (Cambridge, MA: Harvard University Press, 2104), especially the introduction.
5.   Hendrik De Leeuw, *Conquest of the Air: The History and Future of Aviation* (New York: Vantage Press, 1959), 32, 40, 69; Alfred F. Hurley and William C. Heimdahl, "The Roots of US Military Aviation," in *Winged Shield, Winged Sword: A History of the United States Air Force, vol. 1, 1907–1950*, ed. Bernard C. Nalty (Washington, DC:

Air Force History and Museums Program, 1997), 3–34, https://permanent.access
.gpo.gov/gpo88214/Vol_1_a495279.pdf.

6. Francesco Gerali and Jenny Gregory, "Understanding and Finding Oil over the
Centuries: The Case of the Wallachian Petroleum Company in Romania," *Earth
Sciences History* 36, no 1 (January 2017): 41–62; Yergin, *The Prize*, chaps. 1–3;
Vaclav Smil, *Energy and Civilization: A History* (Cambridge, MA: MIT Press, 2017),
227, 249; Robert J. Gordon, *The Rise and Fall of American Growth: The US Standard of
Living Since the Civil War* (Princeton, NJ: Princeton University Press, 2016), chap. 5.

7. De Leeuw, *Conquest of the Air*, 67–68; John H. Morrow, "The Air War," in *The
Cambridge History of the First World War, vol. 1, Global War*, ed. J. M. Winter
(Cambridge, UK: Cambridge University Press, 2014), 349; Smil, *Energy and
Civilization*, 252–53.

8. Richard P. Hallion, "World War I: An Air War of Consequence," *Endeavour* 38, no. 2
(June 2014): 77; Morrow, "Air War," 364; Daniel R. Mortensen, "The Air Service in
the Great War," in *Winged Shield, Winged Sword: A History of the United States Air
Force, vol. 1, 1907–1950*, ed. Bernard C. Nalty (Washington, DC: Air Force History
and Museums Program, 1997), 49; Maurer Maurer, ed., *The US Air Service in World
War I: vol. I, The Final Report and a Tactical History* (Washington DC: US
Government Printing Office, 1978), 51, 17, https://media.defense.gov/2010
/Oct/13/2001329758/-1/-1/0/AFD-101013-007.pdf; Thomas C. Hone, "Fighting
on Our Own Ground: The War of Production, 1920–1942," in *Gearing Up for
Victory: American Military and Industrial Mobilization in World War II*, Colloquium on
Contemporary History, Naval History and Heritage Command, 25 June 1991, no.
5, https://www.history.navy.mil/research/library/online-reading-room/title-list
-alphabetically/g/gearing-up-victory.html.

9. Maurer, *US Air Service*, 90, 128; Alexander R. Ogston, "A Short History of Aviation
Gasoline Development, 1903–1980," *SAE Transactions* 90 (1981): 2591; Mortensen,
"Air Service in the Great War," 47; S. D. Heron, *Development of Aviation Fuels*
(Cambridge, MA: Harvard University Graduate School of Business Administration,
1950), 578–79.

10. I was able to experience *Wings* in this early-twentieth-century manner, as organist
Peter Krasinski performed live accompaniment at Bethany Congregational Church
in Quincy, Massachusetts, during a Veterans Day World War I centennial tribute on
November 10, 2018. Edward Rothstein, "Silent Films Had a Musical Voice," *New
York Times*, February 8, 1981, https://www.nytimes.com/1981/02/08/movies
/silent-films-had-a-musical-voice.html; "The Restoration of WINGS (1927): The
Loudest Silent Movie I've Ever Seen," *Cinematically Insane*, August 2, 2012, https://
willmckinley.wordpress.com/2012/08/08/the-restoration-of-wings-1927-the
-loudest-silent-movie-ive-ever-seen; John Pruitt, "Between Theater and Cinema:
Silent Film Accompaniment in the 1920s," American Symphony Orchestra,
accessed June 30, 2019, https://americansymphony.org/concert-notes/between
-theater-and-cinema-silent-film-accompaniment-in-the-1920s.

11. Ferguson, "Aviation Cinema," 310–11.

12. Turner, "Epic of the Air," 37–38.

13. John M. Barry, *The Great Influenza: The Epic Story of the Deadliest Plague in History*
(New York: Penguin, 2005), 4–5.

14. De Leeuw, *Conquest of the Air*, 84; Herman S. Wolk, "The Quest for Independence,"
in *Winged Shield, Winged Sword: A History of the United States Air Force, vol. 1*,

1907–1950, ed. Bernard C. Nalty (Washington, DC: Air Force History and Museums Program, 1997), 391–92; Maurer, *US Air Service*, 51,17; Mortensen, "Air Service in the Great War," 51.

15. Maurer, *US Air Service*, 34, 64, 81, 104–105; De Leeuw, *Conquest of the Air*, 86; Hallion, "Air War of Consequence," 78; Mortensen, "Air Service in the Great War," 34, 56, 64; Morrow, "Air War," 374.

16. At the *Wings* World War I centennial screening, I spoke with older women who began flying as children in the Quincy airfields where Earhart practiced, inspired by her exploits. Wayne S. Cole, "Lindbergh, Charles Augustus (1902–1974), Aviator," February 1, 2000, *American National Biography*, https://www.anb.org/view /10.1093/anb/9780198606697.001.0001/anb-9780198606697-e-0700367; Dorothy S. Cochrane, "Earhart, Amelia Mary (1897–1937), Aviator," February 1, 2000, *American National Biography*, https://www.anb.org/view/10.1093 /anb/9780198606697.001.0001/anb-9780198606697-e-2000310; De Leeuw, *Conquest of the Air*, 139; Joseph J. Corn, *The Winged Gospel: America's Romance with Aviation, 1900–1950* (New York: Oxford University Press, 1983).

17. Bruce J. Evensen, "Cooper, Gary (1901–1961), Film Actor," *American National Biography*, February 1, 2000, https://www.anb.org/view/10.1093/anb /9780198606697.001.0001/anb-9780198606697-e-1800247.

18. Virtually this exact visual sequence appears in the 2019 Hulu television adaptation of Joseph Heller's best-selling novel *Catch-22* (1961). In the book, a new arrival is killed within hours, but there is no left-behind bar of chocolate.

19. Flying circus: Aaron Norman, *The Great Air War: The Men, the Planes, the Saga of Military Aviation: 1914–1918* (New York: Macmillan, 1968), 156, 191. German fuel shortages: Lee B. Kennett, *The First Air War, 1914–1918* (New York: Free Press, 1991), 214; John H. Morrow Jr., *German Air Power in World War I* (Lincoln: University of Nebraska Press, 1982), 97; John H. Morrow Jr., *The Great War in the Air: Military Aviation from 1909 to 1921* (Washington, DC: Smithsonian Institution Press, 1993), 222, 229, 293–310. I thank Charles Gallagher, SJ, for the insight about fuel efficiency.

20. "Mysterious missing 'WINGS' footage?" discussion commencing February 2010, NitrateVille classic-film fan site, https://www.nitrateville.com/viewtopic.php ?t=5687.

21. Turner, "Epic of the Air," 35–37; Paris, "Wings," 44–45, 50. An episode in the film in which a daring flier tosses a note onto an opposing camp echoes real events: Norman, *The Great War*, 139.

22. Paris, "Wings," 45; David Sirota, "Opinion: 25 Years Later, How 'Top Gun' Made America Love War," *Washington Post*, August 25, 2011, https://www.washington post.com/opinions/25-years-later-remembering-how-top-gun-changed-americas -feelings-about-war/2011/08/15/gIQAU6qJgJ_story.html; Turner, "Epic of the Air," 35, 38; "Wings (1927)," AFI Catalog of Feature Films; Hallion, "Air War of Consequence," 85.

23. Sonia Shechet Epstein, "Lions and Ostrich and Elephants: Carl Akeley and Documentary Cinema," *Sloan Science and Film*, Museum of the Moving Image, January 27, 2017, http://scienceandfilm.org/articles/2845/lions-and-ostrich-and -elephants-carl-akeley-and-documentary-cinema; Sonia Shechet Epstein, "Carl Akeley and Nature's Truth," *Sloan Science and Film*, Museum of the Moving Image, August 15, 2018, http://scienceandfilm.org/articles/3130/carl-akeley-and-natures -truth; "Carl Akeley: Taxidermy," n.d., LibGuides, Field Museum, Chicago, https://

libguides.fieldmuseum.org/c.php?g=560440&p=3855405; Turner, "Epic of the Air,"
36–39; Paris, "Wings," 47–48.

24. Turner, "Epic of the Air," 37, 40.
25. Eberwein, "Wings," 439; Turner, "Epic of the Air," 40; Everett, "Wings"; K. Austin
Collins and Dana Stevens, "*Wings* (1927)," June 30, 2019, *Flashback*, produced by
Chau Tu, podcast, MP3 audio, 11:11, https://slate.com/culture/2019/06/flashback
-wings-movie-1927.html; Gordon, *Rise and Fall of American Growth*, 201.

Chapter 7

Derricks and Skulls: Filming and Promoting the Extractive Landscapes of *Boom Town* (1940)

Michaela Rife

W hen MGM's blockbuster *Boom Town* spread across the United States in the late summer of 1940, oil derricks followed in its wake. The big-budget drama was intentionally designed for widespread appeal and much of its promotion emphasized its four stars: Clark Gable, Spencer Tracy, Claudette Colbert, and Hedy Lamarr. With the focus on the actors and a tagline proclaiming "Four Pictures in One," the oil industry could be dismissed as nothing more than the setting for a romantic melodrama.[1] However, oil is central to the film's plot, and reports from trade publications reveal the prominence of oil in its promotion. Throughout the United States, theater owners and MGM promoters worked with oil companies to connect the film to local industry. In New Orleans, Gulf Oil toured a "marsh buggy" through the city as part of a parade for the film, and Loew's Theatres coordinated with a St. Louis oil company to link their twentieth anniversary with the theater's *Boom Town* run.[2] Tulsa, which features in the film and hosted one of its earliest premieres, received an eighty-foot portable derrick for the city's courthouse lawn. A fifteen-foot model rig originating in a Houston theater also traveled to Victoria, Texas.[3] The *Motion Picture Herald* even reported that a theater in Fort Morgan, Colorado, installed a miniature oil derrick in front of the building that "actually pumped oil."[4]

Film historian Catherine Jurca has examined *Boom Town* in the context of Hollywood's own Depression-era crisis, arguing that the tale of oil and romance was conceived as something of a "test case" for the ailing industry. As Jurca explains, the highest-grossing film of 1940 was explicitly designed to appeal to wide audiences and to make America's support of Hollywood a patriotic issue, a goal achieved through the elevation of the oil industry through the wildcatting main characters.[5] Building on this analysis, I argue that oil is more than a vehicle for *Boom Town*'s romantic plot. In fact, the film explicitly employs the oil industry setting to valorize America's extractive landscapes and respond to Depression-era narratives of decline. Through its celebration of the oil business, *Boom Town* pushes the narrative that capitalism is a series of booms and busts, a natural, even necessary, cycle to be weathered and enjoyed. This essay explains these ideological goals through a discussion of *Boom Town*'s plot structure, its relationship to the Great Depression, and its use of the paired symbols of the oil derrick and the bleached steer skull.

Boom Town and "A Lady Comes to Burkburnett"

John Lee Mahin based his screenplay for *Boom Town* on James Edward Grant's novella "A Lady Comes to Burkburnett," published in the August 1939 edition of *Cosmopolitan*.[6] Grant's story extracts dramatic tension from Betsy Bartlett's (Colbert) arrival in the rough boomtown of Burkburnett, Texas, in the early years of the North Texas oil boom. Mahin's screenplay largely adheres to Grant's plot structure with a few notable differences. Both texts tell the story of two oilmen: "Big John" McMasters and "Square John" Sand (played by Gable and Tracy). They meet in Burkburnett, and each recognizes a kindred spirit in the other. Both men are wildcatting drillers, willing to work and steal to bring in their next gusher. In both narratives, it is ostensibly Bartlett's arrival that drives a wedge between the two men. She travels to Texas for Sand but marries McMasters. Grant dispatches with this plot point quickly, and while Bartlett is presented as the narrator at the beginning of the novella, she primarily operates as a frustration for McMasters's wildcatting and philandering ways. Her femininity and domesticity serve as impediments for him, though she experiences more violence at his hand in the novella.[7] In both plots, Sand is driven by his unrequited love for Bartlett, but in *Boom Town* his desire for her to be happy supersedes his own business interests; in "A Lady Comes to Burkburnett," his eventual enmity with McMasters is also based in their competing oil empires. In *Boom Town*, though her homemaking initially frustrates McMasters's wildcatting spirit, it is ultimately Bartlett who laments their distance from the "smell of fresh oil."[8] The film's three main characters find their happy ending when they join forces at a remote drilling site in California, an outcome that Bartlett equally desires. In *Boom Town*, both McMasters and Bartlett are truly happy only when they are poor and wildcatting or moving between wage work at oil camps.

Grant's novella and Mahin's screenplay share many of the same landscapes of extraction: North Texas, Veracruz (described as "the Tropics" in the film), Oklahoma, and California's Kettleman Hills. In Texas, the two Johns initially drill a dry well and must take on wage work to earn enough money to drill a new site. Upon their return to Burkburnett, they finally find a gusher: "Beautiful Darling Betsy No. 1." The film sets McMasters and Betsy Bartlett's love story against the backdrop of Burkburnett as an oil boomtown; promenades amid the town's pumpjacks and muddy streets afford McMasters the opportunity to woo Bartlett with tales of mining and oil. Their personal love story is bound up in their mutual love of the work of oil extraction. Though their meeting is brief in the novella, Grant later devotes a full paragraph to a tender description of the oil landscape of North Texas:

> Maybe you've driven through Twelve Section. You should, because it's an impressive sight. Eight miles of derricks standing almost side by side, and good high-gravity oil flowing out of every well. You get to speculating how many millions of dollars came out of that field, and the figures make your head spin. Then maybe you think about it another way. You think of that money flowing out all over the county, spreading around and making life richer for ever so many people. And you think of the heavy work that oil has saved and the billion people it has warmed and it takes on a significance other than financial; maybe a social significance.[9]

Grant's words could signify disaster (oil "flowing" and "spreading" across the country) but instead he crafts a morally significant tale of oil improving billions of lives. The love story at the core of Grant's novella is between America and oil.

In both texts, the two Johns initially plan to share their empire, but the partnership falls apart over McMasters's treatment of Bartlett. At the site of their oil fire, Sand wins the entire operation in a coin toss with a counterfeit silver dollar, initiating a pattern in which the two can never experience oil wealth at the same time. In the film, the coin flip also launches a cycle in which Sand must bankrupt his former partner in order to repeatedly save the McMasterses' marriage. Now poor, John and Betsy McMasters are shown in a montage happily traveling through oil sites until they arrive at "the Tropics." McMasters refuses work from Sand, who is unhappy as the wealthy head of an oil company in an apparently corrupt location. While Sand's tropical oil empire burns in a coup, the McMasterses move on to Oklahoma, where we watch as Big John secures land through a deal with a Native man.[10] We see a montage of multiplying derricks and other signs of the family's newfound wealth.[11] As McMasters negotiates with New York refiner and distributor Harry Compton (Lionel Atwill), temptation appears in the form of Compton's assistant, Karen Vanmeer (Lamarr). Soon after, a penniless Sand arrives in Oklahoma on a McMasters oil train, where he will spurn his former partner's attempt to help him get back on his feet in the oil business, echoing in reverse their situation in Veracruz.

In the final act, the film departs significantly from the novella. On screen, the McMasterses move to New York City at the end of the 1920s, a chronological detail that viewers learn from the date on a plan for a McMasters cracking plant superimposed over an image of the New York skyline. In the city, McMasters is deep into an affair with Vanmeer when Sand arrives with new oil wealth. The two men plan to work together at long last, but when Bartlett attempts suicide because of the affair, the lovesick Sand again tries to bankrupt McMasters. This time, however, McMasters is able to defeat Sand in their business war, but his methods leave him vulnerable to an antitrust suit. Tried by a zealous government prosecutor, McMasters's stock plummets, which bankrupts him anyway. The film reaches a climax when Sand arrives to testify against McMasters, but instead defends him with an impassioned pro-business soliloquy that likens McMasters to the pioneers who "opened up the country." The film implies that this speech so moved the jury that McMasters is acquitted. *Boom Town* concludes in California's Kettleman Hills, where the McMasterses (including their young son, Jack) reunite with Sand and their Burkburnett backer, Luther Aldrich (Frank Morgan). The protagonists link arms and walk through the mountainous landscape.

Boom Town and the Depression

The events of the film occur over the course of the 1920s but in Grant's novella, Sand departs Oklahoma for the Kettleman Hills to make his fortune in Western oil plays. Given the historic Kettleman Hills boom in the late 1920s and early 1930s, the film and the story clearly have different chronological trajectories. Furthermore, rather than moving from Oklahoma to New York, Grant's McMasters moves to Washington, DC, and becomes embroiled in the business side of oil, "concerned more with tariffs and proration laws than with drilling wells."[12] After Sand and McMasters's final falling out, Sand heads west to keep wildcatting and McMasters continues to work in Washington, where he is later caught up in a bribery scandal. Sand also delivers a rapturous testimony in the novella, but each man serves a prison sentence thanks to an ambitious New Deal prosecutor. Both texts end at a new drilling site, but the chronological shift is made abundantly clear as the novella concludes with an adult Jack, on a break from his university to learn the oil business firsthand.

Changes between source material and script are certainly not unusual, but while the chronology of "A Lady Comes to Burkburnett" (1939) allows Grant to castigate New Deal regulations specifically, *Boom Town*'s (1940) alternate chronology facilitates a cinematic response to the economic woes of the 1930s.[13] While screenwriter Mahin was politically conservative and later described himself as "an old rightist," Sand's defense of McMasters near the end of the film argues that his old friend was employing patriotic conservation methods.[14] Notably, in the film's timeline, this positions McMasters on the side of New Deal rationing before the New Deal occurred. I contend that, rather than advancing Grant's more specific political ideals, *Boom Town*'s creators used the medium of cinema to respond to the Depression through both visual symbols and the film's cyclical temporal structure, telling a story of resilience through capitalism's inevitable booms and busts. *Boom Town* should thus be seen in relation to and in conversation with John Steinbeck's contemporaneous *The Grapes of Wrath* (already a bestselling novel when Grant's story was published) and larger Depression-era visual culture. In fact, John Ford's film adaptation of *The Grapes of Wrath* debuted on March 15, 1940, before production began on *Boom Town* later that same month. In some ways, the films mirror one another.[15] For example, both end in a version of California. For the Joads, the Californian promised land is a mirage until they reach the government-sponsored Wheat Patch camp at the end of the film.[16] In *Boom Town*, though we do not see them dreaming of California throughout the film, it is only there that the McMasters family, Sand, and Luther Aldrich can finally coexist as happy wildcatters.

Over the course of both films, the central families are forced back out onto the road. In *The Grapes of Wrath*, the Joads lose their Oklahoma home and must crowd into a car and head west; never able to rest, little joy remains and they are unhappy in their poverty. Their melancholic existence starkly contrasts with that of the McMasterses, who are also forced back on the road in their own periodic poverty. But the McMasterses' financial losses are also paired with Big John's return to Bartlett and matrimonial happiness. Rather than signaling a break, it is in their impoverished interludes that the pair are happy, traveling between work sites and reveling in the nobility of the working class. Following their departure from Burkburnett, we see the McMasterses smiling at each other on the train and winking over shared laundry. These montages operate in opposition to depictions of the Joads on the road and in scenes set in the California work camps.[17] In their final cycle of poverty, the McMasterses head west to California in their car, this time with their son, Jack. The small family is jubilant and beaming at each other; Big John begins to whistle the refrain of "Polly Wolly Doodle," a song that reappears throughout the film during scenes of drilling and other new beginnings. Their happiness contrasts sharply with scenes of the dejected Joads, crammed into their overfilled car. But the McMasterses' joy also suggests something about the specific mythology of oil work, distinct from migratory agricultural work—namely, that the next lucrative gusher is just around the corner.

In addition, *Boom Town*'s periods of wage work are distinct in that they are always in support of wildcatting. Notably, the film ends with wildcatting rather than the wage work depicted after the Texas duster and the falling out in Burkburnett. Throughout the film, the figure of the wildcatter (typically McMasters) is linked to the American pioneer.[18] As discussed above, Sand compares McMasters to a pioneer in his climactic testimony, but the film foregrounds this connection between the wildcatter and the pioneer from the very beginning. After a few brief scenes of American landscapes (mountains, deserts), *Boom Town* is introduced with text scrolling over the screen: "This is the story of a hard-driving breed of Americans—oil prospectors—'wildcatters.' Made of the bone and blood of pioneers—men born of the lasting miracle that is America—they probed the earth from early Pennsylvania to California's Kettleman Hills to bring forth America's greatest treasure, the life blood of today's world—Oil!" The introductory text establishes our view of McMasters and Sand. Despite their flaws, these men are a noble "breed" of pioneer stock, positioned between the earliest oil wildcatters in Pennsylvania and the Kettleman Hills (where the film ends).[19] *Oil*, the final word of the introductory text, is superimposed over a mountain scene before dissolving into the first shot of Burkburnett, a town squeezed in among crowds of derricks with bustling muddy streets that all serve the oil economy. It is important that the prologue culminates in an image of oil derricks; the film consistently valorizes the machinery of extraction, using it as a symbol of McMasters's return to a moral life and thereby linking happiness and wellbeing to extractive landscapes.

Derricks

Tracing how derricks are presented throughout *Boom Town* reveals both its veneration of extractive landscapes and oil's centrality to the film. For example, after the two Johns initially fail to strike oil, we see the first montage of their wage work at a string of oil landscapes. The machinery of extraction is lovingly filmed, and the two Johns are frequently shown grinning as they operate drills, establishing both the joy they find in oil work and their technical prowess. When they make it back to Burkburnett, we see an establishing shot of a derrick on a dusty plain followed by McMasters operating a drill and

Sand painting a sign. This is the derrick that will make them rich and serve as the origin point for their doomed empire. But before the gusher begins, the film follows McMasters into town where he will meet and fall in love with Bartlett against the backdrop of the rough oil town. The pair walk along the muddy streets with derricks rising up above them, and McMasters tells Bartlett about his past in logging and mining. They happen upon a pumpjack operating inside a church. At first, Bartlett seems startled: "Here? But it looks like a church!" McMasters explains that this has happened all over Texas. Bartlett contemplates the scene and reverently states, "And ye shall rise out of the earth," a phrase that has no direct referent but recalls biblical language, particularly given the setting. At that moment, the well's owner, a man named Springtime (John T. Murray), arrives. McMasters later explains that he was twice a millionaire but is now broke again, a cycle that foreshadows McMasters's own story. He describes oil like an addiction; after getting away from it, suddenly "those darn pumps start pounding in your ears . . ." He trails off, and Bartlett softly intones, "Like a heartbeat."

To twenty-first-century ears and eyes, this scene can be jarring. Oil extraction seems out of place in the center of a church and unusual as the setting for a love story, but *Boom Town*'s contemporary audience had experience with these themes.[20] A June 1940 *Life* magazine spread on Centralia, Illinois's recent oil boom prominently features a photograph of a derrick rising up behind a church with a pumpjack at work in the foreground. The caption explains, "The Young's Chapel Christian Church of Centralia has just been built with $20,000 derived from five wells on church property, pumping 350 barrels of oil daily."[21] On a Centralia theater screen only two months later, McMasters will declare of Texas churches: "Now there are churches all over the state spreading happy days and hallelujahs right out of these holes." In fact, *Boom Town* debuted in Centralia with significant fanfare. As the *Motion Picture Herald* reported, the city's mayor declared it "Boom Town Week" to coincide with "Boom Town Sales" from local merchants. The article continued, "With oil derricks decorating the lawns of many homes, it was a natural to plant a 20-foot model, plus drilling machinery, in the intersection of two of the city's busiest streets. Cards placed on all four sides sold the picture, cast and playdates. Two weeks ahead street signs were planted on all highways leading into the city with copy reading: 'You are now entering the biggest oil Boom Town in America . . .'"[22]

The city's promotion of a romantic oil film makes sense given its own boomtown status. Indeed, the *Life* feature aimed to chronicle the new oil field in southern Illinois and accompanying photographs demonstrate that the industry had already seeped into every aspect of life and death. In a photograph showing oil in a graveyard, the caption reads, "Oil surges up between the bodies of the dead." Others depict Centralia's booming nightlife, described as full of "happily oiled petroleumfolk."[23] *Boom Town* animates these petroleumfolk with a story of romance, business, and intrigue among oil landscapes.

Furthermore, the film romanticizes the landscapes of extraction themselves. Betsy Bartlett and John McMasters fall in love amid the derricks pumping oil from beneath a church. In fact, the pair get married that very night and are greeted in the morning with the news that Beautiful Darling Betsy No. 1 is a gusher. However, the audience learns of this before the new McMasterses do, as a shot of the newlyweds in a passionate embrace dissolves into a scene of the derrick, the approaching gusher anticipated by a deep, intensifying rumble. A close-up allows viewers to see the moment that oil breaks through the earth, before the camera pulls back to allow for a wide shot of the gusher. The scene lasts for nearly a minute, and we see the surge from a variety of angles, sharing in Sand's joy as oil rains down upon him. According to historian Kathryn Morse, the media enthusiastically described and pictured oil gushers throughout the early decades of the twentieth century. She explains, "To pose with an oil gusher was to embrace a limitless future."[24] *Boom Town*

Fig. 7.1. Betsy and McMasters (Colbert and Gable) fall in love surrounded by oil extraction in *Boom Town* (MGM, 1940).

fits into this lineage of media depictions relishing oil gushers as symbols of fabulous instant wealth.

In Grant's novella, the first well immediately catches fire and sows the seeds of the feud between the Johns. In the film, however, we see Sand come to terms with McMasters's marriage alongside the growth of their shared oil empire, represented by an image of multiplying derricks all named "Beautiful Darling Betsy." The first sign of trouble for the McMasterses does not come until the Murphy Brothers (Joe Yule and Horace Murphy), a pair of wildcatters, arrive back in town after striking oil in Arizona. A wistful and restless look plays across Gable's face as Big John is compelled to leave his own one-year anniversary party to meet the brothers at the local brothel, where his wife later catches him dancing and drinking. Yet we are not meant to understand his behavior as the result of marital unhappiness; rather, it is a reaction to the stifling domesticity of his well-appointed Burkburnett house and distance from oil extraction itself. This incident sparks Sand's first bankrupting of his former partner and launches a new period of happiness for the McMasterses as they travel through landscapes of American extraction.

The next roadblock appears when McMasters is again invited to stray from Bartlett (and the landscapes of extraction to which she is tied), this time in the form of Karen Vanmeer and the linked allure of an integrated business that would allow control of his oil from well to filling station. This temptation precipitates McMasters's move to New York, distancing him from the derricks once again. Here, that chasm is represented most vividly in his lush corporate office, where he is surrounded by images of extraction. Large panels depicting derricks line the office walls, poor facsimiles of his proper environment. These panels are later destroyed when Sand and McMasters fight about Bartlett for the last time. Though the film is certainly kind to oil corporations, it does not lavish the same attention on depicting oil once it leaves the ground. Pipelines, refining, and processing are all stages that take the Johns away from the work they were destined for: wildcatting.

In some ways, *Boom Town*'s ending feels like both a continuation and a return to the film's beginning. The main characters, along with their backer Luther Aldrich, are in a new oil landscape, ready to begin wildcatting again. At this point, we have watched these characters repeat the same cycle throughout the film, but now a key difference disrupts the sequence: the group begins this new chapter on the same page, with a renewed love of the work and sites of extraction. Yet this happy ending is complicated by the location (California) and by the film's final shot (a crowd of derricks). Attentive viewers will note that this is the mountainous Western landscape referenced at the beginning of the film, the specific site noted in the introductory text: "From early Pennsylvania to California's Kettleman Hills." The oil history of the Kettleman Hills is significant here. The timing of the boom means that at the film's conclusion, the Kettleman Hills were a site of policy contestation, as the government and oil producers struggled to develop a conservation plan for an already flooded oil market.[25] If *Boom Town* positions the main characters as symbols of the larger oil industry, periodically cycling through booms and busts, then one way to read the ending has our wildcatters profiting from the California boom before bottoming out once again.

However, an alternate reading sees the group learning their lesson and practicing conservation. Sand's testimony at the trial seemingly supports this interpretation. To refute the idea that McMasters broke antitrust laws, he argues that his former partner intuitively exercised conservation:

> But what he was doing, although he didn't know it, he was working for the United States too. He wanted these guys to produce less oil so that their wells would flow years longer and not ruin the fields. That way they'd get all the oil there was to get out of the wells. Don't you get the idea, he was for conservation! Now how can a guy be breaking the law when he's trying to save the natural resources of the country? Well he didn't know that he was doing anything that you might call noble but being one of the best oil men there is, he's got the right hunch about oil.

In addition, as Jurca notes, MGM was involved in its own legal troubles at the end of the 1930s. For her, Sand's speech also serves as the studio's "apology" in the face of an antitrust suit, claiming to remake their monopoly into a servant of the "public interest." [26] Thus, Sand's oration and the happy Hollywood ending promote the idea that the oil industry could self-regulate, or at least weather downturns (despite ample evidence to the contrary), all while retaining a frontier patina, emblematized by the symbol of the wildcatter's derrick. But *Boom Town*'s viewers also knew that the main characters are headed toward a decade of economic depression and fluctuating oil prices. *Boom Town* accounts for this fact of history by countering Depression-era disaster imagery and embracing a cyclical plot.

Skulls

Boom Town's central plot structure offers a message that hard times in a booming capitalist economy are cyclical and destined to pass, an idea that brings another recurrent symbol into view: the bleached steer skull. *Boom Town*'s skull first appears on the dusty plain outside Burkburnett, which Sand believes contains oil. The two Johns argue about where to begin drilling: the skull or the bubbling pool of water? The argument prompts the pair's first coin flip, and though McMasters wins, they ultimately decide to drill at the bubbling water, Sand's preferred site. This failed well leads to the first round of wage work, but it is to the skull that they return to drill the successful Beautiful Darling Betsy No. 1. In fact, the skull reappears throughout the film, and its transformation from plains detritus to polished trophy in a New York penthouse mirrors McMasters's own transformation from wildcatter to corrupt businessman.

Fig. 7.2. Arthur Rothstein, *The bleached skull of a steer on the dry sunbaked earth of the South Dakota Badlands*. Farm Security Administration, May 1936. Office of War Information Photograph Collection. Courtesy of Library of Congress Prints and Photographs Division.

Like oil machinery's invasion of the vernacular landscape, bleached skulls were prominent in the visual culture of the 1930s. In 1936, Arthur Rothstein's well-publicized photograph of a skull in the South Dakota Badlands prompted a controversy when it was discovered that he had moved it around as a prop. This "discovery" allowed anti–New Deal journalists to accuse government agencies of manipulation and it became a national story.[27] For Rothstein and the Resettlement Administration, which distributed the photograph, the skull was intended to serve as a symbol of decline and devastation.[28] However, the bleached skull also occupies a complicated place within the history of American art and in the visual culture of the American West. The bison skull could be used to signal the alleged decline of Native America, as in Frederic Remington's many depictions of skulls and Native people to evoke a "passing frontier." But a bleached skull could also be a token of the West to mount on the wall.[29]

For a 1940 audience, *Boom Town*'s introduction to the skull on an arid stretch of land may have prompted associations with Rothstein's controversy. McMasters points directly to it and the camera lingers on a shot of the skull centered against a slight ridge—framing that recalls one of Rothstein's photographs. Both the photographic and cinematic skulls appear isolated on the dry land; no further skeletal remains are immediately visible. However, unlike Rothstein's, *Boom Town*'s skull is a longhorn, which lends itself to more dramatic effect and links the wildcatters to frontier cattle trails. The two Johns evidently keep the object, and when they return to Burkburnett, the camera lingers on the skull, which is now mounted on the derrick at their new well. We have already learned that the pair resolved to drill at the site of the skull when they returned, and here it is further linked to successful oil extraction, snatching the symbol away from Rothstein's context and claiming frontier credentials. When the first gusher comes in, we see oil pour over its bleached white bones.

The skull next appears shined and stripped to just the horns, mounted over the mantel in the McMasterses' luxurious Burkburnett home. Bartlett even points the horns out to Sand during the fateful first anniversary dinner. Now, stripped of their rough oil context, the horns mirror Big John McMasters, both ensconced in ill-suited domesticity. The mounted horns do not surface again until they are hanging in McMasters's New York office, surrounded by large, two-dimensional renderings of oil extraction. The horns are sporadically visible in the scene as McMasters negotiates his integrated oil empire; they are only foregrounded when Sand visits and the pair hang their hats from the horns while celebrating their newly joined interests. Of course, this détente does not last. Instead, the horns finally serve as the backdrop of the two Johns' long-awaited fistfight, the culmination of jousting over business and Betsy Bartlett.

Fig. 7.3. The longhorn skull is now mounted on the two Johns' derrick as the gusher comes in. *Boom Town* (MGM, 1940).

Notably, the skull does not appear in California, which may be a signal that this oil play is a different and new beginning, rather than the start of the same old cycle.

Conclusion

Boom Town was released and promoted in an increasingly oil-fueled world. The film presented a romantic past in an oil setting, while valorizing the very mechanics and landscapes of extraction that surrounded theatergoers' homes. By elevating petroleum symbols, *Boom Town* also sold the myth that oil extraction was an intrinsically patriotic and noble activity. This message explicitly bookends the film, from the opening text, in which oil is described as "America's greatest treasure, the life blood of today's world," to Sand's speech at the end, which anticipates the coming war and worries that without McMasters's skills there will be nothing to heat American schools and homes or power "airplanes and battleships."[30] Moreover, whether or not *Boom Town*'s creators intended to respond to the Rothstein skull photograph or the narratives around *The Grapes of Wrath,* the film was crafted in a Depression-era context that fretted over decline and emphasized the need for regulation. With oil at the fore, *Boom Town*'s symbolism and cyclical storytelling offered a response to this context, emphasizing capitalism's cycles of booms and busts and perhaps, in the process, providing audiences with some comfort that, like Betsy and the two Johns, they too could have a happy ending.

Notes

1. A two-page spread in the August 3, 1940 *Motion Picture Herald* is indicative of a certain strand of *Boom Town* advertising. Photographs of Gable, Tracy, Colbert, and Lamarr are all featured, while disembodied hands indicate the numbers one through four next to their names. "Boom Town Is Four Pictures in One!" is spelled out in large letters across the bottom of the page. *Motion Picture Herald,* August 3, 1940, 2–3.
2. "Illinois Oil Boom Sells 'Boom Town' on Civic Campaign," *Motion Picture Herald,* August 24, 1940, 80; "Theatre and Oil Company Celebrate Anniversary," *Motion Picture Herald,* December 28, 1940, 66.
3. "Exploitation Briefs from A-Field," *Motion Picture Herald*, September 14, 1940, 52; "An Endless Chain," *Motion Picture Herald*, December 7, 1940, 65.
4. "Exploitation Briefs from A-Field," *Motion Picture Herald*, October 26, 1940, 56. The elevation of the derrick as a symbol of oil extraction and a promotional tool for the film is intriguing but not surprising. Kathryn Morse, for example, has shown that oil could represent sudden, fantastic wealth, particularly in the form of gushers. Kathryn Morse, "There Will Be Birds: Images of Oil Disaster in the Nineteenth and Twentieth Centuries," *Journal of American History* 99, no. 1 (June 2012): 125.
5. Catherine Jurca, "What the Public Wanted: Hollywood, 1937–1942," *Cinema Journal* 47, no. 2 (Winter 2008): 17–20.
6. James Edward Grant, "A Lady Comes to Burkburnett," *Cosmopolitan,* August 1939, 34–37, 106–14.
7. In Grant's story, as in the film, Sand suggests that McMasters divorce Betsy Bartlett. In the film this prompts a reconciliation for the married couple, in part because Sand has caused him oil troubles, but in the story their reunion is physically violent and McMasters is praised for slapping Bartlett. Grant, "A Lady Comes to Burkburnett," 114.
8. Jack Conway, dir., *Boom Town* (Beverly Hills, CA: MGM Studios, 1940).
9. Grant, "A Lady Comes to Burkburnett," 106.
10. *Boom Town*'s presentation of Native peoples in oil landscapes are highly racist and in keeping with contemporary depictions of Osage oil wealth. For example, a Native man drives Sand to Tulsa and brags about his many cars in different colors. See Alexandra Harmon, *Rich Indians: Native People and the Problem of Wealth in American History* (Chapel Hill: University of North Carolina Press, 2010), 171–208; Hanna Musiol, "Liquid Modernity: *Sundown* in Pawhuska, Oklahoma," in *Oil Culture,* ed. Ross Barrett and Daniel Worden (Minneapolis: University of Minnesota Press, 2014), 129–44.
11. For example, as McMasters is talking to a refiner about expanding into distribution, Bartlett and their son Jack arrive in a car with the architect of their

new home. Bartlett is dressed in fine clothes, in obvious contrast to her more modest dresses during their periods of wage work.

12. Grant, "A Lady Comes to Burkburnett," 111.

13. Grant's story includes editorial asides that make his negative feelings toward New Deal regulations clear. For example, McMasters is the victim of public hunger for a scapegoat responsible for the market crash. Grant's description of the prosecutor, Ferdinand Barber, is also telling: "Barber was the new type of politician. His demagoguery was based on the flamboyant use of the new economic bromides that sound so scientific. He used the new lexicon of semitechnical phrases which had crept into our language since the depression." Grant, "A Lady Comes to Burkburnett," 114. Here, Barber is portrayed as the aggressor, akin to the similarly derided geologists. Notably, Grant went on to become a favored collaborator of John Wayne.

14. For more on Mahin, see Todd McCarthy and Joseph McBride, "John Lee Mahin: Team Player," in *Interviews with Screenwriters of Hollywood's Golden Age*, ed. Patrick McGilligan (Berkeley: University of California Press, 1986), 241–65.

15. As Kathryn S. Olmsted explains, *The Grapes of Wrath* and Carey McWilliams's *Factories in the Field* both prompted angry reactions from Republican politicians and businessmen. Steinbeck's book was both banned and burned. But, as Olmstead also notes, Steinbeck's revolutionary vision was one that whitewashed California agriculture and employed racist arguments to elevate white Dust Bowl refugees. In this worldview, *The Grapes of Wrath* and *Boom Town* are aligned. Kathryn S. Olmsted, *Right Out of California: The 1930s and the Big Business Roots of Modern Conservatism* (New York: New Press, 2015), 222–23.

16. In Steinbeck's novel, the camp is called Weedpatch.

17. On the visual culture of and surrounding *The Grapes of Wrath*, see James R. Swensen, *Picturing Migrants: The Grapes of Wrath and New Deal Documentary Photography* (Norman: University of Oklahoma Press, 2015).

18. Depression-era visual and print culture also likened Dust Bowl migrants to noble pioneers. For example, a June 1937 *Life* magazine feature on the Dust Bowl, which was accompanied by Resettlement Administration photographs of families driving toward California, makes this analogy. The surrounding text reads: "A new caravan of covered wagons." "Dust Bowl Farmer is the New Pioneer," *Life*, June 21, 1937, 65.

19. Robert Lifset and Brian C. Black also note the "pioneer" character in oil films in "Imaging the 'Devil's Excrement': Big Oil in Petroleum Cinema, 1940–2007," *Journal of American History* 99, no. 1 (May 2012): 137.

20. On oil and Christianity in the United States, see Darren Dochuk, *Anointed with Oil: How Christianity and Crude Made Modern America* (New York: Basic Books, 2019).

21. "Oil in Illinois: Rigs Rise over Field and Farm as Boom Unlocks a New U.S. Frontier," *Life*, June 10, 1940, 63.

22. "Illinois Oil Boom Sells 'Boom Town' on Civic Campaign," *Motion Picture Herald*, August 24, 1940, 80.

23. "Oil in Illinois," 64, 66.

24. Morse, "There Will Be Birds," 126.

25. Paul Sabin, *Crude Politics: The California Oil Market, 1900–1940* (Berkeley: University of California Press, 2004), 111–33.

26. Jurca, "What the Public Wanted," 17–18.

27. On the controversy surrounding Rothstein's photograph, see Cara A. Finnegan,

"The Naturalistic Enthymeme and Visual Argument: Photographic Representation in the 'Skull Controversy,'" *Argumentation and Advocacy* 37, no. 3 (Winter 2001): 133–49.

28. A bleached skull and bones also appear on the parched earth in New Deal filmmaker Pare Lorentz's 1936 *The Plow that Broke the Plains*. For an analysis of Lorentz's film as a narrative of decline, see Finis Dunaway, *Natural Visions: The Power of Images in American Environmental Reform* (Chicago: University of Chicago Press, 2005), 33–59.

29. For example, Remington's 1900 *The Signal (If Skulls Could Speak)* depicts a lone Native horseman swinging a buffalo robe over his head at the sight of a bleached bison skull. Of course, Georgia O'Keeffe also painted bleached skulls, which became synonymous with her life in the Southwest. Art historian Wanda M. Corn discusses O'Keeffe's use of skulls in *The Great American Thing: Modern Art and National Identity, 1915–1935* (Berkeley: University of California Press, 1999), 265–86. Also see Lauren Kroiz on O'Keeffe's skulls and the American desert, *Creative Composites: Modernism, Race, and the Stieglitz Circle* (Berkeley: University of California Press, 2012), 175–82.

30. Invoking military vehicles in light of the coming oil-powered war is notable. For an analysis of oil as a "life blood" and the Depression as a turning point, see Matthew T. Huber, *Lifeblood: Oil, Freedom, and the Forces of Capital* (Minneapolis: University of Minnesota, 2013), 27–59.

Chapter 8

Petrodocumentary in the 1940s: The Standard Oil Photography Project, *Louisiana Story* (1948), and the Domestication of the US Oil Industry

Emily Roehl

How much energy does it take to boil an egg? This is the question ExxonMobil poses in their 2014 advertisement "Enabling Everyday Progress: Egg."[1] An attractive white woman in the kitchen of her chic urban condo fills a pot with water, opens the refrigerator, grabs an egg, and clicks on a gas burner. The scene shifts to a montage of energy exploration, extraction, and shipment, accompanied by fanciful chimes, bells, and swelling strings reminiscent of a Danny Elfman film score. At two points during the montage, the commercial cuts back to the woman in her kitchen; she is drinking coffee, reading her electronic tablet, at ease in her comfortable domestic space as she waits for the water to boil. The sixty-second commercial has a brief voice-over that begins just past the halfway point: a male voice delivers ExxonMobil's paternalistic maxim: "You don't need to think about the energy that makes our lives possible. Because we do."[2] ExxonMobil is not interested in answering the question of how much energy it takes to boil an egg. They want you to know that it is too complicated a question for this woman—a stand-in for the viewer—to worry about. The company has her life under control, all the way down to her most mundane tasks.

The oil industry has a long history of celebrating the intricacy of its labyrinthine operations in an attempt to convince the oil-consuming public that they are responsible stewards of the world's resources.[3] Oil companies also have a track record of linking their far-flung industrial enterprises to the daily rhythms and comforts of home.[4] This is a message that ExxonMobil's corporate ancestors, Standard Oil of New Jersey (SONJ), broadcasted in the mid-twentieth century through ambitious film and photography projects like the ones addressed in this essay: Robert Flaherty's *Louisiana Story* (1948) and a set of photographs by Edwin and Louise Rosskam, who worked under Roy Stryker on the SONJ Photography Project. The 2014 commercial's voiceover aptly concludes, "Life takes energy. Energy lives here," suggesting the co-constitutive relationship between oil and domestic life.[5] As in this advertisement from 2014, the industry-sponsored petrodocumentary of the 1940s employed a distinctly gendered, white, and middle-class vision of "the good life" made possible by oil—a vision that obscures the externalities of energy production and consumption.

A brief corporate history is necessary to appreciate the continuities between twentieth- and twenty-first-century oil industry advertising tactics. In 1911, a Supreme Court antimonopoly decision divided Standard Oil into thirty four "baby Standards," seven of which dominated the industry for much of the twentieth century.[6] One of these "Seven Sisters" was Standard Oil of New Jersey, which remains one of the largest multinational corporations in the world, having merged first with Humble Oil and later with Mobil to become ExxonMobil in 1999.[7] In the 1940s, SONJ's newly formed public relations department hired not one but two giants of midcentury documentary: Roy Stryker, who had overseen one of the most celebrated documentary photography surveys in US history, and Robert Flaherty, the "father of documentary" and director of quasi-ethnographic films like *Nanook of the North* (1922).[8] In the years during and immediately following World War II, SONJ financed two extensive documentary projects: a nearly seven-year photographic survey overseen by Stryker (1943–1950) and Flaherty's award-winning docufiction film *Louisiana Story* (1948).[9] SONJ public relations documents from the 1940s reveal that both projects had a similar goal: to rehabilitate the company's image in the aftermath of the antitrust decision as well as wartime investigations into their patent arrangements with German petrochemical firm IG Farben.[10] These projects aimed to convince consumers that the oil industry was not only a responsible corporation but also a trusted partner in ensuring domestic comforts and conveniences.

As in the ExxonMobil commercial, so too in the petrodocumentary of the 1940s: cheap fossil fuels provide ease and the privilege of not having to worry about the energy expenditures of modern life. While the 2014 commercial depicts an apparently single woman (there are no familial symbols on display, such as children's artwork on the refrigerator or toys on the countertop), the petrodocumentary of the 1940s was committed to an image of the white heterosexual family unit. In this image, the father is a productive worker either in or adjacent to the oil fields, the mother is a doting homemaker, and the children are the beneficiaries of the wonders that appear when oil moves into the neighborhood. Flaherty's and the Rosskams' work in Louisiana aimed to offset oil's risks by illustrating its compatibility with rural families' domestic lives. However, it did so while overlooking those who bore the greatest burden of these risks: those who lived outside of the white middle-class family frame.

Petrodocumentary in the 1940s

In 1942, SONJ hired pollster Elmo Roper to survey public opinion of the oil industry in general and SONJ in particular. Much to the company's dismay, they discovered that the highly publicized probes into the company's prewar involvement with German petrochemical firm IG Farben—which may have contributed to US rubber shortages—had harmed their reputation, particularly among the nation's "thought leaders," academics, and other white-collar types that the company believed could turn the tide of public opinion.[11] Carl Maas, an art consultant hired by SONJ, concluded that this demographic was more art conscious than the general public, so the company embarked on a number of projects to create and distribute art around the world. Painting and photography exhibitions as well as film screenings were all part of the company's multipronged, multimedia mission to rehabilitate its image.[12]

SONJ public relations chairman George Freyermuth wasn't convinced that art and other media could polish the company's tarnished reputation. In a transcript of a SONJ working public relations conference in December 1947, Freyermuth compared "entertainment" films, like Standard Oil's state-by-state travel documentaries, to more informational films that illustrated various facets of the industry. An entertainment film, according to Freyermuth, "gives the audience a pleasant half hour in which they don't learn anything about us except that we are nice people to show them the film."[13] He wondered, "How can we raise the public relations value of showing films? . . . Now take this entertainment-type film, would it hurt it or would it help it if you were to run a leader on it saying something like, 'The oil industry has made possible travel within the states. Thank God for the American oil industry'?"[14] Later in the conference, G. A. Lawrence, a public relations representative from Imperial Oil, responded to Freyermuth, explaining, "We have been complimented that our Company promotion is so small. Somehow I think it has worked in reverse."[15] This is what SONJ was hoping to get when they hired Stryker and Flaherty: public relations in reverse, an angle on oil that didn't let the industry's technological and logistical complexity detract from a story about a place and its people, even as oil was transforming the ecological and social landscapes being documented.

By sponsoring Stryker's photography project and Flaherty's film, SONJ amassed a visual archive of a country in the midst of an environmental, social, and energy transition. SONJ paid the era's most celebrated documentary media producers to spend long stretches of time embedded in southern Louisiana so that they might capture the look and feel of oil in a place that, due to the industry, was rapidly changing. In *Carbon Nation*, Bob Johnson argues that Flaherty's work "neutralized" the destructive force of oil development in Louisiana "by drawing on the authenticating power of the region's local Cajun culture" to suggest that "oil and its culture were not at odds with the rhythms and values of the somatic world."[16] This neutralization of oil's inherent risks was accomplished in large part by midcentury petrodocumentary makers' insistence that oil was interlaced with some of the era's most treasured ideals: the white heterosexual family unit and the comforts of postwar economic abundance—a material and emotional windfall in the post-Depression, post–World War II context of the US South. At the same time, this neutralization domesticated the oil industry; it made oil seem not only safe and in step with rural lifeways, but also a valuable feature of the home.

Living Well on Dry Land

An image fades in from black: it is a close-up shot of water, lily pads floating lazily along the surface. The camera pulls wider as a boy navigates his long, narrow canoe—a pirogue—amid the drifting vegetation and low-hanging tree branches. An alligator glides menacingly nearby. The camera hovers just above the water, capturing flashes of light through the dense, lush foliage. A voiceover speaks of mermaids, "their hair green [who] swim up these waters from the sea," and of werewolves with "big red eyes [who] come to dance on moonless nights."[17] This scene, peopled with mythological creatures and thick with emblems of primordial nature, is the opening sequence to Flaherty's *Louisiana Story*. In the years leading up to the making of this film, Roy Stryker deployed photographers in the Bayou State to document SONJ's expanding oil operations. Many of their images, while lacking in mermaids and werewolves, also featured the distinctive watery landscapes of southern Louisiana. What emerges in many of these photographs is a vision of progress that centers the modernized space of the home.

Much has been said about the way Flaherty depicts oil infrastructure in *Louisiana Story*; Janet Walker refers to the film as "a 78-minute oil extraction montage" that reaches its climax when the oil well comes gushing in during a dramatic sequence of spouting water and exploding gas.[18] This essay, however, focuses on some of the quieter but no less critical moments of the film in order to tease out the way that these scenes, like the Rosskams' photographs, link gender, domestic space, and the benefits of energy in an oil frontier. In 1944, Roy Stryker hired Edwin and Louise Rosskam to take pictures of oil infrastructure and daily life along the Mississippi River, in Baton Rouge, and in the Choctaw Oil Field in Louisiana.[19] Edwin had been a writer and editor with the Farm Security Administration (FSA), but he agreed to join the Standard Oil project on one condition: that he be permitted to take his own photographs.[20] Edwin was joined by his wife, Louise, who left her training in genetics to pursue a photographic career with her husband that would span more than five decades. The Rosskams created a photo story on the Moseley family in southern Louisiana that features images of the father at work, the mother performing domestic duties like cooking and cleaning, and the daughter playing with dolls, all in the shadow of oil infrastructure. The Moseley family photo story documents the intersection of oil infrastructure, labor, and domestic life in a developing oil field. In these photographs, oil isn't just in sync with the rhythms of work and leisure; it is a member of the family.

The Moseley family photo story begins at the Moseley residence, a house that was constructed on the site of a dry well (fig. 8.1).[21] According to the photograph's caption, the Moseleys lived in a houseboat in this location when it was covered with water, before the oil industry drained the region to begin drilling. The house in this photograph is long and low, with a porch that stretches along the façade and a wooden staircase leading to the front door. The image would be rather bland, like a poorly framed real estate photo, if not for the derrick that seems to rise like a chimney out of the center of the house and the oil tanks that flank the right side of the photograph. The white figures of oil infrastructure in this black-and-white image, the derrick and storage tanks, are interwoven with the bare February tree branches surrounding the Moseley property. Closer inspection reveals that the Moseleys themselves are posing for the photograph on their front steps: an agrarian family, *American Gothic* at a distance.

In this photograph, oil infrastructure literally intersects with the domestic space of the home—a home built by the oil industry for former houseboat dwellers. The line formed by the Moseleys' bodies and the railing of the wooden stairs extends up through the house to the top of the derrick in the center of the frame. The modern lifestyle the image depicts is one shot through with oil in a way that is exemplified by the derrick rising from the center of the house. This is an oil landscape photograph that blends the space of the home and the space of the industry, which are nearly indistinguishable on the Moseleys' property. The house is an image of progress, of modernized domesticity, albeit a humble one.

Unlike this deceptively simple photograph of a house on dry land, the

Fig. 8.1. Edwin and Louise Rosskam, "Choctaw Oil Field, La. C. F. Moseley Picture Story: The house of the Moseley family" (January 1944), SONJ_01600d, Standard Oil (New Jersey) Collection, Photographic Archives, University of Louisville, Louisville, Kentucky.

National Board of Review of Motion Pictures described the setting for *Louisiana Story* as "the weirdly picturesque and beautiful swamplands and bayous of Louisiana."[22] In spite of their aesthetic differences—their penchant for mermaids and werewolves or social documentary realism—both Flaherty and the Rosskams illustrated extraction in Louisiana in the 1940s as an inflow of material wealth that maintained domestic bonds. A scene near the end of *Louisiana Story* makes it clear that oil has not only preserved Acadian culture but improved upon it. After the dramatic climax, when the well surges forth, we see the boy and his mother unwrapping gifts; a new pot and rifle. In the final shot of the film, the boy and his raccoon climb to the top of the oil well's "Christmas tree," which regulates the flow of oil in pipelines beneath the water, as the derrick is towed away. The boy smiles and waves as the raccoon climbs across his shoulders. In these scenes, the holiday tradition of gift-giving links oil infrastructure and family life. The material goods ostensibly begotten by oil money reinforce the mother's domestic duty as a cook and the male child's role as a hunter.

The Rosskams' images evoke similar familial feelings, which appear in a photograph that depicts the Moseleys at home in their living room surrounded by their material possessions (fig. 8.2).[23] According to the caption, "The whole house is spick and span. The antiques are partly inherited, partly collected by Mrs. Moseley. Note treating tanks outside window."[24] In almost the same breath, the caption comments on the cozy family in their tidy dwelling as well as the fourth member of the family: a treating tank. This quiet domestic scene incorporates the infrastructure of oil into its construction of familial sentiment, mixing inherited goods—their link to the past—and new acquisitions, which promise a comfortable future. In the photograph, the daughter smiles as she reads a book. Her father looks over her shoulder, and her mother touches her arm. The family is physically connected to one another and visually surrounded by the comforts of upholstered furniture and collected belongings. They are clothed, perhaps, for church or visiting on a Sunday in collared dresses and a jacket and tie. The photograph is likely staged, though the expressions on the Moseleys' faces appear unforced. The choice to draw attention to the treating tanks in the caption can be read as a fulfillment of the SONJ project brief—to document the oil industry's positive impact on local communities— but also as an indication of the subtler message about oil and everyday life that the company promoted at midcentury: the inextricable relationship between industry and family, the feel of home and the feel of the landscape.

Like *Louisiana Story*, the Rosskams' work in Louisiana made the oil industry seem not only innocuous but advantageous. And for some people, it was. Reflecting on his time with the project, Edwin Rosskam noted, "The environment we lived in was a middle-class environment, even the roughnecks on the rigs. They were the most highly paid people around . . . so you didn't have the impulse to photograph the broken-down, the tragic . . . things didn't look the way they looked at the time of Farm Security."[25] Unlike FSA photographs of rural poverty, *Louisiana Story* and the Moseley family photos depict rural spaces in the midst of a seemingly smooth transition from agrarian labor to well-paid working-class jobs in the oil industry. Both Flaherty and the Rosskams leave the social and ecological externalities of oil off-screen and outside of the photographic frame. These externalities are easier to discern from a twenty-first-century vantage point, but even in the mid-twentieth century they loomed large on the horizon.[26] While midcentury petrodocumentary subsumes these dangers within domestic scenes of plenty, gendered labor, and heterosexual family life, the transformation of the Bayou State was already well underway.

Oil industry-sponsored documentary media from the 1940s displaced the dangers of the oil industry by domesticating it, by representing its far-flung and complicated operations as a series of stories that centered the white

Fig. 8.2. Edwin and Louise Rosskam, "C. F. Mosely Picture Story: The Mosely family in their living room" (January 1944), SONJ_01835, Standard Oil (New Jersey) Collection, Photographic Archives, University of Louisville, Louisville, Kentucky.

middle-class or rising working-class family participating in gendered labor and familial intimacy. The Rosskams' photos and *Louisiana Story* use Louisiana as a figure for rural simplicity tilting toward industrial modernity, painting the extractive process as harmonious with family life while bolstering the idea of abundant, consequence-free fossil energy. This idea has lubricated many of SONJ's public relations efforts and flows through twenty-first-century advertisements. While Stryker's and Flaherty's efforts did not immediately improve public perceptions of SONJ in the 1940s, they did stock the petrodocumentary archive with images that would link oil with the comforts of home for a specific group of people: white middle-class families in heterosexual units.[27] SONJ may have failed in their immediate PR goals, but they created a template for oil industry marketing with remarkable staying power.

Notes

1. ExxonMobil, "Enabling Everyday Progress: Egg," television advertisement, 2014, https://www.ispot.tv/ad/7Ecg/exxon-mobil-enabling-everyday-progress-egg#.
2. ExxonMobil, "Egg."
3. Stephanie LeMenager, *Living Oil: Petroleum Culture in the American Century* (New York: Oxford University Press, 2014), 177–78.
4. Matthew Huber, *Lifeblood: Oil, Freedom, and the Forces of Capital* (Minneapolis: University of Minnesota Press, 2013), 83–85.
5. ExxonMobil, "Egg."
6. Standard Oil Co. of New Jersey v. United States, 221 U.S. 1 (1911).
7. For a more detailed corporate history of Standard Oil, see the online finding aid for the ExxonMobil Historical Collection, Dolph Briscoe Center for American History, University of Texas at Austin, https://legacy.lib.utexas.edu/taro/utcah/00352/cah-00352.html.
8. Stryker was the head of the historical section of the Resettlement Administration (later called the Farm Security Administration) from 1935 to 1943. For reference to Flaherty as the "father of documentary," see "Robert Flaherty, Film Producer, 67; 'Father' of Documentary Dies—Made 'Louisiana Story,' 'Man of Aran' and 'Elephant Boy,'" *New York Times*, July 24, 1951.
9. Standard Oil wasn't the only company using documentary media in the 1940s to market an image of the good life. As Rachel Webb Jekanowski argues in her assessment of Canadian "petro-films" of the same era, industry-sponsored documentaries like Imperial Oil's *A Mile below the Wheat* (1949) normalized extraction in rural landscapes by identifying oil as "another one of nature's bounties," like wheat or cattle, "one which co-exists in harmony with agrarian traditions" and fits neatly within settler narratives of national identity and development. Rachel Webb Jekanowski, "Fuelling the Nation: Imaginaries of Western Oil in Canadian Nontheatrical Film," *Canadian Journal of Communication* 43 (2018): 112.
10. Steven Plattner, *Roy Stryker: U.S.A., 1943–1950: The Standard Oil (New Jersey) Photography Project* (Austin: University of Texas Press, 1983), 12.
11. Plattner, *Roy Stryker*, 11.
12. For example, SONJ sponsored an art exhibition called *Oil: 1940–1945*, which included over three hundred paintings and traveled to forty-one museums, galleries, and universities around the world. Standard Oil (New Jersey) public relations report, 1948, box 2.207, ExxonMobil Historical Collection, Dolph Briscoe Center for American History, University of Texas at Austin.
13. Standard Oil (New Jersey) working public relations conference, December 1947, 34, transcript, box 2.207, ExxonMobil Historical Collection, Dolph Briscoe Center for American History, University of Texas at Austin.
14. SONJ working public relations conference, 34.
15. SONJ working public relations conference, 38.

16. Bob Johnson, *Carbon Nation: Fossil Fuels in the Making of American Culture* (Lawrence: University of Kansas Press, 2014), 149.
17. Robert Flaherty, dir., *Louisiana Story* (1948; New York: Home Vision Studio, 2003).
18. Janet Walker, "Media Mapping and Oil Extraction: A Louisiana Story," *NECSUS: European Journal of Media Studies* 7, no. 2 (Autumn 2018): 235.
19. *Louisiana Story* and many of the Stryker photographs from Louisiana were shot in and around the Choctaw Oil Field, an extractive landscape named for the Indigenous people whose ancestral territories spanned the southeastern portion of what is now called the United States. Though the population of Choctaw citizens in Louisiana remains small, they have lived in the region since well before the oil industry arrived. For more on the history of the Jena Band of Choctaw Indians, see http://www.jenachoctaw.org.
20. Plattner, *Roy Stryker*, 45.
21. Edwin and Louise Rosskam, "Choctaw Oil Field, La. C. F. Moseley Picture Story: The house of the Moseley family," January 1944, photographic print, SONJ_01600d, Standard Oil (New Jersey) Collection, Photographic Archives, University of Louisville, Louisville, Kentucky.
22. Postcard for *Louisiana Story* from the National Board of Review of Motion Pictures, 1948, box 2.207, ExxonMobil Historical Collection, Dolph Briscoe Center for American History, University of Texas at Austin.
23. Edwin and Louise Rosskam, "C. F. Moseley Picture Story: The Moseley family in their living room," January 1944, photographic print, SONJ_01835, Standard Oil (New Jersey) Collection, Photographic Archives, University of Louisville, Louisville, Kentucky.
24. Rosskam and Rosskam, "C. F. Moseley Picture Story."
25. Edwin Rosskam quoted in Plattner, *Roy Stryker*, 22.
26. Walker, "Media Mapping and Oil Extraction," 231. Walker cites a number of sources on the history of industrial impacts on southern Louisiana. For example, see William Freudenburg et al., *Catastrophe in the Making: The Engineering of Katrina and the Disasters of Tomorrow* (Washington, DC: Shearwater Books, 2009), which reports that between 1937 and 1977 sixty-three thousand exploratory wells and twenty-one thousand development wells were drilled in eight Louisiana parishes, and ten thousand miles of canals and pipeline corridors were dredged.
27. In 1948, when Flaherty's film premiered, polls revealed that public opinion of the oil industry had not improved much since Roper's 1942 study, and the photography project budget was cut in half. Plattner, *Roy Stryker*, 23.

Chapter 9

TVA and the Price of Progress: Elia Kazan's *Wild River* (1960)

Donald C. Jackson

he Tennessee Valley Authority (TVA) reigns in popular lore as a great tri-umph of President Franklin D. Roosevelt's New Deal.[1] With the nation struggling to survive the Great Depression, a new federal agency marched into the economic morass of the rural South. Its mission: to bestow the benefits of "planning" and massive funding for hydropower dams upon the peoples of Appalachia and bring modernity—centered around a capacious electric power network—to the Tennessee River Valley. Authorized by Congress in May 1933 and signed into law by FDR during his landmark "First Hundred Days," TVA had its critics—most prominently utility executive and future Republican presidential nominee Wendell Willkie—who objected to the federal govern-ment's entry into the business of electric power.[2] But the agency proved re-markably successful in promoting itself as a beneficent organization battling the rapacious capitalists of Wall Street. In the finger-pointing that followed the stock market crash of 1929, no corporate villain loomed larger than the electric power industry, often derided as the "Power Trust." To FDR and early TVA directors Arthur Morgan and David Lilienthal, the new agency offered a way to counter the Power Trust and make public ownership a key component of the nation's electric power grid.[3]

Produced more than twenty years after TVA became a nationally recog-nized symbol of the New Deal, the film *Wild River* does not address the issue of public versus private power. Instead, it offers a provocative perspective on TVA that was often overlooked, if not purposely ignored, during the agency's early years. The regional economic benefits brought by TVA dams were substantial, but they also came at great cost for those unfortunate rural folk who would be flooded out by expansive storage reservoirs. The price paid by some valley residents to foster the progress of others comprises the thematic heart of *Wild River*, and it is a theme that broadly reflects not so much what people may have been concerned with in the 1930s, but rather how (some) Americans of the late 1950s and early 1960s were willing to question both governmental activism and a dominant social norm that celebrated a materialist ethos of unbridled consumptive growth.

While the arguments and agendas that director Elia Kazan embedded into *Wild River* can be seen as precursors of the antidam environmental protests that flourished in the 1970s, they are in fact more aligned with a conservative critique of big government—a critique concerned not so much with environmental degradation as with the diminution of private property rights in the face of an expanding public infrastructure. Although it did not achieve great box office success, *Wild River* is a thoughtful and important film that offers a revealing window into an America that, by the early 1960s, was on the verge of confronting the costs incurred by incessant escalation in energy use. As such, it stands as a leading film in the demesne of energy history, one of the few major Hollywood films of any era to seriously address the proliferation of electric power systems and the concomitant impact on individuals and local communities.

During FDR's presidency (1933–1945), Hollywood produced no notable films depicting the myriad transformations brought by TVA. Certainly there is nothing comparable to director John Ford's 1940 adaptation of *The Grapes of Wrath*, which posits the federal government as the savior of "Okie" migrants forced out of dust bowl Oklahoma. Beyond Hollywood, the story of—and need for—government involvement in the nation's economic resurgence was cinematically rendered in a variety of public domain films. These included *The Plow That Broke the Plains* (1937) and *The River* (1938), produced under the aegis of the Farm Security Administration, *Power and the Land* (1940) by the Rural Electrification Administration, and TVA's *A National Program in the Tennessee Valley* (1936) and *The TVA at Work* (1935).[4] Intended to promote the social benefits of New Deal conservation and public works programs, these documentaries display considerable visual flair but are hobbled by a ponderous narrative styling.[5] The film *Wild River* offers something quite different—a dramatization of Tennessee Valley life in the 1930s where both the costs and benefits of material progress are given a compelling human face.

Released in May 1960 by 20th Century Fox, *Wild River* was a major CinemaScope production.[6] Directed by Elia Kazan—previously honored with two Academy Awards for Best Directing: *Gentleman's Agreement* (1947) and *On the Waterfront* (1954)—all filming took place on location in and around Bradley County, Tennessee, during the fall of 1959.[7] Costing an estimated $1.5 million, Kazan's film featured an A-list cast, including Montgomery Clift (four-time Academy Award nominee) as TVA emissary Chuck Glover; Jo Van Fleet (Academy Award winner in the 1955 Kazan-directed *East of Eden*) as

Ella Garth, a domineering matriarch whose family farm is marked for inundation by a TVA dam; and Lee Remick (future Academy Award nominee) as Ella Garth's widowed granddaughter-in-law, Carol.[8]

Despite Clift's relatively constrained performance, the film overall exhibits superb production values, highlighted by Van Fleet's stellar turn as an aggrieved landowner facing eviction from her ancestral home. *Wild River* does not attempt to offer a sweeping history of TVA, focusing instead on how the often-praised federal program also required tremendous sacrifice from some valley residents. But before considering the film as a historical artifact reflecting America's complex relationship with electric power, we need to consider the origins of TVA and issues driving its early growth.

Origins and Implementation of the TVA

The genesis of TVA lies not in some utopian scheme to transform Appalachia, but rather in the tumult of World War I military planning. Fearful that nitrate imports from Chile might be interrupted, Congress and President Woodrow Wilson enacted the National Defense Act of 1916 and authorized federal financing for a hydroelectric power dam across the Tennessee River at Muscle Shoals, Alabama.[9] The aim was to insure a domestic supply of nitrate—an essential component of explosive weapons—in case the United States needed to defend itself against foreign aggression. America did indeed enter the war in April 1917, but construction of Muscle Shoals Dam (later renamed Wilson Dam) was far from complete when the armistice was signed in November 1918. The question then became what to do with this huge, partially completed, federally owned dam. The electric power industry wanted it sold to private investors or to have its power leased on a long-term basis, Henry Ford lobbied Congress for a hundred-year lease to support a huge Ford-managed industrial complex at Muscle Shoals, farming interests believed the dam best suited to support the manufacture of nitrate-based agricultural fertilizer, and progressive conservationists led by Senator George Norris of Nebraska envisioned it as the core of a government-owned regional power system.[10]

Republican presidents of the 1920s (Warren G. Harding, Calvin Coolidge, and Herbert Hoover) opposed the federal government's entry into the electric power business, and during their administrations no agreement could be reached on Wilson Dam's future, even after it began generating power in 1925. Although a short-term renewable lease with the local Alabama Power Company provided a modicum of revenue to help repay a federal investment of some $47 million, long-term use of the dam remained in limbo through the early 1930s.[11]

In the meantime, hydroelectric power had become an issue of national

Fig. 9.1. Interior of Wilson Dam powerhouse at Muscles Shoals, Alabama. The electricity generated at Wilson Dam was originally intended to produce nitrates as part of defense planning for World War I. But the war was over by the time the federally financed dam across the Tennessee River became operational in 1925. After Franklin D. Roosevelt became president in 1933, the dam and powerhouse became the foundation of the newly created Tennessee Valley Authority (TVA). Author's collection; public domain.

import, spurring the creation of the Federal Power Commission in 1920 (later renamed the Federal Energy Regulatory Commission). In addition, a desire for comprehensive natural resource planning impelled Congress to authorize the Army Corps of Engineers to undertake detailed studies of the nation's river basins. By 1928, the Corps envisaged a plan for the Tennessee Valley that included twenty-three dams. As part of this work, Corps engineers made estimates for a major dam across the Clinch River, a tributary draining much of northeastern Tennessee. Designated Cove Creek Dam, this structure was to be approximately two thousand feet long and over two hundred feet high, creating a reservoir with a storage capacity of more than 800 billion gallons; the estimated generating capacity of the planned powerhouse approached 150,000 kilowatts.[12]

The Army Corps's study of the Tennessee River made no recommendations that the federal government build any dams. Instead, the Corps's charge was to study the watershed's navigation and power potential, leaving it to other parties—such as private power companies—to finance construction. Congress was willing to fund regional studies of water basin development, but as long as Republican presidents held the White House, no federal agency would develop Tennessee River hydropower beyond the existing Wilson Dam.

All changed when FDR took office in March 1933. As president, he supported federal involvement in the electric power business, and when campaigning in 1932 had asserted government's "undeniable basic right" to both generate electricity and "transmit and distribute [power] where reasonable and good service is refused by private capital." While disagreeing "with those who advocate Government ownership or Government indiscriminate operation of all utilities," he believed the federal government should engage in such work if deemed appropriate. And nowhere would it be more appropriate than in the Tennessee River Valley.[13]

FDR's interest in public power extended beyond the Tennessee River, but the facts that the federally owned Wilson Dam was already operational and that the Army Corps had completed a detailed study of the watershed gave impetus to making the valley the focus of a great social, economic, and technological experiment. Joining with Senator Norris, FDR selected the Tennessee Valley for a grandly ambitious project, one not centered solely on electric power but also dedicated to uplifting the "forgotten" and "uneducated" Americans of Appalachia who would receive "schools and electric lights . . . and industries."[14] In terms of the "forgotten," it is fair to point out that investor-owned electric power companies had largely left rural America in the literal dark; when Roosevelt became president, only 10 percent of America's farmers were served by electric power lines.[15] Endorsing the project in a speech to the National Emergency Council, the president broadly proclaimed, "When you build a dam as an incident to this entire program [of revitalizing the Tennessee Valley], you get probably a certain amount of water power development out of it. We are going to try to use that water power to its best advantage."[16]

Upon the enactment of TVA legislation in May 1933, the agency set out to remake the valley. The Corps's Cove Creek Dam project was quickly renamed Norris Dam and approved as one of the agency's first ventures. Engineering issues related to building the dam were hardly minor, but they comprised only part of the challenges TVA faced. With a planned height of about 250 feet (reaching an elevation of 1,020 feet above sea level), Norris Dam would impound a reservoir stretching seventy miles up the Clinch River (and another fifty miles up the tributary Powell River). Overall, the TVA would purchase over 150,000

Fig. 9.2. TVA's Norris Dam nearing completion in 1936. The reservoir impounded by the hydroelectric dam (generating capacity: 132,000 kilowatts) stretches seventy miles up the Clinch River and required the "relocation" of some three thousand families. The sacrifice demanded of these families to help bring electricity to the Tennessee Valley became an inspiration for the 1960 film *Wild River*. Author's collection; public domain.

acres of land in the "take zone" and surrounding hill country; as a result, some three thousand families would need "relocation" from the greater Norris Basin.[17]

The new agency now confronted an unavoidable cost engendered by its dam-building ambitions. Yes, many people would benefit from TVA's new hydropower plants, but some would suffer in service to a larger public good. Notably, the people of the Clinch and Powell River Valleys forced from their homes were not scheming capitalists cosseted away in the aeries of Wall Street. In fact, they were just the type of people that the agency was intended to succor. As late as 1933, "94 percent of the [farm] owners and 98 percent of the tenants [above Norris Dam] were without electricity or phones. . . . Indoor toilet facilities were just about as rare as lighting systems."[18]

The sacrifice required of families residing above Norris Dam was not something that TVA wanted to publicize. In their book *The Greater Good*, Laura Beth Daws and Susan Brinson make this point explicit: "[TVA's] Information Office primarily focused on sharing [stories] which shed favorable light on the TVA.

. . . Two potentially contentious issues were noticeably absent from press releases: the removal of families and displacement of graves from the reservoir areas." At TVA's behest, local newspaper editors also discouraged discussion of negative aspects of the agency's program: "There was little criticism of the TVA in local newspapers in the early years of the agency's existence. . . . [They] largely ignored the realities of life for families living on the riverbanks who sacrificed much in the name of progress."[19] Legally, the agency had the right to buy all the land and property necessary to build and operate Norris Dam. But how that mission could be carried out with minimal turmoil remained uncertain. As historians Michael McDonald and John Muldowny note in their 1982 study *TVA and the Dispossessed*, "The resolution of what was psychologically and emotionally a holistic problem for the dispossessed became for TVA an agonizing and continual appraisal of its role at the grass roots."[20]

The easy story to tell about TVA's history is one of a determined cadre of social planners, progressive politicians, and dedicated engineers taking on the Power Trust and bringing modernity to a "forgotten" part of America. Illuminating—or even acknowledging—the sacrifices made by those people who suffered in the name of progress is a harder one. It was this latter story that Elia Kazan sought to underscore and humanize in *Wild River*.

A Synopsis of *Wild River*

Kazan's film starts with newsreel footage documenting destruction brought by rampaging urban floods. In close-up, a distraught man describes how the rising water drowned three of his children. This poignant portrayal of a family shattered by a "wild river" sets the stage for why large storage dams are needed in a modernizing America. The point seems obvious. Who could object to a carefully planned dam in the face of such devastation? Who would want families to suffer as raging waters kill helpless children?

A dramatic narrative then begins with the arrival of Chuck Glover, a Northerner sent from Washington, DC, to a TVA office in a small, mid-1930s Tennessee town. His mission: to persuade an obstinate old woman (Ella Garth) that she and her family must leave their home and farm (which encompasses a large island) because it will soon be flooded by an almost completed dam. She is refusing the agency's offer to buy her holdings, and the TVA hierarchy back in the nation's capital fears the publicity that might result if she is forcibly dragged from her home. In a long-distance phone call, Glover's superiors caution that the situation is politically perilous: "Well we can't use force [to remove her]. . . . There are a couple of senators up here who've really got their teeth into us. They're just waiting for something like this to put on the docket and we're through." Thus, the outsider from Washington must find a way to convince her to prioritize the greater public good over her seemingly personal whims. The entire region will benefit from flood control and the copious hydroelectric power generated at the new dam. Why can't she understand?

The plot includes a prominent racial element, with African Americans comprising the bulk of workers on the Garth farm. There is also a love-interest storyline centered on the matriarch's widowed granddaughter-in-law, Carol, a young woman (with two infants) seeking a future in the rapidly changing Tennessee Valley. Both race and the sociopolitical status of women are aspects of the film that speak to the contentious character of mid-twentieth-century America (and both are worthy of analysis in studies separate from this essay). But it is the battle over private property rights in the face of a government Leviathan that occupies the film's epicenter. And here is where *Wild River* is willing to critique TVA as a social experiment and foreground the plight of people facing forced removal from their homes.[21]

In this latter context, the most powerful scene in the film comes early on when the elderly Garth speaks to a gathering of Black field hands about what the government intends for the island farm: "Well, they say President Roosevelt has got some kind of new government, you know, it's called the New Deal. . . . Well I tell ya, Mr. Roosevelt is going to flood this island, yes sir, yes sir . . . He's gonna take the best piece of land in these here parts and put it right smack under the Tennessee River. . . . You see, he sets up there in that big white house and he says this country, he says is just a-goin' to the dogs and that the only way that he can figure to do anything to stop it is to put my land under water." Seeing that Glover has arrived within earshot, Garth seemingly ignores him. Instead, she engages with Sam Johnson (Robert Earl Jones), a field hand and owner of a dog named Old Blue, in an attempt to illustrate—through parable—the injustice of TVA's claim on her property. Suddenly, she proposes purchasing Old Blue, paying no heed to what Sam might want:

GARTH: Well you know, I decided I'm gonna buy Old Blue, Sam.

SAM: What's that, Miss Ella?

GARTH: You heard me. I want to buy Old Blue, now how much you want for him?

SAM: Oh, I wouldn't want to sell Old Blue, Miss Ella.

GARTH: Well I didn't ask if you wanted to sell him, did I? I say I'm gonna buy him. I'm gonna give you, oh, I'll give you fifteen dollars for him. What's the matter? He ain't worth more than that, is he?

SAM: No, no, ma'am, he ain't worth nuthin'. But I ain't a-gonna sell him.

GARTH: Well you got to sell him, Sam, because I'm gonna buy him. Now how am I gonna buy him lessin' you sell him?

SAM: I don't know, but I ain't a-selling him.

GARTH: Sam Johnson, you're sellin' him and that's that.

SAM: No I ain't gonna sell him. Old Blue is mine and I ain't gonna sell even to you. You ain't got no right to make me.

(Pause)

GARTH: Well now, that's true. Come to think of it, I don't have the right, do I?

On the page, Garth's faux attempt to force Old Blue's sale might seem contrived. But on screen, Van Fleet and Jones bring the allegory to life with enormous pathos and power. Of course, some might question if the sale of Old Blue is really comparable to what TVA is asking of Garth. This issue arises as she turns to Glover and speaks to him directly.

GARTH: You see, young man, Sam and me don't sell. Sam don't sell his dog and I don't sell my land that I put my heart's blood into. . . .

GLOVER: Mrs. Garth, uh, sometimes it happens we can't remain true to our beliefs without hurting a great many people. And I'm afraid this is one of those times. You're the only person who hasn't sold in this valley. . . . You know the Tennessee River has been a killer for years. Year after year it's taken God knows how many lives. Isn't it just plain common sense to want to harness it? And you know what that will mean? Today 98 percent of the people in this valley have no electricity. The dam will bring them the electricity.

GARTH: I expect that's what you call progress, isn't it?

GLOVER: And you don't?

GARTH: No sir, I don't. Takin' away people's souls, puttin' electricity in place of them, ain't progress, not the way I see it.

GLOVER: We're not taking away people's souls. Just the opposite. We're giving them a chance to have a soul. And it isn't just this dam. It's dam after dam after dam. We aim to tame this whole river.

GARTH: You do? Well I like things runnin' wild. Like nature meant. There's already enough dams lockin' things up. Tamin' 'em. Making them go against their natural wants and needs. I'm agin' dams of any kind.

Garth soon guides Glover to the family cemetery atop a nearby hill, showing him the gravestone of her husband next to the one already in place for her. She tells him, "My husband came down this river in a flatboat when he was nothin' but a boy. . . . He was a-lookin' for an island and he took this one. . . . He drained the fields, he cleared the brush. He cut down them trees. He worked hisself to death just to make these fields. And he told me never to get off and I ain't. I ain't." After Garth heads back to her farmhouse, Glover turns to her granddaughter-in-law, Carol, and describes the good life awaiting the family matriarch when she leaves the island at TVA's behest: "We'll get her a nice house. She'll have a radio. She'll have a modern kitchen." But Carol is unconvinced that the trappings of modernity will ever mean much to Ella Garth, and tersely responds, "You better believe it. If she has to leave this island it'll kill her."

As the story plays out, Glover hits upon the idea of drawing the African American workers off the island by offering them jobs with TVA. This angers the valley's white power structure because TVA wages exceed what Black people are typically paid in the local labor market. The conflict eventually leads to a nighttime assault on the TVA agent that resembles a Ku Klux Klan terror attack. Glover also becomes romantically involved with Carol, who then sides with him in the battle with her late husband's grandmother. In the end, Ella Garth—abandoned by most of her longtime field hands (but not Sam Johnson, owner of Old Blue) as well as her lackadaisical sons—leaves Garth Island to its fate, but only after a marshal serves a judicial decree demanding her eviction. She walks proudly to the ferry, departing under the legal force and directive of the federal government. Soon the family homestead is ablaze as the clearing crews move in.

Relocated to a wooden cottage abutting a busy road, Garth steps onto the porch of her new home but evinces no interest in going inside, where a radio might connect her to a wider world. A final scene brings closure to her life, as she tells Carol, "I owe Frank Zachary sixteen cents for two pounds of sugar. You see that he gets it the next time you go in." Then, after a pause, "That's all I owe, anybody." Her final request made, she dies within hours and is soon buried next to her husband in the family plot.

Not long after Garth's death, Carol—who has married Glover in a stark civil ceremony—heads north with her children and husband to begin life anew. For all the wondrous things that the dam and hydroelectricity are supposed to bring to a presumed "New South," young Carol still wants to escape; her future lies elsewhere. As the new family flies out of the valley, they pass over the Garth clan's hilltop cemetery, now surrounded by the reservoir. The movie's last scene features a stunning aerial shot of a massive TVA dam (Fontana

Fig. 9.3. Still photo from *Wild River*, showing matriarch Ella Garth (played by Jo Van Fleet) being removed under legal force from her ancestral home to make way for a TVA dam and reservoir. Courtesy Tennessee State Library and Archives, Photo ID 24125.

Dam, completed in 1944). The dam no doubt represents a powerful monument to modernity—a symbol of government providing the "greatest good for the greatest number"—but anyone who has witnessed the fate of Ella Garth should now appreciate the individual sacrifices it required.

Switching Sides: Kazan and 1950s America

Although *Wild River* focuses on a nation grappling with the Great Depression and the ramifications of FDR's New Deal, the film was a cultural artifact of 1950s America. While Democratic presidents Franklin D. Roosevelt and Harry S. Truman had embraced TVA as a venerable example of a publicly owned utility, Dwight Eisenhower (elected in 1952 as the first Republican president since Herbert Hoover) was inclined to see the agency as a dangerous step toward socialism, if not communism. Eisenhower and his supporters failed to dismantle TVA, but the political demonization of investor-owned power companies was checked during his administration.[22]

The US in the 1950s also witnessed the resurgence of a free market ideology exemplified by the novels of Ayn Rand and writings emanating from the economics department at the University of Chicago. Kazan did not necessarily share in the ideals of Rand and the Chicago school, but the one-time member of the Communist Party in the 1930s had now come to reject the precepts of totalitarian socialism. In 1952, as the Red Scare roiled Hollywood, he had testified before the House Committee on Un-American Activities (HUAC) and "named names" of his one-time fellow travelers.[23] The genesis and ultimate message expressed in *Wild River* reflects his political transformation (or evolution). As Kazan describes in his 1988 autobiography:

> I'd switched sides. I'd conceived of this film years before as homage to the spirit of FDR, my hero was to be a resolute New Dealer engaged in the difficult task of convincing "reactionary" country people that it was necessary, in the name of the public good, for them to move off their land. . . . Now I found my sympathies were with the obdurate old lady who lived on the island that was to be inundated. . . . I was all for her. Something more than the shreds of my liberal ideology was at work now, something truer perhaps, and certainly stronger. While my man from Washington had the "social" right on his side, the picture I made was in sympathy with the old woman obstructing progress.[24]

In 1960, New Deal historian (and, later, speechwriter for President John F. Kennedy) Arthur Schlesinger Jr. took a different, more conventional, tack, effusing how "TVA built twenty-one dams . . . [their] copper and aluminum wires, glistening from steel transmission towers, carried new life from the foaming waters of the river to the farthest corners of the Valley . . . there now was the magic of electricity." [25] This praise for FDR's landmark federal agency diverged from Kazan's view of TVA dams, or at least it lacked any of the ambivalence or nuance offered in *Wild River*. As reflected in Schlesinger's sermonizing, in the early 1960s the wonders promised by an ever-expanding supply of energy still enthralled many Americans and the nation's political leadership. Of course, this would significantly change in a few years, when, for example, plans to build dams in the lower Grand Canyon and amid the highlands of the Hudson River Valley, and an oil spill despoiling the beaches of Southern California helped foster growing anxiety over the ecological damage incurred by rising energy consumption.[26] Perhaps these newfound concerns deviated from Ella Garth's property rights defense in her attack on TVA dam building, but her proclamation that she was "agin' dams of any kind" would have resonated with many environmentalists in the late twentieth century. In challenging a pro-growth ethos of ever-expanding energy use, *Wild River* proved to be—in ways largely unforeseen by director Kazan—a prescient piece of art ahead of its time.

Commercial Failure, Belated Acclaim

When released in May 1960, *Wild River* generated little box office buzz, with the studio hesitant to promote the film as some kind of paean to the (potential) abuses of big government in transgressing upon individual property rights or as a statement about civil rights and Southern white hegemony.[27] Selling *Wild River* as a thought-provoking battle over a TVA dam held little appeal to the business moguls at 20th Century Fox as, in historian Richard Schickel's view, company leaders feared that "TVA was old and irrelevant news to a mass audience."[28] Instead, studio flacks emphasized the love story between Lee Remick and Montgomery Clift, depicting the film, in the words of a theater lobby card, as a "Smouldering Story of the South. You Can't Hold Back a Wild River, A Deep Longing, A Sudden Love!" Yet heralding the film as a love story is likely why it failed to attract much popular interest. Despite Remick's considerable charm and talent, her supposed romance with Clift lacks any on-screen spark.[29] Lobby cards may have primed audiences for a "smouldering story," but the actual film falls short in delivering on this promise. Rather, the evocative power of the film resides in Van Fleet's poignant defense of her island homestead and the sacrifice forced upon her by a government bureaucracy.

Wild River received no Academy Award nominations and quickly faded from the nation's consciousness. Conceivably, followers of Ayn Rand and the Chicago school (and perhaps even conservatives in the mold of General Electric spokesman Ronald Reagan) could have championed the film as a testimony to how big government deprives people of hard-earned property rights. But in the end, Ella Garth is removed from her island, and the film's final, glorious shot of a massive concrete dam signals that—despite the costs incurred—TVA has done the right thing in providing for the valley's larger public good. Ella Garth may not have wanted electricity to enter her life, but the film evinces no evidence that her views were shared by many, if any, local residents. Early on in the film, Kazan allows Garth to make an eloquent defense of property rights, but as the story unfolds she becomes ever more isolated from the valley's broader culture. TVA threatens the local power structure not because it strips landowners of long-held property rights, but because—at least as portrayed in the film—it upends the norms of segregated Southern culture. In truth, the TVA of the 1930s offered no challenge to a political economy founded upon racial exploitation.[30] The film, however, projects the agency as an instrument of positive social change operating outside the supposed "free market" of the South's Jim Crow labor regime. In this, the fate of Ella Garth and her cherished island are eventually registered as acceptable collateral damage. Such a conclusion is likely not one around which Rand or the Chicago school (or Ronald Reagan) would have rallied.

Despite disappearing from the American cultural landscape soon after its release, *Wild River* nonetheless holds the respect of film devotees and admirers of Elia Kazan. In particular, famed director Martin Scorsese and actor Robert De Niro championed the film as a cinema classic, and with their support, it was added to the National Film Registry as a "culturally, historically, or aesthetically significant" film in 2002. This represents no small honor, as the National Film Registry was created by Congress to identify major works of cinema and, in concert with the Library of Congress, ensure the long-term preservation of films deemed "of enduring importance to American culture."[31]

For many years, *Wild River* was available only on hard-to-find VHS cassettes, but the 20th Century Fox Studio Classic series released high-quality DVDs starting in 2006. After languishing almost unseen for decades, through DVDs and streaming sites the film can once again draw public attention to how a great filmmaker brought to life complicated relationships connecting energy, property rights, socioeconomic progress, and environmental change. Viewed today, Elia Kazan's *Wild River* endures as a story of modernity, electric power, and the price of progress. It also offers insight into a time when America was both enthralled by a future promising the limitless growth of electric power and, conversely, fearful that such growth might diminish, if not destroy, the character of American society and the landscape that sustains it. As a work of cinema, *Wild River* is complex and far from perfect. But in transcending the film's imperfections, Kazan brings to the screen the struggles of modern

America, evocatively dramatizing the way that Americans have come to view energy as both a blessing and a curse. What could be more relevant, now and for decades to come?

Notes

1. Willson Whitman, *God's Valley: People and Power along the Tennessee River* (New York: Viking Press, 1939); David E. Lilienthal, *TVA: Democracy on the March* (New York: Harper and Row, 1944); R. L. Duffis, *The Valley and Its People* (New York: Alfred A. Knopf, 1944); Gordon R. Clapp, *TVA: An Approach to the Development of a Region* (Chicago: University of Chicago Press, 1955); North Callahan, *TVA: Bridge over Troubled Water; A History of the Tennessee Valley Authority* (New York: A. S. Barnes, 1980).

2. David Levering Lewis, *The Improbable Wendell Willkie: The Businessman Who Saved the Republican Party and His Country, and Conceived a New World Order* (New York: Liveright, 2018), 65–102.

3. For discussion of the Power Trust, see Thomas K. McGraw, *TVA and the Public Power Fight: 1933–1939* (Philadelphia: Lippincott, 1971), 1–46; John L. Neufeld, *Selling Power: Economics, Policy, and Electric Utilities before 1940* (Chicago: University of Chicago Press, 2016).

4. Pare Lorentz, dir., *The Plow That Broke the Plains* (Washington, DC: US Resettlement Administration, 1936), FDR Presidential Library and Museum, YouTube video, 28:40, https://www.youtube.com/watch?v=hzaV5FdZMUQ; Pare Lorentz, dir., *The River* (Washington, DC: USDA Farm Security Administration, 1938), FDR Presidential Library and Museum, YouTube video, 31:56, https://www.youtube.com/watch?v=fpz0XI6U97U; Joris Ivans, dir., *Power and the Land* (Washington, DC: US Rural Electrification Administration, 1940), YouTube video, 38:02, https://www.youtube.com/watch?v=-KVwWAJBJUA; Tennessee Valley Authority, *A National Program in the Tennessee Valley* (Washington, DC: US Department of the Interior, 1936), US National Archive, YouTube video, 47:23, https://www.youtube.com/watch?v=Xv0dPCIl7io; Tennessee Valley Authority, *The TVA at Work*, (Washington, DC: US Department of the Interior, 1935), US National Archive, YouTube video, 13:28, https://www.youtube.com/watch?v=idCwqXju7w0.

5. Film historian Richard Schickel describes this genre of 1930s documentaries as "embracing Soviet-style montage," with narration in the "mock simple proletarian stylings of the day." Richard Schickel, *Elia Kazan: A Biography* (New York: Harper Collins, 2005), 60.

6. Elia Kazan, dir., *Wild River* (Los Angeles: 20th Century Fox, 1960).

7. Ted Strong, "Charting a 'Wild River' Tennessee Style," *New York Times*, November 29, 1959. Paul Ostrom's screenplay for *Wild River* was nominally based upon two novels: Borden Deal's *Dunbar's Cove* (New York: Scribner, 1957) and William Bradford Huie's *Mud on the Stars* (New York: L. B. Fischer, 1942). However, while these books narrate TVA dam building's impact on rural life in the Tennessee Valley, neither feature any character comparable to Ella Garth in her resolute opposition to TVA.

8. Aubrey Solomon, *Twentieth Century Fox: A Corporate and Financial History* (Lanham, MD: Scarecrow Press, 1989), 252.

9. National Defense Act of 1916, Pub. L. No. 64-85, 39 Stat. 166 (1916).

10. Preston J. Hubbard, *Origins of the TVA: The Muscle Shoals Controversy* (Nashville: Vanderbilt University Press, 1960).
11. Hubbard, *Origins of the TVA*.
12. Leland R. Johnson, *Engineers on the Twin Rivers: A History of the Nashville District, Corps of Engineers* (Nashville: US Army District, 1978), 9–186; also see David P. Billington and Donald C. Jackson, *Big Dams of the New Deal Era: A Confluence of Engineering and Politics* (Norman: University of Oklahoma Press, 2006), 84–91.
13. McGraw, *TVA and the Public Power Fight*, 27–34; Franklin D. Roosevelt, "Campaign Address in Portland, Oregon on Public Utilities and Development of Hydro-Electric Power," September 21, 1932, American Presidency Project, UC Santa Barbara, Santa Barbara, California, https://www.presidency.ucsb.edu/node/289311.
14. FDR speech to National Emergency Council, December 11, 1934, quoted in Michael J. McDonald and John Muldowny, *TVA and the Dispossessed: The Resettlement of Population in the Norris Dam Area* (Knoxville: University of Tennessee Press, 1982), 263.
15. McGraw, *TVA and the Public Power Fight*, 86; Neufeld, *Selling Power*, 203.
16. FDR speech, December 11, 1934, quoted in McDonald and Muldowny, *TVA and the Dispossessed*, 263.
17. McDonald and Muldowny, *TVA and the Dispossessed*, 4.
18. McDonald and Muldowny, *TVA and the Dispossessed*, 108.
19. Laura Beth Daws and Susan Brinson, *The Greater Good: Media, Family Removal, and TVA Dam Construction in Northern Alabama* (Tuscaloosa: University of Alabama Press, 2019), 105, 109.
20. McDonald and Muldowny, *TVA and the Dispossessed*, 125.
21. It should be noted that privately financed hydroelectric projects could also be granted powers of eminent domain, allowing the forced displacement of landowners on grounds that a reservoir would provide a valuable public service. Such displacements were contingent upon "fair" compensation for property owners, but this was no different than a government-financed project like Norris Dam. *Wild River* narrates a dispute between a governmental agency and a private landowner, but many of the same essential issues could have arisen in a story pitting a private power company (with powers of eminent domain) against private property owners.
22. Eisenhower's opposition to TVA is described in Aaron Wildavsky, *Dixon-Yates: A Study in Power Politics* (New Haven, CT: Yale University Press, 1962).
23. Elia Kazan, *A Life* (New York: Doubleday, 1988), 101–104, 128–33, 440–43, 448–66.
24. Kazan, *A Life*, 896–97.
25. Arthur Meier Schlesinger Jr., *The Age of Roosevelt: The Politics of Upheaval*, vol. 3 (New York: Houghton Mifflin, 1960), 373.
26. Byron E. Pearson, *Still the Wild River Runs: Congress, the Sierra Club, and the Fight to Save Grand Canyon* (Tucson: University of Arizona Press, 2002); Robert D. Lifset, *Power on the Hudson: Storm King Mountain and the Emergence of Modern American Environmentalism* (Pittsburgh: Pittsburgh University Press, 2014); Teresa Sabol Spezio, *Slick Policy: Environmental and Science Policy in the Aftermath of the Santa Barbara Oil Spill* (Pittsburgh: Pittsburgh University Press, 2014).
27. *Wild River* accrued gross rentals of about $1.5 million, which was close to its production cost. In the end, the studio essentially broke even on the film as a financial venture. "Rental Potentials of 1960," *Variety*, January 4, 1961, 47.

28. Schickel, *Elia Kazan*, 369. In a caustic review, nationally syndicated columnist Dorothy Kilgallen offers evidence that studio executives rightly appraised the film's potential mass appeal: "Mr. Kazan's new movie 'Wild River' isn't advertised as a mystery, but that's what it is. The mystery: Why would anyone want to do a full length drama on the problems of the Tennessee Valley Authority? . . . He established in the first five minutes of the film that an old lady living on an island in Tennessee didn't want to sell her property to the TVA, and almost an hour later the situation remained unchanged. And who cares?" Dorothy Kilgallen, "On Broadway," *Pittsburgh Post-Gazette*, May 30, 1960. In contrast, a highly favorable review appeared in the *Philadelphia Inquirer*: "*Wild River* [is] Elia Kazan's moving, stunningly performed study of rugged individualism at war with the forces of paternalistic government. . . . Jo Van Fleet makes a powerful bid for an academy award." "Capsule Film Reviews," *Philadelphia Inquirer*, June 5, 1960.

29. The *New York Times* noted that "[Kazan] distracts a viewer with a romance that shares importance with the social and economic upheaval that unquestionably is closest to the heart of this movie matter." A. H. Weiler, "Kazan Film is Drawn from Two Novels," *New York Times*, May 27, 1960.

30. McGraw specifically notes that TVA "had a unique opportunity to ameliorate the racial situation [in the Tennessee Valley but] made little effort to do so, despite repeated protests from the NAACP." *TVA and the Power Fight*, 61.

31. "Librarian of Congress Adds 25 Films to National Film Registry," December 17, 2002, Library of Congress, Washington, DC, https://www.loc.gov/item/prn-02 -176/. Prior to this, Kazan received an Oscar for Lifetime Achievement in 1998, with Scorsese and DeNiro serving as on-stage presenters. Because of Kazan's HUAC testimony, his appearance at the Academy Awards prompted protest from some Academy members who did not wish to celebrate someone who had, in their view, facilitated Hollywood "blacklisting" in the era of Joe McCarthy. "Elia Kazan Receiving an Honorary Oscar," 71st Annual Academy Awards, March 21, 1999, YouTube video, 3:19, https://www.youtube.com/watch?v=3YziNNCZeNs; Patrick Goldstein, "Many Refuse to Clap as Kazan Receives Oscar," *Los Angeles Times*, March 22, 1999, https://www.latimes.com/archives/la-xpm-1999-mar-22-mn -19738-story.html.

Chapter 10

Do Action Movies and Environmental Messages Mix? About as Much as Oil and Water: *On Deadly Ground* (1994)

Teresa Sabol Spezio

There are many movies with environmental messages but few, if any, action movies have met this challenge. In 1993, Steven Seagal attempted to make an action movie with an environmental message with his directorial debut, *On Deadly Ground* (1994). The early 1990s were an opportune time to develop a movie with a grandiose environmental villain, especially one from the oil industry. In 1989, the *Exxon Valdez* oil tanker split open and polluted Prince William Sound in Alaska with millions of gallons of crude oil. Soon after, in the early 1990s, the First Gulf War accentuated the US economy's dependence on imported oil and the pollution from hundreds of Kuwaiti oil wells blown up during Saddam Hussein's retreat led to untold ecological devastation. Thus, Hussein and Exxon's CEO were perfect targets for the "all-or-nothing" and "good-versus-evil" dichotomies of the action movie genre. Mix the anxieties of the early 1990s over oil dependence and pollution with some good old-fashioned "slash-and-burn" violence, throw in a protagonist whose environmental sensibilities are awakened during the action, and there is a chance for environmental redemption for both the action movie hero (as well as the audience). But is this genre, with its death, destruction, and mayhem, an appropriate avenue for a message of environmental protection?

In this essay, I argue that although *On Deadly Ground* was poorly directed and ravaged by critics, it is the action movie genre itself that prevents an adequate cinematic representation of the world's complex relationship with oil in the 1990s. In *On Deadly Ground*, Seagal fails on three counts. First, the explosions and mayhem of any action movie pollute and harm the surrounding ecosystems—in this case, the very ecosystems the narrative attempts to protect. Second, because the American public's relationship with oil was fraught with ambiguity and fear in the early 1990s, vilifying the *domestic* production of oil after the First Gulf War complicates the environmental message of the movie. And third, Seagal's antipollution message gets lost in the movie's overall incoherence. *On Deadly Ground* thus demonstrates that action movies and environmental messaging do not mix.

Creating *On Deadly Ground*

In 1994, Steven Seagal was an action hero at the peak of his stardom. Two years earlier, Seagal starred in *Under Siege*, which grossed $83 million in the United States and $156 million worldwide.[1] The movie was nominated for two technical Oscars, for sound and sound effects editing, made more money than the Harrison Ford–led *Patriot Games* (1992), and was number 13 in box office sales. Warner Brothers considered Seagal a meal ticket, hoping for another Bruce Willis or Harrison Ford, whose roles as John McClane (*Die Hard* and its many sequels) and Jack Ryan (*Patriot Games* and *Clear and Present Danger*), respectively, expanded to create franchises and brought in millions of dollars for 20th Century Fox and Paramount Pictures. In fact, it has been reported that *Under Siege* was initially pitched as *Die Hard* on a battleship.[2] As with many male actors with strong box office hits, Warner Brothers signed Seagal to a four-picture contact—a type of deal that usually included a vanity project that gave the male actor directorial control over his next film. Some, like Kevin Costner's *Dances with Wolves* (1990), became Oscar winners and made millions.

From the beginning of production, Seagal wanted his directorial debut to be an action movie with an environmental message. Throughout development and production, he lobbied to end the movie with a speech that discussed the perils of oil production and the need for alternative technologies. In reviews of the movie, critics stated that the final speech was planned to be between ten and fourteen minutes long, but the studios balked at its length. Seagal worked with screenwriters Ed Horowitz and Robin U. Russin to create a story that included an evil oil industry CEO and a race against the threat of catastrophic oil pollution on the North Slope of Alaska. In 1993, when they wrote the script, legal suits addressing the disastrous *Exxon Valdez* spill were still ongoing between Exxon and Alaska residents and Native populations. In this context, an antagonist attempting to further contaminate Alaska's pristine waters had the potential to fit into the simple narrative of an action movie. The story also allowed the action hero to save the people and the environment with few complications. Of course, what the writers failed to take into consideration was that they had to blow up the forest and tundra and spill millions of gallons of oil into the water to "save" the environment from the oil industry's pollution.

Action movies were a fairly new genre in the early 1990s. According to film writer Eric Lichtenfeld, action movies are derived from both Westerns and film noir. From Westerns, the genre takes the lone hero seeking justice but working outside the law using violence; from film noir, it takes the flawed male antihero who attempts but often fails to understand his modern and contemporary surroundings.[3] Many consider Don Siegel's *Dirty Harry* (1971) to be the first modern action movie. Siegel introduces Inspector "Dirty" Harry Callahan as a lone vigilante who fights the film's villain, Scorpio, as well as the largely unseen mayor of San Francisco. Significantly, Harry is played by Clint Eastwood, who made his fame in Westerns, now in modern San Francisco pursuing the same kind of justice. With this direct tie to Westerns, Harry is very much an antihero, shunning modern ideas of justice as he fights city hall and catches Scorpio. Moreover, with an obsessive use of violence and the predator/prey relationship between Harry and Scorpio, *Dirty Harry* created the action movie genre.

In addition, the movie incorporates what film scholar Rikke Schubart argues are central to the genre: passion and acceleration. Harry is emotionally invested in catching the villain and rectifying injustice. In fact, the viewer never glimpses Harry's life outside of work. He is a martyr, the only person with the ability to prevail against Scorpio and the system that protects him.[4] As Harry fights to stop Scorpio's killing spree, Seagal intensifies the action and violence throughout the movie until its final climax, when Harry kills Scorpio and then throws away his police badge. Employing a now standard feature of the genre, the director cycles from drama to action, never letting the audience wait more than ten minutes between action sequences. These methodically timed scenes create tension, constantly reminding the audience that this is not film noir or a police procedural; it is an action movie.

The action genre is about the hunt and, ultimately, the redemption of the hero. Such films certainly engage critical issues, but because they prioritize the frenzied thrill of destruction and violence, issues generally take a back seat. Although *Dirty Harry is* now part of the Library of Congress National Film Registry, no viewer would argue that *Dirty Harry* is a statement about the status of the criminal justice system in the United States. Likewise, with *On Deadly Ground*, Seagal attempted to use a film genre that lacks nuance to critique oil—a substance that powers the world's economy, particularly during the era in which he produced the movie.

Oil in the 1990s

In 1992, the same time that Seagal was developing *On Deadly Ground*, Amitav Ghosh wrote in a piece, considered seminal to the field of petroculture studies, that few people truly understand oil and its exploration and production. Ghosh asserts that these activities are removed from view, as US-based (and now multinational) corporations travel to faraway lands to penetrate the earth with grotesque machinery to obtain a dirty liquid that the corporations steal and then transport to far-off locations for use by Americans and Europeans, leaving behind pollution, poverty, and instability. Within this context, Ghosh remarks on the muteness of the oil worker. Few tell their stories. He blames some of it on the banality of their circumstances in the Middle East, where corporations create entire Western style complexes for their workers so they do not experience new cultures. The places are hidden away from the insecurity of the oil fields and the surrounding landscapes. Using fiction writing as his lens, Ghosh argues that for these reasons, few writing programs have the knowledge to assist students in understanding the geopolitical, technical, and environmental entanglements required to tell stories that transcend these complications.[5]

According to Peter Hitchcock, social critics and observers were seeing and experiencing something new in the early 1990s. Oil, the lifeblood of twentieth-century society and culture, had become a weapon to destabilize a world that had just overthrown Communism and ended the Cold War. With the Soviet Union vanquished, the next wars would be over resources, and, indeed, the oil industry and its drive for profits became the catalyst for war, instability, and pollution.[6] In the years leading up to the First Gulf War, the US avoided direct intervention in the Iran-Iraq War, but Iraq's invasion of Kuwait in 1990 forced the George H. W. Bush administration's hand. The US launched Operation Desert Storm in January 1991. With Kuwait, Iraq would have possessed 20 percent of the world's petroleum reserves, and the US assault punished Hussein for adding volatility to the world's oil market. While Hussein had expected to escape sanctions from the US and the United Nations Security Council, he miscalculated the role of oil and oil hegemony in post–Cold War geopolitics.[7] With the UN Security Council's unanimous vote for economic sanctions, Hussein quickly became a pariah. The rules of global politics were indeed changing.

The Bush administration never specifically stated that protecting the oil industry's investments in Kuwait and other Middle Eastern countries was the sole reason for the war. However, many critics and protesters accused them of it. Analysts at the time instead used phrases like "a war of resources" or the desire of Saddam Hussein to make Iraq a global superpower. The first combat activities after the Cold War were about oil production and control. Protests against the hostilities concentrated on its connection to oil, as demonstrators took to the streets shouting, "No blood for oil!" One of the most iconic cartoons from the era lampooned Bush's statement about the reasons for the war with oil company logos: "We *SHELL* not *EXXON*erate Saddam Hussein for his actions. We will *MOBIL*ize to meet this threat to our vital interests in the Persian *GULF* until an *AMOCO*ble solution is reached."[8] Although historians and others have argued that US involvement in twentieth-century wars and foreign policy revolved around access to oil, the First Gulf War laid the argument bare.[9] Protesters and critics believed that American soldiers were dying to protect oil companies' profits. Moreover, gas prices increased and never again dropped below $1 per gallon for the American consumer, and a lack of transparency regarding how oil was delivered to the gas pump made the post–Cold War resource wars even more complicated.

After achieving "victory" in 1991, television viewers watched a different type of devastation unfold in the region. As Iraqi troops pulled out of Kuwait, they detonated more than eight hundred oil production wells, leaving 656 wells ablaze and 74 spewing oil. Approximately 42 billion gallons of crude oil were ultimately either spilled or burned.[10] Inky smoke blackened the sky, polluting the air with sulfur dioxide, nitrogen oxide, and carbon dioxide and covering land, homes, and bodies with oil, particulates, and ash. The oil well fires provided the American imagination with a nonmilitary hero: oil well firefighters, specifically Red Adair. Adair, a Texan and World War II veteran, had made a career fighting oil well fires for close to fifty years.[11] Over six months, Adair and his crew (among others) worked to control and extinguish fires in Kuwait. Although defeated and ousted from Kuwait, Hussein had gotten his revenge on the United States and local governments, showing how easy it was to create instability in the world's oil market.

On the domestic side, the United States was confronting the role of oil and its pollution on many fronts. In January 1988, a newly installed 1 million gallon oil storage tank in Floreffe, Pennsylvania, catastrophically failed and released approximately 750,000 gallons of oil into the Monongahela River, about twenty-five miles upstream from Pittsburgh.[12] The oil flowed into the Ohio River and through Pittsburgh, Wheeling, and Cincinnati during the months of January and February, until it eventually dispersed and diluted into the Mississippi River. The resulting spill caused more than 1 million people to be without water for up to eight days and the death of countless fish and birds. Just fifteen months later, the *Exxon Valdez* grounded in Prince William Sound.

The spill covered the sound with oil, killed innumerable birds and marine organisms, destroyed the ecosystem, and devastated the commercial fishing industry as well as the subsistence traditions of Alaskan Native groups.

In response, Congress passed and George H. W. Bush signed two major pieces of legislation. The Oil Pollution Act of 1990 (OPA) dealt directly with the two disasters. The bill required oil storage facilities and tankers to develop detailed plans to respond to catastrophic spills and created detailed regulations for the storage and handling of oil in aboveground storage tanks and oil tankers.[13] Moving beyond industrial processes, Congress and the Bush administration also concentrated their efforts on air pollution from automobiles and trucks. The Clean Air Act of 1990 (CAA) addressed the major reason for the United States economy's reliance on fossil fuels—cars, trucks, and buses. The CAA established standards that reduced cars' tailpipe emissions and required the use of new technologies for bus fleets, which would eventually pave the way for hybrid, plug-in hybrid, and electric vehicles.[14] Thus, although the early 1990s was a time of heightened cultural awareness of oil and its environmental and geopolitical effects in the US and abroad, the issues were multifaceted, complex, and ultimately unknown.

On Deadly Ground and the Limitations of the Action Movie Genre

How did writers and filmmakers make sense of this new geopolitical reality? As Hitchcock shows, few if any movies address the First Gulf War, providing only *Courage under Fire* (1996), *Three Kings* (1999), and *Jarhead* (2005) as examples. He argues that filmmakers who attempted to confront the changing and unfamiliar geopolitics of the early 1990s ultimately failed.[15] Seagal—developing *On Deadly Ground* just as oil had become the driver for global conflict—was no exception.

Although *On Deadly Ground* does not deal directly with the First Gulf War, it does confront the hegemony of the oil industry and its ubiquity in American culture. Having replaced Communism as the new villain in international relations, Seagal and the screenwriters must have believed that using the oil industry as the antagonist in an action movie was a slam dunk. But while the movie's aims were in line with concurrent problems in the oil industry and its complicity in worldwide pollution and instability, they unfortunately did not account for how Americans' views on oil production had changed. Namely, due to the oil spills and the resulting regulations, by 1994 domestic production enabled a way to avoid the geopolitical conflicts associated with foreign oil. Accordingly, *On Deadly Ground* is set (and filmed) in Alaska, a dominant site of domestic oil production and of the recent *Exxon Valdez* spill. Yet despite the aptness of this setting for depicting oil's environmental devastation, the limitations of the action movie genre hurt the narrative, which, to make matters worse, further suffers under Seagal's almost incoherent direction. These shortcomings ultimately prevent the movie from effectively conveying a coherent environmental message.

Seagal begins the movie with spectacular views of snow-covered mountains, a bald eagle, and a polar bear. Although these species were not directly impacted by the *Exxon Valdez* grounding, the bald eagle was considered an endangered species in 1994, and the US Fish and Wildlife Service elevated its status to threatened one year later, while the polar bear's habitat has been affected by the climate crisis.[16] The images do evoke photographs used to show Prince William Sound before the *Exxon Valdez* spill. There is no doubt that Seagal is playing to environmentalists with these scenes of the pristine Alaskan wilderness.

The movie then cuts to a chaotic oil well blowout in which three crew members are killed. Forrest Taft, the movie's protagonist, played by Seagal himself, methodically contains the blowout with a large explosion (the first of many) that prevents more oil from escaping the wellhead. The first image of Taft highlights his cowboy boots, signaling the action genre's Western roots. In addition, by centering the movie on an oil well firefighter in the vein of Red Adair, Seagal is counting on his viewers to accept Taft as an environmental hero. With these two scenes, Seagal establishes that the oil industry is polluting the land and stealing resources from Native peoples, but Taft's response—the explosion—foreshadows that he will, contrary to Seagal's intention, actually pollute the environment as much as his oil industry villain.

Over the next ninety-five minutes, the viewer watches the story of Aegis Oil, a company that plans to begin production at a large oil well and refinery on the North Slope of Alaska, and Native Alaskans' struggle to stop its opening. Aegis Oil has fewer than twelve days to begin production from the well (Aegis-1) or the company's title to the oil rights will return to the Alaskan Natives. The deadline forces the company to cut corners, and CEO Michael Jennings (played by Michael Caine) orders his workers to use faulty blowout preventers—the source of the blowout that caused three employees' deaths and thousands of gallons of oil to spill into the Pacific Ocean at the movie's start. When Taft learns that the blowout preventers for Aegis-1 are compromised, he asks Jennings for a clarification. In response, Jennings plots to kill Taft, sending him to a sabotaged well, where he narrowly escapes an explosion. Taft is rescued by a group of Inuit and, while with them, goes through a "vision quest" that endears him to the chief. Taft then travels with the chief's daughter

Masu (played by Joan Chen) to the North Slope to stop Aegis-1's production. Taft and Masu battle Aegis-hired mercenaries using explosives, rocket launchers, and guns through the Alaskan rainforests and tundra. They make it to the well and methodically destroy it, the refinery, and every structure in the area before it can be brought into production. The movie ends with Taft's speech in front of an audience preaching about the dangers of oil production and the need for new technologies that do not pollute the air and water.

Since the debut of *Dirty Harry*, the violence in action movies has exponentially increased to include explosions and other forms of pyrotechnics while continuing to amplify the hero as an emotionally flawed loner, working for justice outside the boundaries of the law. Believing in his cause and relying on violent and explosive methods, Seagal's Taft clearly fits the bill. Moreover, as a student of action movies, Seagal uses the genre's interval method (one scene focusing on the drama, followed by one spotlighting action), the story crisscrossing between environmental-themed narrative scenes and those in which Taft and his adversaries harm the land and people that Seagal purportedly wants to protect. This cyclical structure, so essential to action movies, impedes his ability to concentrate on the environmental message.

In addition, considering the genre's need for a simple narrative in which the flawed hero finds redemption or deliverance, the oil industry has the potential to be a successful action movie antagonist, with or without a message. From each violent scene, Seagal switches to a series of scenes that tie directly to the oil industry's role in Alaska. One involves Aegis CEO Jennings preparing to shoot a commercial, during which he yells and condescends to everyone around him. When his staff explains that the networks will be leading with the spill and that "EPA, OSHA, and the Department of Environmental Concerns" will be investigating the accident that killed three people, Jennings responds, "For God's sake, why all the heat? It's a small oil spill. Accidents happen." [17] Immediately following this retort, Jennings walks onto a sound stage to create a commercial demonstrating that Aegis Oil cares about the environment. Caine does a remarkable job transforming from a heartless corporate executive to a corporate leader who purportedly loves and safeguards the Alaskan wilderness. In one take, he speaks of his love for the porcupine caribou, asserting that Aegis Oil believes in protecting them and the earth. Jennings tenderly pets the caribou, but when the taping ends, he barks that they stink and walks away.

The fictive Aegis commercial bluntly ties the movie to one of the reactions to the *Exxon Valdez* spill. In response to criticisms observing that using double-hulled tankers would have prevented the spill, the federal government required all new oil tankers built for use between US ports be double-hulled. In 1990, Dupont-Conoco developed a commercial that included clapping seals and otters, dancing dolphins, flipping orcas, and other wildlife celebrating their use of double-hulled tankers.[18] The commercial pioneered the use of greenwashing by industrial corporations since it ignored the fact that double-hulled tankers were not new technology and the oil industry had for years hindered their rollout because of cost. At the same time, though, the American Petroleum Institute opposed congressional attempts to mandate double hulls, and while many environmental groups lauded Conoco's use of them, Friends of the Earth and others published criticisms of the commercial as it related to Dupont and Conoco's corporate malfeasance.[19] Later, Seagal makes another allusion to DuPont in the movie when Taft learns that Aegis Oil plans to use abandoned oil wells for underground injection of wastewater. In 1994, Dupont was the leader in the use of underground injection for waste disposal.[20] By including the porcupine caribou in the commercial, Seagal links the movie with another long-running conflict: opening the Arctic National Wildlife Refuge (ANWR) to oil drilling. ANWR is the calving grounds of these animals as well as home to the Gwichyaa Zhee Gwich'in people. Prior to the grounding of the *Exxon Valdez*, Congress had the momentum to open the refuge, but the spill forced congressional leaders to drop the proposal.[21] By 1994, Republicans in Congress were again working to open the refuge for drilling.[22]

The next scene features Jennings gleefully asking his lawyers how to minimize insurance payments to his dead employees. Again, this episode mirrors Exxon's desire to minimize penalties and compensation for the people harmed by the *Exxon Valdez* spill. In 1991, Exxon had agreed to pay $900 million over a ten-year period. After the settlement, individuals worked to sue Exxon for civil damages incurred by fishers and other businesses and residents in the spill's aftermath. As filming *On Deadly Ground* commenced in 1993, federal courts were still determining how to manage the complicated case as Exxon and its lawyers fought to minimize compensation to Alaskan natives and residents.[23] Thus, in a span of less than three minutes, Seagal connects Jennings to corporate greenwashing, the opening of ANWR, the perils of underground injection, and corporate resistance to compensation for oil spill victims. A better director may have been able to gracefully transition from this oil industry critique to the next scene, but the action movie genre requires a return to even more action and mayhem. Therefore, over the next five minutes, Aegis Oil's henchmen torture and kill the well supervisor who informed Taft of the company's malfeasance.

Pivoting to another environmental issue, in the next scene, Jennings is confronted by a member of the tribal council about the poisons and increased rates of cancer and stillbirths from Aegis Oil's activities. Jennings ridicules him and accuses the tribal council of reneging on their agreement for the oil and mineral rights. At that point, Masu throws oil on Jennings's suit and, uses a slight modification of the Gulf War protest slogan "No blood for oil!": "Blood of our people is upon you." He responds, "The hell with the [bleep] Eskimos." One of the movie's fatal flaws that ultimately dilutes the impact of its environmental and Native rights messaging is Seagal's treatment of Native Alaskans. With the success of *Dances with Wolves*, Seagal promised to include Native Alaskan and other Native American actors in the movie and to accurately portray their cultures on screen. However, those cast to play Inuit and other Natives were actually of Japanese and Chinese descent. In addition, although Seagal includes a beautiful short scene in which an Inuit group is shown living in harmony with the ecosystem—one of the few to honor his promise—*On Deadly Ground* contains a number of jumbled cultural inaccuracies that caused pushback from the movie's "cultural advisor" Apanguluk Charlie Kairaiuak and others. The problems are large and small: the erroneous presence of nudity in the context of Native Alaskan rituals and jewelry from the Great Plains tribe, one of the few Native American actors portrays a "drunken Eskimo," the North Slope is in Inupiat territory but the actors speak Yup'ik, and a featured raven tradition originates with the Tligits of southeastern Alaska. Taft's interactions with Intuits and other groups smack of cultural appropriation.[24] In Taft's "vision quest" scene, he sees an old woman representing Mother Earth, who tells him he must save the earth from oil production. Predictably, Mother Earth is not part of Inupiat traditions.

Of course, Seagal and his character's high regard for Native culture disappears due to the rules of a standard action movie. The genre requires more violence and bigger and louder explosions. Despite being in direct conflict with the movie's environmental message, Taft must blow up the earth in order to save it. From that point forward, he destroys more of the Alaskan landscape than Aegis Oil as he travels to the Aegis-1 oil facility, killing Jennings's mercenaries when they attempt to stop his progress, while the audience revels in the just retribution against evil villains and escapes the heavy-handed and confusing environmental sermonizing. As Taft gets closer to stopping the oil well, Jennings describes him as someone that when you "delve down into the deepest bowels of your soul, try to imagine the ultimate (bleeping) nightmare and that won't come close to this son of bitch when he gets pissed." As viewers watch Taft blow up refinery equipment, spill oil into the ocean, and kill his adversaries including Jennings and his attorney, they see that Jennings is right; Taft is a bad guy or, according to the action movie genre, a flawed hero. He manages to stop oil production from Aegis-1, but at what price? He disregards the guidance of the Inuit chief, destroys the pristine arboreal forests with explosions, and causes countless gallons of oil to pollute the ocean.

Seagal ends his movies by pedantically emphasizing his environmental message as Taft speaks to a group of Alaskan Natives about the perils of oil industry hegemony. Footage from the *Exxon Valdez* oil spill and of air and water pollution in US cities accompanies his speech. Stating that "the internal combustion engine has been obsolete for over fifty years," Seagal/Taft goes on to reference the Dupont-Conoco commercial and greenwashing, claiming that oil companies are using the media to "control our minds." By the end of the speech, all eyes are on the hero—Forrest Taft/Steven Seagal—who has the solution to humanity's reliance on oil and the oil industry. Pollution is humanity's fault, and humans need to change. If they would only listen to the hero and follow his lead, humans could overthrow the oil industry and create new, cleaner products. But the hero is covered in oil and blood, as action heroes are supposed to be. Action movies are not about protecting Native cultures and critiquing America's ambiguous relationship with oil after the First Gulf War. The explosions and the resulting escapism are integral to the genre.

Martin Scorsese argues that although action movies are most often at the top at the box office, they are not real films.[25] Seagal and the screenwriters hoped to bring an environmental message to an action movie audience—an audience that relies on an inherently violent and explosive genre to offer an escape from their everyday problems. Is it even possible to effectively convey an environmental message with this genre? *On Deadly Ground* is not the answer, but it does provide some clues. First, screenwriters must work to minimize the amount of environmental destruction in their movies and find other ways to deliver tension and escapism for their viewers. Second, oil and energy production are complex issues that do not have simple answers. In the early 1990s, the American public was struggling with the new reality of the post–Cold War resource wars and their impact on daily life.[26] Therefore, the action movie antagonist must be a straightforward villain, like the Soviet spies in Cold War action movies, not oil industry executives. Third, the movie must have a skillful director, great screenwriters, and good actors. *On Deadly Ground* has none of these characteristics; it is an incoherent movie that won Seagal the Razzie for worst director.

In the 1990s, most humans needed oil for almost every facet of their lives. It was oil that drove politics and conflict. The movie's failings do not lie solely at the feet of the director but also with human's complicated relationship with oil. The movie may be terrible, but it shows that humans want simple solutions to complicated issues, just as Seagal's final speech attempts to provide. The movie reveals that the viewers themselves—humanity—are both part of the problem and the solution; something that an action movie simply may not be able to portray.

Notes

1. "Under Siege," IMDB.com, https://www.imdb.com (June 10, 2019).

2. Everett Weinberger, *Wannabe: A Would-Be Player's Misadventures in Hollywood* (New York: St. Martin's Griffin, 1997), 52.

3. Eric Lichtenfeld, *Action Speaks Louder: Violence, Spectacle, and the American Action Movie* (Middletown: Praeger, 2007), xvi.

4. Lichtenfeld, *Action Speaks Louder*, 27. "Dirty Harry (1971)," accessed December 1, 2019, https://www.imdb.com.

5. Amitav Ghosh, "Petrofiction," *New Republic* 206, no. 9 (1992).

6. Peter Hitchcock, "Oil in an American Imaginary," *New Formations* 69 (Spring 2010): 81–97.

7. R.W. Apple Jr., "Invading Iraqis Seize Kuwait and Its Oil; U.S. Condemns Attack, Urges United Action," *New York Times*, August 3, 1990, https://www.nytimes.com/1990/08/03/world/worldspecial/invading-iraqis-seize-kuwait-and-its-oil-us-condemns.html.

8. See http://besser.tsoa.nyu.edu/T-Shirts/rbkemp/george.jpg, accessed July 12, 2019.

9. David S. Painter, "Oil and the American Century," *Journal of American History* 99, no. 1 (2012): 24–39.

10. Tahir Husain, "Kuwaiti Oil Fires—Source Estimates and Plume Characterization," *Atmospheric Environment* 28, no. 13 (1994): 2149–58.

11. "Obituary: Red Adair," *The Economist*, August 14, 2004, 74. Robert Mowris, "Dousing the Devil's Cigarette Lighter," *Earth Island Journal* 6, no. 3 (1991), 44. See Ila Tyagi's essay "Ranches to Oil Wells: Reconfiguring the Western Hero in *Hellfighters* (1968) and *Fires of Kuwait* (1992) in this volume for information on the heroics of Red Adair.

12. Andrew Sheehan, "Oil Oozes for 33 Miles," *Pittsburgh Post-Gazette*, January 4, 1988, 1; Lynda Guydon, "Oil Affects People, Wildlife; Families in District Evacuated Overnight, *Pittsburgh Post-Gazette*, January 4, 1988, 5; "The Nation: Cincinnati Shuts River Valves as Oil Hits," *Los Angeles Times*, January 25, 1988.

13. Oil Pollution Act of 1990, Public Law 101-380, August 18, 1990.

14. Clean Air Act Amendments of 1990, 104 Stat. 2399, Public Law 101-549, November 15, 1990

15. Hitchcock, "Oil in an American Imaginary," 81–97.

16. US Fish and Wildlife Service, "Fact Sheet: Natural History, Ecology and History of Recovery," March 4, 2019, https://www.fws.gov/midwest/eagle/recovery/biologue.html.

17. Steven Seagal, dir., *On Deadly Ground* (Burbank, CA: Warner Bros., 1994).

18. Dupont-Conoco, "Applause," October 1991, https://www.youtube.com/watch?v=zJZFfeLRCJs.

19. Jack Doyle, *Hold the Applause: A Case Study of Corporate Environmentalism as Practiced at Dupont*, Washington, DC, 1991.

20. Adam Rome, "DuPont and the Limits of Corporate Environmentalism," *Business History Review* 93 (Spring 2019): 87.

21. E. J. Dionne, "Big Oil Spill Leaves Its Mark on Politics of Environment," *New York Times*, April 3, 1989, 1.

22. Bill Clinton would veto a bill to open ANWR in 1996. It would take until 2017 for Republicans to open ANWR for oil drilling, and they needed to bury the opening in

a tax bill that barely passed in the Senate. On the first day of his presidency, January 20, 2021, Joe Biden halted all drilling in ANWR using the power of the executive order. The saga of drilling in ANWR continues.

23. Kathryn Jones, "A Collision in Court on Exxon's Oil Spill," *New York Times*, October 10, 1993, https://www.nytimes.com/1993/10/10/business/a-collision-in-court-on -exxon-s-oil-spill.html.

24. According to the website NativeCelebs.com, Jules Desjarlais identifies as a Metis/ Saulteaux. In the credits, the actor's character is not given a name but only the identifier "drunken Eskimo" (accessed June 22, 2019). Anthony Newman, "Movies: Native Americans and Oil Executives Agree: 'On Deadly Ground' Got Everything Dead Wrong," *Los Angeles Times*, March 4, 1994.

25. Martin Scorsese, "I Said Marvel Movies Aren't Cinema. Let Me Explain," *New York Times*, November 4, 2019, https://www.nytimes.com/2019/11/04/opinion/martin -scorsese-marvel.html.

26. Even in the second decade of the 2000s with the threat of the climate crisis, making oil the antagonist is complicated.

PART 3

Critiquing the Western

Selling the American "Oil Frontier": *Tulsa* (1949), *Giant* (1956), and American Resource Politics during the Early Cold War

Sarah Stanford-McIntyre

Tulsa and *Giant* are sweeping midcentury films that dramatize the early days of American oil exploration. Both are relatively critical of the oil industry.[1] However, they are also politicized vehicles for American free enterprise, elevating oil speculation to the stuff of myth for audiences at home and abroad. Their creators, producer Walter Wanger and director George Stevens, were very conscious of the political power of the moving image, and both had a background in diplomatic service. Walter Wanger was a self-proscribed "New Deal liberal" who served as attaché to Woodrow Wilson at the Paris Peace Conference after World War I. He also saw Hollywood—and his 1949 oil industry epic—as a vehicle to promote America. According to Wanger, *Tulsa* would "spread the good news of what this wonderful country has and what it's willing to do to assist other countries to build up their industries."[2] When *Giant* premiered in 1956, George Stevens had already directed several blockbusters and was well connected in Washington. *Giant* was the third in a trilogy of films that self-consciously addressed the contradictions within American identity.[3] During World War II, Stevens had been a member of the US Army Signal Corps, shooting color footage of the US liberation of Paris, and his wartime experience shaped his filmmaking career. His son and biographer, George Stevens Jr., was the director of the United States Information Agency Motion Picture Service and a close friend of Robert Kennedy's.[4]

Given this context, it is no surprise that the two films have many similarities, reflecting a thematic tension between nostalgia for a transformative period in American industrial history and a critique of the industry's excesses. Both films critique racial and ethnic injustice in early-twentieth-century America. Both feature strong female leads who rail against the limitations of a patriarchal society. And both depict an American oil industry that slowly and inevitably corrupts the individuals who attempt to "play the oil game." Crucially, however, in both cases such heavy-handed social critiques are tempered by lush cinematic spectacles. Wide-screen shots of breathtaking sunsets, sweeping deserts, and towering oil fields draw heavily from the Western genre to create a sense of nostalgia for a mythical American past filled with natural splendor and untapped resource wealth. Both films are set in the early days of midcontinent oil exploration, and explosions, well fires, and gushers showcase oil production as dangerous, exiting, and visually spectacular. According to these films, while the oil industry has its problems, it is also a big, loud, and exciting free-for-all in which anyone can instantly become fabulously rich regardless of background or personal wealth. A quintessentially American enterprise, the oil industry is built off of American land and fundamental to American individualism and success. Understanding the early 1950s as a period of anxiety within the industry over its consolidation and the waning importance of domestic oil production allows us to read both films and their creators as appealing to Cold War nostalgia for a fictional industry past built on limited government interference and domestic resource sovereignty.

An Uneasy Environmentalism

The films' juxtaposition between plot and visual spectacle reflect cultural and political tensions of the early 1950s. Just as President Harry Truman announced the Truman Doctrine in 1947, vowing to support anticommunism abroad through all military and economic means necessary, America became a net oil importer for the first time. Truman made the decision to preserve domestic oil reserves in favor of international exploration, led by American multinationals.[5] This constrained small independent oil producers who did not operate internationally. In 1948, one year before *Tulsa* was released, the discovery of the monumental Ghawar oil field in Saudi Arabia further increased concern among independents in Texas and Oklahoma that their domestic operations were under threat.

In response to these events, American oil companies desperately worked to solidify control over oil reserves both at home and abroad, battling the federal government to control access to untapped oil in the Gulf of Mexico. However, it became increasingly clear that the sheer size of Middle Eastern oil deposits and skyrocketing global consumption had shifted the center of oil production eastward, out of Texas and Oklahoma. The industry's role in US foreign policy would only deepen over the next decade. Standard Oil, Texaco, and other multinationals partnered with the US State Department, the CIA, and other organizations to secure allies—and oil—in the Middle East. Yet nationalist movements in Egypt and Iran would complicate these efforts. For example, just as *Giant* premiered in 1956, Egypt seized and then closed the Suez Canal, creating an oil transport crisis in Europe that foreshowed the oil embargoes and fuel shortages of the 1970s.

The US government and American oil companies met this changing oil landscape with a variety of tools, including widespread public relations campaigns. Both government and private organizations promoted American oil multinationals as vehicles for anticommunist foreign policy and as demonstrative of American business success. The industry lobbyist group the American Petroleum Institute and the US State Department were quick to counter any foreign and domestic industry criticism by reminding the public that Standard, Texaco, and other large companies had been crucial partners during World War II, helping the military to coordinate infrastructure that very literally fueled American victory. They praised the industry as a tool of American foreign aid and development. *Tulsa* and *Giant* were released into this mix, soothing public concerns by looking backward to draw a through line between American multinationals of the 1950s and independent wildcatters of the early 1900s.

Tulsa was released in 1949, at the beginning of this period, and anxiety about the changing American oil industry can be felt in the film. While the plot is tinged with deep nostalgia for the independent, locally autonomous American wildcatters of the early twentieth century, it is also highly critical of the industry's culture of greed and the environmental consequences of intemperate oil exploration. The film opens with a scene of towering conflagration as a gusher well disrupts the bucolic life of rancher Cherokee Lansing, played by Susan Hayward. The name is descriptive, as Lansing quickly informs the audience that she is Native American with deep roots in Oklahoma. Lansing then discovers that her prized Hereford cattle have been killed, poisoned by stream water contaminated with drilling waste. Her father attempts to confront the perpetrator, Bruce Tanner (Lloyd Gough) of Tanner Petroleum, only to be killed by an explosion from the same offending well. In a bid for revenge, Lansing thrusts herself into the dangerous world of oil prospecting. She hopes to strike oil before Tanner is able to profit from the oil beneath her land. Along the way, she meets self-assured geologist Brad Brady (Robert Preston), who convinces her to pair her money with his scientific knowledge to strike it rich. The two fall in love. However, this is not a simple Horatio Alger story. Over the second half of the film, Lansing slowly devolves into the same kind of greedy, amoral petrocapitalist who had caused her pain and suffering, gambling with both lives and fortunes in the spirit of competition. At the end of the film, Lansing's cousin Jim Redbird (Pedro Armendáriz) sets her oilfields afire, seemingly purifying the land and freeing Lansing—and his people—from the corrupting forces of oil.

Through this narrative, *Tulsa* engages with period industry criticisms. The American environmental movement expanded rapidly in the postwar era.[6] *Tulsa* appeared at the same moment as Marjory Stoneman Douglas's *The Everglades* (1947) and Aldo Leopold's *A Sand County Almanac* (1949). Both wildly popular, these books saw America's irreplaceable natural beauty threatened by human development and called for conservation. Similarly, by the end of the 1940s oil companies were already well-established villains in American cinema. In films such as *Oil for the Lamps of China* (1935), *Black Gold* (1936), *Boom Town* (1940), and *Conquest of Cheyenne* (1946), oil development alternately stood in for American corporate greed, moral corruption, environmental exploitation, and hubristic foreign policy. Echoing Douglas's and Leopold's sense of loss, such energy cinema most often represents the oil landscape as the antithesis of the natural or the beautiful. The industry is analogous to a natural disaster, as the viscous black fluid pumped out of the ground destroys nearby plant and animal life. Even as oil's circulation and sale built a new economic lifecycle of royalties, rents, and further investments, its landscapes were also dead zones, and according to these films, those physically closest to their source were often deeply harmed by the industry.[7]

We see some of this tradition in *Tulsa*. The film was shot in Technicolor on location near Ada, Oklahoma. Oklahoma governor and oilman Roy Turner lent his ten-thousand-acre ranch to the production team, intending for the film to showcase Oklahoma as a prime spot for future Hollywood Westerns.[8] The film makes full use of the landscape. *Tulsa* opens on a scene of the ultimate American pastoral. Cherokee Lansing rides through rolling, vividly green hills under a blue sky. Fields of waving tall grasses are dotted with placidly munching cattle. Both roads and significant human populations are notably absent. Such preindustrial bliss is shattered, however, by the discovery of the bloated carcasses of the Lansings' dead Herefords. In a foreshadowing of cataclysmic oil fires to come, Jim Redbird ignites the oil slick on top of the contaminated water. Throughout the remainder of the film, Oklahoma's natural beauty is juxtaposed with the degradation of industrialization. At mid-film, the sea of oil derricks on the Tanner fields are as ominous as they are awe-inspiring. Detailed watercolor backdrops and panoramic camerawork make the Lansings and their employees tiny as they work amid a hulking field of derricks.

However, *Tulsa* refuses to completely villainize the industry. In fact, Wagner's initial plans for the film did not include an industry critique at all. Rather, he planned to produce a film that would act as a "celebration of robust capitalism" and "showcase American free industry and enterprise." [9] The film was supposed to be the first in a series on the "American free enterprise system" that would "show the entire world how great America was." Planned *Tulsa* sequels included films on the airline industry, the free press, and coal mining.[10]

In this context, it is not surprising that the film counters environmental destruction with images of grand hotels and rowdy saloons, depicting a boom-town-era Tulsa teaming with life. The city is full of exciting and colorful people celebrating the possibility of future wealth. Midcentury Western singer and actor Chill Wills narrates the film and appears in full cowboy regalia to lead a folksy barroom sing-along. Later in the film, geologist Brad Brady implies that such exuberance and resource stability can exist in tandem, dimming the lights to provide both on- and off-screen audiences with a slide presentation on resource conservation.

Crucially, however, in contrast to the measured, scientific petroleum engineer, *Tulsa* depicts Native American landholders as impulsive, emotional, and irresponsible. Cherokee's more stereotypically Indian relatives and neighbors, represented predominately by Mexican actor Pedro Armendáriz and Italian American Iron Eyes Cody, are unable to resist the corrupting forces of oil wealth. Midway through Cherokee's drilling efforts, Iron Eyes Cody arrives in an expensive red convertible to announce that he wants drilling to speed up. Other Native landholders dismiss appeals for communal resource conservation in the name of immediate gratification. Later, Cherokee's cousin Jim is destructively ruled by his emotions, as his love for Cherokee and distaste for oil lead him to arson. In a scene of breathtaking visual chaos, flames consume an entire field of closely spaced wooden derricks. As Jim looks on, his face locked in a rictus grin bathed in the blaze's light, Cherokee and her employees work desperately to extinguish the rising flames. Smoke billows from hundreds of derricks, which begin crashing to the ground in cataclysmic explosions.

Such stereotypes have a long history in America's paternalistic and exploit-ative relationship with Native peoples. These are particularly damning in light of the infamous Osage murders, in which a number of Native American oil royalty holders were killed under mysterious circumstances in 1920s Oklahoma. Scholars such as Robin Murray and Joseph Heumann have argued that this history—and the spectacle of towering conflagration at the end of the film—fatally detracts from *Tulsa*'s attempt at industry critique.[11] Although this is true, the postwar global petroleum landscape provides further context for the film's mixed messages.

Through both visual and narrative means, *Tulsa* suggests that while intemperate oil production can be destructive, a properly managed oil industry ultimately brings life, excitement, and culture to previously sleepy settlements. With such a juxtaposition, *Tulsa* sells the industry using the same strain of Cold War corporate paternalism promoted by the American Petroleum Institute, the State Department, and other oil industry advocates after World War II. In an era of growing fear that oil-producing nations would nationalize their resource wealth, the US marketed American oil exploration in the Middle East as a humanitarian expedition. According to industry publications, American petroleum engineers would not only drill for oil but also provide needed technical know-how to better the lives of "primitive peoples." They promised to build infrastructure, improve healthcare, and build schools.[12]

Tulsa audiences were likely intended to make a comparison between irresponsible Native royalty holders in early-twentieth-century Oklahoma and growing 1950s tensions between the United States and Saudi Arabia, Iran, and other oil-rich postcolonial nations. Jim Redbird's spectacular arson attempt might be read as a statement of Native sovereignty, using fire in a purifying effort to return Oklahoma to a preindustrial, preconquest ideal. However, presented alongside Brad Brady's scientifically backed and carefully detailed plans for long-term energy extraction, Redbird's actions become the self-destructive, impulsive revenge of a jilted lover. Similarly, while filmmakers probably assumed audiences would agree that oil nationalization was impulsive and unnecessary, viewers outside of American oil-producing regions were unlikely to follow the film's allusions to industry conflicts between independent domestic producers and the multinationals. Other midcentury concerns, such as the strain that Middle Eastern oil production placed on carefully negotiated domestic proration agreements, were not referenced. As a result, Brady provides audiences with simplified answers to complex industry controversies couched within *Tulsa*'s nostalgic vision of the global oil industry. According to *Tulsa*, the path to global energy stability is through support for measured, rational energy extraction led by American oil companies, which could maintain prosperity for all.

Oil Progress Is Inevitable?

The early days of midcontinent oil exploration continued to appear in cultural productions and debates about oil's role in the American Cold War project. Into this mix, an ongoing battle between the state of Texas, oil producers, and the federal government increasingly concerned US oil companies. In 1949, President Truman declared all subsurface oil along the Gulf of Mexico's continental shelf to be the property of the US federal government. In his announcement, Truman cited his newly articulated Truman Doctrine and the need to secure military oil reserves in the event of a war with the Soviet Union.[13] Not satisfied with such expediency, oil companies in Texas and Louisiana were angered at what they saw as a clear usurpation of local sovereignty—and a threat to their profit margins. In their minds, while the largest American oil companies continued to reap massive profits abroad, the nascent domestic offshore industry floundered due to federal interference. Called the Tidelands controversy, the issue wound its way through the courts for the next several years, with Texas governors and senators campaigning heavily against federal control.

In 1952, four years into the Tidelands battle, best-selling novelist Edna Ferber wrote *Giant* based upon extensive field research among Texas's nouveau-riche oil elites. The book caused a sensation, and in 1956 *Giant* was adapted into a major motion picture. While *Tulsa* was produced by Eagle Lion, a British movie house that made "respectable" B films, *Giant* was produced by Warner Bros. and starred some of the biggest Hollywood actors of the day, including Elizabeth Taylor, Rock Hudson, and James Dean. *Giant* was directed by Oscar nominee George Stevens, who would go on to chair the Academy of Motion Picture Arts and Sciences. Stevens saw the oil industry as a backdrop from which to explore larger philosophical and moral issues. Like *Tulsa*, *Giant* employs spectacular visual aesthetics and didactic social criticism to generate a conflicted message about the American oil industry. And, as in *Tulsa*, *Giant* is also steeped in the Cold War energy politics of the early 1950s.

Giant tells the sweeping tale of the mixed blessings and curses of oil and power for one wealthy Texas family. Rancher Bick Benedict Jr. (Rock Hudson) marries Maryland socialite Leslie Lynton (Elizabeth Taylor) after a whirlwind romance. They return to Texas where rough-and-tumble ranch hand Jett Rink (James Dean) falls in unrequited love with Leslie. After Bick's older sister Luz is killed in a fall from Leslie's horse, Rink inherits a small patch of Bick's expansive ranch, the Riata. He strikes oil on this land, immediately attempting to win Leslie's heart with his newfound wealth. Although he is rebuffed, Rink's fortune grows over the next several years, and it becomes clear that wealth only amplifies his many demons. In contrast, Benedict patriarch Bick attempts to uphold his own honor and confronts race and class inequity in midcentury Texas. His son falls in love with a Tejano woman, and after overcoming his own bigotry, Bick becomes a defender of their relationship.

Time passes. Both families grow. And the Benedicts and the Rinks continue to feud. Many times, Bick refuses to allow Jett to drill for oil on the Riata, attempting to maintain the family's ranching traditions. When Bick ultimately permits oil drilling on Benedict land, much to his chagrin, oil only makes the Rink family even more wealthy and powerful. The film ends with a final confrontation between the two men after Jett refuses to allow Bick's Tejano relatives into his newly built glamorous hotel. In these closing scenes, Jett has become an isolated alcoholic. Publicly embarrassing himself with his bigotry and drunken rambling, he has come to embody the worst of Texas oil excess.

Oil lurks in the background throughout the film, a catalyst that amplifies individual failings and virtues. Oil is the fuel that prevents social stagnation and allows agrarian traditions to continue. However, in the wrong hands it is also a lubricant for excess, embarrassment, and personal alienation. While the catalyst is oil, the film seeks to provide more universal commentary on wealth and the seeming immutability of racial and class divisions in America. In doing so, *Giant* paints oil as the quintessential American industry and the narrative pushes forward with a self-conscious sense of inevitability. It is not a question of *if* oil will be drilled on the Riata, but a question of *when*. The film takes place over a span of thirty years and has a similarly lengthy running time of 201 minutes. Texas oil production grows and the industry expands during this time. While Stevens clearly wants audiences to critique the moral failings of this process, neither resource depletion nor an end to Texas's preeminence are in sight.

Ferber's novel was the result of field research in Texas during the 1940s, and her narrative choices reflect this high point in Texas oil production. The characters are amalgamations of real people. Bick Benedict is Bob Kleberg, and the Riata parallels his massive 8.25 million acre King Ranch in far South Texas. Kleberg inherited the ranch through marriage in the 1880s and expanded it over the next several decades. Humble Oil, which would later merge with Exxon, produced numerous dry holes on the King Ranch in the 1920s, but it wasn't until the 1940s that oil prospecting began to make a profit. The character of Jett Rink was designed to parallel the life of real rags-to-riches oilman Glenn McCarthy. McCarthy was born to a poor family in Beaumont, near Houston. He struck oil in Hardin County, Texas, near the Texas-Louisiana border and far from King Ranch. His sudden success in the 1940s made him fabulously wealthy. By the mid-1950s, his flamboyant lifestyle had already put him in economic trouble.

In his film, Stevens puts these characters together against a stark desert backdrop. *Giant* is a study in contrasts, and the film's desolate, windswept landscape reflects its epic scope and sense of allegorical self-importance. Rather than setting the film in the swampy, oil-rich forests of East Texas, principal shooting was done near the isolated town of Marfa six hundred miles to the west, approximately 4,600 feet above sea level, and an hour's drive from the Mexican border. Stevens paid local a local family, the Ryans, $20,000 for the use of their cattle ranch—animals included.[14] The Ryan ranch is dominated by scrub desert covered in dry streambeds that fill with water during sudden rainstorms. The air is dry, and the blue Davis Mountains loom far in the distance. While Marfa's population had peaked at five thousand during World War II, by 1956 the region was again hit by hard times.

The contrast between this landscape, a place of extreme isolation and perennial economic decline, and the trappings of oil wealth and production reinforce a perception of the industry as a force of dramatic and irreversible change. The façade of the Benedicts' three-story Victorian mansion was built in Burbank, California, and shipped to Marfa in six pieces. The visual conflict between the desert backdrop, the working ranch, and the Benedicts' prim Victorian house is symbolic of the film's ideological conflicts, first between East Coast gentility and Western impropriety, and later between traditional agrarianism and the mechanized future offered by oil exploration. Marfa's desolate arid landscape emphasizes the house's stark verticality against the distant skyline.

Unlike the Benedict house, *Giant* depicts oil production as a natural part of the landscape. While the mansion is regularly shot from far away or from below, we experience Jett's big oil discovery through a series of establishing shots. With the rig itself off-screen, oil begins to rain down on Jett's face and body, quickly soaking him. Rather than explosive or destructive, oil discovery is as unpredictable and inevitable as the rain. Covered in oil, Jett immediately rushes to the Benedict house and attempts to seduce Leslie with his newfound wealth. His oil-drenched hands dirty the porch railings, showing the contrast between genteel wealth and those who work to make that lifestyle possible. Later, as the Benedict family grows in wealth and power due to oil exploration, the house becomes a symbol of stability, indicative of the industry's deep mark on Texas's social and economic fortunes.

Such a larger-than-life depiction glorifies the industry, portraying it unequivocally as a catalyst for the inevitable forward march of industrial progress and urbanization. The implication is that even though Jett Rink—and the industry—are responsible for both raucous excess and moral bankruptcy, they are also responsible for transformative industrial change. Scholars have studied Jett Rink as a conflicted antihero.[15] His desire for acceptance and economic security are as relatable as his methods are deplorable. To this end, Rink's construction of the Emperador Hotel, modeled after McCarthy's famously green Shamrock Hotel in Houston, can be understood as his effort to leave some kind of lasting legacy. While Rink's conflict with Bick and closing monologue reveal the hollowness of these aspirations, the hotel's size and grandeur attest to the creation of a monolithic and fabulously important industry.

Giant capitalized on a midcentury fascination with Texas oil money, just as the stability of that newfound wealth was looking increasingly uncertain. Articles in *Life* and *Look* magazines from this period describe a new generation of the "Texas ultra-rich."[16] Even though architect Frank Lloyd Wright reportedly described the Shamrock, which was styled in sixty-three shades of Irish green, as "architectural venereal disease," NBC broadcast the hotel's St. Patrick's Day opening live.[17] However, even in 1956 the importance of the Texas oilman was already waning. McCarthy was forced to sell the hotel to Conrad Hilton in 1955, signaling the beginning of his downfall and a period of decline for Texas oil profits.

The Oil Film and Resource Sovereignty

The year 1956 was also filled with growing questions about the worsening Cold War and the viability of American ambitions for global oil sovereignty. While the Railroad Commission of Texas still controlled global prices, Texas oil production had been fully eclipsed by Saudi Arabia and other Middle Eastern nations. American oil companies operating in the region, including Aramco, made tidy profits, but Middle Eastern nationalists increasingly agitated for local control over oil production and oil money. In 1956, the anticolonial Egyptian president Gamal Abdel Nasser nationalized control over the Suez Canal. In response, Israel, aided by the United Kingdom and France, invaded Egypt, hoping to regain control of the key trade route. Israel and its allies were unsuccessful, leaving the canal closed for almost a year. This created a dramatic disruption in the global movement of Middle Eastern oil, especially to Europe. While US oil supplies were not disrupted during the crisis, the idea that another nation could so fully upset the global supply was a source of anxiety for US officials and major American oil companies. While in 1956 the US imported far less oil from the Middle East than Europe, this number was increasing steadily. In 1959, Dwight Eisenhower, pushed by Texas independents, would put quotas on foreign oil imports.[18]

As if offering a panacea for such big-picture anxiety about American natural resource sovereignty, both *Tulsa* and *Giant* provide nostalgic dreams of an oil industry in which systemic evils were the result of individual moral failings and could be fixed through technical know-how or one-on-one fistfights. These films shrink an industry that was already multinational by 1900 to the level of individual wildcatters and single families. This, combined with both films' cinematography—they were shot on location on ranchland near historic centers for US oil production—situates the industry within well-trodden American myths of Western expansion and industrialization.

The Western was the most popular genre of the 1950s and the creative team behind both films knew their Westerns. *Tulsa* screenwriter Frank Nugent often collaborated with director John Ford, and Nugent also wrote the screenplay for *The Searchers* (1956), one of the highest-grossing Westerns of all time. *Giant* director George Stevens was nominated for an Oscar in 1953 for the classic Western *Shane*. Scholars of the postwar Western connect their popularity to America's expanded international influence during the Cold War. Richard Slotkin characterizes the Western genre as an explicit retreat from fears about Cold War nuclear armament and a reaction to cultural changes brought by new technologies.[19] A stereotype in the John Ford Western is a didactic narrative of national expansion in which white settlers are the victims of hostile inhuman savages. In the Western, the globally dominant American is made small—the victim of forces beyond his control—and in both *Tulsa* and *Giant*, the global oil industry is reduced to personal battles between a few individuals.

At their core, Westerns are also about conquest, and conflict is most often derived from efforts to either maintain control over land or to wrest it from another.[20] As Westerns, *Tulsa* and *Giant* are defined by a conflict between ranching and oil and who is best equipped to control that transition. However, neither film questions the inevitability of industrialization. Tellingly, *Tulsa*'s narrator—folksy Western actor Chill Wills—explains that while Oklahoma residents had known about subsurface oil for generations, by the twentieth century, "it just had to come out." *Giant* provides a similar narrative, like most oil films focusing on extraction rather than what would become the long-term source of Texas oil wealth: the international expansion of Texas oil service companies and the rise of offshore oil production in the Gulf of Mexico.

By the early 1950s, Houston and its adjacent cities Beaumont and Baytown were already industrial centers with skylines dotted with oil refineries. By the end of the decade, this oil processing center would become a sprawling suburbia, connected by a growing network of civil defense highways. The region was a hub for new technological industries, such as Everette DeGolyer's Geophysical Service (later Texas Instruments), that served an oil industry that looked to the Middle East, South America, and the North Sea rather than to the midcontinent. For Texas audiences, *Giant* appealed to a nostalgic version of an industry increasingly at odds with reality.

Audiences clearly appreciated this nostalgia. Nationally, *Giant* was both a critical and popular success, given singular mystique as James Dean's final film before his death at age twenty-three. *Giant* was praised by critics as a mature and nuanced indictment of Texas culture and the pitfalls that come with oil wealth. The film won George Stevens an Oscar for Best Director, and he would go on to continue a highly successful Hollywood career. *Giant* had a large production budget, which only ballooned during shooting, but it made $12 million in the US and Canada, and would go on to be Warner Bros.' highest-grossing film until *The Exorcist* (1973).[21]

Tulsa, in contrast, was panned by critics and audiences alike as a cliché-ridden, over-budget last gasp from a failing B-movie studio. *Time* called it "rambling and logy with clichés." The *New York Times* echoed this appraisal with "cliché-loaded."[22] In 1949, *Tulsa* made only $2.34 million at the box office, about one-eighth of the year's the highest-grossing film, *Samson and Delilah*.[23] Even though *Tulsa* was nominated for a 1950 special effects Oscar almost completely based upon the minutes-long towering inferno in the film's final scenes, *Tulsa*'s bad box office numbers meant that Wanger's two planned sequels were not filmed.[24] In an effort to recoup some of the film's exorbitant costs, *Tulsa* spent the next decade as a B listing at drive-in double features.

Tulsa's poor domestic showing was not necessarily a surprise to Walter Wanger. In a post-premiere Q&A session, Wanger described the film as "Not the best effort but a stab in the right direction."[25] He was probably more disappointed, however, that it did not do well abroad. Possibly more surprisingly, *Giant* also did poorly internationally, only making $6 million overseas. This was a problem for an American film industry that was actively engaged in the American Cold War project and desperately working to court international audiences.[26] The arrival of television had dramatically reduced ticket sales, and Hollywood was looking to redefine itself by providing spectacle that could not be seen on the small screen.[27] The epic vistas and towering oil conflagrations in both films speak as much to this concern as to a desire to promote American industry to foreign audiences. Epic or not, 1950s American oil films did not seem to resonate with international audiences.

It might be that these films' perspectives on land, industry, and progress reflected particularly American sensibilities. Even though both Cherokee Lansing and Jett Rink become paragons of industry greed and excess, they are also very compelling characters. At the heart of both films are underdog stories of individual perseverance in the face of gender, racial, and class bigotry. Cherokee Lansing is snubbed at the craps table by Brad's aristocratic ex-girlfriend: "Why, that name, its sounds positively . . . Indian." Cherokee responds mockingly and proceeds to win exorbitant sums of money gambling. As Jett Rink is discussing his ambitions with Leslie, she reminds him, "Money isn't everything, Jett." He replies, "Not when you've got it." Such statements shrink global American oil giants such as Texaco or Exxon or Phillips down to the level of relatable, if flawed, underdogs. This sense of victimhood in the face of global Cold War preeminence is common to American cinema but might not have appealed to audiences outside of the US.

It is clear, however, that people in Tulsa and Texas welcomed both films with open arms. In Tulsa, Eagle Lion approached William "Bill" Skelly, founder of the International Petroleum Exhibition, as a promoter. He convinced local oilmen to provide $1 million to finance the film premiere, complete with a three-hour, five-mile-long "International Petroleum Exposition on Wheels" parade through downtown.[28] According to one effusive report, the parade included the "world's largest portable oil rig" as well as local marching bands, the American Legion, and a flyby from the "125th Army Air Force fighter squadron." The Tulsa Chamber printed *Tulsa* inserts for all local papers and schools excused children to attend the parade as an "educational event."[29] However, it is clear that this spectacle was not about education, but rather about highlighting Tulsa's economic potential. Skelly and the other promoters chartered an airliner to transport sixty reporters from major metropolitan areas to cover the premiere. A local auto dealership provided twenty new Lincoln convertibles, and twenty young women from the Bannister Modeling Agency were hired to escort the journalists. These efforts drew an estimated one hundred thousand people. While locals' initial reactions to the film are not recorded, they did pack the city's four theaters, which hosted multiple screenings.[30]

Due to James Dean's recent death, *Giant* opened with far less fanfare on October 10, 1956, in New York City and a second premiere was held at Grauman's Chinese Theater in Los Angeles one week later.[31] Despite reports of threats to kill both Edna Thurber and George Stevens for their negative depictions of the industry and of Texas, *Giant* was very popular in the state. It opened in nine theaters in Houston, six in Fort Worth, and five in Dallas. People saw it multiple times.[32]

British film critic Gilbert Adair remarked that George Stevens "might be described as a chronicler of the pursuit of happiness, that craving for self-betterment." Both *Tulsa* and *Giant* dare to bluntly critique the American oil industry in an era of growing international uncertainty and carefully curated PR. However, such critique is couched in a romanticized understanding of American free enterprise that assumes an extremely high level of local control over the industry's destiny, reflecting an underlying desire for domestic control over an international industry. Both films are about efforts to regulate industrialization in the rural American heartland, highlighting postwar anxieties about the changing roles of US oil companies in an increasingly global industry. They each attempted to reassure audiences that the future of oil lay in American-led technological development and that the monuments to American oil wealth built over the past century would not be toppled by either the rise of foreign oil producers or the era's skyrocketing demand.

Notes

1. *Tulsa*, directed by Stuart Heisler (1949; Ada, OK: RCF, 2008), DVD.; *Giant*, directed by George Stevens (1956; Marfa, TX: Warner Bros, 2005), DVD.
2. J. Hoberman, *An Army of Phantoms: American Movies and the Making of the Cold War* (New York: New Press, 2012), chap. 2.
3. Other films in this series included *A Place in the Sun* (1951) and *Shane* (1953).
4. George Stevens Jr., Oral History Interview, April 10, 1969, John F. Kennedy Presidential Library and Museum, Accessed 2.7.2020, https://www.jfklibrary.org /asset-viewer/archives/RFKOH/Stevens%2C%20George%2C%20Jr/RFKOH -GCS-01/RFKOH-GCS-01.
5. Tyler Priest, "The Dilemmas of Oil Empire," *Journal of American History* 99, no. 1 (June 2012): 236–51.
6. The Nature Conservancy was founded in 1951 and Fairfield Osborn's *Our Plundered Planet* was also published in 1949. See also Robert Gotlieb, *Forcing the Spring: The Transformation of the American Environmental Movement* (New York: Island Press, 1993).
7. Robert Lifset and Brian Black, "Imaging the 'Devil's Excrement': Big Oil in Petroleum Cinema, 1940–2007," *Journal of American History* 99, no. 1 (June 2012): 135–44.
8. "State May Be Ideal Spot for Making Movies," *Ponca City News*, Ponca City, Oklahoma, December 30, 1947, 1. See also John Wooley, *Shot in Oklahoma: A Century of Sooner State Cinema* (Norman: University of Oklahoma Press, 2011).
9. Hoberman, *Army of Phantoms*.
10. "Tulsa Speech, April 12, 1949," Walter F. Wanger Papers, 1908–1967, Box 37, Folder 4, Wisconsin Historical Society Archives, Madison, Wisconsin. See also Matthew Bernstein, *Walter Wanger: Hollywood Independent* (Minneapolis: University of Minnesota Press, 2000).
11. Robin Murray and Joseph Heumann, *Gunfight at the Eco-Corral: Western Cinema and the Environment* (Norman: University of Oklahoma Press, 2012), chap. 4.
12. For example see "US Oil Improves Nation's Foreign Relations," *National Petroleum News*, and "Hope in the Harbor," *Petroleum Today*. Box 1, API Photo and Film Collection, Smithsonian Archives Center, Washington, DC. See also Robert Vitalis, *America's Kingdom: Mythmaking on the Saudi Oil Frontier* (New York: Verso, 2007).
13. Edward A. Fitzgerald, "The Tidelands Controversy Revisited," *Environmental Law* 19, no. 2 (1989): 209–55.
14. Marilyn Ann Moss, *Giant: George Stevens, a Life on Film* (Madison: University of Wisconsin Press, 2004).

15. J. E. Smythe, "Jim Crow, Jett Rink, and James Dean: Reconstructing Ferber's Giant (1952–1956)," *American Studies* 48, no. 3 (2007): 5–27.

16. "Southwest Has a New Crop of Super-Rich," *Life*, April 5, 1948, ExxonMobil Collection, Briscoe Center, Austin, Texas. Karen Merrill further contextualizes this tendency in "Texas Metropole: Oil, the American West, and U.S. Power in the Postwar Years," *Journal of American History* 99, no. 1 (2012): 197–207.

17. Mark Lardas, *Vanished Houston Landmarks* (Cheltenham, UK: History Press Library Editions, 2020), 62.

18. John Lewis Gaddis, *We Now Know: Rethinking Cold War History* (Oxford: Oxford University Press, 1998); Daniel Yergen, *The Prize: The Epic Quest for Oil Money and Power* (New York: Simon and Schuster, 1990), 480.

19. Rickard Slotkin, *Gunfighter Nation: Myth of the Frontier in Twentieth Century America* (Norman: University of Oklahoma Press, 1998). See also Scott Simmon, *The Invention of the Western Film: A Cultural History of the Genre's First Half Century* (Cambridge, UK: Cambridge University Press, 2003).

20. For classic examples see *Shane* (1953) and *The Sons of Katie Elder* (1965). This trope is later parodied in *Cat Ballou* (1965) and *Blazing Saddles* (1974). See also Jim Kitses, *Horizons West: The Western from John Ford to Clint Eastwood* (London: British Film Institute, 2007), and Stanley Corkin, *Cowboys as Cold Warriors: The Western and US History* (Philadelphia: Temple University Press, 2004).

21. Originally budgeted just shy of $2 million, the film ended up costing over $5 million. "Vagaries of Overseas Playoff," *Variety*, May 27, 1959, 3.

22. "Tulsa," *Time*, June 20, 1949; Bosley Crowther, "'Tulsa,' Story about Oil Fields, with Susan Hayward, New Feature at the Capitol," *New York Times*, May 27, 1949.

23. *Sampson and Delilah* made $28.3 million.

24. Bernstein, *Walter Wanger*.

25. Bernstein, *Walter Wanger*.

26. "Vagaries of Overseas Playoff," *Variety*, May 27, 1959, 3.

27. Peter Lev, *The Fifties: Transforming the Screen 1950–1959* (Berkeley: University of California Press, 2006), chap. 7.

28. Inez Gerhard, "Star Dust," *Verden News* (Verden, OK), May 6, 1949, 3.; "Governor's Fanciest Proclamation, *The Alva Review-Courier* (Alva, OK), March 30, 1949, 2. See also John Wooley, *Shot in Oklahoma: A Century of Sooner State Cinema* (Norman: University of Oklahoma Press, 2011).

29. Wooley, *Shot in Oklahoma*.

30. Wooley, *Shot in Oklahoma*.

31. George Stevens Papers, Academy of Motion Pictures, Margaret Herrick Library Digital Collections, accessed February 7, 2020.

32. Larry McMurtry, "Men Swaggered, Women Warred, Oil Flowed," *New York Times*, September 29, 1996.

Chapter 12

Ranches to Oil Wells: Reconfiguring the Western Hero in *Hellfighters* (1968) and *Fires of Kuwait* (1992)

Ila Tyagi

Adaptation unfolds as a theme across numerous horizons in *Hellfighters* and *Fires of Kuwait*. The first is a Hollywood film starring John Wayne as Chance Buckman, a swashbuckling oil well firefighter based on real celebrity firefighter Paul Neal "Red" Adair. In other words, *Hellfighters* is an adaptation of Adair's life story, which, due to his job's frequent and thrilling hazards, was ripe for conversion into a good old-fashioned American action picture. *Fires of Kuwait*, on the other hand, is an IMAX documentary chronicling multinational oil well firefighting teams' cleanup efforts in the wake of the Gulf War (1990–1991), when Saddam Hussein's retreating army set some six hundred Kuwaiti oil wells ablaze, triggering an environmental catastrophe. *Fires of Kuwait* adapts complex, concurrent events to a neat teleological narrative, which casts the firefighters in Kuwait—especially the American ones—as heroes, bravely putting their lives on the line for the sake of an ecosystem that, thanks to their presence, is converting from black to green.

Both films, in fact, are invested in depicting their oil well firefighter protagonists as heroes, and engage in a third kind of adaptation to do so. They take the mythic frontier hero around which countless American Western movies revolve and pour into the mold new professions and places. Instead of cattle driving or gunfighting, the heroes of *Hellfighters* and *Fires of Kuwait* extinguish infernos; instead of roaming the American West, they find themselves in Canada or Malaysia or Venezuela or the Middle East. The desert frontier, holding both extreme dangers and the exciting promise of adventure, is endlessly adaptable to fresh settings. However, amid these contextual changes, the hero's basic characteristics remain the same.

Successful adaptations take a core idea and utilize it to unveil previously hidden dimensions, facets to which the idea's earlier mediums could not easily gain access. In *Hellfighters* and *Fires of Kuwait*, the core idea is the mythic hero of umpteen Westerns preceding them. By casting ecological disasters like oil well fires as the dominant threat, rather than the usual human obstacles like tribes of "savages," *Hellfighters* and *Fires of Kuwait* expose how the qualities of the mythic hero change in response to the environmentally debilitating consequences of the Vietnam War and the Gulf War. Ostensibly timeless, the hero's characteristic strength and independence are tinged with obsolescence in 1968. By 1992, they have transformed into an understanding that despite a lingering toughness, his deleterious environment is tougher, and building alliances with others, not isolation, is the only way to survive in it. Toughness and independence are rendered anachronistic by environmental consciousness; natural forces are stronger than humankind, and they affect us all.

This essay examines how *Hellfighters* and *Fires of Kuwait* establish their heroes as tough by tapping into the myth surrounding the man of the American West peddled by Hollywood's dream factory. I suggest that although Wayne clings to vestiges of his image's legendary resilience and independence in *Hellfighters*, he is clearly aging rapidly and thus cannot persuasively portray the brawn he once did. This dissonance messily undercuts his own propagandistic agenda, mirroring coeval transformations in American domestic identity and uncertainty regarding the US military presence in Vietnam. In addition, the essay argues that Wayne's relative frailty in his role as Chance augurs the way that *Fires of Kuwait*'s firefighters jettison the more hubristic aspects of the mythic Western hero in favor of acknowledging their own smallness and vulnerability amid colossal environmental devastation. Significantly, this recognition manifests as a preference for collective action to undo the horrific aftermath of the war, rather than Wayne's preoccupation with solitary American exceptionalism. Adapting the frontier hero mold across time and space reveals that his characteristic toughness and autonomy simply cannot hold within the anarchy of climatic degradation set loose upon the world.

Tough Heroes

By now, the Western is an expansive, long-running genre with familiar tropes and includes films that push against its conventions in diverse and complex ways. Even the revisionist Western hero, though, has a great deal in common with his classical Hollywood antecedent. The Western hero is taciturn. "Let's skip talking about it," Chance says in *Hellfighters*.[1] "There's no words around to describe what we saw," a Texan firefighter insists in *Fires of Kuwait*.[2] Suspicious of words and impatient with their limitations, the Western hero prefers to let his actions speak for themselves. He is a loner—the word *lonesome* is indeed "almost a Western patent"—and keeping to himself hints at a melancholy past.[3] Accordingly, Chance is haunted by a sad history in *Hellfighters*. He begins the film estranged from his wife and daughter, whose existence comes as a surprise to characters who thought they knew him; he has kept determinedly mum about his lost family for ten years. Perhaps to escape such troubled memories, the Western hero is extraordinarily mobile, lighting out for open territory whenever he feels like it. The men in *Fires of Kuwait* and *Hellfighters* freely go wherever their work takes them, embodying the image of the Western hero as a drifter, the man forever wandering on his steed and living off his knowledge of the land. But above all, as both films plainly convey, the Western hero is tough.

There are many celluloid iterations of this legendary Western hero, from Alan Ladd's Shane to Gene Autry's singing cowboy to William Boyd's Hopalong Cassidy. Arguably, though, none are as iconic as John Wayne's. If his many biographers are to be believed, the rugged fortitude and self-reliance of Wayne's performances epitomize what Americans consider to be their purest national virtues. A quick glance at the titles of these biographies affirms their part in indelibly linking him to his country: *John Wayne: American*, *John Wayne: Prophet of the American Way of Life*, *American Titan: Searching for John Wayne*, and *John Wayne's America: The Politics of Celebrity*, among others. According to Michael Munn in *John Wayne: The Man behind the Myth*, person aligned perfectly with persona. Wayne's on-screen all-American individualism found expression off-screen in ultraconservative politics. His anticommunism combined with enthusiasm for American intervention abroad yielded ardent support for the Vietnam War (1956–1975). In his mind, as the greatest country on the globe, the United States singlehandedly bore the difficult but essential responsibility to defend the interests of the free world. Wayne visited Vietnam in 1966, returning home so impressed by what he saw as the nobility of American troops that he decided to make a film about them. *The Green Berets* (1968) was produced by his own company, Batjac Productions, and Wayne also directed and starred as Colonel Michael Kirby, a dedicated career officer flatteringly contrasted with prissy, pacifist war correspondent George Beckworth (David Janssen).

Hellfighters was Wayne's next project after *The Green Berets*, and Vietnam was still very much on his mind. The opening scene in *The Green Berets*, in which George asks soldiers impertinent questions, reappears in almost identical form early in *Hellfighters*, when an ineffectual television anchor interviewing Chance about firefighting procedures causes a bulldozer to crash into the hero and break his ribs. While *Hellfighters* was produced by Universal Pictures rather than Batjac, Wayne was still closely involved in its development, specifically requesting that certain episodes from Adair's life be written into the script.[4] For example, he was intrigued when Adair told him that oil well fires were not always the greatest threat to his crew. In Africa, Asia, and South America, they also had to worry about communist snipers. The film translates this detail into a protracted sequence in which Chance dodges guerrilla bullets while bringing under control flaming wells that have been bombed outside of Caracas, Venezuela, acting as a surrogate for Vietnam. Even though the task is a challenging one—for the first time in the film, Chance is handling multiple, deliberately sabotaged wells instead of accidental fires—there is no doubt that he will ultimately prevail. As with *The Green Berets*, Wayne's image as a durable Western hero in *Hellfighters* has ideological motives: to show that his country has the necessary grit to succeed in Vietnam.

By all accounts, Red Adair was every bit as stalwart as Wayne tried to make him seem on-screen. Born in Houston in 1915, he had his first brush with the petroleum industry in 1940. After convincing an Otis Pressure Control foreman to hire him, Adair learned how the oil field service company cleaned and adjusted the large valves that prevented wellhead blowouts. He met Myron M. Kinley, a well control pioneer, in the spring of 1941, when Kinley was called in to extinguish an Otis blowout that had caught fire. Kinley and his father had begun putting out well fires using explosives in 1913. While taming combustion with dynamite seems counterintuitive, a properly calibrated explosion momentarily sucks the oxygen from a given area, starving the flames for long enough to get a cap on the spurting well.[5] In 1923, Kinley formed the M. M. Kinley Company, specializing in blasting fires into submission using this technique. By the time he met and recruited Adair, he was well established in the industry.

Working for Kinley after World War II, Adair and his colleagues Asger "Boots" Hansen and Edward "Coots" Matthews made up a fearless firefighting team. When the injuries Kinley had sustained over many decades began to catch up with him, Adair, Hansen, and Matthews started to handle jobs by themselves. In 1959, Adair decided to strike out on his own, taking Hansen and Matthews with him.[6] The Red Adair Company had a monopoly on managing oil and gas fires until 1975, when "Big Joe" Bowden established Adair's first major rival, Wild Well Control, whose work is featured in *Fires of Kuwait*. Hansen and Matthews also parted ways with Adair in 1977 to form another rival, Boots & Coots. The Kuwaiti government hired all three Houston companies in 1991, along with others from around the world, to stamp out the fires that were wasting six million barrels of the country's oil reserves per day.[7] At age seventy-five, Adair supervised the capping of 117 wells, taking only six months to complete his portion of a task that had collectively been expected to last up to a decade. Strong, commanding, and effectively navigating danger, Adair fit the hero mold perfectly.

Moreover, like the Western hero, oil well firefighters must possess the toughness necessary to withstand severe physical hardships. Adair met with many accidents during his high-risk career, including a smashed pelvis and blinding by hydrogen sulfide, but the damage was never permanent. He nonchalantly shrugged off these blows in a 1977 *People* magazine profile, simply saying, "Injuries aren't serious if you don't have to stay in the hospital more than a week."[8] *Hellfighters* and *Fires of Kuwait* also depict such perilous outcomes, their intensity matched by the grueling conditions under which both crews suffered while shooting. When early in the film the hapless television interviewer causes the bulldozer to crush Chance at the site of a Baytown fire, the dialogue makes it clear that such wounds are routine for him. His doctor bemusedly tells waiting coworkers and friends, "Halfway out of the anesthetic, he wanted to leave the hospital." Though Chance supposedly has broken ribs and a punctured lung, he merely wears his arm in a sling, and only for a few minutes of screen time, before deciding that he is sufficiently healed and abruptly dispensing with that too. Likewise, *Fires of Kuwait* reminds viewers that the firefighters must display a fortitude commensurate with the enormity of their mission. As two firefighters gingerly approach a towering inferno, voiceover narrator Rip Torn reveals, "Staying upwind of the two-thousand-degree heat is a matter of life and death. But even here, you'll sweat a quart an hour. And twelve hours is an average day."

The *Fires of Kuwait* crew did not escape the arduous conditions they were recording. Director David Douglas had originally arrived in Kuwait to make a documentary about the interdependence of plant and animal life. However, seeing the raging oil well fires blanketing the landscape like a vision of hell made him realize that they should be the centerpiece of his film instead. Douglas and his four-person team lugged hundred-pound cameras, seventy-pound tripods, and forty-pound batteries everywhere they went for the twenty-seven scorching days it took to collect all the footage they needed.[9] *Fires of Kuwait* particularly lauds Wild Well Control employees because they lent the crew protective uniforms and invited them to get close enough to capture the tensest moments up until each fire was smothered.[10]

Hellfighters' director, Andrew V. McLaglen, also braved fierce temperatures to get close-ups of the thirty-five thousand gallons of diesel and sixty thousand gallons of raw propane that his special effects engineers ignited into geysers of flames over a hundred feet high to simulate crude oil fires.[11] He recalled that the plastic webbing on his director's chair melted as they filmed five adjacent fires for the Venezuela sequence, "even though [they were] some thirty or forty feet away."[12] Wayne himself practiced capping wells for the film, getting pummeled by spewing oil in the process. During filming, McLaglen sent him within spitting distance of the fires, hosing him down with water that bubbled and steamed as Wayne inched closer and closer to the skin-peeling heat. The searing heat even caused Wayne's hair to catch fire under his helmet. The actor dove headfirst into a nearby lake.

Tough Heroes Become Vulnerable

The *Hellfighters* script describes Chance as "about forty, a powerfully built, rugged, good-looking man."[13] Wayne turned sixty-one during the three-month shoot, making him a good twenty years older than his character's scripted age. *Hellfighters'* herculean shoot would have been an ordeal for Wayne regardless of his age, as he had undergone surgery to treat lung cancer in 1964. A rib and a lung were removed, making exercise and dieting more onerous, and Wayne grew paunchy and prone to shortness of breath.[14]

Interestingly, Wayne's character in *Hellfighters* mirrors some of this vulnerability. Chance appears in a hospital room in two scenes after his cracked ribs tear one of his lungs in the bulldozer accident. In the first, his daughter, Tish (Katharine Ross), visits him while he is still sedated, his hand hooked to an intravenous drip. In the second, he is conscious and furious at his raffish employee Greg—played, at Wayne's request, by Jim Hutton, his costar in *The Green Berets*—for marrying his daughter after only having known her for five days. His anger quickly turns to joy when he realizes that Tish and Greg genuinely love each other, and he bolts out of bed to celebrate with them despite the protestations of his nurse, Mrs. Thistlewaite (uncredited role). The nurse's frumpy name and mealy-mouthed cautiousness contrast unfavorably with Chance's ability to take firm charge of his own destiny.

However, the scene is undercut by Wayne's demeanor; he is supposed to be radiating youthful vigor, yet seems disoriented and weak. Defenders may contend that this is appropriate for a character recovering from a life-threatening accident, but Wayne's slurred speech, labored movements, cloudy eyes, and wrinkles on his haggard face betray an encroaching infirmity well beyond his characterization. Compared with his granite slab of an image in *Stagecoach* (1939), the film that lifted him out of bit parts in B Westerns, the effect is one of Ozymandias lying ruined in the sands of time.

Wayne's growing frailty was not lost on his contemporaries. *Los Angeles Times* journalist Kevin Thomas noted that time was chipping away at Wayne's persona in *The Green Berets*. Describing the film as a "sincere but dismayingly clumsy patriotic gesture," Thomas identifies a scene in which Wayne comforts a small Vietnamese boy as ringing particularly false, maintaining, "We're not at all assured the way we used to be back when Wayne was fighting World War II at the Saturday matinee. He simply looks too old to do the job." [15] Critics reviewing *Hellfighters* picked up on Thomas's observation that Wayne inspired less confidence in his dotage than earlier in his career. The *Globe and Mail*'s Melinda McCracken called Chance's attempt "an obsolete concept of manhood." [16] Moreover, Wayne's efforts to rally his fading image of mythic strength in support of an unpopular war were disturbingly and curiously out of step with the times. His shadow falls over virtually every subsequent noteworthy Hollywood movie addressing the conflict. In *Full Metal Jacket* (1987), Matthew Modine's Private Joker—on whose helmet is scrawled both a peace sign and the slogan "Born to Kill," reflecting the Jungian "duality of man"—repeatedly asks, "Is that you, John Wayne? Is this me?" [17] Significantly, Vietnam had a hand in eroding the very brand of masculinity Wayne espoused. According to a March 1969 editorial in the *Journal of Higher Education* titled "John Wayne Is Irrelevant,"

> When our young men wear long hair, love beads, peace medallions, earrings, and in other ways dress unconventionally, they may be expressing some confusion about sex roles, but more often, we suggest, they are challenging the traditional image of masculinity—that style of manhood by which we conquered a frontier, won two world wars, and overcame an economic depression. . . . The student will be very much aware that adherence to the values which his father wishes to instill in him have resulted in pollution and blight along with efficient production, in continued confidence in violence as a way of resolving conflicts. . . . Our youth see more clearly than we what our sojourns in Korea and Vietnam, our blighted and troubled cities, our racial unrest, and even the sterility of the suburbs should have taught us—that no one wins unless everyone wins. [18]

As the editorial indicates, not only was the nature of American manhood up for grabs in the Vietnam era but Americans' relationship with the environment was newly in flux as well. A November 1969 *New York Times* article reported on the environmental "new wave" blooming across college campuses nationwide in response to pollution generated by "efficient production." The article features a photograph of University of Minnesota students staging a mock funeral for the gasoline engine and quotes a Berkeley student emphasizing the importance of collective action. "There's a role for everybody," he says. "People with widely different styles and politics can talk to each other with no more tension than a Presbyterian talks with a Methodist."[19]

This domestic environmental consciousness in the late 1960s was closely linked to the Vietnam War, as revelations surfaced about the role of the United States as a heavy international polluter. Between 1961 and 1971, the US army and its South Vietnamese allies sprayed over 19 million gallons of chemical agents over 2.5 million acres in South and Central Vietnam. Their goal was to destroy the forests and jungles the Viet Cong used for cover, expose supply trails to air observation, and cut down the rice crop feeding enemy troops.[20] A February 1968 *Washington Post* article raised the alarm about the ravages of Agent Orange and other "rainbow herbicides." Citing a report commissioned by the Pentagon from the independent Midwest Research Institute, it warned that "the use of defoliants over the past five years could be disrupting the Vietnamese balance of nature." The piece went on to explain that this chemical warfare was causing permanent damage to soils, streams, and wildlife, including endangered tree-dwelling monkeys like the douc langur and crested gibbon, as well as microorganisms essential to the food chain.[21] Such articles incited unease about mounting environmental degradation.

Perhaps in consideration of these growing ecological concerns, *Hellfighters* dispensed with a few lines found in a draft of the script that did not make the final cut. In this draft, also from February 1968 (the film began shooting in mid-March and wrapped in early June), Chance bemoans the Venezuelan communists hiding in the brush around the burning oil wells, irritated by the havoc they are causing. To the platoons the government has provided for his protection, he orders, "Have some napalm flame throwers brought in. I want every bush on that mountain burned over—so that not even a snake can hide."[22] Eliding such explicit references to the napalm bombs and defoliation tactics then being used in Vietnam makes Chance a tad less arrogant in the final version of this sequence, even as he continues posturing at other moments left untouched in the transition from page to screen.

Consequently, despite this concession, the aging Wayne's ideology of tough, independent masculinity remains intact. Chance's friend Jack Lomax (Jay C. Flippen) praises him as "one-of-a-kind . . . the best there is at what he does." While looking at a framed photograph of an underground Mexican volcano in Chance's office, Greg tells Tish that her father capped its six-thousand-pound pressure steam all by himself, while also managing to convince his clients to build a power plant that will "supply eight Mexican towns for the next hundred years." The implication is clear: a Western hero meets challenges with an unyielding commitment to standing alone. Wayne had yet to adjust to a social revolution that sought to remold American masculinity along more compassionate lines, and that recognized that an individual's fate is intertwined with that of all who share the earth with him.

Vulnerable Heroes Seek Company

In *Fires of Kuwait*, the heroes cannot escape this lesson. The film champions their esprit de corps as painstakingly as *Hellfighters* attempts to elevate Chance above the rest of the population, and its protagonists possess the characteristic toughness of the mythic Western hero for very different reasons. The Gulf War was not entirely like Vietnam. Instead of a lonely eighteen-year quagmire ending in humiliating defeat, the United States led a coalition of thirty-two nations that triumphantly drove back occupying Iraqi forces in a mere six weeks. Just as America apparently learned from the Vietnam debacle not to go it alone, *Fires of Kuwait* repeatedly emphasizes the power of communal effort and goodwill. These Western heroes use their strength in collaboration with foreign firefighting teams to repair a toxic environment for everyone's benefit.

The scale of the obstacle in Kuwait decisively removed the possibility of overcoming it unaided, no matter how tough the persons involved. The more than six hundred torched wells were belching sixty thousand tons of sulfur, forty-five thousand tons of soot, three thousand tons of nitrogen oxides, and thousands of tons of greenhouse gases into the air every day via smoke plumes nearly three miles high.[23] Torn's voiceover informs the audience, "The whole desert ecosystem is smothered under a blanket of tar for hundreds of square miles. Oases, once havens for desert wildlife, now lie under lakes of oil. Sulfur dioxide, hydrogen sulfide, trace metals, unburned hydrocarbons, and salt combine with the oil to encrust the trees. For thousands of migrating birds, the journey ended here." Additional menaces included poisoned water sources and unexploded Iraqi mines and coalition bombs buried under the oleaginous black flood.

Collaboration was key in this intensely toxic environment, man-made in cause but natural in effect. Torn remarks, "Like oil-soaked shore birds, human beings can overheat when their pores are clogged. You can pass out without warning. You're trusting your life to the men around you." Community meant survival in Kuwait at this time, and solitude meant suicide. With the exception of the Venezuela sequence, *Hellfighters'* Chance remains blissfully untethered from the social, cultural, economic, and political contexts enmeshing the fires he has been hired to fight. He zips in and out of nations at will, while the firefighters in Douglas's documentary, legacies of combat permeating every atom of their existence, cannot glibly flit about. All equally at risk, they must dig in their heels for the long-term commitment required to undo this colossal damage, and they must do so in cooperation with other firefighting teams. The documentary shows various Texan firms deploying the dynamiting technique that Adair borrowed from Kinley and then perfected. Once Adair's unique claim, this now commonplace technique is one of many, and additional methods to tame the fires have been devised beyond American borders with similar results. The Hungarian team, for instance, ingeniously replaces the gun turret on a Russian T-34 tank with engines from MiG-21 fighter planes. The team is shown injecting water into the jet stream, then simply opening the throttle and blowing out their allotted fires.

What is more, ten thousand firefighters from a total of forty countries gathered in Kuwait after the Gulf War in the largest nonmilitary mobilization in history, far too many for *Fires of Kuwait* to imbue with the individuality Chance enjoys in *Hellfighters*. Though he starts out refusing to discuss his past, *Hellfighters* devotes about half of its eventual runtime to his reconciliation with his wife and daughter. It is replete with personal details, from the squeaking live monkey Chance bought Tish when she was a child to first meeting his wife at her family's department store when he was buying a fur coat for another girl. In contrast, *Fires of Kuwait* obscures any identifying traces of its firefighters. Each one is part of an anonymous mass—unnamed when speaking, faces usually hidden behind protective eyewear and headgear. Their sheer numbers mean that we know them through the result of their aggregate labor, rather than from the distinctive personalities that coordinated and completed it.

All the fires were extinguished in just nine months, four years ahead of predictions. A job that would have been too big to pull off singlehandedly was finished in record time through unified action. Sara Akbar, cofounder of the Kuwaiti firefighting team (and, as a woman, the only consistently recognizable voice besides Torn's), ascribes the cleanup's resounding success to its collectivity, asserting, "Teamwork is the best way to go about things." *Fires of Kuwait* is a paean to teamwork, and this cooperation on the ground in Kuwait represents a larger, more significant kind: our collective responsibility to protect a planetary ecosystem woven into all of us. As Torn notes, human beings drenched in oil and oil-soaked shore birds can be indistinguishable. "It's a global thing," one firefighter says. "You're actually helping wildlife, you know, the seas, everything." In other words, *Fires of Kuwait* extends people's connections in working together to their connections to the environment, recognizing that Kuwait is linked to the rest of the world. A natural disaster left unchecked in one minuscule country has the potential to bring everything down with it in a house-of-cards collapse.

No One Wins Unless Everyone Wins

In his *People* profile, Adair says, "Nature causes more catastrophes than man, so we may be overdoing all this ecology business. The good Lord put oil and gas there for us to find and use, and we'd better do it." [24] Adair, like Wayne, came of age at a time when the environment was a battlefield on which man had to prove his superiority. His "me versus them" mentality served him well in a capitalist system prizing ambition, competition, aggression, and unshakable confidence. As the *Journal of Higher Education* editorial concedes, "These are the attitudes which have brought our nation its power and our economy its strength." [25]

Adair's attitude lives on today in an exacerbated form, nourished by neoliberalism. At the Heartland Institute's Sixth International Conference on Climate Change in 2011, detractor Patrick Michaels suggested that those worried about global warming should do what the French allegedly did after a 2003 heat wave killed fourteen thousand citizens: "They discovered Walmart and air-conditioning." The solution to the costliness of adapting to a warmer climate, he added, is to further free trade. [26] This perspective is illuminating for a number of reasons. It trumpets an utter lack of empathy for climate change's victims. It reveals that a deteriorating environment affects some of us more than others, as the rich retreat further into comfort while the poor become climate refugees. Most of all, it exposes the foolishness of overlooking *Fires of Kuwait*'s advice. Wealth camouflages connections between people and their environment, but cannot eradicate them. They persist. A new kind of toughness is necessary to grapple with the crisis that men like Adair and Wayne have created. Like the documentary's firefighters, this toughness, adapted from older templates, should emphasize "interdependence rather than hyper-individualism, reciprocity rather than dominance, and cooperation rather than hierarchy." [27] We must reevaluate such relics from the Western frontier when man is the cause of nature's catastrophes.

Notes

1. Andrew V. McLaglen, dir., *Hellfighters* (Universal City, CA: Universal Pictures, 1968).
2. David Douglas, dir., *Fires of Kuwait* (Mississauga, ON: IMAX, 1992).
3. Roger Horrocks, *Male Myths and Icons: Masculinity in Popular Culture* (New York: St. Martin's Press, 1995), 67.

4. James S. Olson and Randy Roberts, *John Wayne: American* (New York: Free Press, 1995), 552.
5. Sean Flynn, "The Big Heat," *New York Times Magazine*, December 26, 2004, 46.
6. Philip Singerman, *An American Hero: The Red Adair Story* (Boston: Little, Brown, 1990), 197.
7. Joe Treen, "Fields of Fire," *People*, April 29, 1991, 42.
8. Kent Demaret, "When the Shout 'Wild Well!' Is Heard in the Oil Fields, Red Adair Puts a Lid on the Crisis," *People*, May 23, 1977, 38.
9. Noel Taylor, "Canadian Imax Film Up for Rare Oscar," *Ottawa Citizen*, March 26, 1993, E1.
10. Richard H. Curtiss, "Fourth Anniversary Report: Giant-Screen Film Records Horrors of Kuwait's Flaming Oil," *Washington Report on Middle East Affairs* 13, no. 6 (March 1995): 30, https://www.wrmea.org/1995-march/giant-screen-film-records -horrors-of-kuwait-s-flaming-oil.html.
11. Stephen B. Armstrong, *Andrew V. McLaglen: The Life and Hollywood Career* (Jefferson, NC: McFarland and Company, 2011), 152.
12. Michael Munn, *John Wayne: The Man behind the Myth* (New York: New American Library, 2003), 285.
13. John Lee Mahin, *The Hellfighters* (script), February 27, 1968, 4, box 90, *Hellfighters* folder, Western Filmscript Collection, Beinecke Rare Book and Manuscript Library, Yale University, New Haven, Connecticut.
14. Garry Wills, *John Wayne's America: The Politics of Celebrity* (New York: Simon and Schuster, 1997), 283.
15. Kevin Thomas, "John Wayne, 'Green Berets' in Multiples," *Los Angeles Times*, July 3, 1968, G1.
16. Melinda McCracken, "John Wayne Is John Wayne Is John . . ." *Globe and Mail*, December 28, 1968, 22.
17. Stanley Kubrick, dir., *Full Metal Jacket* (Burbank, CA: Warner Bros., 1987).
18. C. G. A., "John Wayne Is Irrelevant," *Journal of Higher Education* 40, no. 3 (March 1969): 235–36.
19. Gladwin Hill, "Environment May Eclipse Vietnam as College Issue," *New York Times*, November 30, 1969, 57.
20. Edwin A. Martini, *Agent Orange: History, Science, and the Politics of Uncertainty* (Amherst: University of Massachusetts Press, 2012), 2.
21. Tomas O'Toole, "Vietnam Defoliation Seen Wildlife Threat," *Washington Post*, February 11, 1968, A1.
22. Mahin, *Hellfighters*, 128.
23. Brian Gorman, "IMAX Takes a Peek into Hell and Puts It on the BIG Screen," *Toronto Star*, December 4, 1992, C3.
24. Demaret, "When the Shout 'Wild Well!' Is Heard," 38.
25. C. G. A., "Irrelevant," 235.
26. Quoted in Naomi Klein, "Capitalism vs. the Climate," *The Nation*, November 28, 2011, 19, https://www.thenation.com/article/archive/capitalism-vs-climate.
27. Klein, "Capitalism vs. the Climate," 19.

Chapter 13

Revisiting *Matewan* (1987): Upending the Appalachian "Western" and Broadening an Old Labor Tale

James R. Allison III

Set deep within the hollows of West Virginia, along the same Tug River Valley of Hatfield and McCoy fame, the 1987 film *Matewan* depicts an infamous 1920 labor strike that culminated in a dramatic shootout leaving ten men dead.[1] As movies are apt to do, this one largely ends with that climactic violence. Yet the real "Matewan Massacre" served merely as a prelude to a much larger contest between the forces of capital and organized labor in the Mountain State. The following year, in the Battle of Blair Mountain, roughly ten thousand striking coal miners squared off against three thousand lawmen and strikebreakers in what is routinely characterized as America's largest armed labor uprising. The workers did not fare well. After a week of fighting required federal intervention to restore the peace, dozens of combatants lay dead, nearly one thousand miners faced indictments, and the United Mine Workers of America was eviscerated in southern West Virginia.[2]

The telling of this remarkable confrontation and the events leading up to it have long been the domain of labor historians. Almost immediately following the events, the first news reports filtering out of the region cast the conflict as a simple clash between capital and labor. Radical organizations touted the miners' actions as the start of the inevitable class war, while Progressive muckrakers focused on the exploitative labor practices that triggered the violence. By midcentury, "institutional" labor historians from the Wisconsin School, who relied heavily on union and media sources, had turned their attention to the subject, largely adopting the Progressive perspective. These consensus historians muted the miners' militancy and collectivist goals, foregrounding instead the hard-earned partnership forged between union and management that supposedly addressed workers' concerns and kept the coal industry viable. The new labor historians of the 1960s and 1970s, however, saw things differently. Employing alternative sources and innovative techniques, these scholars opened up the "workers' world" by exploring the lived experiences of individuals, both at work and at home, rather than merely following labor leaders, institutions, and strikes. What these scholars found was a thick menagerie of interpersonal relations that cultivated an evolving—and radical—sense of class, which often transcended ethnic and racial divides. From this community-level perspective, the West Virginia mine wars were, in the words of David Corbin, "collective and militant acts of aggression, interconnected and conditioned by decades (beginning in the 1890s) of social change, economic exploitation and oppression, political corruption, and tyranny."[3]

Matewan reflects the best and worst of this new labor historiography. It is a gritty, on-the-ground portrayal of how coal miners lived, worked, and interacted with one another to negotiate and overcome their cultural differences and shared subjugation. But it is also very much a film about an exceptional moment in time that remains detached from its broader context. This deliberate depiction of a diverse community combating its exploitation comes at the expense of any historical understanding of how that community became dependent on forces beyond its control or how decades of oppression fostered the solidarity to fight such dependency. It is rich in texture but narrow in scope.

There is good reason for this emphasis, however. John Sayles, the film's writer and director, is less concerned with providing a nuanced history lesson and more interested in delivering a powerful message of unity to a polarized 1980s America. This essay thus assesses *Matewan*'s effectiveness as a medium for that message. The first part explores Sayles's use of the Hollywood Western as a narrative device to set audience expectations before dashing those assumptions with plot twists that force a reexamination of American exceptionalism. Once properly unsettled, the audience is then ripe for accepting Sayles's counterargument that American greatness stems from its diversity, not individual heroics. Such a conclusion clearly reflects the filmmaker's (incomplete) reading of the new labor history, which the second part of this essay explores in more detail before then discussing the broader story that Sayles's perspective obscures. As a whole, the essay sings *Matewan*'s praises for its vivid depiction of a coal mining community but argues that greater attention to that community's changing economic and ecological context would strengthen the film's message.

Narratives, Myths, and Genre Films

For even the most casual history buff, *Matewan*'s story should ring familiar. The film portrays a greedy coal operator, the Stone Mountain Coal Company, seeking to squeeze more work for less pay from its downtrodden workers. The miners resist, of course, but the terms of the contest are not evenly set. Living in company housing and subsisting on scrip, the workers' only recourse is to strike. In response, the coal company brings in African Americans and European immigrants to continue the work and break the strike. The predictable skirmishes erupt between scabs and strikers, but eventually class unites people divided by race and culture. A heterogeneous labor force forms "one big union" to protect its collective interests.

But then the hammer drops. Faced with unexpected solidarity and a continued work stoppage, the coal company dispatches the despised Baldwin-Felts detectives to rough up, intimidate, and throw out the troublemakers. Once again, an inevitable gunfight ensues. There is even a heroic Hatfield—the town's pro-union sheriff—who rides to the rescue, personally dislodging several Baldwin-Felts goons. In the end, blood is spilled and a union organizer is martyred, but the good guys prevail. The union is saved, evil capitalism is checked, and a community is forged.

Matewan works as a compelling, if familiar, narrative precisely because it plays upon some of America's most fundamental myths. These half-truths that Americans tell about and among themselves embody widely held values or beliefs, demonstrating right from wrong and generally helping to make sense of the world and each person's position in it. Repeated often enough, these myths can also serve to cohere the nation around a shared perspective, even if that understanding sometimes distorts historical reality. One of the most effective methods for disseminating these myths is through popular media like music, literature, and, of course, films. In Hollywood, America's sacred myths take secular form.

The most common cinematic vehicle for delivering national myths is the genre film. These productions contain familiar plotlines, characters, and outcomes that resonate with the moviegoing public and reassure them of their beliefs. The film industry has made a living off of selling America's dreams back to its citizens. According to film critic Barry Keith Grant, genre films have "made up the bulk of film practice, the iceberg of film history beneath the visible tip that in the past has commonly been understood as film art."[4] There are good reasons for such prominence, ranging from the efficiency genre films afford an industrialized film industry to the relatively safe expectation of box office sales.

But despite the success of these packaged products, it would be misleading to view genre films as overly formulaic and unchanging. They tell familiar stories with familiar characters, yet as with all narrative forms (including histories), they relay these tales in ways that evolve with the times. And because genre films occupy such a central place in popular culture, they can serve as good barometers of contemporary thought. As Grant once again explains, "Whether they are set in the past or in the future, on the mean streets of contemporary New York or long ago in a galaxy far away, genre movies are always about the time and place in which they are made. Inevitably, they are expressions of the cultural *zeitgeist*, instances of society engaging in dialogue with itself. . . . They speak to cultural issues both timely and timeless, and attempt to resolve them as narrative rituals."[5] Myths thus become embodied as genres, and then the evolving portrayal of those familiar tales through individual films reflect society's shifting interpretations of its central myths.

So what then can *Matewan*, the movie, tell us about 1980s America and its relationship to the nation's foundational myths? And what, if anything, can this film about Appalachian coal tell us about how the nation viewed the energy resource most responsible for its meteoric rise to global power? To begin with, assigning this film a particular genre is trickier than it first appears. Tucked away in a remote wilderness and culminating with a high-noon shootout on Main Street, the film cannot help but be part Western. Filmmaker John Sayles admits as much, explaining in a 2017 interview that what first drew him to the Matewan Massacre was its "movie-like quality of being like a Western."[6] This most enduring of all Hollywood genres rests upon the familiar narrative of a lone gunman—and it is nearly always a man—pitted against uncivilized evildoers and a wild landscape, ultimately dispensing justice, restoring order, and establishing civilization before riding off into the sunset to do it all again.[7] Such a structure barely conceals the genre's formulating myth of American exceptionalism, expressed most forcefully in its nineteenth-century tropes of manifest destiny and Frederick Jackson Turner's frontier thesis. Both of these doctrines assert the primacy of the American frontier as a force for national greatness, particularly as rugged individuals civilized it, extracted its wealth, and in the process became self-sufficient democrats undergirding American strength.[8]

In the character of Sid Hatfield, the pro-union sheriff who boldly stands up to the Baldwin-Felts detectives and shoots several of them down, *Matewan* clearly has its rugged individual. A man of few words, Sid takes decisive action. Yet, as other Westerns from the Vietnam era forward have done, this film blurs the traditional lines between good and evil. Sid is a lawman and thus thought to be a force for justice. But there are badges on both sides of this conflict, complicating familiar markers of morality. Further, the sheriff's propensity for violence, bordering on a desire for it, gives the viewer pause to consider who the real instigators are. This deliberation is cut short, however, by the rather ham-handed portrayal of the Baldwin-Felts detectives as simple, cold-blooded sociopaths. Detectives Hickey (Kevin Tighe) and Griggs (Gordon Clapp) are played with little nuance, leaving the audience with no doubt of who to root for. As tensions mount between gun-toting factions—one representing the humane, the other heartless injustice—all the trappings of the Western are present. We expect, almost demand, a bloody shootout to restore order.

But what happens when that violence arrives and leaves several of the film's most endearing characters dead without providing a final resolution to the conflict? John Sayles is an award-winning fiction writer whose accolades include a nomination for the National Book Award, an O. Henry Prize for short stories, and a MacArthur Fellowship. He understands better than most the power of a good narrative to hold an audience. But in *Matewan*, Sayles sees the real payoff in challenging the genre's expectations in a manner realistic enough to compel viewers to question their underlying assumptions about American myths. He does this in two primary ways. The first is by delivering a climactic violent encounter that resolves nothing. Yes, Sid and the miners kill more than get killed, but the final scene is not the actual shootout. Instead, the film concludes with Danny, a young preacher boy swayed to the union cause (played skillfully by a fourteen-year-old Will Oldham, better known as the American singer-songwriter Bonnie "Prince" Billy) returning to the mines. As the audience watches the teenage Danny hobble underground, it hears an elderly version of the boy narrate the details of Sid Hatfield's death a year later at the hands of Baldwin-Felts agents. For the first time, we learn that the film's events triggered, not resolved, the great coalfield wars of the 1920s.

So unlike the typical Western where the shootout restores order, here the cycle of violence continues. This dissonance is intentional. As Sayles explains in *Thinking in Pictures*, a book he wrote about the making of *Matewan*,

> If all the movie is about is who got shot and who didn't, the history ends there—it doesn't inform anything we do today. But people still go underground to mine coal [and] people with power still pit races and ethnic groups against each other to keep them from taking control of their own lives. . . . [In the final shootout,] we have seen only a piece of an ongoing battle, a cycle of violence and revenge with no definite end.[9]

By replacing the climactic resolution with a cyclical time structure in which miners return to their arduous work, Sayles connects the violence depicted in the film to what he sees as an ongoing struggle for justice in Appalachia. In the 1980s, this meant less pay for fewer jobs due to the consolidation of mine ownership by massive out-of-state conglomerates; advanced mining technology and techniques that shifted the industry from labor-heavy, deep-shaft mining to technology-dependent, mountain-top removal; and the further integration of Appalachian coal into global markets that increased competition and depressed prices. Each of these trends worked to exacerbate the fundamental problem Matewan miners faced in the 1920s: dependency on an industry unconcerned with the health of the local community.[10]

In connecting the historical events depicted in this Appalachian "Western" to contemporary conditions (in this case, the 1980s), John Sayles echoes one of the more forceful critiques of Turner's frontier thesis, and with it the notion of American exceptionalism. Turner's exceptionalism rests upon the supposed existence of "free land" in the West, which Americans constantly moved into, discarding their European ways and becoming self-sufficient pragmatists with a disdain for concentrated authority. But as Patricia Limerick and others have noted, this emphasis on a teleological frontier *process* as the mechanism for American greatness means that once the frontier was closed—as the 1890 census declared it to be—the American past was severed from its present. An orphaned and exotic past could then offer few insights into contemporary conditions, and an explanation for American exceptionalism based upon a completed process could hardly foster future progress.[11] Within academic circles, this argument has been recited so often as to become trite. Yet the broader public remains reticent to accept such a damning critique of one of its most cherished intellectual traditions. Sayles, however, does not let us avoid the issue. By concluding the film with this alternative time structure, he forces the audience to confront their assumptions about the supposed linear march of progress that produced American greatness.

If *Matewan*'s first challenge to standard expectations of the Western is to complicate notions of American progress, the second entails rethinking who our real heroes are. With a famous last name, a gunslinger's mentality, and a historical record that largely supports the film's depiction of him as a charismatic agitator, there is a natural tendency for the audience to focus on Sid Hatfield.[12] But Sid is not the movie's protagonist. Instead, *Matewan*'s primary point of view is provided by Joe Kenehan, a fictional union organizer, socialist, and avowed pacifist. Historians will scoff at Kenehan's identification as a Wobbly, seeing it as incongruous with his declared pacifism and knowing that the Industrial Workers of the World had little presence in southern West Virginia. But in his efforts to organize a diverse labor force into a cohesive community, Kenehan's character (played by an understated Chris Cooper) introduces a second great tension in the film that moves beyond the obvious conflict between "good" miners and "evil" coal operators. This one posits whether "one big union" can overcome ethnic divisions to achieve collective goals without the use of violence.

The results are mixed. Kenehan's death in the final shootout, Danny's return to the mines, and the subsequent murder of Sid Hatfield would all suggest that not much came of this moment of interethnic cooperation. But connected as it is to the present, *Matewan*'s more hopeful—and in Sayles's eyes, more useful—message centers on the feel-good federation of laboring white, Black, and Italian people that Joe Kenehan helps to forge. This storyline is developed beautifully, if comically at times, with intimate and sometimes awkward scenes of life within a striking coal camp. There, we see miners' wives from divergent backgrounds initially fighting over meager rations before ultimately sharing meals and knowledge about one another's customs and foodways. We watch as campfire musicians move gingerly from solo performances toward a blended bluegrass style that incorporates white miners' guitars, African Americans' harmonicas, and Italians' mandolins (though, curiously, the African banjo is missing). And we see distrustful men slowly building solidarity, though this coalition is constantly tested, such as when a ridiculous plot twist has Kenehan falsely accused of sexual misconduct with a local girl. Despite this narrative misstep, these scenes of coal camp life provide the real grist for the film's message, which again defies genre expectations of a lone individual meting out justice. Whereas the typical Western, according to film critic John Hellman, "deals with the conflict created by the dominant direction of American experience, the flight from community (Europe, the East, restraint, the conscious) into a wilderness (America, the West, freedom, the unconscious)," *Matewan* runs in the opposite direction.[13] It makes the case that a diverse and segregated community can come together to rectify injustice. Thus, while this film's skeletal structure may be all Western, its narrative heart taps into another of America's foundational myths: its supposed melting pot origins. Clearly, this conception of the nation is also problematic. But like all good myths, it possesses at least a kernel of truth, particularly in southern West Virginia, where historians have uncovered a robust record of minority miners and interethnic cooperation.[14]

Labor Historiography and an Enviro-Energy Perspective

Matewan's focus on the fine-grained interactions of a diverse community coming together can be traced to John Sayles's own intellectual journey to this historical subject. In *Thinking in Pictures*, the filmmaker explains how his path to the Matewan Massacre traveled through the work of new labor historians, who by the 1970s were dismantling their field's dominant "institutional" approach, which focused on labor's most visible components: trade unions, labor leaders, and strikes. In contrast, these new labor historians were interested in better understanding workers, and they did so by exploring the intricate social relations forged within their workplaces and communities.[15] This turn reflected the discipline's broader interest in the social history of everyday folk, and it produced significant insights into the long-term, multigenerational process of class development. As E. P. Thompson, a leading advocate of this new approach, explained, "We cannot understand class unless we see it as a social and cultural formation, arising from the process which can only be studied as [workers] work themselves out over a considerable historical period."[16] The new labor history, in other words, went to the ground to get to know the people, but then remained there over time to best explain the development of working-class culture.

Converted to the cause, Sayles's film excels in the former but has no time for the latter. In *Matewan*, typically abstract institutions like "the company," "the company town," and "the union" get transformed into a collection of personal relationships worked out in this particular place. As such, the specifics of place matter quite a bit to understanding these interactions, as well as to the film's success in portraying the workers' world. So while John Sayles's familiar Western narrative carries the audience along, Oscar-winning cinematographer Haskell Wexler frames the narrow verticality of this Appalachian hollow in such a way as to make inescapable the intimate entwinement of workplace with homelife. In this tight space, there are few unfamiliar faces or single-layered relationships. Danny must share his rooming house with the hated Baldwins, Sid Hatfield regularly crosses paths with his adversaries as he patrols Main Street, and ethnically diverse communities are "segregated" by just a few hundred yards, if at all. This intimate and textured look at mining life is further enhanced by *Matewan*'s use of local actors, whose regional accents and dialects provide some stilted prose but also lend an air of authenticity to these Appalachian scenes. Even the largely amateur cast's uneven performances somehow contribute to the film's credibility, similar to a Coen Brothers' production like *Fargo* (1996) or *No Country for Old Men* (2007). In other words, this is not some sweeping Hollywood epic, but a grainy, realistic depiction of life in an Appalachian coal town.

And yet, despite all the benefits of this layered portrayal of interpersonal relations, *Matewan*'s lack of historical perspective leaves it susceptible to a long-running criticism of popular depictions of Appalachia. That is, the film fails to connect these events in Mingo County to larger processes being worked out in the region and the nation over time. Since at least the late 1970s, Appalachian scholars have been combating explanations of the region's problems that center on the uniqueness of its people and its isolation in the mountains. Current scholarship emphasizes the dynamic and diverse history of Appalachian communities, rejecting the static and stereotypical "culture-of-poverty" portrayals recently (re)made popular by J. D. Vance's *Hillbilly Elegy*.[17] This scholarship also reveals the region's longstanding connection to larger capitalist networks, its preindustrial characteristics that shaped later industrial exploitation, and the partnership between absentee capitalists and local elites that produced corrupt state apparatuses to plunder the province.[18] But sadly, none of this broader picture is present in *Matewan*. As historian Eric Foner noted twenty years ago when reviewing this film, "The relentless concentration on the local community, *Matewan*'s greatest strength, also contributes to its most glaring weakness—the absence of context, both historical and political."[19] That critique still resonates today.

And I think I know why. For a film that ostensibly is about the coal mining industry, Sayles and his cast say remarkably little about coal or the land from which it is mined. Instead, the film's focus, like the vast majority of academic attention paid to Appalachia, remains on the plight of laborers. This is not necessarily a bad thing, particularly as new labor historians have deepened our understanding of the relations between workers and how categories of race, gender, and class can both structure working communities and sometimes be transcended for the greater good. These are invaluable insights and are central to Sayles's message. But what gets lost in these vivid portrayals of Appalachian coal miners is a sense that their social interactions occurred within a wider world of economic and ecological change. Miners were not always so destitute, their options were not always so limited, and the tensions between them and mine operators did not constantly erupt into work stoppages and violence. This is not to say that the work was ever easy or safe, the wages fair, or the struggle to survive in this exploitative labor regime merely episodic. But less spectacular everyday struggles were key to developing a class consciousness that could sustain labor solidarity, and open conflicts like the one portrayed in *Matewan* occurred mainly at significant inflection points within the broader coal industry. These were moments of crisis produced by local reactions to shifting external forces, not workers simply reaching a "tipping point" of frustration with existing conditions. The real Matewan Massacre, for example, came at the end of southern West Virginia's greatest economic boom, when World War I's extraordinary demand for and federal oversight of the nation's coal supplies emboldened the United Mine Workers of America to expand into Mingo County. Such expansion, however, ran headfirst into a postwar recession that brought declining coal demand and a new era of relative stagnation that would dominate the industry for the next fifty years. "Thus, the violence in West Virginia," according to historian John Williams, "was symptomatic both of a sharp short-run downturn in the coal industry and the onset of long-term stagnation." [20] Local factors certainly mattered: Mingo County's relatively poor coal quality meant that it felt the brunt of this slowdown first, and Matewan's position as one of the few "free" towns not owned by a coal company allowed for the presence of independent political actors like Sheriff Sid Hatfield and Mayor Cabell Testerman. [21] But these local forces operated within broader structural changes that the film ignores.

In addition to larger economic trends, labor violence was also the result of working people running out of other options. Again, *Matewan* does an excellent job of conveying the desperate sense of dependency that pervaded most coal communities by the early twentieth century. In the film, we see mining families reliant on the Stone Mountain Coal Company for nearly everything, from housing to jobs to food to medical care and even currency in the form of company scrip. But while this dependency is palpable and was real, the film offers little explanation for how it came to be. Environmental historians have done better, particularly Steven Stoll in his recent account of how mountain folk were dispossessed of the private property and shared commons that previously provided subsistence. According to Stoll, as Northern capitalists and local elites sought to develop West Virginia's vast resources in the years following the Civil War, their corporate "fixers" exploited discrepancies in land deeds to establish superior title or strong-armed uninformed mountaineers to sell mineral and timber rights for which they had little obvious use. This mass transfer of property from small holders to capitalists enabled new land practices, such as large-scale timbering and mining, that undercut the ecological base of the old subsistence system. When denuded commons could no longer support the game and gardens that had sustained previous generations, mountain farmers drifted into coal camps with little option of returning to their previous lives. [22] The situation grew worse after 1900, when coal operators began recruiting a "judicious mixture" of African Americans and European immigrants to undercut labor solidarity. [23] These newcomers had even less recourse to the land once the exploitative nature of the labor regime became apparent.

Matewan beautifully depicts the heroic efforts to overcome ethnic divisions and combat the exploitation derived from dependency, but it glosses over the longer history that made direct confrontation through strikes seem the only viable option.

And so, for all its rich renderings of life within a mining community, *Matewan*'s myopic lens of labor history renders opaque the broader tale of Appalachia's industrial exploitation, ecological destruction, and the increasingly limited options of its people. The film offers snippets of this deeper understanding, such as when absurdly stereotypical "genuine hill people," who we are told "had most their land stole by the company," emerge out of the forest to defend a striking coal camp. In another scene, we see an entire community provision that same camp with resources from the surrounding mountainside, reflecting the enduring knowledge of a previous subsistence system. But like the mysterious hill people who simply disappear back into the woods in search of game and free-range hogs, these insights are ephemeral. They provide hints of a significant, deeper history that the film leaves unexplored. Instead, *Matewan* offers a trade-off, providing a close look at the interpersonal relations of a mining community driven to the edge at the expense of a broader understanding of the forces that brought them there.

Conclusion

No film can be all things to all people, perhaps especially one that attempts to unsettle such supposedly settled notions as the source of American greatness. *Matewan* does this by deploying the most familiar of all genre narratives, the Western, to lure the audience into a familiar and entertaining tale, only to defy expectations with an unexpected message. The real-life events upon which the film is based assist in the ruse: there is injustice, a lone gunfighter, and climactic violence. But in the hands of master storyteller John Sayles, a climax without resolution provides the opportunity to rethink foundational myths. Instead of rooting American exceptionalism in a citizenry of freedom-loving individuals, Sayles offers America's diversity and tradition of community building as the nation's true bedrock. Delivered to Ronald Reagan's deeply divided country, and with the understanding that our stories about the past must provide wisdom for the present, this message resonates powerfully then and now.

It is also a message that is beautifully delivered. By tightening the scope on a small coal-mining community, *Matewan* provides the layered, intimate portrayal of intertwined lives that residents of such towns know well. The acting, cinematography, and score are superb, and each plays a significant role in building this nuanced portrait. But the rich detail also comes at a cost. Missing is a broader understanding of the economic forces acting upon this mountain hamlet, as well as the longer patterns of dispossession and despoliation that left its inhabitants with few viable options. Without attention to these factors, *Matewan* flirts with discredited Appalachian stereotypes of a unique and isolated people permanently awash in poverty and prone to violence. Such is the risk in applying only half of the insights of the new labor historiography. Excelling in its vivid portrayal of a working-class community and its culture, the film fails to explain how these came to be and why they were suddenly imperiled. A broader energy and environmental history perspective reminds us that even the best of stories operate within larger and longer histories.

Notes

1. John Sayles, dir., *Matewan* (New York: Cinecom Pictures, 1987). The conflict between, and among, the Hatfields and McCoys is perhaps the most celebrated family feud in American history. Its origins remain murky, but nearly three decades of violence at the end of the nineteenth century left dozens dead on either side of the Tug River, which separated the largely West Virginia–based Hatfields and the eastern Kentucky McCoys. The feud has inspired countless popular films, songs, works of fiction, and amateur histories, but for the best scholarly examinations of its origins, development, and impacts, see Altina L. Waller, *Feud: Hatfields, McCoys, and Social Change in Appalachia, 1860–1900* (Chapel Hill: University of North Carolina Press, 1988); Otis K. Rice, *The Hatfields and the McCoys* (Lexington: University Press of Kentucky, 1982).
2. Much recent attention has been paid to the Battle of Blair Mountain. See Lon Savage, *Thunder in the Mountains: The West Virginia Mine War, 1920–21* (Pittsburgh: University of Pittsburgh Press, 1990); Robert Shogan, *The Battle of Blair Mountain: The Story of America's Largest Labor Uprising* (Boulder, CO: Westview Press, 2004); William C. Blizzard, *When Miners March* (Oakland, CA: PM Press, 2010); James R. Green, *The Devil Is Here in These Hills: West Virginia's Coal Miners and Their Battle for Freedom* (New York: Grove Press, 2016), esp. part 3.
3. David Corbin, *Life, Work, and Rebellion in the Coal Fields: The Southern West Virginia Miners, 1880–1922*, 2nd ed. (Morgantown: West Virginia University Press, 2015), xxii. Corbin provides an excellent summary of the evolving scholarship on the West Virginia Mine Wars (xvii–xxii). For a more concise historiographical review of the Matewan Massacre, see Rebecca J. Bailey, *Matewan before the Massacre: Politics, Coal, and the Roots of Conflict in a West Virginia Mining Community* (Morgantown: West Virginia University Press, 2008), 7–10.
4. Barry Keith Grant, introduction to *Film Genre Reader IV*, ed. Barry Keith Grant (Austin: University of Texas Press, 2012), xvii.
5. Barry Keith Grant, "Genre Films and Cultural Myth," *Genre Films and Cultural Myth* (blog), April 20, 2011, http://filmint.nu/?p=1689.
6. Jeff Young, "'Matewan' Revisited: Film Unearthed Region's Buried Labor History," 89.3 WFPL News Louisville, October 9, 2017, https://wfpl.org/matewan-revisited -film-unearthed-regions-buried-labor-history.

7. Much has been written on the structure and persistence of the Western in popular print and film. For a concise summary of the genre's evolution, see Robert V. Hine and John Mack Faragher, *The American West: A New Interpretive History* (New Haven, CT: Yale University Press, 2000), 472–511. For a more detailed overview, which emphasizes the essential masculinity of Westerns, see Lee Clark Mitchell, *Westerns: Making the Man in Fiction and Film* (Chicago: University of Chicago Press, 1996).

8. The amount of ink spilled by Western historians over the terms *manifest destiny* and *frontier* is absurd, but to begin at the beginning, see Frederick Jackson Turner, "The Significance of the Frontier in American History," in Frederick Jackson Turner, *Rereading Frederick Jackson Turner: The Significance of the Frontier in American History, and Other Essays*, ed. John Mack Faragher (New York: H. Holt, 1994), 31–60. Faragher's afterword provides a nice summary of the long-running, and sometimes heated, debates surrounding Turner's frontier thesis (225–41).

9. John Sayles, *Thinking in Pictures: The Making of the Movie "Matewan"* (Boston: Houghton Mifflin, 1987), 27.

10. Ronald D. Eller, *Uneven Ground: Appalachia since 1945* (Lexington: University Press of Kentucky, 2008), esp. 221–28.

11. Patricia Nelson Limerick, *The Legacy of Conquest: The Unbroken Past of the American West* (New York: Norton, 1987), esp. 17–32.

12. For Sid Hatfield's personal history and reputation, see Savage, *Thunder in the Mountains*, 10–18.

13. John Hellman, "Vietnam and the Hollywood Genre Film: Inversions of American Mythology in *The Deer Hunter* and *Apocalypse Now*," *American Quarterly* 34, no. 4 (Autumn 1982): 419.

14. Herbert G. Gutman, *Work, Culture, and Society in Industrializing America: Essays in American Working-Class and Social History* (New York: Vintage Books, 1976), 121–208; Corbin, *Life, Work, and Rebellion in the Coal Fields*, esp. 61–86; Ronald L. Lewis, *Black Coal Miners in America: Race, Class, and Community Conflict, 1780–1980* (Lexington: University Press of Kentucky, 1987), 121–64; Joe W. Trotter, *Coal, Class, and Color: Blacks in Southern West Virginia, 1915–32* (Urbana: University of Illinois Press, 1990). Herbert Hill argues that too much has been made of this supposed interracial cooperation. Herbert Hill, "Myth-Making as Labor History: Herbert Gutman and the United Mine Workers of America," *International Journal of Politics, Culture, and Society* 2, no. 2 (1988): 132–200. For a response to Hill's critique, see Joe William Trotter, "The Dynamics of Race and Ethnicity in the US Coal Industry," *International Review of Social History* 60 (2015): 145–64.

15. Sayles, *Thinking in Pictures*, 10. For helpful reviews of this historiographical transition, see Gutman, *Work, Culture, and Society in Industrializing America*, 435–37; Corbin, *Life, Work, and Rebellion in the Coal Fields*, xix–xxii.

16. E. P. Thompson, *The Making of the English Working Class* (New York: Vintage Books, 1963), 11, quoted in Corbin, *Life, Work, and Rebellion in the Coal Fields*, xxi.

17. J. D. Vance, *Hillbilly Elegy: A Memoir of a Family and Culture in Crisis* (New York: Harper, 2016). For criticisms of Vance's portrayal of Appalachia, see William R. Schumann and Rebecca Adkins Fletcher, eds., *Appalachia Revisited: New Perspectives on Place, Tradition, and Progress* (Lexington: University Press of Kentucky, 2016); Elizabeth Catte, *What You Are Getting Wrong about Appalachia* (Cleveland: Belt Publishing, 2018); and Anthony Harkins and Meredith McCarroll, eds., *Appalachian*

Reckoning: A Region Responds to "Hillbilly Elegy" (Morgantown: West Virginia University Press, 2019).

18. Ronald D. Eller, *Miners, Millhands, and Mountaineers: Industrialization of the Appalachian South, 1880–1930* (Knoxville: University of Tennessee Press, 1982); Mary Beth Pudup, *Appalachia in the Making: The Mountain South in the Nineteenth Century* (Chapel Hill: University of North Carolina Press, 1995); Ronald L. Lewis, *Transforming the Appalachian Countryside Railroads, Deforestation, and Social Change in West Virginia, 1880–1920* (Chapel Hill: University of North Carolina Press, 1998); Dwight B. Billings and Kathleen M. Blee, *The Road to Poverty: The Making of Wealth and Hardship in Appalachia* (Cambridge, UK: Cambridge University Press, 2000).

19. Eric Foner, "Matewan," in *Past Imperfect: History According to the Movies*, ed. Mark C. Carnes (New York: H. Holt, 1995), 206.

20. John Williams, introduction to Savage, *Thunder in the Mountains*, xi. As for the union's expansion into Mingo County and southern West Virginia, as well as the response it elicited from local coal operators, see Green, *Devil Is Here in These Hills*, 181–214. For the broader coal industry trends, see James Howard Thompson, *Significant Trends in the West Virginia Coal Industry, 1900–1957* (Morgantown: West Virginia University Bureau of Business Research, 1958).

21. Rebecca Bailey's entire book makes the case for the importance of local factors in understanding the violence in Matewan. Bailey, *Matewan before the Massacre*.

22. Steven Stoll, *Ramp Hollow: The Ordeal of Appalachia* (New York: Hill and Wang, 2017), chaps. 4 and 7.

23. Kenneth Bailey, "A Judicious Mixture: Negroes and Immigrants in the West Virginia Mines, 1880–1917," in *Blacks in Appalachia*, ed. William Hobart Turner and Edward J. Cabbell (Lexington: University Press of Kentucky, 1985), 117–32; Lewis, *Black Coal Miners in America*, 121–42.

Chapter 14

"This Is the Third World": Coal-Fired America in *Montana* (1990) and *Powwow Highway* (1989)

Ryan Driskell Tate

In 1971, Kentucky writer Harry Caudill issued a stark warning to the American West: it was on path to become the next Appalachia. "As the demand for coal goes up, the proportion obtained by stripping also rises," he wrote in *My Land Is Dying*. "New power stations near sources of coal supplies may bring the strip mining boom to states like North Dakota, Montana and Wyoming."[1] At that time, few people thought much about coalfields of eastern Montana. The earlier history of mining on these Western prairies harkened back to the Gilded Age, when small coal camps provided a spot on the map for railroad engineers to pause and fuel up on routes to elsewhere. But when the transcontinentals converted to diesel engines in the 1950s, the region's coal sector faded away without much fanfare. The locals made a living off the livestock and prairie grasslands, and few paid much mind to the bounties beneath their feet.[2]

And yet by the early 1970s, Caudill found himself, for better or worse, correct in his predictions about the new geographies of coal production. The national energy crisis revived the Western coal business in its eleventh hour. As the government and energy industry plotted new ways to meet projected energy needs and wean the nation off its addiction to foreign oil, Richard Nixon's plan for "energy independence" called for frenzied build-out of centralized strip mines and power plants to generate cheap electricity through the nation's most abundant fossil fuel: coal. Energy executives knew they'd barely scratched the surface of the fossil landscapes out West. They went on a coal-buying spree and binged on new leases, new mines, and new plants.

Within thirty years, the Western coalfields of Wyoming and Montana became the largest producing region in the nation.[3]

The B movies *Montana* (1990) and *Powwow Highway* (1989) try to explain what happened here, east of Billings. They profile neighboring communities, one white and one Indigenous, to provide a sense of the magnitude of mass extraction in the early years of the coal rush. At times, the scripts read like amusing bits of campy Wild West theater. They're jam-packed with fistfights, damsels in distress, chases on horseback, white hats, and black hats. But the films remain important historical artifacts: fictionalized accounts of an important moment in time, when Western coalfields became ground zero for mass extraction and today's coal-fired climate crisis. These films depict in human terms the return of what Bernard DeVoto once called the "plundered province"—the rural West's position in the United States as a sacrifice zone for the rest of the nation.[4] They provide elegies and farewells to the rural West before energy industrialization, when things felt simpler and more meaningful for white settlers and Indigenous communities alike, even if that feeling was more nominal than real.

These small films, though largely forgotten now, harbor greater importance than their cultural neglect might suggest. They strike at the heart of the "Western paradox" that once bedeviled an entire generation of Western historians. Donald Worster famously puzzled over the white man's Westering dream: to live one life in nature and another life with machines.[5] What's interesting now is how much the attention to fossil fuels and energy transitions has revived this paradox as a subject of study, returning to age-old historical concerns about industrialization.[6] Just as Andrew Needham and Judith Nies make clear for the Southwest, where metropolitan growth in Phoenix, Las Vegas, and Los Angeles relied on the use and abuse of coal-fired electricity, the frenzied pursuit of fossil fuels in the northern plains bound American dreams to Indigenous lands and rural resources.[7] *Montana* and *Powwow Highway* shine a spotlight into the forgotten corners of postindustrial society: the frontline communities that powered the suburban tract houses and strip malls of the consumers' republic. These places felt the promises and perils of "high energy" society at its most extreme.[8]

Both movies sprung from the literary minds of high-profile Western writers—Larry McMurtry and David Seals—and provide early and potent examples of what's now called "post-Western" cinema. Neil Campbell, an American studies scholar, has offered the most clear-cut definition of the term: current art and film about the West, "coming after and going beyond the traditional Western while engaging with and commenting on its deeply haunting assumptions and values."[9] The post-Western, in other words, remains rooted in Western experiences but is shorn of myths and commentary. White men's settler fantasies become actual fantasies. As such, both films provide a view into the region's real-life ranchers and Indigenous communities, who experienced the fracture and heartache of the new coal economy much as they do on-screen: as individuals bound by choices outside their control.

Taken together, *Montana* and *Powwow Highway* offer a massive contribution to energy humanities: they strip away the abstractions and technical details rolled up into so much scholarly commentary on energy and instead glimpse the world of people brought face-to-face with its concrete realities—newcomers and smokestacks and changes in the land.[10] The protagonists and problematic heroes face a catalogue of personal trials and psychological tolls wrought by new energy regimes, as the audience witnesses internal battles for authenticity and identity in a world turned upside down. The films remind us, above all else, that while energy systems and technologies shape politics and economies, they also shape cultures and human relationships, social worlds and personal experiences. Writing at a moment of profound climate crisis, it's necessary to reflect upon how much fossil fuels reconfigure not only economies and global environments, but also peoples and places.

Montana (1990)

During the early 1970s, when Larry McMurtry set to work writing *Montana*—his first original screenplay—he hoped to repeat the magic of the *Last Picture Show*, his semiautobiographical novel that received eight Academy Award nominations when adapted for the screen in 1971. McMurtry applied for a grant from the National Endowment of the Arts and, though frustrated by the strings attached and its "complicated list of stipulations," took the money and headed for the northern plains. He was looking for the just-so story that captured the heart of the modern West. If he had learned anything studying at Stanford under the tutelage of Wallace Stegner, the dean of Western literature, it was to write fiction as truth. At some point, McMurtry read press coverage of real-life ranchers in southeastern Montana trying to protect their land from multinational energy firms. After poking around and talking to a few of them, he settled on translating their stories to the big screen.[11]

The plot of *Montana* could have easily been true to history: the Guthries, a family of cattle ranchers, fall on hard times in a tight cattle market. When a large coal company makes them an offer to strip mine their land, the family splits into factions that resemble a war of words within the broader community. On one side stands Hoyce (Richard Crenna), the family patriarch, who wants to sell the outfit—"I'd like to be out of debt just once before I die"—and son Clyde

(Justin Deas), who wants to make an easy dollar from a coal sale—"I hate to be a slave to a piece of country." On other side stands Bess (Gena Rowlands), the family matriarch, who opposes the sale of land inherited from her family's homestead—"I hate strip mining"—and daughter Peg (Lea Thompson), who is the most environmentally conscious and wants to keep the family property— "You don't want this valley filling up with smokestacks." On the fence stands Jimbo (Darren Dalton), Peg's fiancé, who works in a nearby strip mine for the paycheck, even though he prefers the ranching lifestyle. But Peg worries about his future: "Every year you get further away from ranch life."[12]

The screenplay experiments with McMurtry's favorite theme: the clash of the romantic and the realistic. The film's white people, reared on cowboy myths, face off with a new class of tycoons. After the opening altercations with land surveyors and coal executives, the family tug-of-war takes center screen. The family provides a microcosm for the broader coal fight between protecting the awesome spaciousness or exploiting a rural place. At some point, every family member wonders some version of Peg's line: "Is there a future in cattle? What do you think the future of coal is?"

The opening scene makes clear that the coal boom unsettles existing power relationships on the northern plains. The first prospector (Dean Norris) pits the Guthrie family against one another. Hoyce must convince Bess to let the company drill on the ranch, and the prospectors threaten to leave if Hoyce can't "control [his] woman." The region's white men all face some existential crisis, and in their physic meltdowns lash out at those around them. Hoyce, in his first scene, punches a land agent and then carries his temper into racial and misogynistic violence: he brawls with Native Americans at a roadside bar ("roping Indians") and physically assaults his wife ("I won't stand here and let some old woman insult me"). He wants to sell the property, not just because of cattle markets and economic maelstroms, but because he feels emasculated by the changes afoot.

Hoyce continues to reassure his family that he's got everything under control. "Somebody wears the pants around this ranch," he says, but it's clear he's only fooling himself. The rugged rancher is really an economic dependent. He lives on homesteaded land his father-in-law "proved up" and that he owns only through marriage. The filmmakers carry Hoyce's crisis of masculinity to the most obvious Freudian conclusion. In his redemptive scene, or so it's intended, he explains to his wife, Bess, why he really wants to sell the property: he's been out of sorts and frustrated by a recent bout of sexual impotence. Hoyce remains self-conscious about his lost manhood, of being "over the hill," as he puts it, and though audiences are supposed to take pity and appreciate the honesty, it's hard to ignore the callowness of his motives.

The film's fixation on technology provides a central metaphor in this world where men feel emasculated and inadequate in modern industrial society. The Guthries are at their best as a family and most egalitarian when working the land with simple tools, such as mending a fence, or herding cattle. The freedom from machines and big technologies restores their humanity and even patches over their conflicts to create harmony with the environment and one another. By contrast, the new coal miners embrace a mechanized existence as a sturdy tool for violence and domination over nature, over women, over anachronistic ranchers, over each other. The big machines gouge open the earth, and aerial shots from a single-engine plane provide the audience with a bird's-eye view of the gore within the open pits. Down below, the coal miners hoot and holler and enjoy the power of machines. They control the might to raze the prairie with the crank of a wheel.

At its worst, the Western genre has a tendency to ridicule women, and in *Montana* coal miners rely on the new technologies to settle personal scores with women in their lives. When young miner Willie (Scott Coffey) discovers that his fiancée moonlights as a prostitute, he drives his titanic earthmover to her mobile home and bulldozes the trailer with her inside. She escapes the near-death experience while he yawps, "The wedding's off." Then there's the worksite bully, a violent-tempered coal miner named Pierce (Michael Madsen), who beats his girlfriend for hanging out with Clyde, the rancher's son. When Clyde arrives on horseback to rescue her, Pierce chases the pair in his massive pickup truck. He can't catch them, but in the film's climactic scene, Pierce seeks vengeance with the most vintage technology the Wild West has ever known: the barrel of a gun.

It took eighteen years before *Montana*'s script ever made it to screen. Ted Turner's new television network TNT picked up McMurtry's screenplay and released it as a direct-to-cable movie. But by then, the hook of strip mining and environmental ruin stories, told by Harry Caudill, had passed from the nightly news. Director William Graham decided to soft focus the screenplay's critiques of unbridled capitalism and instead sharpen the hijinks of good-time cowboys. The film turned tragedy into a comedy of errors, and McMurtry distanced himself from the project. He wrote later that he "had trouble getting in sync with" the film and even speculated that Turner, a media mogul who had recently purchased a ranch in Montana, bankrolled the "virtuous little film" as a tax write-off.[13]

The film zooms in so much on the family's squabbles that it sacrifices the bigger picture of extractive exploitation, some of which appears in the original script.[14] The entire community comes to blows over the decisions of faceless energy executives, but no one dares to call them out. Strip mining becomes nothing more than a matter of personal grievance. *Montana* barely even nods to the broader regional impacts of fossil fuel development. Hoyce, at one point, asks his "big Injun" friend, a Northern Cheyenne whose reservation is practically on his doorstep, why the tribal council has refused to sell its coal rights: "You and your people sell your coal, you'd be able to buy a big old purple Cadillac." The Northern Cheyenne responds: "I don't know what the grass would say. They'd make a mess out there."

Powwow Highway (1989)

The Northern Cheyenne's struggle against the same coal companies comes to the fore in *Powwow Highway* (1989), a film based on a novel by David Seals, which he initially published privately by Xerox copy in 1978. The buddy film follows a Cheyenne named Philbert Bono (Gary Farmer) crossing the countryside in a rusted '64 Buick LeSabre with his friend Buddy Red Bow (A Martinez). Buddy and Philbert must drive from Lame Deer, Montana, to Santa Fe to rescue Buddy's sister Bonnie (Joanelle Romero). The local police have conspired with corporate land-grabbers to jail Bonnie on trumped-up charges in order to lure Buddy off the reservation before a controversial tribal council vote: whether or not to lease Northern Cheyenne coal to a large energy conglomerate. Buddy, a Vietnam veteran and sympathizer with the American Indian Movement (AIM), is outspoken against strip mining. As one executive complains, he's "got a bunch of radicals on the loose up there."[15]

The first major scene of the film portrays a sales pitch from Sandy Youngblood (Geoffrey Rivas), an Indigenous man who works for a white-owned coal company. His slick presentation, complete with graphs and charts, assures the Northern Cheyenne that the multinational energy company has their best interests in mind. Buddy rejects the claims. "It's always the same deal," he hollers from the back of the room. "You get what you want, and we get the shaft." Youngblood tells Buddy he's out of line and tries to smooth things over, before Buddy fires back: "Seventy-five percent of our reservation is living below the poverty line. You tell us stripping off what's left of our resources is going to change that? Maybe you better tell us something different. This ain't the American dream we're living in. This here is the Third World."

The film explores the depths of "Indianness" and authenticity in an extractive landscape. The clash between Buddy Red Bow and Sandy Youngblood generates the incident that sets the whole plot in motion. The two men represent opposing interests on the coal issue. Youngblood's polished economic plans earn favor within the tribal council, which believes their poverty-stricken community needs well-paying jobs—as one executive puts it, "economic autonomy for the entire Lame Deer community." The tribe's anticoal activists, though, view the well-heeled Youngblood as a fake Cheyenne and decry him as an "apple"—red on the outside and white on the inside—for trying to exploit Indigenous peoples for profit. At one point, the film makes it seem likely that the Northern Cheyenne will vote in favor of signing away their coal rights, though the real-life history of coal leasing on the reservation, as historians Jamie Allison and Teresa Houser have shown, was far more complicated.[16]

The film presents political conflicts within Indigenous communities to counter popular caricatures of innate "Indianness." *Powwow Highway*, like most road movies, pairs its male characters in an adventure to learn and bond, and Buddy and Philbert spend much of the film's rising action at odds over their worldviews. Buddy thinks his people's histories and stories are inadequate for handling new political problems. He tries to get out of participating in a Christmas powwow at Pine Ridge because he's unconformable with Indigenous traditions, asking, "You think a few lousy beads and feathers are a culture or something?" He dismisses the Northern Cheyenne's "fairy stories" as useless and apolitical. "It's just too bad those stories don't tell us why our reservations turned into sewers," he says. "White American won't hold off much longer. They're hungry and they want our coal. . . . They're gonna take it." By contrast, Philbert believes in the beauty of old and new, and prizes the survival of his people. He views the road trip as a "vision quest"—a way to claim Cheyenne status as a warrior—and names his car a "pony" and "Protector," which will carry him to sacred cultural sites.

By portraying Northern Cheyenne diversity, the film breaks the mold of Indigenous typecasts. At Pine Ridge, one group of Indigenous leaders try to rough up Buddy. "All you AIM sonsofbitches are going to rot in prison," a member of the Oglala Sioux taunts, "just like your friend Peltier," referencing AIM activist *Leonard* Peltier. Presenting the conflict in this way enables *Powwow Highway* to push beyond the boundaries of the "Hollywood Indian." Literary scholar Jane Tompkins provides a good description of how Native Americans have been typically cast in Western film: "The ones I saw functioned as props, bits of local color, textual effects. As people they had no presence. Quite often they filled the role of villains."[17] Instead, *Powwow Highway* grounds itself in Indian Country and, unlike many cinematic predecessors, presents "Indian material from an Indian perspective."[18] That's not to say the film is without its problems (stereotypes of "drunken Indians" and "broken English") but it more often than not acknowledges rather than embraces such racist stereotypes.

In the film, Buddy and Philbert hatch an action-filled plot to bust Bonnie out of jail. There's a deliberate homage to old-fashioned Westerns, first in the treatment of women as game pieces, then in the jailbreak, and finally in the subsequent chase. The true character journeys, though, occur in the scenes intended to contrast Native American worldviews and white capitalist ideologies. At one point, Philbert and Buddy confront each other while standing, not so subtly, in front of a gigantic Wyoming coal-fired power plant. The chimney stacks and hulking steel in the background dwarf the human beings in the foreground of the frame. The men eat gas station hot dogs and drink cheap Miller beer, while Philbert tells Buddy about his people's oral tradition of "Wihio the trickster." He explains that the "trickster"—"sometimes a man, sometimes an animal"—mostly likes "pulling antics" at people's expense. Buddy rejects the notion that he has anything to learn from these stories, but the industrial backdrop makes it clear that Philbert is speaking in parable. The white corporate land-grabbers, intent on turning the Northern Cheyenne reservation into a coal-fired power plant, are Wihio the trickster, and the Cheyenne people have seen him before. There's much to learn and remember, Philbert is saying, from ancestors and history.

The film differs from David Seals's novel in its preference for Philbert's worldview. The book portrays Philbert as a loveable goof who provides comic relief.[19] But Seals was himself a member of AIM and likely more aligned politically with Buddy's character. The novel presents strip mining on the reservation as an allegory for what bell hooks would call "*white* supremacist *capitalist patriarchy.*" Seals describes the stacks on the power plant as "penis snouts" and anthropomorphically connects them to white men. Throughout the novel, the power plant "belched," "farted," "pissed," and "shit." "It was the whiteman's contribution to intergalactic space travel," Seals writes. "The mother ship to a scratching brood of space shuttles."[20]

Seals lost considerable control over the project when it passed into the hands of Los Angeles screenwriters Janet Heaney and Jean Stawarz. The screenwriters hired Native American consultants to give their script some authenticity, including former AIM leader John Trudell and Comanche guitarist Jesse Ed Davis. The crucial contact for the film, though, came by happenstance when Davis was performing at the Palomino Club in North Hollywood. His friend, rock star George Harrison, came that night, and Davis apparently told them about *Powwow Highway*. When Harrison, the former Beatle and co-owner of HandMade Films, heard about it, he agreed to produce the film, while Robbie Robertson, lead guitarist and songwriter for The Band, contributed songs for the soundtrack.[21]

This remarkable backstory is part of the film's allure. The rock stars and enhanced script inspired the independent aesthetic that turned *Powwow Highway* into a cult classic. After it received the Sundance Film Festival Filmmaker's Trophy, it won Best Picture, Best Director, and Best Actor at the American

Indian Film Festival, and picked up four nominations at the Independent Spirit Awards. As a result, *Powwow Highway* found a longer shelf life than *Montana*. If *Montana* was about a seemingly bygone world of righteous ranchers that viewers could find while channel surfing, *Powwow Highway* spoke more clearly to the enduring questions of settler colonialism—with a star-studded cast and prizes to boost its long-term reputation.

Montana and *Powwow Highway* provide an important contribution to energy humanities and film studies because they not only depict the cultural mood of the 1970s and 1980s, but they also capture the stakes of energy debates in the rural American West during that period. Just as extraction predominated in the Old West, the films reveal how it lived on in the New West. The boom and bust of the Old West mining frontier, historian Patricia Limerick once wrote, "placed settlements of white people where none had been before. It provoked major conflicts with Indians. It called territories and states into being and forced them to an early maturity." She continued, "Mining set a mood that has never disappeared from the West: the attitude of extractive industry—get in, get rich, get out." [22] The 1970s coal rush on the northern plains continued that "legacy of conquest" and impinged not only on the land but also on relationships among peoples and within communities and families.

At a moment of climate catastrophe, when so much of the political commentary on "energy" remains shrouded in wonkery and policy shoptalk, *Montana* and *Powwow Highway* provide a necessary focus on human interest. Although prone to camp and comedy, the films are rare gems, especially when paired together: they depict the disparate rural constituencies on the front lines of fossil fuel development. While these communities, and the people within them, reacted to the ordeal in disparate ways, they shared in the struggle for self-transformation, authenticity, and identity. These films remind us of the role of energy systems and technologies in shaping not only abstract forces of politics and economies, but also human relationships and everyday life. Those social concerns remain all the more poignant in an age of global climate disaster, when Peg Guthrie's worry in *Montana*—"What do you think the future of coal is?"—has become one for us all.

Notes

1.   Harry Caudill, *My Land Is Dying* (New York: E. P. Dutton, 1971), 129–30.
2.   Energy Information Administration, *Coal Data: A Reference* (Washington, DC: US Department of Energy, 1989), 15. On early Western mines, see Robert A. Chadwick, "Coal: Montana's Prosaic Treasure," *Montana: The Magazine of Western History* 23, no. 4 (Autumn 1973): 18–31; William S. Bryans, "A History of Transcontinental Railroads and Coal Mining on the Northern Plains to 1920" (PhD

diss., University of Wyoming, 1987); Richard White, *It's Your Misfortune and None of My Own: A New History of the American West* (Norman: University of Oklahoma Press, 1991), 256–57.

3. Ben Franklin, "Coal Rush Is on as Strip Mining Spreads into West," *New York Times*, August 22, 1971, 1, 49; Thomas Bass, "Moving Gary, Indiana to the Great Plains: The Oil Companies Head to the Prairies," *Mother Jones*, July 1976. On "energy independence," see Meg Jacobs, *Panic at the Pump: The Energy Crisis and the Transformation of American Politics in the 1970s* (New York: Hill and Wang, 2016).

4. Bernard Augustine DeVoto, "The West: A Plundered Province," *Harper's* 169 (August 1934): 355–64.

5. On the Western paradox, see Donald Worster, *Under Western Skies: Nature and History in the American West* (New York: Oxford University Press, 1992).

6. On this concern in earlier periods, see Allan Kulikoff, *The Agrarian Origins of American Capitalism* (Charlottesville: University Press of Virginia, 1992).

7. Andrew Needham, *Power Lines: Phoenix and the Making of the Modern Southwest* (Princeton, NJ: Princeton University Press, 2015); Judith Nies, *Unreal City: Las Vegas, Black Mesa, and the Fate of the West* (New York: Nation Books, 2014); Teresa Houser, "Native American Sovereignty and Coal Mining in the Powder River Basin," *Mining History Journal* 20 (2013): 53–67; James Robert Allison III, *Sovereignty for Survival: American Energy Development and Indian Self-Determination* (New Haven, CT: Yale University Press, 2015).

8. On "high energy" society, see David Nye, *Consuming Power: A Social History of American Energies* (Cambridge, MA: MIT Press, 1999). On consumers' republic, see Lizabeth Cohen, *A Consumers' Republic: The Politics of Mass Consumption in Postwar America* (New York: Vintage, 2003).

9. Neil Campbell, *Post-Westerns: Cinema, Region, West* (Lincoln: University of Nebraska Press, 2013), 31. The term *post-Western* was first applied to cinema in Philip French, *Westerns: Aspects of a Movie Genre* (London: Secker and Warburg, 1973). Campbell offers the best elaboration of the idea, along with White, *It's Your Misfortune*, 537.

10. For a critique of energy studies' preference for the technical over the human, see the introduction to On Barak, *Powering Empire: How Coal Made the Middle East and Sparked Global Carbonization* (Berkeley: University of California Press, 2020).

11. Larry McMurtry, *Hollywood: A Third Memoir* (New York: Simon and Schuster, 2010), 100; Wallace Stegner, *On Teaching and Writing Fiction* (New York: Penguin, 2002).

12. William A. Graham, dir., *Montana* (1990; Burbank, CA: Warner Home Video, 1990), VHS.

13. McMurtry, *Hollywood*, 100.

14. Larry McMurtry, "Montana, an Original Screenplay," folder 3, box 1, Larry McMurtry Screenplays, 1979–1988 and undated, Southwest Collection, Special Collections Library, Texas Tech University, Lubbock, Texas.

15. Jonathan Wacks, dir., *Powwow Highway* (1989; Los Angeles: Image Entertainment, 2011), DVD.

16. See Houser, "Native American Sovereignty"; Allison, *Sovereignty for Survival*.

17. Jane Tompkins, *West of Everything: The Inner Life of Westerns* (New York: Oxford University Press, 1992), 8.

18. Eric Gary Anderson, "Driving the Red Road: Powwow Highway," in *Hollywood's Indian: The Portrayal of the Native American in Film*, eds Peter Rollins and John E. O'Connor (Louisville: University Press of Kentucky, 1998), 143.

19. David Seals, *The Powwow Highway: A Novel* (Albuquerque: University of New Mexico Press, 2014).

20. Seals, *Powwow Highway*, 94.

21. Thomas Vernon Reed, *The Art of Protest: Culture and Activism from the Civil Rights Movement to the Streets of Seattle* (Minneapolis: University of Minnesota Press, 2005), 137–38.

22. Patricia Nelson Limerick, *The Legacy of Conquest: The Unbroken Past of the American West* (New York: W. W. Norton, 1987), 99–100; Patricia Nelson Limerick, "Of Forty-Niners, Oilmen, and the Dot-Com Boom," *New York Times*, May 7, 2000, BU4.

Chapter 15

Hydrocarbon Nostalgia and Climate Disaster: An Environmental History of *Hell or High Water* (2016)

Mark Boxell

In the spring of 2011, historic, drought-fueled wildfires raged across Central and West Texas. Amid the smoke and heat, an aspiring Hollywood screenwriter found inspiration for one of the decade's most critically acclaimed independent films. Taylor Sheridan, a native Texan and longtime bit actor in search of a better career behind the camera, encountered a rural region on the brink. In 2010, wildfires had consumed 3.4 million acres across the entire United States, yet by late spring 2011, 1.5 million acres of Texas wildland, cropland, and pasture had already burned, badly undermining farmers and ranchers still recovering from a similar disaster that occurred just two years earlier. On top of this, the effects of the Great Recession rippled across the rural Southwest. In Sheridan's words, "Texas was on fire and markets were collapsing and the way of life that I grew up with was failing and dying." This combination of climatic and financial disaster inspired Sheridan to write *Hell or High Water* (2016), a neo-Western featuring a series of antihero bank heists carried out in response to intergenerational poverty and rampant economic inequality.[1]

Sheridan's story is heavily rooted in a post-2008 culture of resentment and mistrust aimed at financial institutions, bankers, and other parties guilty of precipitating the Great Recession. While anger toward finance capital permeates the film, Sheridan situates another institution, the petroleum industry, in a peculiar role: not as a villain, but as a passive source of economic justice for the downtrodden, premised on the assumption that poor landowners can find prosperity through oil extraction. This essay argues that such a story both ignores the role of anthropogenic climate change in triggering contemporary economic disasters in West Texas and rests upon a longing for a mineral property regime that has mostly disappeared. Despite a growing ecological crisis driven by fossil fuel companies, *Hell or High Water* reflects what I call hydrocarbon nostalgia, resurrecting longstanding myths about the power of "black gold" to enrich rural communities and reinforcing popular conservative tropes centered on the liberation of poor, white Americans through collaboration with fossil fuel producers.[2]

While this piece is a reflection on how *Hell or High Water* is situated within the context of contemporary energy history, it is also a history of that film's origins from the perspective of its screenwriter. This means that I deal with both what is and is not depicted in the film, with a focus on elements of the story's origin, as Sheridan tells it, that were ultimately left out of the final product. Both the film's emphases and its silences reveal how certain social and political critiques lend themselves to popular, mainstream narratives while others seemingly do not. The story's anger toward financial institutions marks it as an example of post-2008 political critique, but Sheridan's insistence that the destruction wrought by climate change in Central and West Texas inspired the script is not clearly evidenced by the film. Climate disaster does not yet fit easily into a mainstream Western lexicon the way Robin Hood–style bank robbers and poor landowners striking "black gold" do. This suggests that the fight against fossil fuel capitalism requires stories that resonate with an idiom of justice, just as in these latter narratives that have long reverberated in depictions of the American West.[3]

Grassroots on Fire

Films focused on the oil industry in the American West often emphasize the explosive nature of petroleum production, the social pathologies that oil wealth produces, and the people those pathologies infect. Sheridan's screenplay opts for a different perspective, situating petroleum as a source of socioeconomic emancipation that operates, at least on the surface, in contrast to manipulative bankers and the financial markets they exploit. No Jett Rinks, Daniel Plainviews, gushing oil wells, or tank farm fires appear in *Hell or High Water*. Instead, the film tells the story of Toby and Tanner Howard (played by Chris Pine and Ben Foster, respectively), two brothers from a poor rural white family who plan and carry out a string of bank robberies in a series of worn-out, depressed Texas towns. The robberies are a scheme to raise cash to pay off a predatory mortgage on their deceased mother's ranch. Chevron has discovered that the land is oil-rich and desires a drilling lease, but the property is at risk of being seized by the family's creditor, the fictional Texas Midlands Bank. By robbing different branches of Texas Midlands, the Howard brothers hope to pay off the mortgage with the bank's own money, secure the ranch and its future oil royalties, and provide a path for Toby's estranged teenage sons to escape poverty.

The story that Sheridan chose to tell is premised on specific calamities that affected both Texas and the wider world between 2008 and 2012. First, the West Texas depicted in *Hell or High Water* is heavily influenced by the national experience of the 2008 financial crisis and the subsequent Great Recession. At some level this is ironic, as Texas stood out as a state that buffered the worst of the economic shocks that struck the United States during the period. Counties in Texas averaged a 7 percent unemployment rate in 2009, well below other Southwestern states, such as California and Arizona, where unemployment rose to nearly 13 percent. Overall, employment in Texas fell nearly 3 percent between 2007 and 2009, much lower than the national decline of almost 7 percent during the same period. These relatively stable conditions were connected to the sustained growth that the Texas economy enjoyed in the years preceding the recession. Petroleum resources were implicated in the larger history of the recession in their own way. Among the scant number of regions that experienced employment growth during the recession were sections of the Dakotas that underwent an oil and natural gas boom. Furthermore, some economists have suggested that a historic spike in oil prices in the runup to the initial crisis—the price of West Texas Intermediate crude doubled to $145 a barrel between the summers of 2008 and 2009—exacerbated instability.[4]

Regardless, the existing socioeconomic context that pushed Sheridan to create a film about oil, finance, and the contemporary history of West Texas was premised on an overwhelming state of global economic insecurity. This instability and its overwhelming costs are central to *Hell or High Water*. The story presented in the film reflects an ascendant populist conservatism that rhetorically opposes Wall Street while doubling down on petroleum extraction as a source of liberation, at least for one fictional family. The film's anti–Wall Street politics combine an old vein of late-nineteenth-century Populist revolt with more recent threads of working- and middle-class economic anxiety that grew especially acute after 2008. Toby Howard embodies the Western masculine tropes of ruggedness, quiet resolve, and disdain for established authority that reflect a long tradition of modest Western landowners' opposition to powerful economic interests, whether they be railroads, absentee landlords, or financiers. What separates the character from the classic male Western hero is the acknowledgment that he is not a self-sufficient farmer or rancher, but someone reliant on wage labor in an increasingly precarious and postindustrial twenty-first century. Oil and gas production stalk from the margins of this particular narrative thread. At one point, Toby tells a waitress that his most recent job was for a natural gas company, but that no one seems to be drilling for gas any longer. The character adds, "There ain't nothing high-dollar about drilling," suggesting that the persistent poverty that motivates his spree of robberies has been exacerbated by the tenuous nature of his oil-and-gas employment. Nevertheless, amid a plot brimming with anti-corporate venom, fossil fuels—whether as a generator of royalties or a source of wages—remain the only viable source of redemptive income.[5]

The film's visual depictions of Central and West Texas reinforce the often heavy-handed critique of finance capital while simultaneously revealing little about the petroleum industry's place within a faltering economy. Sheridan asserts that one of his goals when making the film was to portray large corporations preying upon vulnerable people through predatory loans and debt relief programs. The film achieves this in several scenes, as billboards advertising debt relief programs appear along isolated stretches of highway, situating the sparse built environment as a reflection of a broader social, environmental, and economic collapse. The viewer also gets glimpses of Texas's oil richness through brief images of tank farms, fields full of pumpjacks, oil and gas freight cars, and refineries. However, unlike the billboards, which serve a clearly didactic purpose, oil and gas infrastructure merely coexists alongside social and economic deterioration. Twice in the film, oil refineries appear in the background of the aforementioned billboards, and at one point a sprawling junkyard full of old vehicles and rusted, broken-down oil field equipment fills the screen. These scenes are empty of people. Besides the two brothers themselves, there is no sign that anyone lives near or works in the oil fields or junkyard. Even the refinery is shown from a long-distance perspective, obscuring any evidence of workers benefiting from its existence. However, there is never a clear indication that these fossil fuel technologies represent a source of the backbreaking problems that the film depicts.

Ironically, although the petroleum industry's culpability in creating climate change and other social and ecological problems is absent from the film, historic drought conditions and numerous destructive wildfires across Texas between 2009 and 2011 proved just as impactful as the financial crisis in inspiring Sheridan to write Hell or High Water. These droughts and fires caused serious harm to Texas ranchers and farmers during the period, increasing the state's reliance on a petroleum industry responsible for fueling climatic changes that only deepened agroecological crises. In the spring of 2009, cata-strophic drought gripped Garza County, Young County, Archer County, and other parts of Central and West Texas that serve as the setting for the film. By April, sixty-day rain totals in parts of the region had fallen below 1 percent, and exceptionally low humidity, strong winds, and vulnerable energy infrastruc-tures exacerbated the growing threat of fire. Fallen power lines ignited one fire in Central Texas that destroyed twenty-eight buildings, two businesses, and twenty barns and burned over a thousand acres. Authorities suspected that sparks from an operating pumpjack caused another blaze. Over a dozen fires were burning by the second week of April, consuming nearly 150,000 acres of grass and timber. In July, the state of Texas declared extreme fire-hazard conditions in 167 counties. One rancher, who sold 165 of his 225 cows amid the flames and dying pasture, said, "I'm eighty years old, and it's the worst I've seen in my lifetime." The director of the Texas and Southwestern Cattle Raisers Association lamented that ranchers "are always talking about which disaster was the worst." In his experience, "The answer is easy. It is the one you are currently dealing with . . . Mother Nature is dealing Texas cattlemen some devastating blows through saltwater intrusion from hurricanes, wildfires, and now, severe drought." Indeed, the first two months of 2009 had been the driest in South and Central Texas since 1918. Conditions for a catastrophe abounded, and by September livestock producers had lost nearly a billion dollars.[6]

An even worse disaster struck some of the same regions of Texas just two years later. Exceptional drought levels once again desiccated much of the state's grasslands and wheat fields while La Niña conditions contributed to dangerously low humidity. Texas farmers were hit hard, as the state's aver-age annual wheat harvest of one hundred million bushels fell by two-thirds. Even irrigation-reliant farmers found that the historic drought conditions had depleted groundwater supplies. Some of the worst wildfires in Texas's history raged throughout western parts of the state long before the summer had even begun, starting in January and consuming 1.5 million acres over a span of three months. Despite weeks of firefighting efforts, 573,000 acres continued to burn at the end of April. In July, the US Department of Agriculture declared 86 percent of Texas's pasture and rangeland to be "poor" or "very poor." An agent for Texas's extension service illustrated the depth of the disaster for rural communities: "Ranchers complain that not only did the wildfires destroy the hay population, they also burned summer crops such as wheat or cotton, that usually can be counted on to support rural economies when there are dips in the cattle market." Fraudsters took advantage of the conditions by collecting thousands of dollars from ranchers via wire transfers in exchange for bales of hay that did not exist. By the beginning of the fall, fires had destroyed three million grazing acres, six thousand miles of fence (at a cost of $10,000 per mile), and over fifteen hundred cattle.[7]

The environmental changes that precipitated economic disaster in Texas in the late aughts and early 2010s cannot be credibly decoupled from anthropogenic climate change, yet *Hell or High Water*'s creators included petroleum companies and oil production in the narrative without making the connection. In the wake of the 2011 fires, the climate change advisor to the chief of the US Forest Service attributed increased risk of wildfires in places such as Central and West Texas to climate change. Likewise, Texas's state climatologist, while reluctant to attribute singular weather events to climate change, stressed that the combination of extreme drought and unprecedented heat was "off the charts." Global warming creates greater variability in weather conditions, increasing the chances of both prolonged and intensified rain events and extreme drought—a mix that bolsters vegetation growth and then exposes verdant plant life to prolonged heat and dryness, conditions ideal for fire. Such an environment prevailed in Texas, where the occurrence of tropical storms made the summer of 2010 unusually wet, while subsequent months proved historically dry. Yet, in the aftermath of the drought and wildfires, Texans were mostly mum about the possibility that anthropogenic climate change played a role in the events. One reporter discovered that "The topic appears to have been actively excluded from public discourse." Certainly, this was due in part to the state's history of petroleum production and, moreover, an ongoing oil and gas boom in West Texas. By the end of 2012, oil companies had invested upward of a billion dollars in hydraulic fracturing in the region, which produced forty-eight thousand new jobs. Drought and wildfire thus made Texas that much more dependent on such booms in the fossil fuel energy economy.[8]

Taylor Sheridan's personal reflections on the origins of *Hell or High Water* reveal how these environmental disasters, financial crises, and the specter of oil wealth sowed the seeds for a declensionist narrative about the decline of the rural United States and oil's role in meting out some degree of justice. Sheridan emphasized that the historic drought conditions and wildfires shaped the film's creation. In his own words, "Texas was on fire and markets were collapsing and the way of life that I grew up with was failing and dying. . . . It was really me reexamining my past." Sheridan acknowledged that the drought and fires, anomalies that he "had never even heard of . . . growing up," only strengthened the state's economic reliance on oil production. "At that time oil was the only thing that was funding the economy," the screenwriter stated in one interview. "Texas is tethered to oil. It's its cash crop." In Sheridan's eyes, the oil industry not only stood out as an economic harbor in a storm that badly damaged the state's farmers and ranchers, but it also explained the impetus for the numerous banks that continued to operate in shrinking rural towns. Wondering why these isolated banks kept their doors open, Sheridan assumed that it was because "obviously [lessors] needed to deposit oil royalties." He latched on to the connections between oil and finance when developing the screenplay, saying, "I then worked through in my mind the cycle of poverty, by robbing the people who legally robbed from you. I watched as the recession hit, and there was anger, and I allowed that to manifest."[9]

Longing for the Days of Black Gold

The plot of *Hell or High Water* reflects a culture of unexpected wealth predicated upon a system of land and mineral ownership that by the early twenty-first century no longer existed in most parts of the United States; I call the continued hopes and dreams of hitting it rich via this largely defunct regime of petroleum abundance *hydrocarbon nostalgia*. One reviewer notes that the film is premised on "its anti-hero cultivating a petro-garden" amid a deteriorating rural economy. However, in the real world, landowners in the position in which the Howards find themselves would likely not experience the benefits of their land's subsurface energy wealth. As energy historian Abby Spinak points out in her own reflections on the film, present-day landowners often do not own the rights to the minerals that rest beneath their soil, and likely would not even be informed if an oil company such as Chevron purchases those rights. There's a good chance that the pumpjacks squeaking ominously in the film's final scene—as Toby Howard and a Texas Ranger contemplate an old-fashioned Western duel—would, in reality, not make the Howards much, if any, money.[10]

However, the fortunate circumstances that Toby Howard and his sons stumble upon do reflect an earlier era of oil extraction. When the petroleum industry first boomed in Texas in the early twentieth century, landowners across the Mid-Continent oil fields—including impoverished farmers, both white and Black, as well as Indigenous allottees from the tribal nations of Oklahoma—were much more likely to profit from oil extraction than their twenty-first-century counterparts. The region's early producers found it acceptable to negotiate directly with landowners to set up drilling operations, usually offering a standard 12.5 percent royalty on all production. Shallow oil sands that could be drilled for a few thousand dollars allowed hundreds of small, independent drilling companies to flourish, each competing with one another. This dispersal of drilling power led to the sinking of large numbers of individual wells across numerous properties. Over time, as the region's shallow sands became exhausted and productive wells grew increasingly expensive to drill, independents lost power to highly capitalized companies, whose officials wanted to prop up oil prices by producing less petroleum. This meant fewer leases and a smaller number of royalty owners. Such shifts hearkened the end of an oil production regime that offered some hope to impoverished landowners. This system of mineral leasing enriched a handful of poor farmers and ranchers and, perhaps most influentially, generated a host of popular stories and myths about "black gold" and instant wealth. This trope endured in the mainly Southwestern communities where the twentieth-century oil industry boomed, before being subsumed within a broader American oil culture. Such tales clearly continue to carry narrative power.[11]

The oil industry is certainly not situated as a hero in the film, but the near-total absence of criticism belies the historical context in which the film was created. At one point, Tanner Howard tells his brother that the "the oilman is the enemy, make no mistake. He just ain't ours." Much like many Texans in the aftermath of drought and fire, Sheridan's screenplay never implies that oil companies played any role in the economic and environmental breakdowns that precipitated the film's creation. The industry's place in *Hell or High Water* is rooted in one perspective on the conservative, rural culture that Sheridan sought to depict, a place ravaged by forces bigger than itself and inhabited by down-on-their-luck individuals who get creative to secure a better slice of an unequally-cut pie. As Tanner Howard's quote suggests, this meant bargaining with corporate powers such as Chevron. However, situating the main characters in a reciprocal relationship with Chevron obscures the fact that opposition to petroleum companies increased during the early years of the twenty-first century, even in Texas. This included growing criticism and regulation of hydraulic fracturing, the cancellation of pipeline projects, lawsuits filed by numerous state attorneys general against ExxonMobil for knowingly misleading the public about the dangers of climate change, and new incentives for the purchase of electric vehicles. In particular, the proposed Keystone XL pipeline generated staunch resistance from some rural landowners in Texas, who echoed *Hell or High Water*'s central themes, declaring that "nobody—in Texas, especially—wants to be told someone's going to come in and take your land." Given this historical context, the petroleum industry's benign role in the film was by no means inevitable, but does reflect the assumption—one rooted in both myth and history—that even modest landowners are often wealthy beneficiaries of mineral extraction.[12]

Hell or High Water's embrace of hydrocarbon nostalgia points to the cultural roadblocks that impede movements to wean Americans off fossil fuels.

The film suggests that myths about "black gold" continue to stand at the forefront of American capitalist culture's infatuation with landownership and instant wealth. Even in a world gripped by climate-induced crises, where oil companies are less likely than before to negotiate favorable leasing terms with landowners, *Hell or High Water* insists that the little guy can still cultivate a "petro-garden" and overcome economic inequality and exploitation. Such illusions assist in legitimizing those who excuse oil companies' abuses. Authors of oil industry hagiography rely on the tropes of "black gold" and hydrocarbon nostalgia when defending petroleum producers, while powerful rural political lobbies cite the oil and gas industry's leases on farmer-owned land when arguing against reductions in fossil fuel consumption. The stories that do take center stage in *Hell or High Water*—corrupt banks, justice-seeking robbers, and the experience of rural poverty—resonate with audiences because of their place within both popular and scholarly imaginations, especially within long-standing histories of the American West. These narratives tap into grievances that tie late-nineteenth-century antimonopoly Populists to late-twentieth-century antifederal sagebrush rebels. As this volume reveals, similar narratives do reverberate through numerous cinematic depictions of oil and other energy industries, but how those tales will evolve as fossil fuels wane and climate disasters quicken largely remains to be seen. What is clear is that stories of grassroots justice amid corporate-induced environmental breakdowns provide one avenue through which climate equity might become common sense.[13]

Notes

1. "Drought Leaves Livestock Producers with $974 Million Loss; Producers Can Seek Help from Federal Government," *The Cattleman* 96, no. 4 (September 2009): 1314; David Levitan, "Texas Wildfires Continue to Rage amidst Historic Drought Conditions," *Climate Central*, April 27, 2011, https://www.climatecentral.org/news /texas-wildfires-continue-to-rage-amidst-historic-drought-conditions; Taylor Sheridan, "*Hell or High Water* Screenwriter Taylor Sheridan: 'I'm Allergic to Exposition,'" interview by Stephen Galloway, *The Hollywood Reporter*, uploaded December 17, 2016, video, 2:38–3:15, https://www.youtube.com/watch?v= TTdDZJioYDI.

2. I am indebted to the historian Mark Fiege for the term *hydrocarbon nostalgia*, which he introduced to me several years ago when discussing automobile-centric tourism in the twentieth-century American West.

3. On the history of energy, political economy, and culture in the American West, see Thomas G. Andrews, *Killing for Coal: America's Deadliest Labor War* (Cambridge, MA: Harvard University Press, 2008); Darren Dochuk, *Anointed with Oil: How Christianity and Crude Made Modern America* (New York: Basic Books, 2019); Dochuk, "Blessed by Oil, Cursed with Crude: God and Black Gold in the American Southwest," *Journal of American History* 99, no. 1 (June 2012): 51–61; Wallace Scot

MacFarlane, "Oil on the Farm: The East Texas Oil Boom and the Origins of an Energy Economy," *Journal of Southern History* 83, no. 4 (November 2017): 853–88; Andrew Needham, *Power Lines: Phoenix and the Making of the Modern Southwest* (Princeton, NJ: Princeton University Press, 2014).

4. Brian C. Thiede and Shannon M. Monnat, "The Great Recession and America's Geography of Unemployment, *Demographic Research* 35 (2016): 21, doi:10.4054 /DemRes.2016.35.30; John E. Connaughton and Ronald A. Madsen, "U.S. State and Regional Economic Impact of the 2008/2009 Recession," *Journal of Regional Analysis and Policy* 42, no. 3 (2012): 178–82, https://ageconsearch.umn.edu /bitstream/143779/2/12-3-1.pdf; David Luttrell, Tyler Atkinson, and Harvey Rosenblum, "Assessing the Costs and Consequences of the 2007–09 Financial Crisis and Its Aftermath," *Federal Reserve Bank of Dallas Economic Letter* 8, no. 7 (September, 2013), https://www.dallasfed.org/~/media/documents/research /eclett/2013/el1307.pdf; Tom Hertz, Lauren Kusmin, Alex Marré, and Tim Parker, *Rural Employment Trends in Recession and Recovery*, United States Department of Agriculture, August 2014, 5, https://www.ers.usda.gov/webdocs/publications /45258/48731_err172.pdf.

5. Former Texas governor Rick Perry was head of the United States Department of Energy under President Donald Trump when the agency branded liquified natural gas as "Freedom Gas" and "Molecules of U.S. Freedom" to be exported around the world. See James Ellsmore, "Trump Administration Rebrands Fossil Fuels as 'Molecules of U.S. Freedom,'" *Forbes*, May 30, 2019, accessed October 28, 2019, https://www.forbes.com/sites/jamesellsmoor/2019/05/30/trump-administration -rebrands-carbon-dioxide-as-molecules-of-u-s-freedom/#1a1d4e383a24; Emily S. Reub, "'Freedom Gas' the Next American Export," *New York Times*, May 29, 2019, accessed October 28, 2019, https://www.nytimes.com/2019/05/29/us/freedom -gas-energy-department.html. My assertion that Sheridan's invocation of this strain of fossil fuel conservatism is largely unwitting, based on the fact that the oil industry is never outwardly celebrated in the film, as well as clear anti-Trump statements he makes in a handful of his interviews.

6. Brad Smith and Greg Murdoch, *Overview of the April 9th, 2009 North Central Texas Wildfire Outbreak* (College Station: Texas Forest Service/Texas A&M University, 2009), https://ticc.tamu.edu/Documents/PredictiveServices/Outlooks/outbreak 09.pdf; Drought Impact Reporter, National Drought Mitigation Center, University of Nebraska, accessed April 27, 2019, https://droughtreporter.unl.edu/map/. County-by-county drought reports and data accessible going back to 2009 found via customized searches; "Rio Grande Valley under Extreme Fire Hazard Proclamation," *Brownsville Herald*, July 16, 2009, https://www.brownsvilleherald .com/rio-grande-valley-under-extreme-fire-hazard-proclamation/article_c622c2da -6cb1-513b-bc96-4e0b77584857.html; "High Winds Fuel Wildfires," *NBC Dallas-Fort Worth*, April 9, 2009, https://www.nbcdfw.com/weather/stories/Wild-Fires -Rage-West-of-Fort-Worth.html; "Crews Fight Wildfire in Central Texas," *CNN*, March 2, 2009, http://www.cnn.com/2009/US/03/02/texas.wildfires/index.html; "Drought Grips Texas Cattle Country," *USA Today*, March 17, 2009, https:// usatoday30.usatoday.com/weather/drought/2009-03-17-texas-drought_N.htm; "New Disaster Assistance Program Offered to Texas Ranchers," *The Cattleman*, 96, no. 4 (September 2009): 131; "Drought Leaves Livestock Producers with $974 Million Loss."

7. Blair Fannin, "Texas Drought Losses Are $5.2 Billion and Counting," *Beef*, August

19, 2011; "Wildfires and No Drought Relief in Sight for Southwest," *Climate Central*, May 18, 2011, https://www.climatecentral.org/blogs/wildfires-and-no -drought-relief-in-sight-for-southwest; "Wildfires, Drought Burning Texas Agriculture," *Southwest Farm Press*, April 19, 2011; Levitan, "Texas Wildfires Continue to Rage"; Kay Ledbetter, "Wildfire Claims More Than $150 Million in Texas Agricultural Losses," *Southwest Farm Press*, September 30, 2011.

8. George Marshall, "The Green Star State," *New Scientist* 216, no. 2893 (December 1, 2012): 26–27, doi:10.1016/S0262–4079(12)63063–2; Levitan, "Texas Wildfires Continue to Rage"; Fannin, "Texas Drought Losses Are $5.2 Billion and Counting."

9. Taylor Sheridan, "Taylor Sheridan Delves into Personal and Social Themes with *Hell or High Water*," *Los Angeles Times*, December 15, 2016, https://www.latimes.com /entertainment/envelope/la-en-mn-on-writing-hell-high-water-20161014-snap -20161206-story.html.; Taylor Sheridan, "*Hell or High Water* Screenwriter Taylor Sheridan: 'I'm Allergic to Exposition,'" interview by Stephen Galloway, *Hollywood Reporter*, uploaded December 17, 2016, video, 2:38–3:15, https://www.youtube .com/watch?v=TTdDZJioYDI; Taylor Sheridan, "Taylor Sheridan Talks to Written By about Scripting *Hell or High Water*," interview by Richard Stayton and Louise Farr, *Writers Guild of America West*, uploaded January 4, 2017, video, 7:14–8:20, https://www.youtube.com/watch?v=TTAkcDzrObA; Anthony D'Alessandro, "Encore: Taylor Sheridan & David Mackenzie on Raising Hell or High Water: 'It's about Fatherhood at the End of the Day,'" *Deadline*, February 18, 2017, https:// deadline.com/2017/02/hell-or-high-water-taylor-sheridan-david-mackenzie-wind -river-1201866388.

10. Michael C. Reiff, "Review: *Hell or High Water*," *Film and History: An Interdisciplinary Journal* 46, no. 2 (Winter 2016): 108, https://muse.jhu.edu/article/643321; Abby Spinak, "The Twenty-First Century Oil Encounter: Dispatches from Texas," *Technology's Stories*, August 27, 2017, https://www.technologystories.org/the -twenty-first-century-oil-encounter-dispatches-from-texas.

11. For the history of oil in early-twentieth-century Texas and surrounding states, see Mody C. Boatwright, *Folklore of the Oil Industry* (Dallas: Southern Methodist University Press, 1963); W. L. Connelly, *The Oil Business as I Saw It: Half a Century with Sinclair* (Norman: University of Oklahoma Press, 1954); Darren Dochuk, *Anointed with Oil: How Christianity and Crude Made Modern America* (New York: Basic Books, 2019); Brian Frehner, *Finding Oil: The Nature of Petroleum Geology, 1859–1920* (Lincoln: University of Nebraska Press, 2011); C. B. Glasscock, *Then Came Oil: The Story of the Last Frontier* (Indianapolis: Bobbs-Merrill Company, 1938); Wallace Scot McFarlane, "Oil on the Farm: The East Texas Oil Boom and the Origins of an Energy Economy," *Journal of Southern History* 83, no. 4 (November 2017): 853–88; Diana Davids Olien and Roger M. Olien, *Oil Booms: Social Change in Five Texas Towns* (Lincoln: University of Nebraska Press, 1982); Carl Coke Rister, *Oil! Titan of the Southwest* (Norman: University of Oklahoma Press, 1949); Bobby D. Weaver, *Oilfield Trash: Life and Labor in the Oil Patch* (College Station: Texas A&M University Press, 2010); Daniel Yergin, *The Prize: The Quest for Oil, Money, and Power* (New York: Simon & Schuster, 1991).

12. Jim Krane, "Climate Risk and the Fossil Fuel Industry: Two Feet High and Rising," working paper, Baker Institute for Public Policy, Rice University, 2016, 4–7, https://www.bakerinstitute.org/media/files/research_document/6b58fc69 /WorkingPaper-ClimateRisk-072116.pdf; Terrence Henry, "Life on the Line: Landowners Fight Keystone XL and Eminent Domain," *State Impact*, April 19,

2012, https://stateimpact.npr.org/texas/2012/04/19/lives-on-the-line-landowners
-fight-keystone-xl-and-eminent-domain.

13. Taylor Sheridan, "*Hell or High Water* Screenwriter Taylor Sheridan," 2:38–3:15;
     Michael Watts, "Petro-Violence: Community, Extraction, and Political Ecology of a
     Mythic Commodity," in Michael Watts and Nancy Lee Peluso, eds., *Violent
     Environments* (Ithaca, NY: Cornell University Press, 2001), 205–12; Neela Banerjee,
     Georgina Gustin, and John H. Cushman, Jr., "The Farm Bureau: Big Oil's Unnoticed
     Ally Fighting Climate Science and Policy," Inside Climate News, December 21,
     2018, accessed June 29, 2019, https://insideclimatenews.org/news/20122018
     /american-farm-bureau-fossil-fuel-nexus-climate-change-denial-science
     -agriculture-carbon-policy-opposition.

PART 4

Energy and Morality

Control of the Industry: Nineteenth-Century Oil and Capitalism in *High, Wide and Handsome* (1937)

Alexander Finkelstein

In antebellum western Pennsylvania, a small-town farming community gathers around the town square one evening to hear Doc Watterson (Raymond Walburn) hawk his "Indian Rock Oil." Doc Watterson; his daughter, Sally (Irene Dunne); and his business partner (William Frawley), a white man called Chief Yellow Flower, wearing face paint and a headdress, explain the powers of their special oil to the farmers, claiming it has the potential to cure anything and everything. In the middle of their sales pitch, though, a fire sparks and burns down the traveling sales team's wagon. Sally Watterson and the rest of the medicine show crew find refuge in the home of a reluctant Grandma Cortlandt (Elizabeth Patterson). Both Grandma Cortlandt and Sally Watterson agree that this hospitality is not charity, but rather the Cortlandts' Christian and neighborly duty. This opening scene of *High, Wide and Handsome* exhibits the businesses and community that would be soon transformed by an oil boom.[1]

High, Wide and Handsome offers a picturesque retelling of America's oil history, tying together issues of family, energy, and business in this western Pennsylvania saga. Paramount released the highly anticipated musical in the summer of 1937. This dramatization of the discovery of oil in Pennsylvania and the subsequent struggle for its control included a star-studded cast and an established director. Despite laudatory reviews, however, the picture performed modestly at the box office.[2] Produced by Arthur Hornblow Jr., directed by Rouben Mamoulian, and scored by Jerome Kern and Oscar Hammerstein, critic Idwal Jones called the film a "symphonic drama."[3] After premiering in New York City, reviewer Frank S. Nugent predicted that *High, Wide and Handsome* was "destined to continue for months on a two-a-day basis." Continuing to heap praise, Nugent declared, "A richly produced, spectacular and melodious show, it moves easily into the ranks of the season's best."[4] "Handsome," another review wrote, "is the word for this production, and add colorful, amusing and sometimes thrilling."[5] This chapter asks: why in 1937 was this retelling of America's oil history so captivating?

High, Wide and Handsome offers a history of oil, business, and community intended to explore the ways in which capitalism can be either beneficial or deleterious. Released in 1937, the cultural and political context of the Great Depression and New Deal provide the backdrop for understanding the film. The Depression spurred debates about the future of capitalism and the country's economic system, while the New Deal generally shifted the focus of antitrust ideas from independent producers and businessmen to the consumer.[6] This film attempted to convince viewers that capitalism's democratic success required dismantling concentrated power and capital. The moment that the small town in western Pennsylvania discovered oil under the earth's surface transformed the community, changing everything from decisions about land usage to marital strife to business organization. These transformations could have been beneficial for the area farmers and landowners, yet unethical and domineering corporate business practices and individuals wrought devastation instead. Residents derived their power from oil, and the fight over access and ownership frayed relationships and the community. As part of the "dynamic dialogue over the changing image of oil in American life," the film showcases oil itself as a tool of democratic modernization while simultaneously contributing to the broader project of allowing Americans to "glimpse the power structures that brought them oil."[7] In this case, that power structure exemplified greed and anticompetitive business practices to stifle individual production, creativity, and happiness. This 1930s history of oil hails capitalism as a tool of social regeneration and community development while also deriding unfettered capitalism as unfair and corrupting.

The film portrays the story of America's first oil boom through the lives of Sally Watterson and Peter Cortlandt (Randolph Scott). After Grandma Cortlandt welcomes the traveling sales crew, Sally and Peter fall in love and get married. Then, Peter strikes oil. The subsequent oil boom challenges the community as well as Sally and Peter's life together. Immediately, the small town transforms into a boomtown, as farmers-turned-oilmen pursue lives as independent, self-supporting producers. The economic boom also ushers in self-interested businessmen, vices including alcohol and prostitution, and changes to the local economy. Railroad magnate Walt Brennan (Alan Hale)— the film's antagonist—challenges the viability of independent oilmen by dictating transportation prices and launching a scheme to control the industry. Peter Cortlandt leads the farmers in subverting Brennan's grip by constructing a pipeline directly to the refinery. However, in his dedication to the pipeline project, Peter neglects Sally, and she leaves him to pursue a career as an actress and singer. Brennan tries to stop the pipeline construction through physical violent disruption, buying the rights of way and changing the refiner's contract deadline. In the moment that seems to ensure Peter's failure, Sally returns to urge him to persevere. Peter and his ragtag crew of farmers ultimately overcome the power of concentrated capital, succeed in building the pipeline, and regain control of their natural resource.

High, Wide and Handsome received glowing reviews because it resonated with contemporaneous issues. The hardworking farmers triumph over the ruthless and greedy business trusts; the good guys win, and the bad guys lose. Analyzing this film in the contexts of the period in which it was made (the 1930s) and the period it aspires to depict (the latter half of the nineteenth century) reveals that *High, Wide and Handsome* advances antitrust ideology and small-town community nostalgia. In addition to the argument that hard work trumps greed, the film asserts that an economy of small produces is better than one of consolidated interests. In the depths of the Great Depression, the message that unrestricted capitalism corrupts individuals and communities was a response to debates about how the US economic system ought to be structured.[8] Moreover, by critiquing the concentration of power and capital, the film also emphasizes the importance of human energy and labor. While the transition to the era of oil power required human labor to fell trees, build derricks, and lay pipe, labor also held psychic importance, instilling a sense of dignity and pride through work and production. Thus, this musical portrayal of oil's rise to prominence in the United States reflects important economic concerns of the 1930s.

Rock Oil's Potential

High, Wide and Handsome's quaint opening scene uses symbols of Americana to evoke traditional small-town life, but the trio of outsiders selling Indian Rock Oil heralds the change soon to come with the discovery of crude oil underground. Within a few days of living with the Cortlandts, Sally Watterson's vision of oil expands from a simple healing elixir to something with great potential for the nation. As Peter Cortlandt and his band of farmers erect a wooden oil derrick on the Cortlandt land, Grandma Cortlandt explains to Sally that Peter had a "crazy notion" to use the rock oil to "keep the poor man warm and light up every little shack in the country." In mid-nineteenth-century

America, this indeed was a crazy notion because of its relatively limited use to that point.[9] When Peter's workers deride his oil dream, Sally jumps to his defense: "Blockheads don't know what [oil is] good for maybe. Blockheads haven't figured out that maybe you can light the lamps and make stoves go with rock oil." Sally accepts Peter's idealistic vision, quickly recognizing the potential of accessible mineral energy to remake American society.

The film's focus on the transformative potential of energy consumption reflects the era in which it was produced. During the 1930s, Franklin D. Roosevelt and his New Deal pursued improved access to power all across America—urban and rural. In 1935, only one in every nine farms had electricity. Although oil power remained a crucial source of energy during this period, the New Deal combated the corruption within the private utility industry in order to electrify rural America. While electricity did not displace the importance of oil, it offered a means of improving the lives of rural people living in poverty and connecting them to the national economy.[10] *High, Wide and Handsome* presents a parallel in which democratized access to oil in the 1860s would, as Peter argues, "light up every little shack in the country." Significantly, when expressing his goals for oil, Peter does not include a desire to get rich. Instead, he articulates oil's benefits, essentially arguing for the democratization of access to energy.

While Doc Watterson repairs the wagon and the medicine show crew spends their days with the Cortlandts, Sally and Peter fall in love. This relationship pulls Sally from her father's traveling medicine show, and she chooses to stay behind with Peter. They imagine their new life together as happy and simple; he would provide for her by farming and simultaneously pursue his dream of providing oil to the common man. During their wedding ceremony, Peter surprises Sally with a gift that represents their future. He brings her to the top of the hill on which he courted her and promises to build a house for their family on that spot. Sally responds, "I love you for wanting to build it for me up here on our hill." Then she breaks into song to commemorate this moment:

> Someday we'll build a home on a hilltop high,
> You and I, shiny and new, a cottage that two can fill.
> And we'll be pleased to be called,
> "The folks who live on the hill."
> Someday we may be adding a thing or two, a wing or two,
> We will make changes as any family will,
> But we will always be called,
> "The folks who live on the hill."

Down below the whole town enjoys the wedding festivities, with the newly-weds' hill and Peter's derrick visible in the background. Suddenly, the derrick spews oil. "Black gold" shoots into the sky and rains down on the wedding party. Peter gleefully embraces his new wife for a long kiss while the pure white of her wedding gown darkens with the slimy black oil. Here, the film does not critique the oil itself but foreshadows that it will be inseparable from their family life and unavoidably color the town's future. This development—this resource—will loom over their marriage and shape the reality of their dream of being the folks who live on the hill.

An Oil Town

The discovery of oil in this sleepy farming community was based on real events. In 1859, Edwin Drake's well hit oil in Titusville, Pennsylvania. Before Drake's famous finding, he, like Peter, faced doubt and criticism. In fact, Drake's backers sent a letter calling for him to cease his drilling, which thanks to the slow post reached Drake only after the well had begun to gush. Titusville, like the fictional Pennsylvania town in *High, Wide and Handsome,* also experienced a subsequent boom in the 1860s, as both economies immediately switched from agriculture to oil-related industries, including logging, drilling, transportation, and service. The onslaught of fortune seekers transformed this agricultural region into a "sacrificial landscape" that viewed natural resources as utilitarian and commodified the environment to support their extraction. This capitalistic logic and perspective on the environment ultimately led to technological and cultural ruin in Oil Creek Valley.[11]

Indeed, *High, Wide and Handsome* depicts how the oil boom transformed the landscape itself. In a montage of the town's developments, we see land prepared for resource extraction. Derricks replace wooded areas and farms. The local newspaper announces: "Farmers Drilling for Oil." By switching to the more lucrative oil industry, these farmers rearrange regional economic connections, now supplying urban areas with oil and expecting the market to supply them with agricultural goods from further hinterlands. However, the film does not portray the new landscape as negative. Rather than emphasizing environmental degradation, resource consumption, and ruined farmland, the film employs orderly derricks and felled forests as symbols of progress. This oil-based economy represents the optimal use of resources, echoing the increased scope and scale of natural resource use during the 1930s.[12]

The oil boom brought not only environmental change to western Pennsylvania, but also a cultural change, which the film illustrates through a strained marriage and the arrival of new vices. Peter prioritizes his role in championing and leading independent oil producers, spending long hours planning, organizing, and strategizing. He misses dinners and anniversaries, and Sally realizes that the competition for control of land and oil access has diverted Peter's attention away from her. She longs for the simple life on the hill of which they dreamed, working the land while also earning money from oil, having children and starting a family. But the competitive business practices, not the resource itself, have sullied this dream and their marriage.

Similarly, the town's character changes from the small, intimate community portrayed at the beginning of the film. While local farmers like Peter seek to democratize oil access, the greedy businessmen and opportunists that move to the region to get rich quick bring vice along with them. The film shows a new type of people and businesses materializing with the oil boom—namely, gamblers, drunks, thieves, and prostitutes. At one point, the religious men of the community raid a saloon, trying to drive the prostitutes and drunks across county lines into "Petroleum City." As *High, Wide and Handsome* demonstrates, the social effects of an oil boom proved to be somewhat paradoxical: the democratizing access uplifted rural folk throughout the nation, but the unscrupulous businessmen and practices fostered vice and oil drove apart families.

The Oil Business

As the culture changes in this western Pennsylvania community, so too does the oil business itself. The concentration of capital and control of the oil challenges the farmers' independence in a fight that introduces the film's antagonist, Walt Brennan. This conflict pits the hardworking farmers striving to be independent producers against unrestrained big business, which uses capital and manipulation to control resources and power. The businessmen involved are not bad because they are oilmen (this solidifies as a trope in the 1970s); they are bad because they thwart competitive business ideals.[13] It is not the industry that corrupts the business and individuals involved, but the unrestrained nature of the business that corrupts the industry.

Extractive resource economies require capital to succeed on a large scale.[14] In *High, Wide and Handsome*, the need for capital and infrastructural connections create an opening for the capitalist class to corrupt Peter Cortlandt's dream of democratized consumption. Brennan, an evil railroad magnate modeled after John D. Rockefeller, employs his capital and control of infrastructure to drive personal profit, seeking to command the industry in western Pennsylvania. Rockefeller had consolidated his power over the oil and railroad industries by dominating the refineries. Refineries heated crude oil to separate the vaporized hydrocarbons, which were then treated to produce kerosene. By the 1980s, Rockefeller's Standard Oil controlled over 90 percent of the country's refining capability. Moreover, this control enabled the company to have leverage over transportation costs through rebates and drawbacks. Representing the evil of restrained and unregulated business, *High, Wide and Handsome* uses Rockefeller and Standard Oil's methods as a model for Walt Brennan.[15]

Like Rockefeller, Brennan owns the railroads that the Pennsylvania farmers need to transport oil to the refineries, and he uses his infrastructural power to force independent oil producers to sell their land and mineral rights. "I think it's time," Brennan informs his cigar-smoking co-conspirators, "we went to western Pennsylvania and took control of the industry." Following Rockefeller's logic, Brennan recognizes that oil is no good unless it is refined, that it must be transported to refineries by railroad, and that he can use railroad price schemes to "freeze out" the "hard-headed farmers." Along with co-founder of Standard Oil Henry Flagler, Rockefeller similarly consolidated control of the oil industry in the 1880s and 1890s, excluding independent refiners by negotiating with railroads to control freight rates, and increasing prices while securing deep rebates. This system produced preferential rates for Standard Oil shipments and allowed Flagler and Rockefeller to undercut and eventually buy out their competition. A historical critique of big corporations' triumph at smaller firms' expense resonated with audiences in the 1930s.[16]

In addition, invoking Standard Oil engaged conflicts that were central to the 1930s: who should profit from natural resources, and how should businesses be regulated to support independent laborers and businessowners? While the law and government policy continued to view natural resources as instrumental goods to be used for economic gain, the underlying business model that accumulated and controlled resources like oil was challenged during this period.[17] According to historian Ellis Hawley, the New Deal illuminated the tension between ideas of the traditional self-supporting, independent business and the reality of a highly organized and consolidated business world.[18] New Deal policies were fraught with contradictions; indeed, loosened antitrust regulations actually permitted coordination between prices and policies that allowed thousands of independent oilmen to survive the Great Depression.[19] Yet *High, Wide and Handsome* captures the sentiment that informed the antitrust movement in the 1930s. The demise of the film's fictional boomtown lies not with oil or with Peter's attempt to be a self-supporting businessman, but with the large corporations whose dominant hold on the market allowed them to control production and consumption. As the film advocates, Franklin Roosevelt also tried to deal with the problem of monopoly by coordinating independent business activity to foster a regulated and stable form of capitalism.

Just like New Dealers, the farmers in *High, Wide and Handsome* resist monopoly power. Peter Cortlandt organizes his fellow producers against Brennan and the railroads. However, they underestimate Brennan's ruthlessness. When Peter confronts him, Brennan ridicules Peter and informs him that the railroad rates will now be raised. Gathering the farmers in opposition, Peter declares that the community has to fight "people like Brennan" to the end. Even so, his resolve is fortified by community solidarity, and he is happy that he is "not going to be fighting them alone." At stake in this fight is the ownership of public resources: Brennan claims that oil belongs to whoever grabs it first, while Peter argues that it belongs to all. While Brennan is legally correct—the "rule of capture" states that oil belongs to the owner of the subsoil mineral rights—Peter attacks this rule and argues in favor of public ownership. Some New Deal administrators, such as Harold Ickes, explored the possibility of a national oil company to challenge privatization. Likewise, Peter questions privatization because of monopolies' destructive business practices and the lack of universal access to oil.[20]

Subverting the Railroads

While seemingly at the mercy of Brennan's railroad prices, Peter Cortlandt then has an idea to subvert the railroads entirely: "Iron pipes, miles and miles of them, carrying our oil across the state right to the refinery." Peter rallies the farmers to pool their life savings and invest in this new and unproven long-distance pipeline. The community works through snow and rain, hills, rivers, and valleys to build it, their manual labor serving as the basis of this new energy regime. This great battle between railroads and independent oil producers is based on an 1879 effort to build the world's first long-distance oil pipeline to escape Standard Oil's grip. "Pennsylvania producers," Daniel Yergin writes, "made one last effort to break out of Standard's suffocating embrace with a daring experiment."[21] This daring experiment, the Tidewater Pipeline, was intended to offer a competitive alternative to the railroads, thereby lowering the cost of transporting oil to the refineries. Engineers overcame the technological problems of development—building a pump that pushed oil over mountains while maintaining low and even pipe pressure—a true technological feat. However, the Tidewater Pipeline Company faced a greater threat than the technological challenge: Standard Oil. Standard attempted to crush the pipeline in various ways, including purchasing leases on the expected route, sending gangs to rip up pipeline, misplacing and delaying shipments of pipe and supplies, and threatening refineries. Despite these efforts, in May 1879, the Tidewater Pipeline spewed out oil in Williamsport,

Pennsylvania, after transporting it over one hundred miles. This accomplishment, as observers declared, marked the dawn of a new era.[22]

Just as Rockefeller fought against the Tidewater Pipeline, Walt Brennan attacks Peter Cortlandt's pipeline effort in *High, Wide and Handsome*. In addition to a looming deadline imposed by the refiner and the bank, the farmers face both environmental obstacles and Brennan's obstructions. For example, they struggle to transport the steel pipes through snow on horse-drawn carts, at times losing their loads and having to carry the pipes individually up hills and across rivers. Their fight with Brennan exemplifies the resources at the businessman's disposal and his ruthlessness in maintaining power over the industry, as he hires gangs of thugs to terrorize the farmers and break the constructed sections of pipeline. When human power fails to stop them, Brennan uses his railroad, chaining pipe connections to the locomotive itself to pull them apart and forcing the farmers to spend time and energy repairing what is broken and guarding what they have built. Yet armed farmers and their families protect the pipeline, repair the damages, and continue to build.

Brennan also tries to stop the farmers by buying land and the rights of way connecting the oil field to the refinery. This attempt fails, as well. Peter secures all the rights of way required to build the pipeline, but this comes at a significant cost: the owner of the final plot demands that he sell the hill on which he had promised his wife their family home. Peter chooses his commercial interests over their marital dream. Explaining to Sally why he sold what she calls "our hill," Peter implores, "There are other people to think of, honey. We've got to have that pipeline." But selling the land is the final straw in an already frail marriage, and Sally leaves him. Peter's justification for his decision is revealing; he frames his own commercial interests as a form of service to others. In this way, the film aligns Peter's personal interests with public interests, thereby solving the problem of why we—a society committed to oil consumption—should agree with Peter's position instead of seeing him as another selfish capitalist. Ultimately, the struggle with Brennan forces Peter to acquiesce to the market demand even if it means sacrificing his marriage. Losing the hill means losing the dream of being the "folks who live on the hill."

With the rights of way secured and the pipeline almost completed, Peter's final race is against the clock. His contract with the refinery dictates when the oil must be delivered. Although Peter had arranged for an extension, Brennan squashes it by buying the bank that owns the refinery and reneging on the allowance. Brennan's ability to stifle competition exposes the interconnected and interdependent systems of capital concentration. Meanwhile, Sally, who is no longer involved with Peter and is pursuing a singing and acting career, finds out that Brennan has secretly changed the deadline, and she sacrifices a career opportunity to warn Peter. When he tells her that he is quitting due to what seems to be certain failure, Sally inspires him to persevere: "Not you, Peter! You don't know what it is to quit. You've given up everything for this." Peter has an epiphany, realizing that he can build the pipeline over, not around, the mountains to save time.

With a difficult task before him, Peter decides to do the unprecedented and seemingly impossible. Battling both nature and the thugs Brennan has sent to stymie their progress, Peter and his ragtag group of farmers build the pipeline over the mountain. With just seconds to spare before the deadline, the pumps are turned on and oil spews out of the pipe. A dejected Brennan is soaked in oil, surrounded by gleeful farmers who understand that they have achieved a degree of control over their livelihood and have democratized oil access.

History, however, presents a different ending. Although the good guys win in this triumphant film, Rockefeller regained control of the industry in the late nineteenth century after the Tidewater Pipeline challenge. The Tidewater proved the feasibility of long-distance pipelines and jeopardized Standard Oil's dominance. In response, "Rockefeller wasted little time following suit . . . with the thoroughness, expertise, and ruthlessness that characterized his refining operations," using railroads' rights of way to quickly build his own competing pipelines.[23] Standard Oil failed to purchase the Tidewater Pipeline Company outright, but Rockefeller offered an agreement that fixed prices and oil distribution quotas, transforming his role in the affair from destroyer to pacifier. "Any benefit the oil business might have reaped from natural and decent competition," Ida Tarbell writes in her damning expose of Standard Oil, "was of course ended by the alliance."[24] While this new transportation technology revolutionized oil infrastructure, it failed to upset the fundamental balance of power. In the story of Tidewater and Standard Oil, Tarbell concludes, "In the phrase of the region, the Tidewater had 'gone over to Standard,' and there it has always remained."[25] Producers like Peter Cortlandt did not prevail as in the musical; rather, John D. Rockefeller consolidated control and dominated oil transportation until the early twentieth century.

Conclusion

High, Wide and Handsome ends its dramatized history with a hardworking community's victory over a corrupt and powerful business magnate—not with the magnate regaining control. The film's contest between production and distribution, with its "courageous pioneer fighting to keep the oil industry free from exploiting capital," was meant to entertain, teach, and inspire.[26] Its goal was not to chronicle events, but to use broad historical contours to show that it was possible for a community of independent, self-supporting farmers to triumph over unscrupulous businessmen. The choice to democratize access to energy and the oil industry echoed widespread sentiment in the 1930s, and for many, the film's message was compelling. As one reviewer wrote: "There is no exaggeration in counting this picture one of the most inspiring melodramas that has been brought to the screen."[27]

Interestingly, although economic reformers in the 1930s expressed antitrust sentiment and achieved many political gains through legislation, the film omits the role of the state.[28] Instead, *High, Wide and Handsome* asserts that collective, determined, and local effort can succeed without government aid. Peter Cortlandt does not espouse a radical vision of economic transformation but seeks to return the capitalist system to a more competitive and equitable form. Insisting that capitalism and oil could be democratic, the spirit of this key moment in US energy history resonated with 1930s audiences, reflecting contemporaneous debates about energy access and monopolies more broadly.

Notes

1. Rouben Mamoulian, dir., *High, Wide and Handsome* (Hollywood, CA: Paramount Pictures, 1937).
2. The author has been unable to find any further information about the film's box office performance beyond the descriptor "modest," which is used in both Thomas S. Hischak, *The Rodgers and Hammerstein Encyclopedia* (Westport, CT: Greenwood, 2007), 112, and Thomas S. Hischak, *The Oxford Companion to the American Musical: Theatre, Film, and Television* (New York: Oxford University Press, 2008), 117.
3. Idwal Jones, "Hollywood Strikes Oil," *New York Times*, July 4, 1937.
4. Frank S. Nugent, "The Screen: 'High, Wide and Handsome,' a Story of the Oil Rush Opens at the Astor," *New York Times*, July 22, 1937.
5. "High, Wide and Handsome," *Marion Progress*, February 3, 1938.
6. On the Great Depression and New Deal debate over the meaning of capitalism and shifting ideas about antitrust and monopolies, see Alan Brinkley, *The End of Reform: New Deal Liberalism in Recession and War* (New York: Vintage Books, 1995), 63–64, 106–36; on the monopolies of the Great Depression and the campaign to regulate them, see Charlies R. Geisst, *Monopolies in America: Empire Builders and Their Enemies from Jay Gould to Bill Gates* (New York: Oxford University Press, 2000), 126–66.
7. Robert Lifset and Brian C. Black, "Imaging the 'Devil's Excrement': Big Oil in Petroleum Cinema, 1940–2000," *Journal of American History* 99, no. 1 (June 2012): 135, 138.
8. For examples of radical critiques of capitalism and structuring the US economy, see Alan Brinkley, *Voices of Protest: Huey Long, Father Coughlin, and the Great Depression* (New York: Vintage Books, 1983); Mary Stanton, *Red, Black, White: The Alabama Communist Party, 1930–1950* (Athens: University of Georgia Press, 2019), 1–12.
9. For the social history and conception of energy and oil in the nineteenth century, see David E. Nye, *Consuming Power: A Social History of American Energies* (Cambridge: MIT Press, 1998), 121–24.

10. David E. Nye, *Electrifying America: Social Meanings of a New Technology, 1880–1940* (Cambridge: MIT Press, 1990), 299. On electricity in the US, particularly federal efforts to expand its reach to rural America, see Julie A. Cohn, *The Grid: Biography of an American Technology* (Cambridge: MIT Press, 2017), 78–86, 101–104.

11. Brian Black, *Petrolia: The Landscape of America's First Oil Boom* (Baltimore: Johns Hopkins University Press, 2000), 13–36.

12. For an example of the increased scale of natural resource management during the 1930s, see David P. Billington and Donald Jackson, *Big Dams of the New Deal Era: A Confluence of Engineering and Politics* (Norman: University of Oklahoma Press, 2006), 13–70.

13. On the way American culture has grown to accept the business of oil, oil as a commodity, and the mythologizing of oil businesses that comes from cheap and plentiful oil, see Bob Johnson, *Carbon Nation: Fossil Fuels in the Making of American Culture* (Lawrence: University Press of Kansas, 2017), 132–62.

14. On an example of the role of external capital in extractive resource economies, see William G. Robbins, *Colony and Empire: The Capitalist Transformation of the American West* (Lawrence: University Press of Kansas, 1994), 103–42.

15. Daniel Yergin, *The Prize: The Epic Quest for Oil, Money, and Power* (New York: Simon and Schuster, 1991), 40.

16. On Flagler and Rockefeller's success in dominating and organizing the oil economy through refineries, see Richard White, *The Republic for Which It Stands: The United States during Reconstruction and the Gilded Age, 1865–1896* (New York: Oxford University Press, 342–44.

17. For an overview of the legal construction of instrumentalism in US history, see Kathleen Brosnan, "Law and the Environment," in *The Oxford Handbook of Environmental History*, ed. Andrew Isenberg (New York: Oxford University Press, 2014), 513–52.

18. Ellis W. Hawley, *The New Deal and the Problem of Monopoly: A Study in Economic Ambivalence* (Princeton, NJ: Princeton University Press, 1966), 213–20.

19. David M. Kennedy, *Freedom from Fear: The American People in Depression and War, 1929–1945* (New York: Oxford University Press, 1999), 181–89.

20. On Harold Ickes's philosophy on oil and business as secretary of interior and petroleum administrator for war, see Stephen J. Randall, "Harold Ickes and United States Foreign Petroleum Policy Planning, 1939–1945," *Business History Review* 57, no. 3 (Autumn 1983): 367–87.

21. Yergin, *The Prize*, 43.

22. Christopher F. Jones, *Routes of Power: Energy and Modern American* (Cambridge, MA: Harvard University Press), 131–33, 123.

23. Jones, *Routes of Power*, 135.

24. Ida M. Tarbell, *The History of the Standard Oil Company* (New York: McClure and Phillips, 1904), 2:22.

25. Tarbell, *History of Standard Oil*, 2:22.

26. "Irene Dunne and Randolph Scott in Peoples Film," *The Roanoke Rapids Herald*, October 21, 1937.

27. "Irene Dunne and Randolph Scott in Peoples Film," *Roanoke Rapids Herald*, October 21, 1937.

28. On New Dealers' regulatory and legislative impulse, see Brinkley, *End of Reform*, 48–64.

Chapter 17

The Formula (1980): Corporate Villains, Synthetic Fuel, and Environmental Fantasies

Raechel Lutz

In the opening scenes of *The Formula* (1980), General Helmut Kladen (Richard Lynch) of the Nazi Panzer Corps is given an important mission—to bring a truckload of Nazi science and engineering secrets to the Swiss border, including a secret formula explaining how to make gasoline from coal. Kladen's purpose is to use these secrets to bargain for leniency with the victorious American and Allied forces. Kladen, however, is disgusted by his task, which he views as cowardly. Upon meeting Major Tom Neely (Robin Clarke) at the Swiss border, Kladen needs some convincing as to why he should cooperate with American troops and explain the German documents. Neely confidently replies, "Because the war is over, General, and from now on the world is gonna be one big happy corporation. No more secrets. No more enemies. Just customers."[1]

This scene is the key to the puzzle the rest of the movie attempts to put together. From here, viewers are led through a fast-moving and confusing film that begins with Neely's murder and ends with a criminal cover-up of a German formula for pure synthetic gasoline. The movie has all the tropes of classic film noir: a bumbling protagonist struggling to unravel a mystery, a femme fatale whom he falls for despite her undermining his work, and a complex narrative that is not easily resolved and often hard to follow.[2] Alongside *Chinatown* (1974), the film represents a rare return to the genre in the era.[3] Based on the bestselling book by screenwriter Steve Shagan, the movie argues that oil executives' corporate villainy is responsible for the nation's reliance on oil. It asserts that the oil industry will stop at nothing to protect its profit source and will squash technological advances that would make crude oil less valuable. Perhaps building on the popularity of organized crime films, *The Formula* painted the oil industry as an insidious criminal cartel.

Depicting the oil industry as the villain, here epitomized by eccentric and ostentatious Titan Oil chairman Adam Steiffel (Marlon Brando), is not a new narrative. Since the 1904 publication of Ida Tarbell's muckraking book on Standard Oil, the industry's abuses have been part of civil and cultural discourse.[4] Given the political turmoil surrounding oil shortages and rising environmental consciousness in the 1970s, portraying the oil industry as a villain makes sense.[5] In addition, visual media was an important venue through which Americans created cultural meaning about the energy crises, and *The Formula* is evidence of that effort.[6] Moviemakers and screenwriters built the narrative foundation of the film upon contemporary cultural and political anger toward oil companies. With ambivalence toward those critiques, the movie's villain, oil executive Steiffel, explains to Detective Barney Caine (George C. Scott), who has just confronted him about Neely's murder, "Oil nourished the great American dream. . . . Without it, ain't no America."

What is unique about this story of corporate villainy is that *The Formula* weaponizes oil refining technologies as a powerful vehicle for societal control. Here, the portrayal of Titan Oil (likely a symbolic stand-in for Exxon) turns oil companies' self-image upside down. Throughout the twentieth century and especially during the 1960s, 1970s, and 1980s, Exxon worked hard to craft a public image as a scientific and technological expert.[7] *The Formula* corrupts that narrative by having Titan Oil attempt to withhold the Nazis' formula for synthetic fuels, when in reality oil companies worked to develop and improve synthetic fuel technologies throughout the twentieth century. The plot speaks directly to the existing anger at corporations like Exxon and the rest of the oil industry during the 1970s, and depicts oil companies as all-powerful agents of evil at a time when their size and cooperation within the industry created significant antitrust concerns. However, what is most surprising about *The Formula*'s use of petroleum technologies is that the movie employs the idea that synfuels could be the symbolic savior of an America struggling against stagflation, hostile corporations, and social discontent.

A Failed Formula

On December 19, 1980, Metro-Goldwyn-Mayer (MGM) Studios released *The Formula* to national audiences. It was produced by Steve Shagan (who was also the movie's screenwriter and author of the novel on which the film was based) and directed by John J. Avildsen. It was the third movie this pair had worked on together, though none were blockbuster successes.[8] The film notably employed two Oscar-winning stars: George C. Scott and Marlon Brando. Though Scott got the lion's share of the screen time as Detective Caine, some reviews claimed that Brando's portrayal of oil magnate Adam Steiffel was more memorable due to his eccentricity and magnetism.[9] However, even with two powerhouse actors and an estimated budget of $13.2 million, the film underperformed at the box office, pulling in only approximately $850,000 on opening weekend and grossing nearly $8.9 million nationally.[10] In retrospect, the complex plot as well as disagreements between Avildsen and Shagan over the final scenes made it a confusing film to watch and likely hindered enthusiastic reception of the international thriller.[11]

Overall, reviews were lackluster if not downright deprecating. One writer from the *Boston Globe* warned, "'The Formula's' plot is so labyrinthine that the viewer is advised not to worry about it."[12] Other reviewers also chastised the film's complicated narrative, especially the frequency of Detective Caine's leads being murdered shortly after or during their interviews. A writer for the *New York Times* complained about one such occurrence: "The murder scene is littered with so many red herrings it might as well be a delicatessen."[13] "Being the narrative shambles it is," exclaimed film critic Vincent Canby from the *New York Times*, the film was "unintentionally comic." Canby continued, "Relentless murk is the style of the movie and it successfully neutralizes the effects of the talents of Mr. Brando and Mr. Scott. They look absurd."[14] Roger Ebert called the film's premise a "fantasy" and, to counter the filmmakers' claims that the formula was real, cited *Science* magazine in his review as proof.[15]

Despite its specious scientific claims and convoluted plot, *The Formula* very clearly expressed that the oil industry was the cause of America's problems. This message did not go unnoticed by US oil companies. "Every so often," a review from December 1980 warned, "Hollywood makes a movie that treads on the toes of some powerful segment of the American economy." Films in the 1970s stand out for the frequency with which they critiqued big business. A year earlier in 1979, *The China Syndrome* received negative attention from the nuclear industry in response to the film's fictional take on a disastrous accident at a nuclear power plant. General Electric even withdrew sponsorship from a talk show on which Jane Fonda, the female lead, was booked to promote the film. Some Hollywood executives worried that the oil industry would respond similarly to *The Formula*. Frank Rosenfelt, the chairman of MGM, said, "There is no question the heavies in 'The Formula' are big oil. Marlon Brando is almost evil incarnate." Oil company representatives like Anthony Hatch, Atlantic Richfield's manager of corporate media relations, feared the public's response. The company was "worried it could be another 'China Syndrome' where people leave the theaters angry."[16]

Yet there was no public backlash. In fact, Atlantic Richfield invited producer and screenwriter Steve Shagan to speak about the film and its premise with oil company representatives and an academic from Texas A&M University. Their conversation would air on a company-sponsored television program called *Energy Update* that was distributed free of charge to 160 television stations in five different countries. Privately, Mobil also sent representatives to MGM to discuss the film and its implications. In response to this attention from the oil industry, Shagan stood firm in asserting that the studio would not restrict the film's distribution, but that it would also not point a finger at any particular oil company. It is likely that representatives from the oil industry were reluctant to react harshly toward the film, lest they feed conspiracy theories. If they appeared to be secretive or scared of the film, the public could have interpreted such reactions as expressions of guilt. Even so, the implicit tensions here reveal that some oil executives worried about how the film would affect their public image.[17]

Creating Corporate Villains

After the introductory scenes depicting the fall of Berlin, the film takes viewers to 1970s Los Angeles, the first frame exhibiting an aerial view of the city's maze of highways. As the car was often connected with critiques of excess consumption and energy use, featuring highways as a cinematic trope—especially the intertwined loops of Los Angeles's complex interchange, as the film does repeatedly—is a clear visual representation of such criticism.[18] The viewer then meets Detective Barney Caine, whose Sunday visit with his son is cut short just as they are leaving a movie theater. Caine's voice is rife with annoyance at being interrupted, but he quickly learns that his good friend Thomas Neely (the Army major from the first scene) has been brutally murdered in his own home. Caine rushes to the scene, and the investigation of Neely's death begins. Clues found at the site lead Caine to unravel the mysterious circumstances of his old friend's death, including his recent trip to Berlin. After discovering Neely's corrupt dealings with local mafia and apparent social connections to oil tycoon Adam Steiffel, Caine begins to unearth the details of Project Genesis—the Nazi's secret plan to develop synthetic gasoline. Caine suspects that Neely was murdered by a terrorist organization connected to international crime power broker Frank Tedesco, a middleman between what Caine describes as the criminal underworld and the "overworld." What is the "overworld," you might ask? "Big Oil. Big Banking. International cartels like OPEC. Adam Steiffel is Big Oil. OPEC was created by Big Oil," Caine explains to his bewildered police captain. Caine's reasoning here parallels the public belief that there was little difference between Big Oil and OPEC. They were equally bad.[19]

Historical events from the 1970s likely encouraged the filmmakers' willingness to associate Big Oil with criminal cartels. The key events here are undoubtedly the twin oil crises of 1973 and 1979, which dramatically changed American's relationship to energy. The events had disastrous ripple effects throughout the economy and strongly symbolized the destruction of the postwar social contract—the idea that a full-time job in a factory, office, or other economic sector would support a family and provide a comfortable life. Historian Meg Jacobs describes the crises as an "energy Pearl Harbor," which for the first time in nearly three decades challenged the persistence of "big cars, big suburban homes, and boundless consumption."[20] However, the oil crisis is an easy get. Filmmakers might have also been inspired by the Foreign Corrupt Practices Act, which Congress passed and implemented in 1977. The act prohibits US corporations from bribing foreign officials and political organizations, and provided a period during which corporations could report past abuses to the Securities and Exchange Commission without prosecution. For example, this grace period revealed that Exxon gave more than $50 million to political parties in Italy. This outright graft, and similar examples from across the corporate world, infuriated average Americans.[21]

Marlon Brando's character, Adam Steiffel, looms large as the film's symbolic embodiment of the oil industry and its most sinister motives. Caine interviews Steiffel during his initial investigation into Neely's murder (fig. 17.1). Steiffel waxes poetic about the American oil industry being beholden to Arab oil companies, insisting that such dependence is crushing the American dream. He asserts this position despite having learned only moments ago about a large oil field surrounded by hills filled with pure anthracite coal. Steiffel wants Caine to believe that Arab countries are the reason that America's economy and society are struggling. Trying to throw Caine off the scent, Steiffel confirms that Neely was his bagman, employed to deliver bribes to oil producers in the Middle East. Caine, however, sees through Steiffel's subtle deception.

In this discussion with Detective Caine, Steiffel echoes the contemporary oil industry's perspective, which, struggling to reconcile demand and supply, characterized the 1973 crisis as a problem of production and access to crude oil, not consumption. Exxon's quarterly magazine for shareholders, *The Lamp*, published various articles establishing this view. In one such piece from the spring of 1974, chairman of the board J. Kenneth Jamieson undertook damage control of the corporation's image. In "Is the Energy Shortage Real?" he wrote that for some time the industry had been concerned about increasing reliance on oil from the Middle East, and explained that Exxon had been pushing for

Fig. 17.1. In their first meeting in the movie, Adam Steiffel (Marlon Brando) and Detective Barney Caine (George C. Scott) discuss the death of Tom Neely. Caine questions Steiffel's relationship with Neely. A motorcade of guards, employees, and servants follow Steiffel as the two walk, signifying his power in the film's narrative. *The Formula* (MGM, 1980).

access to additional domestic oil sources, like in Alaska, in order to decrease reliance on foreign imports. Working to counter critiques and further Exxon's political agenda, Jamieson specifically focused on the problem of dependence on Middle Eastern oil.[22] Even though the United States remained the world's largest oil producer in the 1970s, oil companies like Exxon asserted that the nation needed to protect its access to oil, as threats to supply and increasing demand were cause for concern in the industry. Other publications, like the *Oil and Gas Journal*, argued that the lesson from the 1973 embargo was to look for new oil supplies elsewhere in order to maintain economic stability.[23] This perspective pushed the blame back onto the Arab nations of OAPEC and created a set of more conservative policies that would not threaten the industry's existing practices.

A subsequent scene reinforces the film's message about the oil industry's role in the supply and demand balancing act. There, viewers find Steiffel dressed in pajamas and a robe, enjoying breakfast outside of his mansion. Mid-meal, an employee approaches Steiffel and announces that OPEC has decided to cut back on oil production by 20 percent. If they move quickly, the employee continues, the company can raise prices by twelve cents on the gallon and blame OPEC for the increase. Steiffel opposes the idea, insisting that Titan Oil should not increase prices by more than seven cents. Confused by the rejection of a nickel profit per gallon, the employee asks, "Our purpose is to raise money, isn't it?" Exasperated, Steiffel sternly responds, "Our purpose is to avoid having people machine gunning us in the gas line."[24] His employee persists, saying that they should inflate prices and blame it on Arab nations. Steiffel ends the conversation by saying, "You're missing the point. We *are* the Arabs."

Regardless of the criminal connections the movie depicts, Steiffel reveals here that oil companies benefited from higher prices during the embargo. Titan Oil shouldn't tip its hand by raising prices too much because it would raise consumer suspicion. This exchange is a nod to popular critiques that surrounded the oil crises. A dominant one suggested that oil companies made it all up in order to raise prices. This was an idea that Jamieson, Exxon's chairman, lamented in his 1974 article. "They accuse us of reaping huge profits at the expense of the consuming public," he wrote, disparaging this idea and attempting to disprove it by describing financial challenges to the industry.[25] The rest of the industry, including other executives, seemed to agree. In a Senate hearing on the issue of extraordinarily high oil prices, oil executives swore under oath that such changes were "unsupported," "absolute nonsense," "erroneous," and "counterproductive" when grilled by senators Henry Jackson, Jacob Javits, and Abraham Ribicoff.[26] Going even further, several editorials from a leading trade magazine, the *Oil and Gas Journal*, suggested that oil prices were not high enough to cover industry costs and expansion.[27] Even so, by agreeing to a smaller price increase, Steiffel addresses a major point of the film: as long as Americans relied on oil, oil companies had the power to inflate prices at will. However, oil supplies became more complicated in the 1970s, and the shortages caused by the oil crises combined with growing demand made oil's products seem highly profitable.[28] Put another way, demand was inelastic and growing, while supply was being more carefully managed for suppliers' benefit. Hence, the more oil Americans used, the more valuable of a commodity it was.

The Promise of Synthetic Fuels

After Steiffel's revealing discussion with his employee, Detective Caine travels to Germany to get some answers. His investigation leads him to German scientist Paul Obermann (David Byrd), who explains Project Genesis: "The entire war-machine ran on synthetic fuel. Germany had no natural crude, but we possessed great quantities of coal. As does your country. The Genesis formula provided us with a pure synthetic oil, producing no pollution." This "no pollution" clause has meaning. Coal hydrogenation is an incredibly polluting process, and mentioning that the fictional formula had solved that problem is a nod to environmentalism's influence on the American public's understanding of energy and the environment. Afterward, Caine learns that Project Genesis was the Nazis' secret weapon that was fueling the war. This, Caine realizes, is the connection between Paul Neely, his murdered friend, and Steiffel. Neely's murder was a necessary step in Steiffel's plan to acquire and suppress the formula. On the way out of their clandestine meeting at the Berlin Zoo, Obermann is killed by an unknown assassin and dies in Caine's arms.

Project Genesis is modeled after real petrochemical processes developed in the late nineteenth century but industrialized by German scientists in the twentieth. It is a fictionalized and perfected version of coal hydrogenation, also known as coal liquefaction, which the Germans used during the 1930s and 1940s to create gasoline.[29] Most simply, the process adds hydrogen molecules to lighten the molecular weight of hydrocarbons wrested from coal. Germany, a nation without natural reserves of petroleum, put effort into developing coal hydrogenation to create the fuel of the future. Only by creating their own independent source of petroleum could Germany fuel its changing energy needs, as gasoline and diesel fuels began to dominate consumer energy demands and coal became less desirable in a quickly urbanizing and industrializing country.[30] The Germans invested in this technology throughout the 1930s, with research conducted largely by the German chemical giant IG Farben. By the 1940s, Germany had more sophisticated, though still very expensive, coal hydrogenation technologies. Even so, a lack of natural oil significantly hampered both the Germans and the Japanese during World War II. In reality, coal hydrogenation produced lower-quality fuel and was very energy intensive. It would have been impossible to fuel the war solely on coal hydrogenation, which supports the real-life significance of oil refineries in Nazi-controlled countries during the war. In addition, the Germans could not compete with the powerful 100-octane aviation fuel produced from crude oil in American oil refineries like Standard Oil of New Jersey.[31]

In *The Formula*, the portrayal of these technologies has racial implications. It is perhaps no coincidence that the film depicts the Germans as capable of creating a pure formula for coal hydrogenation, as it reflects Nazism's focus on racial purity. Even the name of the program, Project Genesis, suggests the formula's ability to buttress Nazi efforts to create a new racially pure society. By using *genesis*, these fictional Nazis could appropriate the word from the Judeo-Christian tradition and redefine it for a new German nation.

Though the movie fetishizes the technology's roots in interwar Germany, it was not solely Germans who worked to develop it.[32] American multinational corporations were part of the effort to develop synfuels, as well. According to historians Joseph Pratt and William Hale, Exxon "had chased the elusive promise of synfuels for more than half a century." However, Exxon's coal lique-faction projects had been continually beset by high input costs in production, and by the 1970s the project was not yet considered industrially viable.[33] Yet the 1973 oil crisis renewed efforts to develop synfuel technologies.[34] Exxon and Mobil Oil Company scientists reignited experiments to improve Germany's Fischer-Tropsch process, which had been abandoned after World War II when cheap crude oil became widely available from the Middle East.[35] In 1974, Exxon publicized efforts to renew these technologies with an article in *The Lamp*, ar-guing, "Coal, and the synthetic fuels derived from it, will be important in our future energy picture." The article assured readers that "Exxon researchers are developing methods to put coal to use in environmentally acceptable ways." [36] Mobil scientists even claimed that the United States was underutilizing its coal resources and that investing in coal liquefaction and gasification technologies could help supply the world with fossil fuel energies in the face of declining domestic oil field production.[37]

The Formula gave viewers a more conspiratorial motive for the development of synfuels. After his unfortunate encounter at the Berlin Zoo, Caine follows the trail created by Obermann's death, leading him—and Obermann's grieving niece and secret assassin Lisa Spangler (Marthe Keller)—to Professor Siebold (Ferdy Mayne). Siebold reveals that German advancements in coal hydrogena-tion began in 1936, when Hitler gave scientists one billion Reichsmarks to develop the technology to mass-produce synthetic fuel. That research produced a "special" catalyst that enabled the Germans to generate enough synthetic fuel to power the war.[38] Siebold goes on to claim that not once during Allied aerial bombings were hydrogenation plants hit: "And why? Because certain American oil companies shared chemical patents with the Third Reich! Americans were in business with the Third Reich then, and the same partnership exists today. There is blood on your hands too, Mr. Caine!" [39] Just as Spangler and Caine leave the room, Professor Siebold is shot in the head through a window.

Environmental Fantasies

Caine, who now recognizes that Adam Steiffel is behind everything, returns to the United States and confronts him at Titan Oil's luxurious high-rise offices. In this final confrontation, Steiffel explains how he set up Neely to create a cover for the murder of Project Genesis scientists—one that wouldn't impli-cate Big Oil and would keep the formula out of the public domain. Synthetic gasoline, from Steiffel's perspective, is just another way to give Americans what they want: cheap energy. This tense exchange in the final minutes of the film illuminates the two characters' starkly different philosophies:

CAINE: You trade lives and human dignity for profit.

STEIFFEL: "Money, not morality, is the principal commerce of civilized nations." Thomas Jefferson, two hundred years ago. That is the philosophy that built this nation.

CAINE: What do you know about this nation? When did you ever give a second thought to American citizens? You're the reason their money's worthless. You're the reason old people are eating out of garbage cans and kids get killed in bullshit wars. You're not in the oil business, you're in the oil shortage business. You're an ivory tower hoodlum. A common street killer. I wish to Christ there was some way I could nail you.

STEIFFEL: Well . . . you're gonna be nailing the American Dream, Barney. Because it all started in the corner gas station. Remember, you used to take your bike down there and get free air. And Daddy said, "Fill them up, Fred." And you go down to Grandma's for Christmas dinner. Yeah. Then, when you got your first car, what did you do? You took your girl for a ride. There was Fred smiling by the pump there. He never let you down, because a gallon of gas never broke down. Well, it was oil that nourished the American Dream. We're the great American tit, Barney. And without it . . . ain't no America.

As Caine charges Steiffel with corruption, he also claims that synthetic fuels have the potential to alleviate these problems. Releasing the formula to the public, as he attempts to do, would not only hurt Steiffel and Titan Oil, but also liberate America from dependence on oil and ease inflation—the major social and economic issues of the 1970s. According to *The Formula*, coal hydrogenation is the solution to America's problems.

Depicting the formula as pollution-free allowed filmmakers to fantasize about a future unencumbered by environmental limits, as long as the nation didn't run out of coal reserves. Unfortunately, this environmental fantasy is baseless, even considering contemporary technologies. Pollution-free synthetic fuel does not exist. The Canadian tar sands project—which some refer to as the biggest industrial and landscape-shaping project ever created—readily demonstrates that the film's vision inverts reality. Perhaps the most visually jarring example of waste from modern tar sands destruction is the tailing ponds— enormous waste ponds filled with toxic sludge. The sludge itself is a distinctive mixture of hydrocarbons and other toxic residues, inextricably merged together in a toxic goo—a form of pollution as permanent as radioactive nuclear waste. Tailings ponds in the Canadian tar sands project hold one trillion liters of industrial by-products, and they are a real environmental threat. Reports of tailings pond spills—sixteen between 2014 and 2018—have begun to inspire charges of corruption.[40] In the film, synthetic fuels are the deus ex machina that solved the problem of energy reliance without environmental destruction.

In focusing on the fantasy of a world without environmental limits, *The Formula* misses a more powerful critique of mass consumption and fossil fuel economies in general. The film could have taken up leftist politics, which in the 1970s began to see consumption as a major problem. As environmentalism grew into a more popular movement, scholars and public figures denounced affluence and consumption in a number of ways.[41] However, even from the very beginning, the film never critiques consumerism. Instead, as the ill-fated Major Neely proclaims in the opening scene, consumerism shaped the postwar world. Mass consumerism fueled by oil and its products isn't the problem, the film claims; it's that crooks are in charge of them. Perhaps addressing consumerism would have made the film too political and turned some viewers away. Fundamentally, the film leaves viewers unsure of the consumer's role in creating this dependent relationship, demonstrating the filmmakers' ultimate unwillingness to tackle more difficult questions. How can society effectively reduce dependence on fossil fuels? What would a world without oil-dependent automobiles look like? The magic of a pollution-free formula for synthetic fuel gave filmmakers an easy out. Big Oil is a simpler villain than American consumers.

At the end of this final argument, Caine reveals to Steiffel that he gave the formula to Swiss businessman Franz Tauber (Wolfgang Preiss) in an attempt to make it public. Afterward, Caine leaves the office, seemingly having pulled one over on Steiffel. Walking outside the high-rise office building, Sergeant Yosuta (Calvin Jung) asks Caine if he thinks Steiffel will go after him. Caine responds, "No. . . . I'm not an adversary anymore. I'm just another customer." The film ends with a fixed frame of Los Angeles highway traffic, reinforcing the car as a symbol of oil consumption. However, Steiffel remains firmly in control, as he calls Tauber as soon as Caine leaves his office and convinces him to maintain the formula's secrecy for ten years in exchange for 30 percent of his anthracite coal holdings. Big Oil outwits the humble LA detective in a conclusion that reinforces the film's main point: Big Oil has outwitted most of us.

Conclusion

The Formula was a problematic international thriller that explored the cultural and social implications of the 1973 oil crisis. It argued that a nefarious oil industry was duping Americans into the mass consumption of oil-fueled and oil-derived products, and that a formula for synthetic fuel—one that could escape environmental limits—could save the nation. Although the film's environmental fantasies allowed it to dodge structural critiques of energy-intensive capitalism, it is a testament to US anxiety about reliance on foreign energy sources, which indeed permeated the American cultural imaginary as result of the 1970s energy crises. In effect, a movie about a formula for synthetic fuel can be interpreted as an exploration of a fictional solution for a prominent social fear. Perhaps the film's poor reception suggests that Americans simply didn't buy into its narrative. Or maybe its narrative confusion merely echoes Americans' confusion about how to approach the complex problems of the 1970s. Either way, *The Formula* demonstrates that oil-refining technologies had permeated America's cultural consciousness.

Notes

1. John G. Avildsen, dir., *The Formula* (Hollywood, CA: Metro-Goldwyn-Mayer Studios, 1980).
2. Sheri Chinen Biesen argues that the uncertainty and trauma of World War II serves as the true origins of the genre and influenced later film noir pictures during the Cold War period. Sheri Chinen Biesen, *Blackout: World War II and the Origins of Film Noir* (Baltimore: Johns Hopkins University Press, 2005), 3.
3. Roman Polanski, dir., *Chinatown* (Hollywood, CA: Paramount Pictures, 1974).
4. Ida Tarbell, *The History of the Standard Oil Company* (New York: McClure, Phillips, and Co., 1904). For more on how historians have analyzed energy use in the 1970s, see Meg Jacobs, *Panic at the Pump: The Energy Crisis and the Transformation of American Politics in the 1970s* (New York: Hill and Wang, 2016); Robert Lifset, ed., *American Energy Policy in the 1970s* (Norman: University of Oklahoma Press, 2014); David E. Nye, "The Energy Crisis of the 1970s as a Cultural Crisis," *European Contributions to American Studies* 38 (March 1997): 82–102; Karen R. Merrill, *The Oil Crisis of 1973–1974: A Brief History with Documents* (Boston: Bedford/St. Martin's, 2007); Daniel Yergin, *The Prize: The Epic Quest for Oil, Money, and Power* (New York: Simon and Schuster, 1991). For an additional work analyzing *The Formula*, see Robert Lifset and Brian C. Black, "Imaging the 'Devil's Excrement': Big Oil in Petroleum Cinema, 1940–2007," *Journal of American History* 99, no. 1 (June 2012): 140–41.
5. Natasha Zaretsky, *No Direction Home: The American Family and the Fear of National Decline, 1968–1980* (Chapel Hill: University of North Carolina Press, 2007), 77–87.
6. Finis Dunaway, *Seeing Green: The Use and Abuse of American Environmental Images* (Chicago: University of Chicago Press, 2015), 113.
7. Raechel Lutz, "Crude Conservation: Nature, Pollution, and Technology at Standard Oil's New Jersey Refineries, 1870–2000" (PhD diss., Rutgers University, 2018), 134–62.
8. Steve Shagan, *The Formula: A Novel* (New York: Morrow, 1979).
9. Vincent Canby, "Film View; On Good Actors in Bad Movies," *New York Times*, January 11, 1981; Janet Maslin, "Film: 'The Formula' For Synthetic Oil: Blood and Oil," *New York Times*, December 19, 1980.

10. "The Formula (1980)," IMDB, accessed March 14, 2019, https://www.imdb.com /title/tt0080754/.
11. Aljean Harmetz, "At the Movies; Producer of 'Popeye' to Try 'Cotton Club,'" *New York Times*, December 12, 1980.
12. Bruce McCabe, "Review/Movie; The Formula Works," *Boston Globe*, December 19, 1980.
13. Maslin, "'The Formula' for Synthetic Oil."
14. Canby, "Good Actors in Bad Movies."
15. Roger Ebert, "The Formula," December 23, 1980, https://www.rogerebert.com /reviews/the-formula-1980.
16. Harmetz, "At the Movies."
17. Harmetz, "At the Movies."
18. Zaretsky, *No Direction Home*, 89.
19. Another confusing plot twist is that Caine's police captain is in the pocket of the "overworld," and reports on Caine's activities.
20. Jacobs, *Panic at the Pump*, 3.
21. Karin M. Lissakers, "Again, Why Congress Barred Bribery Abroad," *New York Times*, June 18, 1981.
22. J. K. Jamieson, "Is the Energy Shortage Real?" *The Lamp* 56, no. 1 (Spring 1974): 1–3. An article in *The Lamp*'s previous issue also argued that the trans-Alaska pipeline would buffet US energy supplies in an increasingly hostile global market. Sanford Brown, "Alaska's New Era," *The Lamp* 56, no. 4 (Winter 1974): 2–11.
23. Frank J. Gardner, "Watching the World: October's Lesson," *Oil and Gas Journal* 72, no. 1 (January 7, 1974): 31.
24. This is a reference to actual gunfights that erupted at trucker strikes resulting from the oil shortage. Jacobs, *Panic at the Pump*, 94.
25. Jamieson, "Energy Shortage," 2–3.
26. "Executives Swear Oil Crisis is Genuine," *Oil and Gas Journal* 72, no. 4 (January 28, 1974): 79. For a discussion of the pressure felt by the industry under such suspicions of foul play, see "U.S. Beginning to Feel Arab Embargo," *Oil and Gas Journal* 72, no. 2 (January 14, 1974): 26.
27. One editorial satirized the profits generated by the oil industry and suggested that they were being unfairly blamed: "The average American, plagued by rising personal costs, is more apt to think current profits make oil companies the sleekest of fat cats. . . . There's too little realization of how desperately the oil industry needs improved profits and needs them consistently over a long period of years." "Oil Profits Not High Enough, but They Must Be Spent Wisely," *Oil and Gas Journal* 71, no. 46 (November 12, 1973): 85. Also see Jim West, "U.S. Oils' Profits Still Short of Expansion Needs," *Oil and Gas Journal* 71, no. 46 (November 12, 1973): 87–89; "Tell it Straight This Time: Higher Oil Profits Are Vital," *Oil and Gas Journal* 72, no. 3 (January 21, 1974): 29.
28. "Demand Outpaces Oil Output," *Oil and Gas Journal* 71, no. 47 (November 19, 1973): 22.
29. Anthony N. Stranges, "Friedrich Bergius and the Rise of the German Synthetic Fuel Industry," *Isis* 75, no. 4 (1984): 643–67.
30. Stranges, "Friedrich Bergius and the Rise of the German Synthetic Fuel Industry," 643–67.
31. Exxon and IG Farben had a scientific partnership in the 1930s that largely dealt with the development of synthetic rubber, though they also had agreements to

work together on coal hydrogenation. Henrietta M. Larson, Evelyn H. Knowlton, and Charles S. Popple, *New Horizons, 1927–1950: History of Standard Oil Company (New Jersey)* (New York: Harper and Row, 1971), 153–59; Anthony N. Stranges, "The US Bureau of Mines' Synthetic Fuel Programme, 1920–1950s: German Connections and American Advances," *Annals of Science* 54 (1997): 39; Yergin, *The Prize*, 328–30.

32. Stranges, "US Bureau of Mines' Synthetic Fuel Programme," 32, 35, 47–49; Richard H. K. Vietor, *Energy Policy in America Since 1945: A Study of Business and Government* (Cambridge: Cambridge University Press, 1987), 44–59, 163–87.

33. Though I mostly use the term *synfuels* as a stand-in for coal hydrogenation or liquefaction, historians Joseph Pratt and William Hale offer a more precise definition: "The word 'synfuels' refers to any number of liquid and gaseous fuels created from hydrocarbons but not originally found as a liquid or a gas. At times, this word is also applied to biomass-derived fuels such as ethanol. The primary synfuels are manufactured from coal, oil shale, oil sands, and heavy oils." Joseph A. Pratt and William E. Hale, *Exxon: Transforming Energy, 1973–2005* (Austin: University of Texas Press, 2013), 197, 526n17.

34. Exxon's developments in synfuel technology led to the technologies necessary to develop the oil sands in Alberta, Canada, which is technically considered synthetic crude because of the significant energy and water needed to produce crude oil from tar sands. Pratt and Hale, *Exxon*, 198–200.

35. Exxon and Mobil merged into one multinational corporation in 1999. The two companies descended from John D. Rockefeller's Standard Oil, which split into Standard Oil of New Jersey and Standard Oil of New York as well as several other similarly named corporations in 1911.

36. Norman Richards, "Coal Comes Back," *The Lamp* 56, no. 1 (Spring 1974): 4.

37. John P. McCullough, "Converting Coal into Gasoline" (lecture, American Chemical Society, Tulsa, OK, May 20, 1976), Box 2.207/D162, Exxon Mobil Historical Collection, Dolph Briscoe Center for American History, University of Texas at Austin.

38. Catalysts are often used in refinery processes, and special formulas could potentially hold significant value.

39. This moment is likely an allusion to Standard Oil of New Jersey's relationship with German chemical company IG Farben.

40. Tzeporah Berman, "Canada's Most Shameful Environmental Secret Must Not Remain Hidden," *Guardian*, November 14, 2017, https://www.theguardian.com /commentisfree/2017/nov/14/canadas-shameful-environmental-secret-tar-sands -tailings-ponds; Judith Lavoie, "Tailings Dam Failures Linked to Hefty Bonuses for Mine Managers: Report," Narwhal, June 24, 2019, https://thenarwhal.ca/tailings -dam-failures-linked-to-hefty-bonuses-for-mine-managers-report.

41. Paul R. Erhlich, *The Population Bomb* (New York: Ballantine Books, 1968); Rachel Carson, *Silent Spring* (Boston: Houghton Mifflin, 1962); Donella H. Meadows and Dennis Meadows, *Limits to Growth: A Report for the Club of Rome's Project on the Predicament of Mankind* (New York: Universe Books, 1972).

Chapter 18

"Keep Moving": *Convoy* (1978), Car Films, and Petropopulism in the 1970s

Caleb Wellum

F ilm," notes critic Eric Mottram, "reflects America as a . . . car culture of
remarkable tenacity."[1] Beginning with the Lumière brothers' iconic 1895
shot of a train gliding into La Ciotat station, to the cruising cars of *American
Graffiti* (1973) and the races of the *Fast and Furious* franchise, cinematic content has been steeped in the imagery, rites, and landscapes of fossil-fueled
culture, valorizing industrial modernity and deriving kinetic excitement from
fossil-fueled mobility.[2] The representation of automobility in particular—the
subject of this essay—has long been a vehicle for dramatizing social and political conflicts in the United States.[3] But what happens when the tenacity and
morality of US car culture comes into question, as it did during the energy
crises of the 1970s? Rising energy consumption, stagnating oil production,
and the OAPEC oil embargo of 1973–1974 led to gasoline shortages and price
increases in many parts of the United States. The resulting uncertainty about
the availability and affordability of fuel inflamed anxieties about the future
of US petroculture and inspired calls for an energy transition. It also reignited
populist resentment toward elite power, as many accused OPEC, Big Oil, and
big government of gouging US citizens. Independent truckers staged slowdowns and blockades to protest rising fuel prices and reduced speed limits.[4]
Popular reportage depicted them as folk heroes, modern day cowboys speaking up for the common man by resisting the powers that threatened the freedom of the open road and working people's ability to earn a decent living on
it.[5] They embodied what we might call a "petropopulist" response to the energy
crisis, framing it as a crisis manufactured by elites, and demanded cheap fuel
and open roads as the right of the people.[6]

American cinema articulated the anxiety and populist discontent of the energy crisis era with a glut of films obsessed with automobility. As citizens fumed and pondered their nation's bicentennial while stuck in a gasoline lineup, car films explored the meaning of American life through stories centered on cars, trucks, and roads.[7] As one critic complained, "Everything of importance [in these films] takes place either in/on a vehicle or in the immediate vicinity of one."[8] By turns nostalgic, aimless, comic, angry, and absurd, 1970s car films signaled a conflicted relationship to fossil-fueled car culture in a decade of national reflection and energy uncertainty. Many such films used unrestrained automobility as a symbol or conduit for individual freedom and self-realization in an overregulated world—the birthright of every free American citizen.

Among the decade's many car films, this essay analyzes automobility in *Convoy*, which skidded into cinemas in June 1978. The last of a short cycle of "trucker films," *Convoy* labored to exploit the cultural capital of truckers in energy crisis America.[9] The film is an apt example of what Nadia Bozak calls the "hydrocarbon imagination" at a moment of crisis in the fossil economy.[10] Filmed on location in New Mexico with dozens of transport trucks, police cars, military vehicles, and a helicopter, *Convoy* was an energy-intensive production.[11] Its story and aesthetics, moreover, articulated the ambivalent petropopulism of US car cinema's engagement with energy in the 1970s. By paying attention to the links between populism and petroculture in *Convoy*, we can get a better sense of the oil-haunted energy unconscious of the United States and the cultural challenge of energy transition.

The concept of an energy unconscious posits that forms of energy play an important but often submerged role in the formation of human subjectivity, culture, and society.[12] Cultural critic and historian Bob Johnson has recently put flesh on the bones of the concept by proposing six "modalities" through which fossil fuels shape the energy unconscious of modernity: ambient energy, congealed energy, polymerized energy, embodied energy, propulsive energy, and entropic energy.[13] Although 1970s energy crisis discourse included ambient (heating), embodied (population), and entropic (pollution and social collapse) energy, car films like *Convoy* operated in terms of congealed (roads and infrastructure) and propulsive (trucks and fossil-fueled mobility) energy— the forms of energy most intimately linked to popular notions of freedom. Examining *Convoy*'s representation of the road, trucks, and motion reveals the tension at the heart of the film between its search for a pluralistic America of freedom and ceaseless motion, its subtle critique of fossil-fueled, hypermasculine autonomy, and its petropopulist celebration of the open road and unlimited automobility as a public good threatened by elites. The popularity of the latter theme suggests the presence of an energy unconscious shaped by the fossil economy. Amid declining fuel supplies and stricter speed limits, *Convoy* articulated a romantic ideal of America as a "saga of motion" structured by the capacities and possibilities of fossil fuels.[14]

An Exploitation Art Film

Based on a popular country song of the same name from 1975, *Convoy* is a strange, visually dynamic, and deeply flawed film about a band of defiant truckers who spontaneously form a convoy that becomes a social movement. It opens on the empty desert roads of Arizona and the adventurous lives of the easygoing truckers who traverse them for a living. The film's protagonist and the convoy's leader, an independent trucker clad in aviator shades and a big black truck who goes by his CB handle, "Rubber Duck" (Kris Kristofferson), roars onto the screen in a sexually charged cat-and-mouse game with a woman driving a Jaguar (Melissa, played by Ali MacGraw). Rubber Duck is soon pulled over, and after talking his way out of a ticket by telling the patrolman that the woman he was chasing "doesn't have any pants on, man," joins up with two truckers who become his companions: a white ethnic man nicknamed "Pig Pen" (Burt Young) and an African American man known as "Spider Mike" (Franklyn Ajaye). As they speed along empty roads, the three are entrapped by the film's villain, "Dirty" Lyle Wallace (Ernest Borgnine), the sadistic sheriff who harasses truckers for pleasure. They pay their fines but enrage Lyle by mocking him over CB radio. The action speeds up at a truck stop diner, where Lyle is revealed as a racist when he tries to arrest Spider Mike for vagrancy. A saloon-style brawl ensues, forcing Rubber Duck, Spider Mike, and Pig Pen to flee to New Mexico, accompanied by Melissa and a few other truckers now implicated in the incident. So begins the convoy.

The narrative shifts as news of the convoy spreads and the mobile gathering swells. More truckers and a van of "Jesus freaks" join the fray in New Mexico to form a miles-long caravan of populist dissent. Through CB chatter and superior driving, the truckers evade Lyle's efforts to thwart their movement, which evolves from physical escape into a self-organizing social and political movement. As media coverage grows, the governor of New Mexico (Seymour Cassel) tries to exploit the convoy's populist appeal for political gain. His advisors think that truckers are "trash," but the governor understands that "this damn convoy has more public support than we do." Rubber Duck and his companions see through the charade and decide to abandon politics. They take off to rescue Spider Mike, whom Lyle had beaten and imprisoned in Texas when he tried to attend the birth of his first child. After liberating Spider Mike from prison, Rubber Duck sacrifices himself in a showdown with the National

Guard, only to be resurrected at a funeral cynically staged by politicians in his honor. The convoy joyously returns to the road while Lyle laughs maniacally.

The tension and dysfunction that afflicted *Convoy*'s production hurt the film artistically but inadvertently worked to more fully reflect populist attitudes toward energy. Executive producer Michael Deeley wanted to create a breezy comedy about CB lingo and fun-loving cowboy truckers, a film for a mass audience that would echo popular sentiments about driving and the freedom of the road. But Deeley hired the talented and increasingly volatile Sam Peckinpah to direct, and Peckinpah wanted to make an art film. Best known for his artistic Westerns, including the elegant *Ride the High Country* (1962) and the bloody ballad *The Wild Bunch* (1969), Peckinpah initially agreed to work on *Convoy* for practical reasons. Box office success had eluded his recent film, so he signed on to *Convoy* while finishing *Cross of Iron* (1977) to secure his next job in the event of another flop.[15] Indeed, Peckinpah's status as a serious director and the film's exploitation cinema roots led critics and industry professionals to dismiss *Convoy* as a money grab by a director on his way down, pointing to its poor acting, stiff dialogue, and hokey premise.[16] But Peckinpah had committed to crafting a statement about American democracy "in the mother tongue," despite the film's aimless script.[17] In his frantic search for a resonant story and images, Peckinpah went over time and budget. His cocaine addiction and drug use by the actors and crew further delayed the film, and an enraged Deeley decided to recut *Convoy* without its director. The result was a film that aimed to reflect popular sentiment *and* make a countercultural statement about the nation. This tension makes *Convoy*, which was ultimately Peckinpah's biggest hit, a compelling artifact of the energy unconscious of middle-class America in the 1970s.

Scholars and critics have noted thematic concerns and historical resonances that establish *Convoy* as a complex cultural artifact. Historians tend to emphasize the film's conservative elements. Derek Nystrom frames *Convoy*'s antiunion conceits as a way to manage "the threat of labor militancy" in the 1970s, while Shane Hamilton sees its rugged individualism as a reflection of the antiregulation trucking culture of the South, which prized the agrarian myth of self-direction and "independence rather than social belonging."[18] Film scholars and critics, however, offer readings that emphasize Peckinpah's creative influence. Frank Burke argues that *Convoy* is a story about spiritual transcendence in which the law/external control is transformed into self-direction, and "mere physical motion" becomes "moral and spiritual action." Rubber Duck sheds his truck and his hypermasculinist individualism for integration into a community through his self-sacrificial death.[19] Burke sees "moving together" and the development of a social unit that represents American society as the heart of the film's effort to "recover and extol the American dream, to resurrect Whitman's America . . . following years of turmoil, paralysis, and shame." [20] Using archival records from the film's production, Elaine Marshall similarly notes that Peckinpah wanted to make a "visual film" that explored the state of America through "the movement and dynamics of the convoy." [21] Peckinpah had been reading Ayn Rand at the time and made a film in which "possibility is not known or designed in advance by its leader, but is an emergent value." [22] The convoy thus represents the "people's energy" and the failed efforts of the law and the state to control it. [23]

Convoy is, of course, all of these things. A reflection of social and creative tensions, it traffics in individualist machismo and trucker romanticism while also telling a story of personal transformation, creative energy, and collective organization to protest elite power. But critics have yet to devote enough attention to its energy crisis context, as well as the fundamental role of the infrastructures and capacities of carbon modernity in the very articulation of these themes and ideals. If *Convoy* tries to represent American democracy as a Whitmanian collective of ceaseless movement, it articulates this vision firmly within a populist vision indebted to fossil fuels. It bespeaks the fossil-fueled energy unconscious of the United States at a moment of crisis.

Freedom of the Road

The energy unconscious in *Convoy*'s petropopulism was predicated first on the congealed energy of the paved highways and roads that support the fossil economy and on US petroculture more broadly. Road construction underlay the expansion of mass automobility early in the twentieth century, creating the endless miles of driveable roads that millions of Americans rely on for work, play, and the transportation of goods and services across the continent. [24] As Bob Johnson argues, now the personal mobility afforded by this road infrastructure has become so basic that it is "something like a social contract." [25]

The paved roads of the American Southwest are *Convoy*'s primary setting, and the film's commonplace treatment of them reflects their socioeconomic significance as well as the tenacity of the energy unconscious to which they contribute. Roads' aesthetic quality and logistical possibilities were so crucial to the basic conception of the film that Deeley chose New Mexico as a filming location for its "miles and miles and miles of often empty roads." [26] The film itself begins on a stretch of desert road that appears completely integrated into the landscape. As Marshall describes it, the desert in this stage-setting scene "is no wasteland, but a fertile field of radiant energy out of which successive events of convoying will be born." [27] Integral to that landscape is the road: sand blows across it as it weaves through the land like a river with tufts of grass along its banks. Never in the film does the road appear to be alienating as in *Two-Lane Blacktop* (1971), dangerous as in *Dirty Mary, Crazy Larry* (1974), or environmentally destructive. Rather, the road is essential to the desert and town landscapes of America, never questioned or made strange. It is the stage on which the drama of American life unfolds.

Just as it naturalizes its existence, *Convoy* imagines the road as a space of social belonging and play. All of the life portrayed in the film takes place on or beside roads: on a gravel shoulder, at a roadside truck stop, in the cabin of a car or truck, at a raceway. The rituals and realities of American life—of working, socializing, reproducing, worshipping, mourning, organizing, policing, and rebelling—take place in and around roads. This sense of social belonging and the promise of the open road was not, of course, a new sentiment. Walt Whitman's "Song of the Open Road" (1856) exclaims, "O public road . . . you express me better than I can express myself," depicting the road as a pluralistic space of social possibility and camaraderie.[28] *Convoy* presents a similar vision, with people from all walks of life—white and black, male and female—uniting in a spontaneous movement on the open roads, where they form deep social bonds. Whereas elites, who are often represented as immobile, as passengers, or as uncomfortable drivers, are willing, in the words of the film's governor, to "sacrifice the individual," the truckers who journey together stick together.

Those truckers who stick together also fight together for freedom on the road, a theme that reflects the larger energy crisis context in which the film was made, wherein the freedom and control of the road were pressing social and political concerns. In December 1973 and February 1974, thousands of mostly nonunionized truckers ("owner-operators") organized slowdowns and roadblocks, primarily in Northeastern states, to protest their economic plight. They decried rising fuel prices in the wake of the OAPEC oil embargo and the fifty-five-mile-per-hour speed limit that the Nixon administration had instituted in November 1973 as an energy conservation measure. The truckers claimed that their vehicles operated more efficiently at higher speeds, so having to drive fifty-five miles per hour not only prevented them from working at a more profitable pace, but also burned through more fuel and ate into profit margins. To broadcast their concerns and compel the government to act, truckers organized ways to slow down traffic, refused to deliver loads, or stayed home. Some protests involved acts of violence and intimidation. As a whole, they demonstrated, however briefly, their revolutionary potential to grind the fossil economy to a halt.[29] As Nystrom notes, US media worried openly about an "explosion of labor unrest" signaled by the trucker strikes.[30] In a matter of weeks, truckers had exposed the road as a prospective choke point in fossil capitalism.

Nystrom argues that trucker films sought to manage the threat of broader labor unrest during the energy crisis by disparaging unions and featuring owner-operator heroes. However, there is a sense in which Convoy posits control of the road as a key social and political struggle within fossil capitalism. Political and police aggression in the effort to control the road propel much of the film's narrative.[31] Each time the convoy adds new members, the group must overcome a new attempt by the law to halt the forward motion of the people.[32] In an echo of the discourse around trucker strikes, the convoy's revolutionary potential is concretized in Rubber Duck's truck, which we learn is full of explosive chemicals when the federal authorities attempt a roadblock.[33] The authorities back off, believing that Rubber Duck is willing to die for his still unknown cause, but they continue trying to control the roads by either cooptation or force. They use several tools of the state, from surveillance networks, helicopters, and police cars to the military power of the National Guard, but they are always derailed by the revolutionary activity of the fun-loving folk truckers. The film's use of military music reinforces this reading of a kind of populist war against illegitimate elite authority over the roads. Numerous and mocking references to the fifty-five-mile-per-hour speed limit, which many Americans resented as an infringement upon their freedom, further broaden the film's antiregulatory appeal beyond trucker concerns. Although Convoy shies away from advocating political revolution, it implicitly acknowledges the road's revolutionary potential while at the same time disparaging state attempts to control everyday drivers.

Despite these occasional references to political revolution, Convoy leans heavily on the myth of the open road to liken its truckers to libertarian cowboys. This was a common association in 1970s popular culture. In her book Trucker: A Portrait of the Last American Cowboy (1975), artist Jane Stern likens the highway to "the long trail" and imagines truckers as inheritors of cowboys' "frontier individualism," whose "freedom to move knows no bounds."[34] Convoy's indulgence in similar comparisons is not surprising given Peckinpah's history with the genre. Early on in the film, Spider Mike claims to have heard more stories about Rubber Duck than about Jesse James, and in their first encounter Rubber Duck and Dirty Lyle lament that independent men like themselves are a dying breed. These are classic themes for Peckinpah, which he consciously adapted to roads and automobility to express his view that the "welfare state" had diminished "people's energies to create, to build, to the satisfaction of their own work."[35] Indeed, the film labored to articulate individualist notions about roaming the open road within a populist frame of cowboy truckers versus the elites, claiming that by attempting to fetter auto-mobility the elites threatened the historic right to individual freedom on the roads.

But the notion of truckers as cowboys who yearn for open pastures sat uneasily with the reality that the road system they traversed was of relatively recent vintage and was itself a technological achievement backed by the state. Less than sixty years before the release of *Convoy*, in 1919, Dwight D. Eisenhower, then a lieutenant colonel (temporary) in the army, embarked on a convoy of his own across the continental United States to determine the state of the nation's roadways. He found a patchwork system of poorly maintained roads that were unpaved west of Illinois.[36] New laws and roads soon followed. In New Mexico, better road construction began in the late 1930s, and in 1956 President Eisenhower initiated construction of the Interstate Highway System. Far from being frontier trails of cowboy freedom, the highways of the twen-tieth century represented a relatively recent engineering achievement—what historian Steve Penfold has called "landscape[s] of petroleum."[37] So while the truckers in *Convoy* and other popular films may have fought for freedom on the road, those roads represented no frontier, and a rather circumscribed expres-sion of freedom. The road had become so integral to everyday American life, however, that it seemed natural and essential, an inheritance for the people that the government dared not restrict.

Truck Aesthetics

Much like the congealed energy of roads, the propulsive energies of mass au-tomobility and the car culture it spawned informed *Convoy*'s petropopulist vision of energy crisis America. Car ownership and dependence had swelled in the postwar years, while transport trucks had supplanted trains as the primary means of transporting goods across the nation.[38] When the energy crisis introduced the prospect of the end of cheap oil, public discourse began to question whether or not US car culture as it existed in the early 1970s had a future. *Time*, for instance, announced that the "romance between Americans and their huge, gleaming cars" could be coming to an end.[39] By the end of the decade, new fuel efficiency standards and competition from smaller Japanese vehicles had begun to change the composition of America's still-growing fleet of automobiles. Yet populist defenses of automobiles and US car culture also appeared, suggesting the durability of US petroculture and its imagined role as a natural benefit for the people.[40]

Convoy aligned with many other popular American films from the 1970s in celebrating the power of big cars and trucks to resist the prospect of their disappearance in an altered energy future. Perhaps most famously, George Lucas's box office smash *American Graffiti* (1973) reflected widespread nostalgia for the youth culture of the 1950s organized around cars and cruising. *Convoy*'s mood was not so much nostalgic as it was brashly defiant in its assertion of the glory of enormous transport trucks. In a production memo, Peckinpah stated that he believed that "the trucks are as important as the actors," and he spent hours filming them in order to lend the film visual and aural excitement.[41] As Marshall notes, "Some of the most beautiful and energetic footage centers on the trucks, their movement in particular—the shimmering emergence from heat waves . . . the lilting slow-motion dissolves in waltz tempo of vehicles and sand . . . the lyrical shots of 18-wheelers traveling in silhouette against a dying sunset."[42] One of the film's first images is of the exhaust from Rubber Duck's imposing black truck cresting a hill and looming into full view. Early on, Melissa abandons her British-made Jaguar to become a passenger in Rubber Duck's American-made Peterbilt. Toward the end of the film, the trucks form an imposing line as they prepare to attack the prison that holds Spider Mike. The scene references Westerns, with the trucks taking the place of horses as expressions of the cowboy truckers' independence and power. The trucks are both literally and figuratively agents of liberation, used to break through prison walls to free Spider Mike, and used to resist the oppressive firepower of the National Guard in the film's climax. The film's narrative imagines the power of collective action through images of groups of trucks far more often than through groups of humans outside of their machinic appendages.

Several film critics noted the allure of the trucks in *Convoy*. Pauline Kael heaped praise on Peckinpah for imbuing the trucks with "alarming individuality":

> Each brawny giant in the procession has its own stride; some are lumbering, others are smooth as adagio dancers, while one bounces along and its trailer shimmies. At night, when a frightened driver pulls out of the line to go off alone in the darkness, the truck itself seems to quaver, childishly. The trucks give the performances in this movie, and they go through changes: when the dust rises around them on rough backcountry roads, they're like sea beasts splashing spume; when two of them squeeze a little police car between their tanklike armored bodies, they're insect titans.[43]

In one of the film's most lyrical passages, several trucks lead the pursuing police cars onto unpaved roads in slow motion. The scene is shot and edited like a dance, with the trucks gracefully accelerating and turning as the white sands of New Mexico spray into the air like fresh alpine snow. The massive transport trucks become objects of aesthetic contemplation and beauty, as well as sources of raw power. Here Peckinpah's aestheticizing treatment of trucks provides, in the context of the energy crisis and swirling questions about the viability of US car culture, what Nicholas Mirzoeff would later call an "Anthropocene visuality [that] keeps us believing that somehow the war against nature that Western society has been waging for centuries is not only right; it is beautiful." [44] If, as film scholar David Laderman argues, "road movies valorize a certain aesthetic thrill related to high-speed car travel," *Convoy* also valorizes the fossil-fueled technologies that make such experiences of propulsive energy possible. [45]

America in Motion

Convoy's fossil-fueled imagination, in which trucks are central characters with personalities, also locates the truckers' identity, freedom, and livelihood in the propulsive energies of automobility that the roads and their trucks provide. As Laderman notes of American road films, "Freedom becomes rediscovered as movement across open space." [46] *Convoy*'s fundamental conflict is between the constant motion of the convoy and the efforts of the sheriff and federal authorities to control it. The film's visuals bask in the size and power of individual trucks and in the truckers' skills to keep them moving. Their aptitude is a form of craftsmanship that provides pride, agency, and income. Rubber Duck is often framed by the window of his rig shot from a low angle, identifying him with the truck and lending him a sense of moral authority that the sheriff lacks. The sheriff's moral inferiority is marked by his inability to drive—to control the motion of a vehicle for his own ends. This visual rhetoric, alongside the absence of energy conservation as a legitimate social aim in an industry built on cheap petroleum, amounts to dismissing the energy crisis as the concern of effete elites, inimical to the primal masculinity and freedom of movement that cheap fuel offers to independent truckers. For a film that rarely steps off the accelerator, fuel is remarkably absent, never used as it could have been as a dramatic threat to the existence and coherence of the convoy. The freedoms afforded by fuel, in the world of the film, are always primary and state authority over them is always illegitimate. When the sheriff protests Spider Mike's attempted jailbreak by appealing to the law, Duck replies, "Well piss on yah and piss on your law." The sheriff and his law are merely forces of oppression for the working men and women who rely on cheap fuel to do their jobs and see automobility as their moral right.

Just as it identifies the truckers with their rigs and fossil-fueled movement, *Convoy* frames automobility as the vehicle for the self-organization of a social movement. Over the course of the film, the size and diversity of the convoy grow into a mosaic of working-class discontent, or what the film's fictional governor calls "a hell of a cross-section of people." As critic Richard Combs wrote, "The film and its ever-growing, road-hogging behemoth become a kind of wish fulfillment machine, to which each individual and community it passes can attach their own banner of protest—a situation which opens up a surprisingly sunny vista of a land running riot with good-natured disrespect for authority, eager to be represented by such a freewheeling symbol but more likely to be exploited by the politicians who gather darkly in the second half of the film."[47] Key here is the propulsive energy of the convoy, which gathers energy, adherents, and the concerns of Americans as it moves through the country. The social and political strength and vitality of the convoy is rooted in its constant movement; to stop is to be threatened with imprisonment or cooptation.

Paradoxically, the film imagines the convoy as a manifestation of working-class consciousness while rejecting the kind of New Deal politics that such solidarity had historically entailed. It insists that the truckers' only shared aim is freedom from regulation, symbolized by uninhibited automobility and driven by a feeling of disenfranchisement in a corrupt polity. When a journalist asks about the purpose of the convoy, responses are varied. For Rubber Duck, "The purpose of the convoy is to keep moving." This could be read as hollow nihilism, or as a political statement about the threat that the energy crisis and regulation posed to trucking, the working class, and to American society in general. As other truckers in the convoy speak up about racial injustice, the fifty-five-mile-per-hour speed limit, Big Oil, and Watergate, it becomes apparent that this working-class solidarity is articulate, but built on the bare fact of grievance and alienation rather than shared interests or political aims. Critics complained about thin plotting and character development, but the lack of a clear motive for the convoy is significant.[48] Aside from mimicking similar energy crisis protests, the individualized variability of the truckers' protest actions suggests that working-class interests exist only at the level of individual trucker-entrepreneur, rather than at a larger class level. Hence, the film repeatedly emphasizes that these are independent, nonunionized truckers who are fed up with their overregulated lives, and it lauds them for it. What unites these truckers is the excitement and possibility they find in fossil-fueled movement itself, which they want to preserve.

Through the pluralistic composition of the convoy, its articulation of contemporary political concerns, and its cynical view of political leadership, *Convoy* is an allegory of bicentennial America. It visualizes American democracy as a self-organizing, pluralistic convoy of jovial and articulate discontent. The truckers are bawdy but kind and intelligent, never posing a threat to the innocent. They are a fossil-fueled version of Whitman's ideal America, in which camaraderie and vitality exist and emerge through the force of propulsive energies on the road, in ceaseless motion. Throughout the film, vulnerability, weakness, and dissension are linked to life off the road, outside of the truck. When the convoy stops to hear the New Mexico governor's offer to take their concerns to Washington, the potential for political manipulation and division threatens the Woodstock-like atmosphere of the trucker gathering. Other moments of stillness are associated with danger and derailment of the convoy by elites—being ticketed, a truck stop brawl with police, imprisonment, and the funeral for Rubber Duck. Automobility is always the vehicle for renewed freedom and vitality—a theme that likely resonated with Americans who sensed a threat to their automobility during the energy crisis as they waited in line for gas, spotted a new speed limit sign, or were cajoled to drive less.[49] As *New York Times* critic Vincent Canby commented about the popular car films of the 1970s, films like *Convoy* "show us that America is the first nation to find heaven on the highway. Heaven is no longer a destination. It's something experienced en route."[50]

Although *Convoy* was ambivalent in its populism, the film ultimately embraced a fossil-fueled vision of American society. It is true, as Frank Burke argues, that Rubber Duck's narrative arc is a spiritual transformation through the sacrifice of his truck and self, which ends with his integration into society in the Jesus freaks' van.[51] There is a sense in which Peckinpah wanted to critique the individualist, masculinist ethos of US car culture through Rubber Duck's transformation from loner to leader to community member. But the Duck is reborn on the road. His joyous reappearance and escape rely on the propulsive energies of US car culture, which are ultimately affirmed. When the convoy takes to the road for a final push to Mexico, it has grown again to include motorcycles, cars, trucks, and a van. The authorities scramble incompetently to halt their return to the road and to freedom. This resolution is foreshadowed earlier in the film by the Jesus freaks' van, whose passengers are a Greek chorus commenting on events through songs and declarations. Rubber Duck initially welcomes them by saying that the convoy could "use some spiritual help," suggesting a spiritual reading of the convoy community. The Reverend later declares: "I don't read nothing in scripture that says though shalt not put the pedal to the metal," offering clear moral sanction to fossil-fueled automobility in the language of popular American Christianity.

Conclusion

This essay has examined the popular film *Convoy* as an artifact of the energy unconscious of the United States in the 1970s. During that decade, oil scarcities and price increases linked to the 1973–1974 OAPEC oil embargo, among other things, threatened the future of mass automobility. Among the most prominent responses was what I am calling a petropopulist framing of this crisis as an elite conspiracy to gouge consumers who depended on automobiles to conduct their lives. In this context, like many of the decade's car films, *Convoy* articulated an ambivalent petropopulism toward automobility that simultaneously critiqued and celebrated the individualist and materialist ethos of US car culture. Ultimately, though, the film demanded freedom of the road as the people's right, not to be gainsaid by elites prescribing when and how to drive. Although its director, Sam Peckinpah, had critical ambitions for the film, he could only express his pluralistic vision of American life in terms of the energy unconscious of US petroculture: of the freedom of the open road, of cars and trucks, and of mass automobility as the conduits of belonging, community, and freedom. In the face of an unprecedented energy crisis, *Convoy*'s equation of automobility with the fundamental interests of everyday people reflects how deeply embedded are the capacities afforded by fossil fuels in everyday lives, beliefs, and expectations. The film's doubling down on fossil-fueled mobility as an unassailable expression of freedom, which persists in present energy and climate politics, suggests the cultural and political challenge that must be overcome in order to realize an energy transition, and the social changes that must accompany it.

Notes

1. Eric Mottram, "Blood on the Nash Ambassador: Cars in American Films," in *Autopia: Cars and Culture*, ed. Peter Wollen and Joel Kerr (London: Reaktion Books, 2002), 106.
2. Nadia Bozak, *The Cinematic Footprint: Lights, Camera, Natural Resources* (New Brunswick, NJ: Rutgers University Press, 2012); Sean Cubitt, "The Ecopolitics of Cinema," in *The Routledge Companion to Cinema and Politics*, ed. Yannis Tzioumakis and Claire Molloy (New York: Routledge, 2016), 40–49. On the "fossil economy," see Bob Johnson, *Mineral Rites: An Archeology of the Fossil Economy* (Baltimore: Johns Hopkins University Press, 2019), 9–10.
3. David Laderman, *Driving Visions: Exploring the Road Movie* (Austin: University of Texas Press, 2002), 3.

4. Shane Hamilton, *Trucking Country: The Road to America's Wal-Mart Economy* (Princeton, NJ: Princeton University Press, 2008), 188–89.

5. Jane Stern, *Trucker: A Portrait of the Last American Cowboy* (New York: McGraw-Hill, 1975), 13; Kenneth L. Woodward, "The Trucker Mystique," *Newsweek*, January 26, 1976, 44. On the political dynamics of the trucker strikes, see Meg Jacobs, *Panic at the Pump: The Energy Crisis and the Transformation of American Politics* (New York: Hill and Wang 2016), 74–79.

6. This is not to be confused with oil states' efforts to secure popular support by financing public works projects with oil revenue. Parvin Alizadeh, "The Political Economy of Petro Populism and Reform, 1997–2011," in *Iran and the Global Economy: Petro Populism, Islam, and Economic Sanctions*, eds. Parvin Alizadeh and Hassan Hakimian (New York: Routledge, 2014), 76–101.

7. Dominic Sandbrook, *Mad as Hell: The Crisis of the 1970s and the Rise of the Populist Right* (New York: Alfred Knopf, 2011), xii. The term *car film* describes films with plots, characterization, and aesthetics that rely heavily on automobility. Examples from the 1970s include *American Graffiti* (1973), *Dirty Mary, Crazy Larry* (1974), *The Sugarland Express* (1974), *Death Race 2000* (1975), *White Line Fever* (1975), *Cannonball!* (1976), *Damnation Alley* (1977), *The Car* (1977), *Smokey and the Bandit* (1977), *The Cannonball Run* (1981), and *The Cannonball Run II* (1984).

8. Vincent Canby, "Why Smokey and the Bandit Is Making a Killing," *New York Times*, December 18, 1977, 109.

9. Derek Nystrom, *Hard Hats, Rednecks, and Macho Men: Class in 1970s American Cinema* (New York: Oxford University Press, 2009), 79–105.

10. Bozak, *Cinematic Footprint*, 12.

11. Garner Simmons, *Peckinpah: A Portrait in Montage* (Austin: University of Texas Press, 1982), 233; Mike Siegel, dir., *Passion and Poetry: Sam's Trucker Movie* (El Dorado Hills, CA: El Dorado Productions, 2013); Sam Peckinpah, dir., *Convoy* (1978; Los Angeles: 20th Century Fox Home Entertainment, 2015), DVD.

12. The term was first advanced in Patricia Yaeger, "Editor's Column: Literature in the Ages of Wood, Tallow, Coal, Whale Oil, Gasoline, Atomic Power, and Other Energy Sources," *PMLA* 126, no. 2 (March 2011): 305–26.

13. Johnson, *Mineral Rites*, 3–5.

14. Stern, *Trucker*, 13.

15. Siegel, *Passion and Poetry*.

16. David Ansen, "On the Skids," *Newsweek*, July 10, 1978, 83.

17. Elaine Marshall, "'We're Always Moving': Sam Peckinpah's Making of *Convoy*," in *Sam Peckinpah's West: New Perspectives*, ed. Leonard Engel (Salt Lake City: University of Utah Press, 2003), 212.

18. Nystrom, *Hard Hats*, 85–86; Hamilton, *Trucking Country*, 189.

19. Frank Burke, "Divining Peckinpah: Religious Paradigm and Ideology in *Convoy* and *The Ballad of Cable Hogue*," in *Sam Peckinpah's West: New Perspectives*, ed. Leonard Engel (Salt Lake City: University of Utah Press, 2003), 132.

20. Burke, "Divining Peckinpah," 132–33.

21. Marshall, "We're Always Moving," 212, 214.

22. Marshall, "We're Always Moving," 222.

23. Marshall, "We're Always Moving," 224.

24. Christopher Wells, *Car Country: An Environmental History* (Seattle: University of Washington Press, 2012).

25. Johnson, *Mineral Rites*, 86.

26. Siegel, *Passion and Poetry*. Deeley mentions approvingly that New Mexico was a right-to-work state.
27. Marshall, "We're Always Moving," 220.
28. Walt Whitman, "Song of the Open Road," in *Leaves of Grass: The Complete 1855 and 1891–92 Editions*, ed. Justin Kaplan (New York: Library of American Paperback Classics, 2011), 299.
29. Hamilton, *Trucking Country*, 216–220.
30. Nystrom, *Hard Hats*, 85.
31. Mottram, "Blood on the Nash Ambassador," 110.
32. Marshall, "We're Always Moving," 220.
33. Bliss's reading of this plot point as "a symbol for the destructive potential of [Duck's] opposition to the smug liberalism of contemporary America" elides the liberalism of the film's truckers. Michael Bliss, *Justified Lives: Morality and Narrative in the Films of Sam Peckinpah* (Carbondale: Southern Illinois University Press, 1993), 293.
34. Stern, *Trucker*, 13, 36.
35. Quoted in Marshall, "We're Always Moving," 214.
36. Johnson, *Mineral Rites*, 87.
37. Steve Penfold, "Petroleum Liquids," in *Powering Up Canada: A History of Power, Fuel, and Energy from 1600*, ed. R. W. Sandwell (Montreal: McGill-Queen's University Press, 2016), 274. See also Cotton Seiler, *Republic of Drivers: A Cultural History of Automobility in America* (Chicago: University of Chicago Press, 2008), 149.
38. Wells, *Car Country*, 279.
39. "The Painful Change to Thinking Small," *Time*, December 31, 1973, 20.
40. See B. Bruce-Briggs, *The War against the Automobile* (New York: E. P. Dutton, 1975).
41. Quoted in Marshall, "We're Always Moving," 213.
42. Marshall, "We're Always Moving," 213.
43. Pauline Kael, "Convoy," *New Yorker*, September 25, 1978.
44. Nicholas Mirzoeff, "Visualizing the Anthropocene," *Public Culture* 26, no. 2 (Spring 2014): 217.
45. Laderman, *Driving Visions*, 16.
46. Laderman, *Driving Visions*, 15.
47. Richard Combs, "Convoy," *Monthly Film Bulletin* (Autumn 1978): 257.
48. "A Hit Song Makes a Strikeout Movie," *Washington Post*, June 30, 1978.
49. "Bitter Thoughts from the 'Gas' Line," *New York Times*, February 19, 1974, 33; "Higher Gas Prices Put Crimp in California 'Cruising,'" *New York Times*, August 23, 1980, 7.
50. Canby, "Smokey and the Bandit," 109.
51. Burke, "Divining Peckinpah," 131, 136–37.

Chapter 19

There Will Be Petroleum Cinema: Portraying the Corrosion of Oil Addiction in *There Will Be Blood* (2007)

Brian C. Black

The deafening silence of the early minutes of *There Will Be Blood* has unnerved viewers since the film's release in 2007. Staged similarly to a horror film, the opening is dominated by a dank view of silent men working inside the earth as we await the sudden arrival of . . . something. Will it be a reptilian monster from the underworld? A maimed human, long trapped in the caves surrounding the earth's innards? As a character literally slogs through the goop within a silver pit mine deep in the bowels of the earth, shrill, hypnotic, and monotone music begins to pulse in the background, seeming to rise and fall while never growing overbearing. Fifteen minutes into the film, viewers are still left waiting for the unknown foe to burst in from off-screen. Yet in many ways, the denouement has already been reached; the film's goal is to depict exactly that suspended moment of discomfort and then to extend it for two hours, eschewing a traditional narrative while unpacking some of the precise origins of this state of agitation.[1]

Although petroleum is the subject of many films, only one can fully be credited with attempting to create a nuanced, in-depth portrait of the resource of crude oil. This is due in part to the folly of such an artistic objective. To be successful, any feature film must be organized around action and populated by aspirants and heroes. Oil's history with human use spans more than two centuries and cannot possibly be framed within a single feature film. Therefore, when Paul Thomas Anderson wrote the script that became *There Will Be Blood*, he made oil its protagonist, rejecting any effort to tell a comprehensive story or even create a narrative around a traditional character. Instead, Anderson's vision is organized around the very essence of crude—its occurrence and the process of acquiring it as well as its effects on the humans who pursue it. But do not be fooled: this film is not about Daniel Plainview (played by Daniel Day-Lewis), a frustratingly flat character. It is about the commodity he seeks and its ability to alter him and his surroundings.

Context matters for *There Will Be Blood*. Some of the film's importance lies in that by the early twenty-first century, petroleum culture—rife with anxiety, gross distaste, and even shame—was part of the framework within which the author could assume viewers might approach the film. Crude is the gorilla in the room—or the film, in this case—and, indeed, in the life of each contemporary human. It is the main character in *There Will Be Blood*, portrayed by a nuanced, timeless narrative structured around oil exploration in the American West during the early 1900s. However, as a work of filmic art, *There Will Be Blood*'s primary story of oil's corruptive capability functions on the microlevel of a single individual: Plainview (after his initial search for silver leads him to crude). But, by association, the film also inculcates each viewer as a consumer of crude in the Anthropocene, an era in which scientists and historians argue that human activity has imperiled Earth's basic ecological systems.[2]

Oil! Provides a Loose Storyline

Proper appreciation of *There Will Be Blood* begins in knowing its literary roots in Upton Sinclair's obscure novel *Oil!* (1926). While the muckraking journalist is best known for *The Jungle*, his 1905 exposé of the meatpacking industry, later in his career Sinclair joined Ida Tarbell, a colleague at *Scribner's Magazine*, to focus his anticorruptive passion on the monolithic oil industry constructed by John D. Rockefeller and others. Even after Tarbell spurred the breakup of Standard Oil in 1911, Sinclair remained awed by petroleum's transformative power. Thus, *Oil!* primarily emphasizes how oil's financial potential changes the novel's characters. However, with Sinclair's keen eye, oil's boom/bust cycle of development also wreaks havoc on everyday American life and particularly on the Western landscape that produced significant amounts of crude in the early twentieth century.

Sinclair's account begins with a great respect for those pursuing oil, which he captures through the youthful narrative voice of his protagonist, Bunny: "Never since the world began had there been men of power equal to this. And Dad was one of them."[3] Published in 1926, *Oil!* tells the story of Bunny's father as he rides through the early oil boom of the American West, particularly emphasizing the technical processes required to bring this commodity to market. Much like Melville captured the early-nineteenth-century whale oil business in *Moby Dick*, these details are an insider's education cast in a personal quest for wealth, making *Oil!* the story of an industry at a specific historical moment.

Oil! contains many unique and surprising aspects of oil development, such as the community meetings in which oilmen (like Plainville in the film) encouraged owners of residential homes or farms to drill for crude; primarily, Sinclair points out how little convincing was necessary.[4] However, he does not imbue oil with any particular insidiousness. Oil is the vehicle for human greed, and the novel uses it to demonstrate how it can corrupt traditional morality and religion. Although the socialist bent of Sinclair's account caused some controversy, it was largely accepted as consistent with much of his other writing. In his introduction to the 1997 edition, Jules Tygiel asserts, "With its unrelenting critique of American society and unapologetic propagandizing for socialist transformation, [the novel] captured a broad American audience during a decade usually celebrated for its conservative politics and pro-business sentiments."[5]

In reinterpreting this story for a new era, *There Will Be Blood* supplements this narrative trope of socialism with a very stiff dose of the culture of crude in the early twenty-first century. Employing Sinclair's novel as a starting point, Anderson's film incorporates the context that had evolved by 2007. In its new form, *There Will Be Blood* offers a narrative less about Plainview's personal demise and more about the film's true protagonist: oil. In casting a natural resource as the primary character in his screenplay, Anderson engages contemporary viewers' angst over this commodity and aligns it with Sinclair's perspective in *Oil!* The portrait of petroleum that takes shape is a severe assessment of the role that humans have allowed oil to play in their lives after just over a century of use. *There Will Be Blood* casts a damning judgement that will likely endure as future generations strain to understand the dominance of oil in the era that historian John McNeill refers to as the Great Acceleration.[6]

Sinclair could not have imagined the ensuing complications of life with petroleum, ranging from geopolitical conflict to climate change. When one considers such "baggage," crude emerges as the single most revealing character of the twentieth century—a period of high energy use that defines our epoch as the Anthropocene. The oil from Signal Hill, California—which features prominently in both the novel and film—and assorted other patches provided the raw material to create more energy for humans to use after 1940 than ever before.[7] This human story also flows though *There Will Be Blood*, and one can assume that Sinclair would have concurred with Anderson's extremely critical view of crude. But while Anderson retains Sinclair's basic plot in following Plainview's effort to develop new oil reserves, he deemphasizes *Oil!*'s focus on labor and class issues. The result is a film that instead demonizes oil and the greed it cultivates for its corruptive influence on the human soul. With this narrative decision, Anderson seems to accept a very dark perspective on crude's inevitable impact on Plainview and, by association, humanity. Whereas Sinclair suggested potential hope through collective action and attention, Anderson's updated account sees only hopelessness.

The Blossoming of "Petromelancholia"

Scholars of cultural studies have proven particularly effective in analyzing the significance of petroleum—a product that achieves an almost grotesque level of ubiquity in modern society. The work of Stephanie LeMenager, Bob Johnson, Karen Pinkus, and Imre Szeman (among others) provides a new language for understanding oil in contemporary human life and has even led to a new scholarly field known as "petrocultures."[8] Their efforts allow us to consider representations of oil such as that in *There Will Be Blood* within the larger, supplementary ideas that grow from its use, including dependence, addiction, scarcity, and environmental degradation.

In our informed twenty-first-century life, filmgoers are cognizant of many of the ills caused by oil. Therefore, cultural representations now move beyond the simplicity of films like *Boom Town* (1940) and require the complexity offered by *There Will Be Blood*. While oil stories still must be told, our culture views petroleum with a visceral hatred—similar to an addict who must admit dependence before coming to grips with its significance on their everyday life. To capture this duality, LeMenager uses the term *petromelancholia*, which she defines as "an unresolved grieving of conventional fossil fuel reserves."[9] Simply put, in LeMenager and others' view, petroleum cannot—and will not—ever again be viewed without its baggage. "Loving oil to the extent that we have done in the twentieth century," she writes, "sets up the conditions of grief as conventional oil resources dwindle."[10] Bob Johnson extends this perspective by describing contemporary Americans as living in a state of being "ashamed of oil."[11]

With this new cultural language for discussing oil, *There Will Be Blood* becomes an artistic icon. LeMenager uses the film to support her terminology, referring to Anderson's notes on his final shooting script, which make clear his intention that the film capture the "sensorial bonanza" of oil's impact on the earth as well as the human body and soul. "Anderson's script," she writes, "obsesses on the resistance of bodies, their heft, the friction of their interaction. He attributes strong agency to both organic and inorganic bodies: arms, mules, deserts, pulleys, trains."[12] Anderson's notes, for instance, demand that a miner's death in the opening scene emphasize the mud's victory over his physical form; he drowns in it. This is no simple oil story. Anderson seeks to condemn the entire society that has compelled such effort and exploration—particularly taking such effort for granted, as we mindlessly visit our local gas pumps. In LeMenager's interpretation, "In a crude Marxian sense, Anderson could be said to pursue the dis-alienation of labor, at sites where human physical energy learns of its own limitations through the resistance of other matter." [13]

There Will Be Blood Transcends Traditional Petroleum Cinema

From the perspective of petromelancholia, *There Will Be Blood* may best be viewed long-term as the headstone for human life with crude and, possibly, for petroleum cinema itself. Its contextual significance and the organic texture of its carefully detailed filmmaking clearly classify it as a landmark cinematic accomplishment, even as its plodding narrative and gratuitous violence frustrate many viewers. While anyone might be able to achieve Plainview's feat—oil wealth—the viewer is left with the question *Who would want to?* The pain, loss, and setbacks he endures grind at the viewer just as they wear at the character. Most importantly, though, we see how valueless oil is before it is accessed through human fortitude and tied into the larger marketplace. There is no glamour in this pursuit. Anderson places the genuine process at the center of the film and creates an amazing sense of continuity in tying the oil process of the 1920s to that of today. With that process at its heart, *There Will Be Blood* remains a timeless classic—the story of oil.

Plainview's quest is clear enough: independently developing the Signal Hill oil reserve in California proves to be only a precursor to the struggle to fight off corporate heavyweights and build a pipeline to the sea in order to access the marketplace. In Anderson's hands, *There Will Be Blood* educates viewers about the industry through demonstration. Process—tedious industrial planning, laborious human effort, and risk-taking—replaces the symbolic gushers of earlier oil films. When a gusher occurs, its result is explosive fire—much closer to realism than, say, James Dean's celebratory oil bath in *Giant* (1956).

In the race for the oil at Signal Hill, Plainview is plainly a success. At the front end of resource development in the West, he is in the right place at the right time. Plainview has the fortitude and focused character to take full advantage of his position by buying (not leasing) most of the empty land around the discovery well before competitors move in. He thus avoids what the film implies is the fate of many independent oilmen (selling to Standard Oil) by privately building a pipeline to the Union refinery (one of Standard's rivals) on the California coast. However, he never achieves moral standing as an honest businessman. The viewer is left to imagine that the promises he makes to the residents at his meetings will likely go unkept. In the end, Plainview is left dogged: a man who sits isolated by his wealth while nursing imagined grievances, only to disown his adopted son in the closing scene of the film, declaring, "I took you for no other reason than I needed a sweet face to buy land."

While Plainview's challenges are consistent with those in efforts to develop crude around the world, as well as in petroleum cinema from *Boom Town* to *Giant*, his demons are unique. Anderson emphasizes these demons to expose the dark connection between oil and human morality, drawing on a primary idea in Sinclair's novel to underscore oil's corruption of the soul, particularly in religious terms. The interplay is so obvious that at times it appears trite. The community sells their land for oil development and applies the funds to the construction of a church; the holdout landowner blocking Plainview's pipeline agrees to concede if the immoral oilman converts and admits his sin; and Plainview agrees, compromising his religious ambivalence in order to complete the process of getting his oil to market.

In gluttonous, overwhelming detail, the narrative is also framed through the experience of an antihero: the congregation's zealous young minister, Eli Sunday (Paul Dano). Plainview's ongoing and violent altercations with Sunday extend the film's dissonance and create a memorable discomfort for the audience. Neither character is redeemable or likable, and the film's climax is likely to leave viewers throwing up their hands in a combination of despair and disgust. Throughout *There Will Be Blood*, Plainview repeatedly beats and berates Sunday, who is obviously the personification of religion in American life—particularly fundamentalism. In the infamous final scene, Plainview has achieved opulent wealth and resides in a drunken stupor, secluded from the world. After refusing his son's last attempt at love and support, Plainview slinks to his mansion's private bowling alley—the setting for his final confrontation with Sunday, now a fallen, drunken minister who has come to ask for financial assistance. In a haphazard, disorganized flurry of activity, Plainview attacks Sunday with relentless fervor. When Sunday falls, Plainview bludgeons him to death with a bowling pin. As the audience sits in stunned, regretful silence, one can almost see Anderson's sneer as he completed the screenplay: Plainview flatly tells his butler, "I am finished." While viewers may interpret this line as a realization that his story—his life—is now hopeless, over, that is not the tone Daniel Day-Lewis takes as Plainview. Instead, his tone makes it clear that it is merely a request that his butler take away the remnants of his meal. As a final reiteration of Plainview's character, now we must accept his grotesque disassociation from the emotion of one of the most violent scenes in American film.

While *There Will Be Blood* extended Sinclair's original juxtaposition of oil and religion, inferring that the oil business is immoral, contemporary scholars have also explored the complex, ongoing interplay between oil and religion. Darren Dochuk, for example, emphasizes "the generations-long workings of established oil corporations like Standard, Union, and Sun, whose calculations for crude dominance mirrored their chiefs' theological aspirations." He argues, "As profoundly as the two absolutes—oil and religion—have shaped modern America and its ascendant moment, scholars and social commentators have tended to analyze them separately, as if they are organically discrete or naturally antagonistic toward each other." Responding to the paradigm portrayed in *There Will Be Blood*, Dochuk stresses that the tension between religion and oil rises steadily, but notes, "Yet, in real life, their two spheres have rarely been held separate or in tension. The Plainviews and Sundays of US history have frequently shared conventional ambitions as well as character traits. Often, they have even been one and the same, their conquering spirit and shared sins far more formidable than Anderson allows."[14] While Dochuk admits that oil and morality often have antithetical implications for humans, his research clearly demonstrates a connection at the corporate level, as well. Such is the complex, embattled culture of crude in the twenty-first century.

Viewers' Changing Perception of Crude

The tradition of using film to tell stories of petroleum development has created important representations of many of the heroic efforts of wildcatters and speculators, ranging from *Giant*'s Jett Rink to *The Beverly Hillbillies*' Jed Clampett. Blending elements of the Western with aspects of the action-adventure genre, films about petroleum remained popular during the twentieth century, even when perspectives on oil itself became a bit more dubious. In films such as *Syriana* (2005) and *The Kingdom* (2007), we find that a more contemporary public is still intrigued by humans' early-twentieth-century relationship with crude, as the reality of Big Oil's dominance is revealed, standing center stage as an inaccessible, now largely foreign entity. Despite Big Oil's evolution into international models of organization, its dark potential persists as part of its appeal and its legend in popular film. In the character of Daniel Plainview, *There Will Be Blood* personifies the industrial end of petroleum culture, reflecting a century of change. "I drink your milkshake," exclaims Plainview in an effort to explain the rule of capture that still guides oil exploration—the operational ethic of Big Oil as one competitor seeks to exploit a reserve before others have the chance. In actuality, the ethic that enabled the trickle of petroleum at Drake Well in 1859 remains at the core of Big Oil's gushers in fields from Baku to Bahrain.

From its start in the 1910s, Big Oil merged myth and reality to create a dynamic transborder entity that evolved along with humans' use of crude, fueling the Great Acceleration of the twentieth century. With a new scale and scope, petroleum's increasing availability changed its economic potential as well as humans' expectations of it. Big Oil, as a term, encompasses all of this, including the mythic dimensions of the resource's past and building resentment toward the commodity's present, binding one to the other in the ongoing narrative of human use of petroleum. Just as petroleum has become a necessity of American life, so, too, it appears, it will remain a mainstay of popular culture as Americans attempt to reconcile their diabolical dependence on the stuff. And that is where we come to the particular and unique significance of *There Will Be Blood*.

Plainview certainly bears a resemblance to Jett Rink, the character meant to demonstrate petroleum's corruptive and financial potential in *Giant*. However, in Anderson's hands, the main character's fall in *There Will Be Blood* is extreme. This is not simply due to Big Oil; in its completeness, it is a dramatization of our own petromelancholia. LeMenager writes:

> Fundamentally, *There Will Be Blood* enacts a mourning for production, oil production specifically and manufacturing more broadly. It makes perfect sense that this mourning would take place in a US film of the early twenty-first century. . . . I do not see *There Will Be Blood* as a peak oil narrative, but as a signal of the tiredness of the twentieth-century stories about modernity, particularly the US frontier myth that explained modernity to the twentieth century.[15]

There Will Be Blood makes no effort to provide a sense of balance by including the benefits of Plainview's crude—casting an explanatory glimpse toward the ease of trade through trucking or the manufacture of lifesaving chemicals and pharmaceuticals, for example. This marks a narrative shift in petroleum cinema that speaks volumes about how oil's role in American life changed over the course of the twentieth century and into the twenty-first. In particular, petroleum's more recent association with powerlessness in films like *There Will Be Blood* represents a significant departure from previous cinematic depictions of oil. Such portrayals suggest a revealing measure of the seriousness of our present reality.[16]

Notes

1. Paul Thomas Anderson, dir., *There Will Be Blood* (Hollywood, CA: Paramount Vantage, 2007).
2. See J. R. McNeill, *Something New under the Sun: An Environmental History of the Twentieth-Century World* (New York: Norton, 2001); J. R. McNeill, *Great Acceleration: An Environmental History of the Anthropocene since 1945* (Cambridge, MA: Harvard University Press, 2016).
3. Upton Sinclair, *Oil!* (1926; repr., Berkeley: University of California Press, 1997), 6.
4. This episode, along with much of the detail in *Oil!*, grew out of Sinclair's firsthand experience. In this case, his residential community was found to contain oil and hosted such meetings.
5. Jules Tygiel, introduction to *Oil!*, by Upton Sinclair, vii.
6. McNeill, *Great Acceleration*.
7. McNeill, *Something New*.
8. On petrocultures, see Imre Szeman, *On Petrocultures: Globalization, Culture, and Energy* (Morgantown: West Virginia University Press, 2019).
9. Stephanie LeMenager, *Living Oil: Petroleum Culture in the American Century* (New York: Oxford University Press, 2014), 16.
10. LeMenager, *Living Oil*, 102.
11. Bob Johnson, *Carbon Nation: Fossil Fuels in the Making of American Culture* (Lawrence: University of Kansas Press, 2014), 137.
12. LeMenager, *Living Oil*, 98. LeMenager credits critic Kent Jones with the phrase *sensorial bonanza*.
13. LeMenager, *Living Oil*, 99.
14. Darren Dochuk, *Anointed with Oil: How Christianity and Crude Made Modern America* (New York: Basic Books, 2019), 14–15.
15. LeMenager, *Living Oil*, 99–100.
16. For a lengthier discussion of petroleum cinema in general, see Robert Lifset and Brian C. Black, "Imaging the 'Devil's Excrement': Big Oil in Petroleum Cinema, 1940–2007," *Journal of American History* 99, no. 1 (July 2012): 135–44.

PART 5

Energy and the State

There's No Business Like Oil Business: The Allure of Tax-Sheltered Oil Income to Hollywood's Wealthy

Yuxun Willy Tan

Hollywood has often villainized the oil industry in its critical on-screen narratives, yet its off-screen participation in the oil business puts this contradictory relationship in the spotlight. A pioneer of this relationship was Bing Crosby, Hollywood's quintessential crooner and one of the first high-income celebrities to invest in the oil business. Crosby and eventually many other Hollywood colleagues bought interests in oil wells to shelter a significant part of their income from taxation. The percentage oil depletion allowance, part of the Revenue Act of 1926, allowed an oil company to reduce its taxable income by 27.5 percent. To combat rapidly rising income tax rates in the 1930s, one Hollywood lawyer approached Congress with a case to gain a similar tax allowance for the entertainment industry. When the attempt failed, Hollywood stars began investing in oil wells to enable the oil depletion allowance to work to their benefit.

By the 1950s, many Hollywood individuals and corporations were extensively invested in the oil business, making the allowance an important component of their financial portfolios. Meanwhile, some prominent oilmen directed parts of their fortunes toward producing Hollywood films, capitalizing on a hit or using a failed film's losses to offset their taxable oil profits. Thus, in the mid-twentieth century, the American oil industry and Hollywood formed a close, mutually reinforcing relationship, and one that academic historians have largely overlooked.

In the aftermath of the 1973 oil shock, the percentage depletion allowance came under threat. In 1975, Congress repealed the provision for major integrated oil companies but retained it for nonintegrated independent producers. To protect it from facing further repeal, the former Hollywood actor and Republican president Ronald Reagan ardently defended the retention of the allowance during his term in the 1980s. Hollywood's role in the oil industry grew from a few casual investors using the oil depletion allowance into a substantial participant and major political defender of oil-specific tax provisions.

Oil Industry's Special Tax Allowance

A year before Crosby's first hit, "My Blue Heaven" (1927), skyrocketed to number one on US charts, the oil depletion allowance catapulted itself to stardom as the biggest tax loophole in US history. The depletion allowance was first introduced in 1913 as a provision to compensate mining and extractive businesses for the diminishing value of their natural resource assets incurred in production.[1] The new term *depletion* was unique to extractive industries, engineered to differentiate its accounting concept from depreciation. While depreciation, used by all other industries, accounts for the decreasing *financial value* of an asset, depletion, applied exclusively to extractive industries, accounts for the decreasing *physical units* of an asset. From 1913 to 1926, Congress, the oil industry, and geologists struggled to value the total assets located in the ground and determine how much depletion expense should be matched to each barrel of oil produced.[2] After trying different ways of financially accounting for the depletion, Congress finally settled on the rate of 27.5 percent for the sake of administrative simplicity.[3]

The percentage depletion allowance was an unprecedented, hugely attractive anomaly in the tax code, as it allowed oil businesses to avoid taxes on 27.5 percent of their total income, even if they had already recovered their initial capital costs.[4] Congress acknowledged this loophole in the Joint Committee's 1926 report by noting that the concept of percentage depletion was "based on no sound economic principle."[5] After its passage in 1926, the percentage depletion allowance made all other industries look upon the oil industry with envy.

The film industry was especially jealous of this special allowance. Many in Hollywood believed that their industry shared similar income patterns and business risks. In January 1938, twelve years after the debut of the oil depletion allowance, Roger Marchetti, one of Hollywood's prominent lawyers, approached Congress to argue that Hollywood should receive a similar allowance. Marchetti claimed that a film star only earns a high salary for an average of five to seven years, likening them to oil wells that only briefly earn their peak income before facing steep decline.[6] "Popularity is the source of their [film stars'] income, and that runs dry as quickly as an oil well does," he explained.

Marchetti's case publicly highlighted the unique tax loophole enjoyed exclusively by oil and questioned the special protection Congress allowed the industry. Although he failed to get a similar allowance for film stars, he succeeded in applying the idea of "depletion" to actors and alerting some of them, like Crosby, to the tax advantages oilmen enjoyed.

Hollywood Discovers Oil

As Crosby became "Hollywood's number one crooner," he also became one of America's top taxpayers. In the 1930s, his income was so high that his name appeared alongside famous oil magnate John D. Rockefeller as one of the nation's wealthiest people.[7] Personal tax rates had steadily increased after 1926, when the highest individual tax bracket was at 25 percent (it peaked at 91 percent in 1964).[8] Since corporate tax rates were much lower than individual rates, Crosby decided to incorporate himself as Bing Crosby Ltd. in 1936.[9] Establishing a personal holding corporation was standard practice for most Hollywood stars, including Kirk Douglas, Frank Sinatra, Robert Mitchum, Joan Crawford, and Henry Fonda.[10] These stars "sold" their talents at a low salary to their corporations, in which they were the sole shareholders. Then their corporations made a profit by matching that expense to the revenues earned from movie contracts. This arrangement effectively shifted taxable income from the actor's higher tax rate return to the corporation's lower tax rate return, resulting in a lower overall tax amount. Developing personal holding corporations was not limited to Hollywood stars, as other wealthy individuals—including former treasury secretary and majority owner of Gulf Oil Andrew Mellon—utilized them to shift their incomes into a lower tax bracket.

Within a year, Congress imposed a "prohibitive penalty tax," which targeted personal holding corporations and raised Crosby's corporate tax rate to one comparable to higher individual rates.[11] The tax penalized Hollywood stars for setting up their own personal holding corporations by slapping an additional tax onto the corporation if a majority of its income was generated from the star's personal service contract. Although this new rule was Congress's attempt to deter the tax-saving activities of personal holding corporations, it left an important provision untouched. This provision allowed companies to avoid being classified as personal holding corporations if more than 20 percent of their income was derived from sources other than dividends, interest, royalties, and personal service contracts. In other words, Hollywood corporations could easily sidestep the prohibitive penalty tax if they invested in and received more than 20 percent of their income in another business.[12] Thus, Congress unintentionally stimulated the business diversification of Hollywood corporations and sent stars looking for profitable businesses outside of the entertainment industry.

It did not take long for Crosby and other Hollywood celebrities to realize that the oil industry was a tax-beneficial investment. Crosby entered into the oil business with his costar and golfing partner, comedian Bob Hope.[13] They each paid Monty Moncrief (a successful Texas oilman also in their golfing cohort) $40,000 for a 25 percent share in a West Texas venture.[14] The investment enabled the stars to sidestep the prohibitive penalty tax on their corporations and earn income that was 27.5 percent tax-free. For this particular venture, both stars earned $5,000,000 on their initial $40,000 investment, $1,375,000 of which was tax-free due to the depletion allowance.[15] Other Hollywood stars experienced similar successes in the oil business, including Jimmy Stewart, Gene Autry, Don Ameche, and Frank Sinatra, who fittingly named his first oil well Crooner No. 1.[16] These famous stars' successes persuaded others in Hollywood to consider the oil business as a strategy to shelter their large earnings.

Not all Hollywood stars, however, found the same fortune. Directors John Huston and Mervyn LeRoy and actor Dennis O'Keefe lost $194,000 financing the drilling of dry holes in Southern California.[17] Although these failures suggested that the oil business was a potentially perilous investment, the risks were not as large as they seemed. The oil business was essentially a safer bet than other ventures due to its tax provisions. A star in the 90 percent tax bracket only risks 10 percent of their investment in unsuccessful oil ventures and can deduct 100 percent of those costs against successful oil ventures that generate 27.5 percent tax-free income.[18]

The United States government was effectively subsidizing the drilling of oil wells with the oil depletion allowance, and these unique tax advantages lured Hollywood stars into oil investments. Oil came to the forefront of Hollywood's consciousness as the newfound business of drilling for oil wells became as much a part of the Hollywood lifestyle as making movies. One oil executive observed in 1949, "When you see a group of movie people talking on the set, you don't know whether they're discussing an oil well or a movie."[19] Numerous reports of celebrity-owned wells in the late 1940s marked the growing use of the oil business as a way for Hollywood's wealthy to shelter their high income.

By the early 1950s, the Hollywood oil phenomenon was in full swing. In 1951, the president of the Music Corporation of America (MCA), Lew Wasserman, entered the oil business by forming the Calgush Oil Company (a combination of the words *California* and *gusher*) with partners Groucho Marx, Leland Hayward, and other Hollywood stars and MCA executives.[20] Finding early successes, MCA continued to invest in oil exploration and became a significant independent oil producer.[21] With increased American demand and the development of oil fields in the Middle East, the 1950s represented one of the greatest periods of growth in the industry's history. As major integrated oil companies shifted their attention toward Middle Eastern investments, the absence of competition from bigger companies allowed smaller independent producers, like Calgush, to develop their presence in the United States. Hollywood's participation in the oil industry expanded from a few casual oil wells owned by personal corporations to oil companies that accounted for a rising portion of US oil production. With the oil depletion allowance as a catalyst for this development, oil became a significant part of the business of Hollywood.

Wasserman was responsible for changing the Hollywood business model in order to accommodate and use the oil depletion allowance to its full effect. Before establishing Calgush, he experimented in oil ventures with a few of his Hollywood colleagues.[22] Wasserman recognized that although a portion of oil income was tax-free, the other 72.5 percent was taxed at a marginal rate depending on the taxpayer's salary. His solution was to broker a famous deal that changed how actors were paid and would go down in film history.[23] As Stewart's booking agent for the film *Winchester '73* (1950), Wasserman negotiated for the actor to receive a percentage of the movie's profits, which would defer Stewart's income over several years, instead of a large salary upfront.[24] This allowed Stewart to stay in a lower tax bracket over several years and permitted his oil income, after the depletion allowance deduction, to be taxed at a lower marginal rate. This arrangement set a precedent for later contracts between studios and actors, and the "deferred salary" model would be a mainstay in the film industry by 1955.[25] Wasserman's shrewd negotiation of Stewart's *Winchester '73* contract helped Hollywood stars stabilize their earnings volatility while reducing their marginal tax rate on their additional oil income.

"Black Gold" on the Silver Screen

After his joint venture with Wasserman sparked his interest in oil, Stewart made a point to integrate the subject into his work. His passion was apparent in his film *Thunder Bay* (1953), the script for which he discovered and sent to director Anthony Mann.[26] Both Mann and producer Aaron Rosenberg were not crazy about it, as it deviated from their practice of making cowboy-themed movies. Stewart, however, was persistent. As Rosenberg recalls, "Jim did the film because he was developing an interest in oil exploration and was—or became—a partner with a Texas oilman. . . . He wanted to deliver a message that oil exploration and production did not affect the environment."[27] Hoping to protect his private financial investments from negative public perceptions, Stewart was determined to convey that oil exploration could coexist with nature.

Three years after *Thunder Bay*, Hollywood again revisited the intricacies of the oil world in *Giant* (1956), an epic feature directed by George Stevens. One memorable scene in the film, based on Edna Ferber's novel about a Texas oil millionaire, features a conversation about the percentage depletion allowance. When the newly oil-rich Texas family sits by their pool and muses wistfully about the allowance, Judge Oliver Whitehead (played by Charles Watts) proclaims it "one of the finest laws ever passed in Washington." Leslie Benedict (the female protagonist and family matriarch, played by Elizabeth Taylor) sharply questions the lack of a tax "exemption for depreciation of first-class brains," alluding to her father's profession as a doctor.[28] This exchange serves to highlight the anomaly of a favorable tax benefit bestowed solely upon the oil industry as opposed to other worthy endeavors. Leslie Benedict's line also echoes Marchetti's argument to Congress almost two decades prior for a special Hollywood exemption for the depreciation of an actor's talent.

Hollywood Stars and Oilmen

Many oilmen resented the fact that Hollywood stars were getting into their business, and they did not respect them as legitimate investors. As one California oilman remarked in 1949, "I can give you an oil well which is actually producing a good amount of oil, and bet you'll go broke if you don't know what you're doing. The stars . . . don't know enough about the business."[29] By the same token, Hollywood stars did not hold many oilmen in high esteem. They questioned whether oilmen's "talent" for discovering oil was due to experience or just plain luck. Crosby and Hope doubted Moncrief after the first well he drilled was a bust. "It came in dry and I'd say those Hollywood friends came in dry too," Moncrief recalled.[30] Crosby and Hope's early misfortune may have convinced Wasserman to form Calgush exclusively with Hollywood partners.

At first glance, Hollywood and the oil industry appear quite different, but they in fact shared some striking similarities. Although Hollywood investors lacked knowledge of oil industry mechanics, they were attracted by its gambling aspect. Both industries experienced sporadic bursts of income when a well, or movie, struck it rich.[31] It is not surprising that both Hollywood and the oil industry prized the oil depletion allowance for minimizing their high taxes. Moreover, the tax benefits did not flow just one way. Oilmen went to Hollywood for the usual "bright lights, the girls, the glamour, the publicity," as well as to seek tax relief. In a 1948 essay for the *Nation*, Carey McWilliams noted that oilmen were "looking around for ways in which they can acquire some 'profitable' business losses for tax-deduction purposes." Using the same rationale as Hollywood stars, oilmen would rather risk money on Hollywood investments than pay it in taxes. Any losses from Hollywood ventures could also offset their large oil incomes, thus reducing their tax burden. McWilliams summed up the oilmen's involvement in Hollywood by proclaiming, "Hollywood is a good place to have an exciting time while losing money—and there is always a chance of making a rich strike." [32] The Hollywood-oil relationship was a two-way street, with both sides reaping tax benefits that were unrelated to their core business.

Oil Seeps into Hollywood

The first oil-rich businessman to enter Hollywood was Howard Hughes Jr., heir to the Hughes Tool Company founded by his father, the legendary Howard Hughes Sr. Hughes Sr. built his oil fortune by inventing the rotary drill bit during the formative years of the Texas oil rush. He founded the successful Hughes Tool Company in 1909. [33] When Hughes Jr. inherited the company, it made him the "wealthiest Texas oilman of all." Hughes Jr., however, was not interested in oil, choosing to leave Houston upon receiving his inheritance to pursue a career in film. [34] He quickly assimilated into Hollywood, producing several films that garnered Academy Award nominations. [35] After his first hit, *Hell's Angels* (1930), the *Los Angeles Times* described him as the "Texas oil tool manufacturer who has successfully crashed the Hollywood gates as an independent picture producer." [36] In 1948, he purchased production company RKO Pictures, securing his place in Hollywood as a "major cog in the industry." [37] Although Hughes Jr. entered the film business to pursue his cinematic dreams rather than tax benefits, he played an important role in bringing Hollywood to oilmen's attention, especially his friend Glenn McCarthy.

It was Glenn McCarthy who brought the image of the "Texas oil millionaire" to national attention, leaving a lasting impression on Hollywood. From humble beginnings, McCarthy grew from the Hughes family's paperboy into one of the wealthiest Texas oilmen, crowning himself the King of Texas. [38] With his newfound wealth, he formed Glenn McCarthy Productions in order to incite Hollywood's interest in a lavish new hotel he was building in Houston called the Shamrock. [39] Hughes Jr.'s RKO helped McCarthy produce a film, *The Green Promise* (1948), which premiered at the grand opening of the Shamrock Hotel on St. Patrick's Day, 1949. [40] Many Hollywood stars attended the opulent and famously chaotic event. [41] The Shamrock fulfilled McCarthy's desire to make Houston the "Hollywood of Texas," drawing crowds from all over the United States and booking entertainers such as Dinah Shore, Mel Tormé, and Frank Sinatra at its famous Cork Club.[42] McCarthy sought fame along with his fortune and emerged as the ultimate representation of an oil-rich Texas millionaire who associated himself with Hollywood's rich and famous. His legend even inspired the character Jett Rink, played by James Dean, in the aforementioned film *Giant*.

McCarthy's fame also brought attention to other oil magnates residing in Hollywood and their tax arrangements. Although it was not explicitly reported that McCarthy reaped any tax benefits from his foray into the film industry, many reporters speculated about his use of business losses for tax-deduction purposes.[43] Besides McCarthy and Hughes Jr., another oilman who became financially successful in Hollywood was Jack Wrather. Wrather, a Dallas oil heir, turned to the film business and made a fortune producing seven movies, investing in television, producing *Lassie* and *The Lone Ranger*, and financing the construction of the Disneyland Hotel in Anaheim.[44]

While McCarthy sought fame and Wrather found riches in Hollywood, other Texas oilmen pursued political power within the Hollywood landscape. For example, instead of bringing Hollywood to Texas, Clint Murchison and Sid Richardson, two of the richest Texas oilmen of the time, brought Texas to California by establishing the Hotel del Charro. In contrast to McCarthy's glitzy eleven-hundred-room Shamrock, which became popular among Houston society, the modest fifty-room Hotel del Charro was an exclusive Hollywood club reserved for the very wealthy and powerful. Murchison and Richardson often invited politicians to stay at their hotel to lobby for their private interests. Murchison understood the interrelationship between money and politics, and once compared money to manure, declaring, "If you spread it around, it does a lot of good."[45] The Texas duo set the foundation for funding politicians that protected their oil income and the tax policies that sheltered it. Influenced by oilmen's tactics, Hollywood soon realized that the best way to protect their own tax arrangements was to get a man of their own into Washington.

Hollywood's Rising Political Star

Despite the ubiquitous use of the oil depletion allowance in Hollywood, the entertainment industry still wanted to attain its own exclusive allowance. In 1959, Ronald Reagan, then a union leader in the Screen Actors Guild, presented a case to Congress that was strikingly similar to Marchetti's plea twenty years earlier. His experience as the star of several movies enabled him to depict actors' perspective firsthand. In his statement to Congress, he again argued that an actor's successful career lasts an average of five and a half years, and complained that they "have no depletion allowance to compensate for the diminishing market value."[46] When offered an alternative to the depletion allowance, Reagan desperately replied, "Yes, of course we will take almost anything we can get. We feel we are about as short lived as an oil well and twice as pretty."[47] Reagan's charm nevertheless failed to attain a favorable tax provision to benefit the entertainment industry. This denial made the oil depletion allowance even more valuable in Hollywood.

That same year, Reagan also made a deal with Wasserman, his boss and mentor, for 25 percent ownership in the *General Electric Theatre*, a radio and television program Reagan had hosted since 1954.[48] MCA owned the *General Electric Theatre*, which made Reagan a formal business partner at MCA, the same corporation that established the Calgush Oil Company eight years prior. Although *General Electric Theatre* was canceled in 1962, Reagan came to appreciate the oil depletion allowance's value in Hollywood through his partnership at MCA and would make it a political priority later in his career.

Both oil and entertainment moguls put faith in Reagan as a political contender. On Tuesday, October 27, 1964, Reagan's televised speech "A Time for Choosing" put him at the forefront of Republican Party politics.[49] An endorsement for Barry Goldwater's presidential campaign, the speech garnered the attention of conservative financiers and helped raise $8 million for the campaign.[50] One of these sponsors, Henry Salvatori (an oilman and founder of seismic exploration contractor Western Geophysical), claimed that Reagan "gave the Goldwater speech better than Goldwater" and expressed interest in funding Reagan's own political career.[51] In 1965, Salvatori helped form the Friends of Reagan Committee—which would evolve into the Reagan for Governor Committee—with MCA's Jules Stein and Taft Schreiber as key supporters.[52] Aided by financial backers from both the oil and entertainment industries, Reagan secured his first political office in 1967 as governor of California. He was reelected for a second term in 1971 but refused to run for a third, instead focusing his energy on his presidential campaign.

Depleting Allowance and the Blockbuster Boom

After remaining unscathed for nearly forty years, the oil depletion allowance was sacrificed to fund the Tax Reform Act of 1969, which reduced the legendary 27.5 percent to 22 percent. Just six years later, its applicability for major integrated oil companies was repealed in light of rising oil prices due to the Arab oil embargo and political backlash against Big Oil.[53] The allowance was retained for independent producers, however, as many oil advocates argued that, with the increased competition from the Middle East, it was the only way such producers could stay in business.[54] Nevertheless, the Tax Reduction Act of 1975 included a timetable that gradually reduced the allowance rate, starting in 1981 at 22 percent (capped at two thousand barrels a day) until it reached a permanent rate of 15 percent (capped at one thousand barrels a day) in 1984. Coupled with the oil markets' volatility, the allure of using the oil depletion allowance as a tax shelter quickly faded.[55]

As the oil industry faced headwinds, Hollywood was discovering newfound prosperity. Steven Spielberg's thriller *Jaws* (1975) astounded the entertainment industry by shattering records for opening weekend, and ushered in a new era of cinema: the age of blockbusters.[56] By the mid-1970s, Hollywood had started to gain an international presence and even tried to flex its influence in light of the oil industry's shifting global role. In response to the Arab oil embargo, Charles Bluhdorn, CEO of Gulf and Western Industries, which owned the Paramount Pictures Corporation, demanded a price increase for American films shown in oil countries, particularly Iran. Bluhdorn compared the price of film rights to barrels of oil: "'The Godfather' in the can will increase in value just the same as oil in the ground."[57] Although Bluhdorn's suggestion to raise film prices failed, the success of blockbusters reignited interest in the entertainment industry as a profitable business, especially for speculators like oilmen. Marvin Davis, chairman of Davis Oil Company and known in the industry as Mr. Wildcatter, recognized this opportunity and in 1981 bought 20th Century Fox with an initial cash investment of $75 million.[58] In true wildcatter fashion, Davis sold his stake in the studio four years later to Rupert Murdoch for $325 million.[59]

The surge in blockbusters was not the only reason new investors were flocking to Hollywood. By 1976, new motion picture tax shelter deals were quickly growing as a result of new tax laws passed to stimulate the economy, fatefully funded by cutting the oil depletion allowance.[60] However, 20th Century Fox, Walt Disney Productions, and MCA—the most successful studios at the time—refused to participate in these tax shelters, recognizing that they were more beneficial for outside investors using borrowed money to deduct a larger amount than they initially invested. Ironically, MCA chairman Wasserman, who formed Calgush decades earlier in order to take advantage of the oil depletion allowance, cunningly declared, "We have never used tax shelter money and we have no intention of doing so," specifically referring to the newer methods. This new influx of investors did not amuse the established studios, their sentiments echoing that of the oil industry when Hollywood flocked to the oilfields almost thirty years prior.[61]

Reagan's Final Act

The impact of cutting the oil depletion allowance was twofold, and both oil and Hollywood lobbyists put their faith in a rising political star to protect their interests. In his first bid for presidency in 1976, Reagan employed the help of many of his oil and Hollywood friends, including Stewart, who used his celebrity status to broadcast public messages to protect his own oil investments. In 1976, Stewart appeared in a Citizens for Reagan political ad explaining how as governor, Reagan had saved "two billion dollars for the [California] taxpayer." [62] In addition to supporting Reagan's tax strategies, Stewart was a public advocate for the continuation of American oil exploration. Throughout the 1980s, he was an active spokesman for the Independent Petroleum Association of America and starred in televised public service announcements touting the importance of oil exploration to America's energy independence. [63] His message stressed the "high risks involved in petroleum exploration" and urged the government to retain the oil depletion allowance for independent producers. [64] Reagan lost the 1976 Republican nomination to Gerald Ford, but his political influence grew and his base of financial backers broadened. In his next bid, he won the 1981 election to become the fortieth president of the United States.

Newly elected with the help of his oil and entertainment supporters, Reagan made it a priority to maintain the oil depletion allowance, even at its reduced rate. When David Stockman, director of the Office of Management and Budget, proposed eliminating the allowance in order to fund certain deficit reduction measures, Reagan immediately shut down the idea. [65] "All of a sudden, the President became animated," Stockman recalled. "Our proposal unleashed a pent-up catechism on the virtues of the oil depletion allowance, followed by a lecture on how the whole idea of 'tax expenditures' was a liberal myth." [66] During this time, journalists reported that Reagan relied on his Kitchen Cabinet more than his officially appointed cabinet members. [67] This group consisted of thirteen close advisers and financiers, including oilmen Wrather, Salvatori, and William Wilson (president of Web Wilson Oil Tools until 1960), all of whom had interest in maintaining the allowance. [68]

Reagan's other priority, which ultimately became his signature piece of social legislation, was to cut taxes to reduce the use of shelters. This would satisfy his entertainment supporters, whose industry had become flooded with newcomers. After a lengthy debate in Congress, Reagan signed the Tax Reform Act of 1986, a landmark overhaul of the nation's tax code. [69] Instead of cutting the oil depletion allowance to fund the tax reform like his predecessors,

Reagan retained it while reducing tax rates. Journalists noted that the bill "attacked tax breaks with an uneven hand—severely paring preferences for real estate developers, for instance, while preserving most of the generous loopholes enjoyed by the oil industry."[70] With that piece of legislation, Reagan satisfied both his oil and entertainment supporters, cutting taxes to reduce the use of tax shelters while protecting the cherished oil depletion allowance. Hollywood had transformed from a casual user of the oil depletion allowance to a major political defender—as personified by Ronald Reagan—of the unique oil-specific tax provision.

Conclusion

The Hollywood oil phenomenon evolved from a mere tax-saving strategy utilized by a few stars to an industry-wide standard. Hollywood had long envied the oil industry for attaining such a unique tax provision and even approached Congress twice to appeal for a similar one. However, when the initial plea for a special entertainment industry tax provision failed, high-earning Hollywood stars funneled their personal incomes into oil exploration and development, taking advantage of the percentage depletion allowance as a key strategy to reduce their tax bills. Many oilmen reciprocated by risking investments in Hollywood films, either to profit from blockbusters or write off money lost on flops against their high oil earnings. With its increased dependence on the allowance, Hollywood backed politicians in order to preserve it, finding tremendous success with Ronald Reagan. Thus, although Hollywood adopted Irving Berlin's "There's No Business Like Show Business" as its theme song after World War II, on some film sets one might have heard a variation sung as "There's No Business Like Oil Business."

Notes

An earlier version of this essay was published as Yuxun Willy Tan, "There's No Business Like Oil Business: The Allure of Tax Sheltered Oil Income to Hollywood's Wealthy," *Iowa Historical Review* 7, no. 1 (May 2017): 37–54. Reprinted with the permission of the Iowa Historical Review.

1. Peter A. Shulman, "The Making of a Tax Break: The Oil Depletion Allowance, Scientific Taxation, and Natural Resources Policy in the Early Twentieth Century," *Journal of Policy* 23, no. 3 (July 2011): 288.
2. Treasury secretary Andrew Mellon, who built his fortune from Gulf Oil, was instrumental in pushing for a generous depletion allowance. Shulman, "Making of a Tax Break," 286–303.
3. Shulman, "Making of a Tax Break," 284, 303. The odd number of 27.5 percent was a

negotiated compromise between the 25 percent desired by House members and the 30 percent in the Senate version of the bill. Philip M. Stern, *The Rape of the Taxpayer* (New York: Random House, 1973), 242.

4. Philip M. Stern, *The Great Treasury Raid* (New York: Random House, 1964), 20.
5. Shulman, "Making of a Tax Break," 307.
6. "Tax Relief Plea to Liken Film Stars to Oil Wells," *Los Angeles Times*, January 3, 1938, 1.
7. "Federal Tax Drive Starts on Wealthy," *Los Angeles Sentinel*, May 30, 1937, 7.
8. "Federal Individual Income Tax Rates History, 1862–2013 (Nominal and Inflation-Adjusted Brackets)," Tax Foundation, October 17, 2013, http://taxfoundation.org /article/us-federal-individual-income-tax-rates-history-1913–2013-nominal-and -inflation-adjusted-brackets.
9. Barbara Miller, "Bing Crosby Forms Own Film Company," *Los Angeles Sentinel*, August 2, 1936, BC1.
10. Stern, *Great Treasury Raid*, 132.
11. Stern, *Great Treasury Raid*, 132.
12. Stern, *Great Treasury Raid*, 133.
13. Bob Hope, "Inside Bob Hope," *Los Angeles Times*, January 2, 1950, H8.
14. Sally Helgesen, *Wildcatters: A Story of Texans, Oil, and Money* (New York: Doubleday and Company, 1981), 89.
15. Helgesen, *Wildcatters*, 89.
16. "The Hollywood Wildcats," *Time*, October 10, 1949, 92–96.
17. "Hollywood Wildcats," 92–96.
18. Stern, *Great Treasury Raid*, 23.
19. "Hollywood Wildcats," 92.
20. Dennis McDougal, *The Last Mogul: Lew Wasserman, MCA, and the Hidden History of Hollywood* (Boston: Da Capo Press, 2001), 113; Connie Bruck, *When Hollywood Had a King: The Reign of Lew Wasserman, Who Leveraged Talent into Power and Influence* (New York: Random House, 2003), 143.
21. McDougal, *Last Mogul*, 113.
22. The most successful was a joint venture with Jimmy Stewart, Frank Sinatra, Robert Six (CEO of Continental Airlines), and producer-director Leland Hayward. Robert J. Serling, *Maverick* (Garden City, NY: Doubleday and Company, 1974), 106.
23. Philip K Scheuer, "Top Stars Now Share in Profits of Major Pictures," *Los Angeles Times*, July 24, 1955, D2.
24. Jeanine Basinger, *Anthony Mann* (Middletown, CT: Wesleyan University Press, 2007), 79–80.
25. Scheuer, "Profits," D2.
26. Basinger, *Anthony Mann*, 132.
27. Michael Munn, *Jimmy Stewart: The Truth Behind the Legend* (Fort Lee, NJ: Barricade Books, 2006), 215–16.
28. George Stevens, dir., *Giant* (Burbank, CA: Warner Bros., 1956).
29. "Hollywood Wildcats," 96.
30. Helgesen, *Wildcatters*, 89.
31. Carey McWilliams, "The Oil Men Invade Hollywood," *Nation*, October 16, 1948, 429.
32. McWilliams, "Invade Hollywood," 429.
33. Bryan Burrough, *The Big Rich: The Rise and Fall of the Greatest Texas Oil Fortunes* (New York: Penguin Press, 2009), 13.

34. Burrough, *Big Rich*, 13.
35. Films that Hughes Jr. produced that received Academy Award nominations include *Two Arabian Knights* (1927) (Lewis Milestone, Best Comedy Direction—winner), *The Racket* (1928) (Best Picture, then called Outstanding Picture—nominated), *The Front Page* (1931) (Best Picture—nominated; Lewis Milestone, Best Director—nominated; Aldophe Menjou, Best Actor—nominated), and *Hell's Angels* (1930) (Best Cinematography—nominated).
36. Earle E. Crowe, "Hughes after Multicolor," *Los Angeles Times*, June 12, 1930, 14.
37. McWilliams, "Invade Hollywood," 429.
38. Burrough, *Big Rich*, 167, 173.
39. Burrough, *Big Rich*, 173–80; "Texas Oil Millionaire Forms Producing Firm," *Hollywood Boxoffice*, May 15, 1948, 47; Thomas F. Brady, "New Film Company Formed by Oil Man," *New York Times*, April 12, 1948, 25.
40. "McCarthy, RKO Talk," *Variety*, March 9, 1949, 22.
41. Burrough, *Big Rich*, 181–86.
42. Burrough, *Big Rich*, 181–86.
43. McWilliams, "Invade Hollywood," 429.
44. Burrough, *Big Rich*, 189.
45. Matt Potter, "Oil and Politics in La Jolla," *San Diego Reader*, January 5, 2011, http://www.sandiegoreader.com/news/2011/jan/05/cover-oil-politics-la-jolla.
46. Ronald Reagan, "Statement to the House, Committee on Ways and Means," *General Revenue Revision*, 85th Cong., 1st sess., January 27, 1958, 1982–91.
47. Reagan, "Statement to the House," 1991.
48. McDougal, *Last Mogul*, 191.
49. Dan E. Moldea, *Dark Victory: Ronald Reagan, MCA, and the Mob* (New York: Penguin Books, 1987), 235.
50. Moldea, *Dark Victory*, 235.
51. Moldea, *Dark Victory*, 238.
52. In order to protect their interests, MCA played both sides of the political coin, with Jules Stein and Taft Schreiber covering the Republicans and Lew Wasserman covering the Democrats. Moldea, *Dark Victory*, 236–38.
53. Yanek Mieczkowski, *Gerald Ford and the Challenges of the 1970s* (Lexington: University Press of Kentucky, 2005), 165–72.
54. Mieczkowski, *Challenges of the 1970s*, 165–72.
55. Robert D. Hershey Jr., "The Boom in Tax Shelters," *New York Times*, July 19, 1983, section D, 1.
56. Mieczkowski, *Challenges of the 1970s*, 157.
57. Frank J. Prial, "Higher Film Fees Urged for Oil Countries," *New York Times*, January 25, 1974, 18.
58. Thomas C. Hayes, "Murdoch Will Buy Out Davis's Holdings in Fox," *New York Times*, September 24, 1985, Section D, 1.
59. Hayes, "Murdoch Will Buy," 1.
60. These new motion picture tax shelter deals used accelerated asset depreciation, investment tax credits, and production service company schemes to shelter income. These were not tax laws specific to the film industry but were used to great effect in the industry due to blockbusters' high earnings potential. Robert Lindsey, "For Best Performing Shelter . . ." *New York Times*, March 28, 1976, 107.
61. Lindsey, "Shelter," 107.
62. Citizens for Reagan, "Ronald Reagan Presidential Campaign TV Ad: 'Jimmy

Stewart,'" March 19, 1976, Citizens for Reagan Records, Archive.org, video, 1:23, https://archive.org/details/csth_000019.

63. "Jimmy Stewart," *Oil and Gas Investor*, July 2004, 88.

64. "Jimmy Stewart," 88.

65. David A. Stockman, *The Triumph of Politics: Why the Reagan Revolution Failed* (New York: PublicAffairs, 1986), 139.

66. Stockman, *Triumph of Politics*, 139.

67. Claudia Wright, "Ronald Reagan's Kitchen Cabinet," *New Statesman*, June 19, 1981, 6–10.

68. Wright, "Kitchen Cabinet," 6–10.

69. Jeffery H. Birnbaum and Alan S. Murray, *Showdown at Gucci Gulch: Lawmakers, Lobbyists, and the Unlikely Triumph of Tax Reform* (New York: Random House, 1987), 284–91.

70. Birnbaum and Murray, *Showdown at Gucci Gulch*, 289.

Chapter 21

"Limitless Power at Man's Command": *A Is for Atom* (1953), the Cold War, and Visions of the Nuclear Future in the 1950s

Sarah E. Robey

On December 20, 1951, a string of four light bulbs lit up at a remote facility in the desert of eastern Idaho. There, at the National Reactor Testing Station, a team of nuclear scientists harnessed the Experimental Breeder Reactor 1 (EBR-1) to produce electricity.[1] The initial demonstration produced one hundred kilowatts of power, just enough to operate a small circuit of lighting and machinery. EBR-1 had been constructed to manufacture plutonium for atomic weapons, but like any reactor pile, the high temperatures involved could be utilized for electrical generation. Even though the production of electricity was not the experimental reactor's primary research goal, the *New York Times* called the milestone the start of "a new chapter in the atomic age."[2] Although a small contingent of advocates had been singing nuclear energy's praises since the early 1940s, the announcement of EBR-1's success reinvigorated a new wave of boosterism. Over the coming years, nuclear energy promoters would emerge from many corners of society with amplified voices, eager to tout the peaceful wonders of the nuclear future.[3]

For nuclear boosters, peaceful nuclear energy served as an antidote to widespread public ambivalence about the world's violent entry into the Atomic Age in August 1945. And in the early 1950s, there were indeed signs that a wholesale peaceful nuclear energy transition was on the horizon, a shift that could eclipse nuclear science's reputation as a tool for destruction. After nuclear electricity had been proven feasible, policymakers in Washington began to consider the possibility of a civilian nuclear power industry. The United States Navy was in the process of building the first nuclear-powered submarine, and many assumed similar technology would someday power all modes of transportation. Radioisotopes had already begun to revolutionize certain aspects of medical practice, agriculture, and industry, and promised more applications in the years to come.[4] Of course, the continued expansion of all these areas would require major legislative reform to break the monopoly the Atomic Energy Commission (AEC) had on nuclear technologies and research. Nevertheless, in the early 1950s, the world seemed poised to be transformed by the benevolent uses of nuclear science.

Yet even before many of these technological developments could be put into practice, American industrial corporations began promoting the peaceful atom through sponsored films. Almost universally framed as scientific education for a general audience, nuclear-themed sponsored films of the 1950s carried strong elements of nuclear boosterism as well. The films intentionally drew the viewer's attention away from nuclear weapons and toward a future of prosperity, health, peace, and continued material abundance and inexpensive energy, all thanks to nuclear science. In doing so, the films' writers, producers, and sponsors worked to reinforce a narrative that nuclear science was a force for good at a moment when many Americans had only ever considered the consequences of its destructive uses.

Energy industries and those adjacent to them were prominent among the firms that sponsored nuclear films. From the late 1940s on, corporations such as Standard Oil of California, Monsanto, Westinghouse, and Union Carbide and Carbon commissioned films that in one way or another promoted the peaceful atom. One of the earliest and most successful, however, was General Electric's (GE) 1953 film, *A Is for Atom*.[5] John Sutherland Productions, Inc., creator of this award-winning short film, claimed it provided "an entertaining but scientifically accurate explanation of the nature and uses of nuclear energy."[6] It reached millions of Americans in the years after its release and won several film industry awards. The film's promotional tone and positive message are representative of the genre, but its timing and accolades also make it a case study worth exploring in more depth.

Despite the boosterism of *A Is for Atom*, the film belies a more ambiguous concurrent story of early nuclear energy in the United States. Although GE partnered with the AEC in early reactor research and development, the energy industry writ large was initially reluctant to dive headlong into the development of utility-scale nuclear power. Corporate questions about regulation, reactor design, and economic feasibility plagued the AEC's plans for the peaceful atom during the 1950s. Despite the persistence of such roadblocks, President

Eisenhower's New Look diplomatic strategy was simultaneously embracing "peaceful atom" as an antidote for the perils of the nuclearized Cold War. *A Is for Atom* was released at the height of these deliberations. Set against the backdrop of these ongoing negotiations between energy industry heavyweights, the AEC, President Eisenhower, and the international diplomatic community, the film takes on a new meaning. In both its messaging and broader context, *A Is for Atom* uncovers how and why a variety of authorities sought to transmute public fears about nuclear energy into hope at the dawn of the age of the peaceful atom. As such, the film demonstrates how popular representations of nuclear energy, like other sources of energy examined in this volume, reflected both cultural anxieties and state power in a complex moment in American energy history.[7]

The Atomic Age Is Born

A loud roar and anxious music herald a flash of light and a growing mushroom cloud. "The Atomic Age was born!" a narrator proclaims. *A Is for Atom* begins like many other sponsored films about nuclear matters: by recognizing the violence that ushered in the Atomic Age. However, the acknowledgment is brief. The narrator is firm in his conviction that "all men of good will earnestly hope that a realistic control of atomic weapons can and will be achieved." But until then, he insists, "Wisdom demands . . . that we take time to understand this force, because here in fact is the answer to a dream as old as man himself: a giant of limitless power at man's command." The giant, of course, is nuclear science, personified as a towering, glowing behemoth straddling the planet (fig. 21.1).

Aside from its ominous opening scene, *A Is for Atom* is an optimistically told lesson in the history, fundamentals, and future of nuclear science. The film is animated in color, giving fanciful form to an atomic realm composed of inconceivably small particles. Early in the film, viewers meet Dr. Atom, whose oversized head is an anthropomorphized atomic diagram (fig. 21.2). He dresses in a mortarboard and gown to convey his professorial role and instructs viewers on the basics of atomic structure. Once leaving his classroom, Dr. Atom arrives in Element Town, a village representing the periodic table. Here, viewers meet other anthropomorphized elements and learn about their differing numbers of protons. Each element lives in a related home: oxygen lives in a pressurized tank, gold in a bank, aluminum in a teakettle. Radioactivity and natural transmutation are explained by a frenetic dancing radium atom that decays until it eventually finds its home in the lead house, wherein the atom tucks itself calmly into bed (fig. 21.3). The effect of humanizing elements is

Fig. 21.1. The nuclear "giant of limitless power at man's command." General Electric Co., *A Is for Atom* (John Sutherland Productions, Inc., 1953), 1:03.

Fig. 21.2. Dr. Atom, "a leading authority on the subject" of nuclear science. General Electric Co., *A Is for Atom* (John Sutherland Productions, Inc., 1953), 1:57.

whimsical but informative, and gives the audience a simplified way to understand nuclear science principles.

Leaving Element Town, the film goes on to explain how "men of science" sought to answer the question "If an atom could change itself," as had radium, "why couldn't man change the atom?" Abandoning the atom characters, the film's animation becomes more technical as the narrator introduces the concept of artificial transmutation of elements and particle accelerators, the machines that led to the discovery of nuclear fission in 1939. The narrator proceeds through a primer in nuclear fission and the research that drove its theorization. Aside from the brief appearance of Albert Einstein, the other figures in this nuclear history are silhouetted men in white lab coats. They are rendered anonymous perhaps to avoid distracting from the story or ostracizing a generalist audience. Whatever the rationale, the labor of nuclear science research is omniscient and authoritative, yet nameless.

The subject of the next brief segment is nuclear weapons, a topic that the script handles carefully. "With this discovery [of nuclear fission] at the time the free world faced a war for survival," the narrator admits, "it was little wonder the first thought was a weapon." However, he goes on, mass cooperation between industry, labor, science, and the military to build facilities—such as those in Oak Ridge, Tennessee, and Hanford, Washington—enabled the mass production of nuclear materials. The narrator uses the facilities as segues into the mechanics of nuclear reactor piles, eliding their explicit wartime—and ongoing—connection to weapons manufacturing, and instead emphasizing the other ways reactors could be used.

The film's final segment explains the manifold current and future peaceful benefits of nuclear energy. First, chain reactions release heat that can be "substituted in many industrial applications where heat is now provided by coal or petroleum," including electrical generation. While the narrator admits there are impediments to its implementation at that moment, "the future supplying of electric power to entire cities is far from impossible." Second, on-board nuclear reactors will revolutionize ground, water, and air transportation, represented by a series of futuristic vehicles. Third, the film demonstrates a variety of uses for radioactive isotope tracers. The animation introduces a detective team called Private "I"-sotopes that viewers follow as they investigate tracer uses in agriculture, industry, and medicine. In all of these applications, nuclear science promises a dazzling future of prosperity, good health, and peace, thanks to "the tireless work of modern pioneers": nuclear researchers.

At its ending, the film returns to the scene of a nuclear giant standing atop the world. "Truly," the narrator concludes, "the super power which man has released from within the atom's heart is not one but many giants." Several

Fig. 21.3. A radium atom experiences radioactive decay by throwing off rays and neutrons as he dances. General Electric Co., *A Is for Atom* (John Sutherland Productions, Inc., 1953), 4:40.

Fig. 21.4. "Not one but many giants." General Electric Co., *A Is for Atom* (John Sutherland Productions, Inc., 1953), 13:44.

other glowing figures appear, standing proudly alongside the warrior giant and representing weaponized uses of the atom (fig. 21.4). The narrator identifies them as the engineer, the farmer, the healer, and the research worker, all shown overseeing benevolent projects to improve the world. Importantly, the narrator states, "All are within man's power, subject to his command," a power that holds no small consequence: the very future of humankind.

Nuclear Science for All

A Is for Atom is a film designed to educate, entertain, and convince. Since the immediate aftermath of Hiroshima and Nagasaki, Americans had confronted a spectrum of cultural messages about the nuclear future, from dystopian nightmares of destruction to utopian dreams of plenty and peace.[8] *A Is for Atom* had the weighty task of offering an optimistic vision that outweighed notions of nuclear energy as a tool exclusively for destruction. Through its production style and script, the film encourages audiences to frame the nuclear future as not only benign but altogether beneficial.

Nuclear science information for a general audience, like that presented in *A Is for Atom*, is a topic well suited for animation. Indeed, many nuclear education films of the era feature animated storytelling. As an advertisement for Sutherland Productions claimed, "If your film problem is abstract, complicated, or just plain tough, animation is your best bet" because it brings "animated screen 'life' to the most difficult static and abstract ideas."[9] Nuclear science is abstract, complicated, and tough par excellence. The topic involves objects that cannot be seen by the human eye and processes that are difficult to conceptualize. Some aspects of nuclear science are so small that they are imperceptible, as with X-rays and radioactive decay. Others, such as nuclear weapons explosions, are so large as to be nearly beyond imagination.

Animation also assigns a recognizable scale to difficult ideas. It allows for easy comparison to relatable concepts. For example, although nuclear explosions are generally described in kilotons (1,000 tons of TNT) or megatons (1,000,000 tons of TNT), such abstract units are difficult to conceptualize. A similar issue arises when attempting to describe the amount of energy released in a nuclear chain reaction. *A Is for Atom* uses familiarly scaled objects to explain the principle. Through the imaginative flexibility of animation, the film portrays Yankee Stadium piled full of dynamite as the energy equivalent of a baseball-sized piece of uranium-235. The illustrated baseball, of course, glows brightly to signal its potential energy.

As in most other sponsored films of the era, whether animated or live action, an omniscient off-screen male narrator tells the story of *A Is for Atom*.

The voice-over style was so ubiquitous for most of the twentieth century that it almost goes without notice. However, in a film such as *A Is for Atom*, the narrator's ultimate authority stems from his gender and implied expertise in the topic at hand. The invisibility of women in this story upholds the maleness of the field. That no practical physicists, male or female, are mentioned by name in some ways explains the exclusion of such important nuclear researchers as Marie Curie or Lise Meitner. However, none of the figures—from the cartoon professor and detectives, to the more realistically drawn accelerator operators, to the nuclear giants themselves—have female forms, which speaks to the dominant idea that science was an exclusively male field. The male narrator, an unquestioned authority, reinforces this messaging.

Together, the content, animation, and narration style of *A Is for Atom* might give the impression of an educational science film meant exclusively for schoolchildren. Yet the film was part of General Electric's *Excursions in Science*, a series designed for audiences of all ages. Thus, although educators undoubtedly used *A Is for Atom* as a classroom presentation—GE distributed a slightly longer nontheatrical version, as well—it also reached a much broader audience. In the first three years of the film's release, nearly eight million people saw it in theaters, while another almost five million saw it elsewhere.[10] Although there is little record of audience reception, the film won multiple awards from film councils and festivals, as well as from the cold warrior Freedoms Foundation. As a reporter for *Business Screen*, an industry publication about sponsored films, put it, the film would be of "interest to every adult in the country" and likely would "be one of the most popular films produced this year."[11]

A Is for Atom sought to mold and correct public opinion, not simply educate about nuclear science. The film positions the Manhattan Project—while never identifying it by name—as the precursor to beneficial nuclear innovations that would someday vastly overshadow the negative consequences of nuclear weapons. The visual elements of the film underscore this idea. As the film begins, the "giant of limitless power" emerges from a mushroom cloud, eventually growing to be many times the size of the bomb's cloud. The giant maintains the smoky, glowing form of the mushroom cloud, but adopts a powerful stance with crossed arms and bulging muscles. The message is clear: the nuclear future will render nuclear weapons inconsequential in comparison. When the giant reappears in many forms in the film's conclusion, he reiterates that nuclear science is much more than weapons.

The film's benevolent giants offer a firm corrective against the association between nuclear science and destruction that had populated American visual and rhetorical culture in the years since Hiroshima. From "The 36-Hour War," *Life*'s horrific feature story that imagined future wars, to federal agencies' own publications about the destruction in Japan, Americans had plenty of imagery—based both in reality and fiction—to conjure images of nuclear devastation.[12] As the frame follows a shadow cloaking an anonymous American landscape in the film's opening moments, the narrator concedes, "There is no denying that since that moment [that the Atomic Age was born], the shadow of the atom bomb has been across all our lives." The exact nature of this shadow goes unsaid. However, since 1945 Americans had witnessed the failure of both a campaign for international control of nuclear weapons and persuasive arguments for disarmament.[13] In 1949, earlier than many experts had predicted, the Soviet Union ended the US nuclear monopoly by testing an atomic weapon of its own. Thus, viewers of A Is for Atom had good reason to fear the nuclear world of the early 1950s. Yet as the narrator insists, until the time when a "realistic control of atomic weapons" is found, a wise person must learn to understand the mysteries—and benefits—of nuclear science.

A Is for Atom's faith in the power of nuclear education tapped into a style of nuclear optimism that had been part of the public conversation since World War II. Advocates on both sides of the fierce debates about disarmament and international control recognized the peaceful uses of nuclear energy.[14] While experts and scientists sometimes attempted to temper runaway optimism, nuclear science as a force for good had a great deal of popular traction.[15] But it was not until the early 1950s that some of the anticipated peaceful uses in electricity, medicine, and transportation had materialized in earnest. In other words, when A Is for Atom reached theaters, the public had reasons to believe that the dawn of a peaceful nuclear future was finally upon them.

As the film's sponsor, GE had much to gain from the nuclear future it describes. In fact, since the 1940s, several divisions of GE had been contracted to assist in nuclear reactor research. Industry partnerships with the AEC were typical in this era, although not widely publicized, given the commission's secrecy mandate.[16] A Is for Atom, of course, conveyed nothing of GE's involvement in classified nuclear research. In fact, aside from the opening and closing title credits, the film does not mention GE by name at all. The public may have seen GE as a firm that would someday produce hardware and infrastructure for civilian nuclear power, but not necessarily as one that was already heavily involved in its development. Notably, however, press reports on the film's release stated that it was "reviewed and indorsed [sic] by the Atomic Energy Commission."[17] If the contractual partnership between the AEC and GE was not publicly apparent, the public relations office responsible for the film was nevertheless eager to wear the badge of the AEC's authority.

At the time of A Is for Atom's release in early 1953, however, the AEC and the US military were opening a new chapter in nuclear weapons development. Despite GE's access to some aspects of AEC research programs, the extent of this knowledge was limited by project compartmentalization and clearance restrictions. It is therefore unlikely that the GE employees involved with the film knew about the AEC's concurrent development of a new class of weapons. In November 1952, just months prior to the film's release, the United States demonstrated the feasibility of thermonuclear weapons. At orders of magnitude more destructive than earlier atomic bombs, thermonuclear bombs—also called hydrogen bombs, or "Supers"—rewrote the terms of nuclear warfare.[18]

The development of the Super would be kept out of public view until early 1954, when the deadly Castle Bravo test in the Marshall Islands brought the new weapons and their dangers to light.[19] The test and its aftermath renewed public controversy and outrage over nuclear science as the enabler of destruction and war. It is perhaps not surprising then that GE continued to distribute *A Is for Atom* into the late 1950s. This film, along with a handful of other boosterish sponsored nuclear films that followed it, suddenly had more of a reason to maintain positive public opinion of nuclear science.[20]

The release of *A Is for Atom* also coincided with a moment in which the idea of commercial nuclear power was merging with Cold War national security imperatives. When President Eisenhower entered office in early 1953, he ushered in a new era in Cold War policy, referred to as the New Look.[21] The broad policy objectives embraced both military and nonmilitary modes of waging the Cold War, including the management of international influence and prestige, domestic economic strength, and public opinion. As a potential field for American technological supremacy and world leadership, nuclear power production certainly fit the New Look bill.

Eisenhower unveiled some aspects of the New Look in front of the United Nations in December 1953 when advocating for a solution to "the awful arithmetic of the atomic bomb." In what became known as his "Atoms for Peace" speech, Eisenhower argued for international cooperation in researching the peaceful uses of nuclear science and pledged the nation's "entire heart and mind to finding the way by which the miraculous inventiveness of man shall not be dedicated to his death, but consecrated to his life." The peaceful atom, he argued, was a way to convert a technology of mass destruction into a force for good.[22]

In asserting moral leadership in nuclear matters, Eisenhower's policy declaration had obvious diplomatic motivations. Indeed, months of difficult deliberations about diplomatic objectives, defense imperatives, and public opinion concerns went into crafting the speech's message. Eisenhower's advisors hoped it would coerce the Soviet Union into productive arms control negotiations and reinforce American leadership among its allies. The public commitment to developing peaceful uses of nuclear science could solidify the United States' global technological and scientific leadership. Eisenhower and his advisors also believed the speech would appeal to the public's desire for transparency about the potential horrors of nuclear war, while simultaneously infusing the same conversations with an overriding hope for positive alternatives. The core of each of these objectives was a peaceful nuclear future.[23]

Nuclear energy also figured prominently in a second "Atoms for Peace" objective: the sharing of peaceful nuclear expertise across borders, especially in nonaligned nations. Such a program could build a cooperative community of nuclear scientists and foster new connections between nations, both of which carried the potential to soften the optics of the nuclear arms race. Accordingly, A Is for Atom was one of fourteen sponsored films that the United States Information Agency translated into thirty languages and took on tour to promote American interests abroad.[24] Within the context of the New Look, peaceful nuclear energy and science education had explicit diplomatic value.

For all of these reasons, federal agencies began to lean hard into establishing a commercial nuclear power industry. In 1954, Eisenhower signed a revised Atomic Energy Act, which enabled the development of a civilian nuclear power industry. Yet industries and utilities were slow to invest, citing high construction costs, skepticism about the ability to compete with abundant and inexpensive existing energy sources, and the risks associated with relatively new technologies. The federal government further incentivized private development by passing the Price-Anderson Nuclear Industries Indemnity Act in 1957, legislation that provided the industry with an unprecedented degree of federally backed liability coverage in the event of a reactor accident. Meanwhile, to demonstrate the feasibility of a private nuclear industry, the AEC commissioned the Shippingport Atomic Power Station, a full-scale commercial reactor in western Pennsylvania. The plant achieved criticality and began powering the grid in late 1957, but only after intensive AEC involvement and funding. Thus, despite over a decade of utopian visions of inexpensive, abundant, and economically viable commercial energy, the nuclear power industry came into being only with a great deal of support from the federal government.[25]

Shifting Terrain

Against the backdrops of shifting Cold War strategy, new motivations for developing nuclear power, and a reluctant nascent nuclear energy industry, the meaning of *A Is for Atom* becomes more complicated. Neither General Electric nor the film's producers could have foreseen in 1953 exactly how nuclear power would develop in the coming years. But given the presence of industry skepticism about civilian nuclear power, even prior to Eisenhower's "Atoms for Peace" speech, it may seem curious that GE would commission a film that conveyed such nuclear boosterism. However, GE was no outsider to the AEC. It enjoyed profitable federal contracts in nuclear research and development, and likely believed it would continue to do so if and when a commercial nuclear power industry got off the ground. If the film accomplished its goal of improving popular opinion about nuclear science, perhaps the public would exert pressure on the federal government to legislate such beneficial developments. As it turned out, GE would be instrumental in convincing electrical utilities to embrace nuclear power in the 1960s and helped to lay the groundwork for a significant, if short-lived, boom in nuclear power plant construction.[26]

There are, of course, other ways to explain why GE commissioned *A Is for Atom*. As part of the *Excursions in Science* series, the film could simply have been meant to promote scientific research and literacy, while indirectly garnering positive publicity for GE. Since 1936, GE had sponsored *Excursions* as a radio show and, less frequently, as a film series.[27] Radio episodes that ran in 1953 included such wide-ranging topics as cortisone, Alaskan anthropology, and "snake facts and fallacies," areas in which GE presumably had little commercial interest.[28] Similarly, since the mid-1940s, GE had also been publishing free comic books in its *Adventure Series*. Alongside such titles as *Adventures in Electricity* (1946) and *Adventures in Jet Propulsion* (1947), *Adventures inside the Atom* (1948) purported to tell the "story of nuclear energy."[29] Thus, GE had been in the business of science boosterism—which included the topic of nuclear science—for many years by the time it sponsored *A Is for Atom*. Such a role could position the company as innovative and exciting as well as transparent and benevolent, traits that did not typically predominate in popular discussions of nuclear energy.

As an entertaining animated film, *A Is for Atom* had the capacity to reach a broader audience than the comic book series and the more technically minded *Excursions* radio show. In its radio format, *Excursions in Science* focused heavily on specific research findings and featured prominent scientists as guest lecturers.[30] *Adventures inside the Atom* is primarily a nuclear history primer. By contrast, *A Is for Atom* presents a broad and benevolent nuclear future in generalities, focusing less on the basic research and more on how an average person might benefit from nuclear science. Although part of the *Excursions* series in name, *A Is for Atom* had different objectives.

Conclusion

In the end, *A Is for Atom* was a sponsored film commissioned by a company with a stake in the nuclear future. Implicitly, GE positioned itself as an authority that bridged the gulf between public knowledge and nuclear secrecy. But more importantly, the timing of the film's release came at a crucial moment of flux in American public conversations about nuclear energy. The film attempted to manage the difficult relationship between atoms for peace and atoms for war. It reinforced political messaging of the era, while attempting to construct a new vocabulary of ideas and opinions about the nuclear future. And like many other films examined in this volume, *A Is for Atom* is a prime example of the complex entanglements between entertainment and the energy industries.

Popular science education is rarely intended as education for its own sake. In the case of *A Is for Atom*, the film's educational and entertaining tone obscures a concurrent and complex set of cultural, economic, and political interests that sought to reorient the conversation about nuclear energy from war to peace. *A Is for Atom* spoke to a public that needed to be convinced and rallied, at least according to organizations poised to benefit from public support for peaceful atoms. By 1953, that group had come to include not only corporations such as GE but also high-ranking bureaucrats and policymakers, including President Eisenhower himself.

For decades to come, nuclear energy's boosters would continue to harness science education as a persuasive device.[31] Historian Paul Boyer characterizes this era as a "systematic effort by opinion-molders in government, education, and the media to reshape public attitudes toward atomic energy."[32] From the 1950s on, however, the nuclear power industry encountered public resistance and controversy. At their core, these debates revolved around the cultural meaning of nuclear energy. Did the benefits outweigh the safety risks? How was scientific information produced, interpreted, and disseminated? And who controlled that information? For many members of the public, the growing weight of these present concerns eclipsed hopes for an abstract prosperous future. In hindsight, the optimistic vision of the future in *A Is for Atom* proved to be mere hubris; nuclear utopia never arrived and the film's predictions have, as of yet, fallen flat.[33] However, viewed as an artifact of the many intersections between political power, industry, and public opinion in the nuclearized Cold War, the film offers yet another frame for understanding the multifaceted role of energy in postwar American life.

Notes

1. The late 1940s and 1950s were an era of rapid development and diversification in nuclear science, resulting in inconsistent vocabulary. In this essay, I use *nuclear* as an umbrella category for different classes of weapons and various peaceful applications.
2. "Electricity Made by Atomic Reactor," *New York Times*, December 30, 1951, 1.
3. For examples of boosterism pre- and post-Hiroshima, see Paul Boyer, *By the Bomb's Early Light: American Thought and Culture at the Dawn of the Atomic Age* (Chapel Hill: University of North Carolina Press, 1994). For examples of newspaper coverage of EBR-1, see Pat Munroe, "First Electric Power from Atom Due Soon," *Daily Boston Globe*, February 11, 1951, C16; and "Breeder Reactors," *New York Times*, March 18, 1951, E9.
4. Angela N. H. Creager, *Life Atomic: A History of Radioisotopes in Science and Medicine* (Chicago: University of Chicago Press, 2013).
5. General Electric Co., *A Is for Atom*, directed by Carl Urbano (Los Angeles: John Sutherland Productions, 1953). Available to view courtesy of the Prelinger Archive at www.archive.org. The existing literature on the history of nuclear energy in the United States has mentioned *A Is for Atom* only in passing. Scott Kaufman and Tony Shaw, for instance, use the film as an early example of official nuclear propaganda simply designed to condition public opinion. Scott Kaufman, *Project Plowshare: The Peaceful Use of Nuclear Explosives in Cold War America* (Ithaca: Cornell University Press, 2013), 19–20; Tony Shaw, "'Rotten to the Core': Exposing America's Energy-Media Complex in 'The China Syndrome,'" *Cinema Journal* 52, no. 2 (Winter 2013): 96.
6. Advertisement for John Sutherland Productions, Inc., *Business Screen Magazine* 13, no. 6 (September 1952): 39.
7. The history of nuclear energy as it came of age in the 1950s in the United States has often been overlooked as an area of study within energy humanities, although the role of nuclear energy in the tumultuous 1970s and beyond has been thoroughly examined. There are several notable exceptions, however. My thinking on this essay has benefited from conceptions of "nuclearity" and "unthinkability" as developed by Gabrielle Hecht and Joseph Masco, respectively. Likewise, although it predates the articulation of energy humanities as a subfield, Spencer Weart's deep exploration of the symbolism of nuclear culture is no less essential. See, for example, Gabrielle Hecht, "Nuclear Ontologies," in *Energy Humanities: An Anthology*, ed. Imre Szeman and Dominic Boyer (Baltimore: Johns Hopkins University Press, 2017), 249–60; Joseph Masco, "Atomic Health, or How the Bomb Altered American Notions of Death," in Szeman and Boyer, eds., *Energy Humanities*, 339–51; and Spencer R. Weart, *Nuclear Fear: A History of Images* (Cambridge, MA: Harvard University Press, 1988).
8. Boyer, *Bomb's Early Light*; Weart, *Nuclear Fear*.
9. Advertisement for John Sutherland Productions, Inc.

10. "Case History of a Successful Business Film," *Business Screen Magazine* 18, no. 7 (November 1957): 5.

11. "'A Is for Atom' Is an Excellent G.E. 'Excursions in Science' Film," *Business Screen Magazine* 14, no. 1 (February 1953): 104.

12. "The 36-Hour War," *Life*, November 19, 1945, 27–35. For an example of early federal publications on Hiroshima and Nagasaki, see United States Strategic Bombing Survey, *The Effects of Atomic Bombs on Hiroshima and Nagasaki* (Washington, DC: Government Printing Office, 1946).

13. Alice Kimball Smith, *A Peril and a Hope: The Scientists' Movement in America, 1945–1947* (Chicago: University of Chicago Press, 1965).

14. Brian Balogh, *Chain Reaction: Expert Debate and Public Participation in American Commercial Nuclear Power, 1945–1975* (New York: Cambridge University Press, 1991); Smith, *Peril and a Hope.*

15. Boyer, *Bomb's Early Light*, 109–21.

16. GE, along with other government contractors such as Westinghouse, did occasionally partner with the AEC in its official public education programming. See Boyer, *Bomb's Early Light*, 296. However, this corporate-federal partnership in information campaigns had been commonplace during World War II and continued into the 1950s via sponsored civil defense initiatives. It is likely that corporate involvement in AEC events and publications would have escaped public attention in the late 1940s and early 1950s.

17. "Atom Educational Film Made Available by GE," *Washington Post*, August 9, 1953, R11.

18. Richard G. Hewlett and Jack M. Holl, *Atoms for Peace and War, 1953–1961* (Berkeley: University of California Press, 1989).

19. Hewlett and Holl, *Atoms for Peace and War*, 172–82.

20. Subsequent sponsored nuclear films include Robert Stevenson, dir., *Atomic Energy as a Force for Good* (The Christophers, 1955); Chamber of Commerce of the United States, *The Atom Comes to Town* (Muller, Jordan, and Herrick, 1957); and Westinghouse Electric Company, *Atomic Power at Shippingport* (Audio Productions, 1958).

21. See Robert R. Bowie and Richard H. Immerman, *Waging Peace: How Eisenhower Shaped an Enduring Cold War Strategy* (New York: Oxford University Press, 1998).

22. Dwight D. Eisenhower, "Atoms for Peace" (speech), December 8, 1953, Dwight D. Eisenhower's Papers as President, Speech Series, Box 5, United Nations Speech 12/8/53, Dwight D. Eisenhower Presidential Library, Abilene, KS, https://www.eisenhowerlibrary.gov/sites/default/files/file/atoms_Binder13.pdf.

23. Hewlett and Holl, *Atoms for Peace and War*; Bowie and Immerman, *Waging Peace*; Ira Chernus, *Eisenhower's Atoms for Peace* (College Station: Texas A&M University Press, 2002); John Krige, "Atoms for Peace, Scientific Internationalism, and Scientific Intelligence," *Osiris* 21, no. 1 (2006): 161–81.

24. "Royalty of Greece Sees 'A Is for Atom' Request Showing in Schools of Their Land," *Business Screen Magazine* 17, no. 1 (February 1956): 86.

25. George T. Mazuzan and J. Samuel Walker, *Controlling the Atom: The Beginnings of Nuclear Regulation, 1946–1962* (Berkeley: University of California Press, 1984); Martin V. Melosi, *Coping with Abundance: Energy and Environment in Industrial America* (Philadelphia: Temple University Press, 1985), 223–33.

26. Robert D. Lifset, "Nuclear Power in America: The Story of a Failed Energy Transition," in "Forum: The Environmental History of Energy Transitions," ed. Ian

Jared Miller, Paul Warde, Ariane Tanner, J. R. McNeill, Victor Seow, Conevery Bolton Valencius, and Robert D. Lifset, *Environmental History* 24, no. 3 (July 2019): 524–33.

27. Until 1949, the series was called *General Electric Research Laboratories' Science Forum*. Marcel Chotkowski LaFollette, *Science on the Air: Popularizers and Personalities on Radio and Early Television* (Chicago: University of Chicago Press, 2008), 135.

28. *Excursions in Science* radio recordings are archived as part of the J. David Goldin Collection, Marr Sound Archives, University of Missouri-Kansas City University Libraries, Kansas City, MO.

29. General Comics, Inc., *Adventures Inside the Atom* (General Electric Company, 1948).

30. LaFollette, *Science on the Air*, 135.

31. See, for example, Jacob Darwin Hamblin, "Exorcising Ghosts in the Age of Automation: United Nations Experts and Atoms for Peace," *Technology and Culture* 47, no. 4 (October 2006): 734–56; and Natasha Zaretsky, *Radiation Nation: Three Mile Island and the Political Transformation of the 1970s* (New York: Columbia University Press, 2018).

32. Boyer, *Bomb's Early Light*, 301.

33. For more on hubris in energy and environmentalism, see Michelle Niemann, "Hubris and Humility in Environmental Thought," in *The Routledge Companion to the Environmental Humanities*, ed. Ursula K. Heise, Jon Christensen, and Michelle Niemann (New York: Routledge, 2017), 247–57; Lifset, "Nuclear Power in America."

Chapter 22

Syriana (2005): The Oil Curse and Hollywood's 9/11 Film

Robert Lifset

n 2005, Hollywood released *Syriana*, a film that explores the root causes of the terrorist attacks on 9/11 and seeks to understand the dynamic linking US foreign policy, oil, and terrorism.[1] While many Hollywood films suggest or assume that US involvement in the Middle East is tied to that region's oil reserves, *Syriana* goes a step further in advancing the idea that US reliance on Middle Eastern oil produced the terrorism that resulted in 9/11. Significantly, the idea that oil was driving American foreign policy in the Middle East was controversial in the early 2000s. The US was attacked by Al-Qaeda on 9/11, and invading Afghanistan was defended as a straightforward response to an unprovoked act of terrorism. The George W. Bush administration worked hard to persuade Americans that Al-Qaeda and Saddam Hussein were connected and that invading Iraq was also a response to 9/11. And since the United States was attacked, any echoes of critiques from the First Gulf War suggesting that US foreign policy in the Middle East was rooted in oil interests were highly controversial.[2]

Over time, however, this view began to change. Alan Greenspan and Hillary Clinton both published memoirs acknowledging the centrality of energy in US foreign policy. Greenspan was particularly blunt: "I am saddened that it is politically inconvenient to acknowledge what everyone knows: the Iraq war is largely about oil."[3] That the war in Afghanistan and Iraq continued for so long without a conclusive and victorious end has also soured public opinion and made the nation more receptive to arguments advanced by the Left in the early to mid-2000s and that scholars have been advancing for decades: that the roots of US foreign policy and action in the Middle East are related to US energy interests.[4]

Arguably ahead of its time in this regard, *Syriana* examined the link between terrorism and US reliance on Middle Eastern oil in 2005. The film is an adaptation of Robert Baer's 2002 memoir of his tenure in the CIA, *See No Evil: The True Story of a Ground Soldier in the CIA's War on Terrorism*. The book argues that the agency had "taken itself out of the business of spying" and thus contributed to international terrorists' success in attacking the United States on 9/11. Baer concludes that political correctness, petty Beltway politics, careerism, and a devaluation of human intelligence and its risks all served to weaken the nation's intelligence community in the 1990s.[5] However, screenwriter Stephen Gaghan used the book to write and direct a far more complicated film. While *Syriana* explores Baer's critiques of American intelligence, it pivots away from a focus on the intelligence community in an effort to understand the connections between the American oil industry, US foreign policy, and terrorism. Indeed, the movie poster depicts an image of Bob Barnes—a character based on Baer and played by George Clooney—blindfolded with the phrase "Everything is connected" covering his mouth in small print. The image reveals the scope of Gaghan's ambition with the film: to explain everything.[6]

But while *Syriana* describes the relationship between oil, the Middle East, and American foreign policy, it fails to explain the dynamic driving these relationships. For that we need to turn to a theory developed by political scientists: the oil curse. The oil curse emerged after the Cold War as scholars began to think about what beyond ideology might motivate future conflict. Essentially, the oil curse argues that the possession and production of large quantities of oil generates several consequences or conditions, which include a weakened economy and tendency toward undemocratic government.[7] In this essay, the oil curse will be deployed as an interpretive lens through which to explain the issues raised by the film. While *Syriana* casts a critical eye on the relationship between oil, the Middle East, and American foreign policy, the film adopts a neoliberal or conservative perspective in finding that America is simply pursuing its interests at the expense of its values. By focusing on the corrosive effects of oil, produced by the oil curse, this essay argues that the film is fundamentally confused about the dynamic powering the relationship between the US and the Middle East. As a result, the film's critique of American foreign policy offers little hope for the future.

Hyperlink Cinema

Syriana is a complex film, often confusing and hard to understand.[8] As one critic noted, "[It] could well be used as the central text of a graduate seminar."[9] Gaghan deploys multiple parallel storylines that quickly jump back and forth between a dozen locations in a style that Alissa Quart describes as "hyperlink cinema."[10] The audience is left, unassisted, to consider how seemingly unrelated stories are in fact intimately connected. It also didn't help that the film does not offer traditional Hollywood light and sound cues to tell the audience what to think and when to think it.[11] Moreover, this approach required a great deal of expository dialogue, and several characters virtually lecture the audience on topics about which most people are ignorant but need to be understood to make sense of the plot (e.g., the Foreign Corrupt Practices Act). Apparently, much of this complexity was intentional. In his production notes, Gaghan wrote, "We are living in complex, difficult times and I wanted *Syriana* to reflect this complexity in a visceral way to embrace it narratively. There are no good guys and no bad guys and there are no easy answers. . . . This seemed like the most honest reflection of this post 9-11 world we all find ourselves in."[12]

This intentional ambiguity may have blunted the film's box office appeal. *Syriana* grossed $50.8 million in North America and $93.9 worldwide, making it the fifty-sixth highest-grossing film of 2005.[13] It was financed by Participant Productions, a company that champions "socially relevant themes . . . [and is] dedicated to entertainment which inspires audiences to engage in positive social change."[14] Bankrolled by the Canadian billionaire Jeffrey Skoll, Participant has backed many of the most prominent socially conscious films and documentaries to emerge from Hollywood in recent years.[15] It is notable that making a film that was partially critical of American foreign policy required foreign financing and the expectation of significant profits from foreign box offices. Even so, the film was generally well received and, significantly, became a Rorschach test for critics' political inclinations. The left-leaning *Guardian newspaper* felt that the film's "reluctance to criticize America too much" was limiting, while conservative commentator Charles Krauthammer asserted, "Osama bin Laden could not have scripted this film with more conviction."[16]

Syriana's narrative style foregrounds the film's economic and political context as opposed to psychological motivations, which can work to obscure characters' intentions.[17] Moreover, rather than a traditional narrative, Gaghan's meandering use of hyperlink cinema depicts networks of characters connected across vast distances by money and power.[18] One storyline follows Bob Barnes, a CIA officer who begins the film in Iran selling a pair of missiles to arms dealers. His mission was to assassinate the arms dealers with a car bomb after the deal was consummated; the explosion would also destroy the missiles. But the deal goes south when the arms dealers sell one of the missiles to an Egyptian Muslim fundamentalist before the car bomb can be detonated. The Egyptian next appears in a *madrassa* (Islamic religious school) where unemployed Pakistanis are being groomed as suicide bombers. From there, a second storyline follows two young Pakistani oil field workers, Wasim (Mazhar Munir) and Farooq (Sonnell Dadral), who attend the *madrassa* because there they are fed and treated well. They don't speak Arabic and were recently beaten by state security officers while waiting in line to extend their visas after being let go from their jobs with Connex, a large multinational American oil company.

Connex, meanwhile, is in the process of merging with Killen, a smaller independent oil company.[19] The US Department of Justice investigates the merger, suspicious that Killen has suddenly gained access to oil in Kazakhstan. As part of their due diligence prior to the merger, Connex has hired a law firm to investigate whether Killen bribed the leader of Kazakhstan to gain access to its oil fields. A third storyline follows the man leading the investigation, Bennett Holiday (Jeffrey Wright). Dean Whiting (Christopher Plummer), a member of the Committee to Liberate Iran, a group that promotes democracy and freedom in Iran, manages Holiday's firm.

Connex's largest holdings are in an unnamed Gulf state ruled by an emir who is about to step down. Vying for the throne are his two sons: Prince Nasir (Alexander Siddig) and Prince Meshal (Akbar Kurtha). Nasir is a reformer, educated at Oxford and Georgetown, and wants to implement democratic reforms, extend the vote to women, and guarantee human rights. However, as Nasir had already secured Connex and the US government's disdain by awarding a large oil contract to China, the CIA, Dean Whiting, and Connex direct their attention to Meshal, a playboy content with maintaining the status quo. A fourth storyline follows energy analyst Bryan Woodman (Matt Damon), who becomes an advisor to Nasir after Woodman's son drowns at a party hosted by the royal family.

When Barnes returns to Washington after his failed mission, he further angers the White House by delivering a pessimistic report on the potential for change in Iran. But the CIA provides Barnes with an opportunity to redeem himself: assassinating Nasir, who they argue has ties to terrorism. The film thus implies that the US oil industry's interest in maintaining access to oil in Syriana led to the US government's desire to assassinate a Western-educated reformer.

Barnes's assassination attempt is unsuccessful, and he is instead kidnapped and tortured by a former asset. He escapes and, realizing he has been betrayed by the CIA, attempts to warn Nasir that the agency wants him dead. Nasir is in the process of organizing a coup against his brother, who has assumed the throne. A drone strike, conducted by the CIA (acting on behalf of Connex), kills Nasir and Barnes, and the film ends with Connex's CEO, Leland Janus (Peter Gerety), receiving an award for orchestrating the merger with Killen. The film cuts between the awards banquet and Wasim and Farooq—the former Connex employees dismissed via the merger—riding a small fishing boat laden with Barnes's missing missile, heading toward a Connex-Killen tanker. Everything is connected.

The Oil Curse Exemplified

The oil curse provides the best lens through which to make sense of how "everything is connected"—the concept that pulls these different and seemingly unconnected storylines together. The oil curse argues that there is a quantifiably direct and proportional correlation between the amount of oil a nation possesses and the weakness of its democratic institutions.[20] *Syriana*'s fictional Gulf kingdom is a monarchy in which the royal family possesses such sufficient wealth that it does not need the support of its citizens—a condition common among states with small populations and large supplies of oil. In these countries, the state lacks legitimacy but secures power by bribing its citizens and maintaining a monopoly on the use of force.[21] And, indeed, the film includes a scene depicting Nasir granting favors to supplicants.

With little political legitimacy due to the lack of democracy, the rulers of a resource-wealthy state have reason to fear internal subversion as well as external invasion. For many, the solution is an expanded and bloated security apparatus and the protection of a patron state (a powerful ally willing to defend the oil wealthy state from external invasion), as we see in *Syriana*. Wasim and Farooq, for example, are viciously beaten by state security officers while standing in line outside a government office. The officers appear to serve no purpose other than to intimidate and harass the people there. The fictional Gulf kingdom in the film enjoys the US as its patron state, a relationship sealed by its hosting a US military base. After Prince Nasir awards a large oil contract to China, the CIA is persuaded that having him in power would jeopardize US interests and assassinates him. Dean Whiting then recruits Prince Meshal and secures the US government's support for his ascension to the throne. Here, the film dramatizes the conflict between US interests and values. Nasir's political and economic reforms reflect Western values, but because they would weaken US hegemony in the kingdom and the larger region, they run counter to US interests. Finally, in the Committee to Liberate Iran we see the oil industry lobbying a superpower (in this case the US) to initiate regime change in an oil rich nation so as to grant the industry access to oil. This is an example of the external threats a resource-wealthy country attracts.[22]

Through US opposition to Nasir's rule, the film suggests that the war on terror can serve as cover for advancing narrow corporate interests. Oil companies can reach more profitable deals with countries suffering from the oil curse.

When a family or small number of elites control the state and the state owns its resources, the state does not need to invest in its people. It can survive without the social investment common in Western societies, and any oil revenue only needs to support the elites, which includes funding a security apparatus to protect the status quo. To the citizens of this state, oil deals appear exploitative, further weakening the state's legitimacy in the eyes of its people. But to an oil company, the risk of doing business with a more unstable government is well worth the increased profitability.

While looking for evidence of corruption during his investigation into Killen, Holiday discovers that Danny Dalton (Tim Blake Nelson), a friend of Killen CEO Jimmy Pope (Chris Cooper), created shell companies for which Killen bore the risk but the president of Kazakhstan's family received the profits. This discovery explains how a small US oil company secured highly lucrative rights to produce oil in that country. When confronted by Holiday, an angry Dalton claims that his violation of the Foreign Corrupt Practices Act is consistent with neoliberalism, consistent with a vision of a laissez-faire economy, and consistent with a government that minimizes its interference in the workings of the economy. "Corruption?" he exclaims. "Corruption ain't nothing more than government intrusion into market efficiencies in the form of regulation. That's Milton Friedman. He got a goddamn Nobel Prize. . . . Corruption is how we win." When the US Attorney (David Clennon) investigating the merger informs Holiday that prosecuting Dalton would not be enough to secure Justice Department approval of the merger, Jimmy Pope warns him, "I'd be real careful. You dig a three-foot hole, you'll find one body, but you dig a six-foot hole and you might find twenty." Holiday satisfies the US Attorney by finding another "body": his immediate boss, Sydney Hewitt (Nicky Henson), who had illegally purchased rights to use excess Iranian pipeline capacity. Hewitt was a member of the Committee to Liberate Iran. As Holiday explains to Pope, the merger is so beneficial to the US that "we're looking for the illusion of due-diligence. Two criminal acts successfully prosecuted gives us that illusion."[23] Harkening back to something Hewitt explained to Holiday in an earlier scene, "If people in oil deals talked to US Attorneys, there'd be no oil business."

The film's argument that the oil industry prefers a corrupt environment because it is "why we win" is unfair to the industry. Given the enormous capital investments involved in oil production, the greater predictability provided by the rule of law is preferable to the corruption and instability endemic in weak states. However, it is also true that the industry has resisted efforts to fight corruption. Europe has no equivalent to the Foreign Corrupt Practices Act, and the American oil industry has lobbied hard for the removal of an SEC requirement (obligated by the Dodd-Frank Act of 2010) that US companies report payments to foreign governments for the commercial development of natural resources.[24]

The oil curse does more than foster the corruption that deprives citizens of the benefits of their state's oil. It actively works to hollow out that country's economy in two ways. The first is through the "Dutch disease"—a reference to economic changes in the Netherlands wrought by the discovery of a large natural gas field in 1959. As a country exports oil, its own currency rises in value, thereby making its exported goods more expensive and imports less expensive. As a result, export-oriented industries unconnected to natural resources decline while domestic industries must now compete with a flood of cheaper imports. The second blow to an oil-rich nation's economy is that natural resources do not need to be produced; they are extracted. Natural resource extraction is isolated from other parts of the economy and requires a relatively small labor force. Countries dependent upon natural resource extraction thus experience economic decline.

When an angry Bryan Woodman confronts Nasir after the death of his son, he describes this dynamic: "Twenty years ago, you had the highest GNP in the world and now you're tied with Paraguay. Your second-biggest export is secondhand goods. Followed by dates on which you lose five cents a pound. You want to know what the business world thinks of you? They think a hundred years ago you were chopping each other's heads off in the desert and that's exactly where you'll be in another hundred." Interestingly, the film never nods toward the oil curse as the cause of the economic decline Woodman describes. Instead, it suggests through Woodman that the problem is a corrupt, undemocratic state and the solution is to implement democratic political reforms and neoliberal or laissez-faire economic policies. If this country were only more like the United States, it wouldn't have these problems. Woodman proposes using excess Iranian pipeline capacity as a means of maximizing profitability for Nasir's country, naively ignoring the geopolitical foolishness of asking a US client state to do business with and strengthen an enemy of the US.[25]

With the economy hollowed out by resource extraction, a country suffering from the oil curse experiences increasing economic inequality. In the film, Wasim and Farooq are radicalized at a *madrassa* by an *imam* who directly attacks the kind of neoliberal reforms that Woodman proposes. He asserts, "The pain of modern life cannot be cured by deregulation, privatization, economic reform or lower taxes. The pain of living in the modern world will never be solved by a liberal society. Liberal societies have failed. Christian theology has failed. The West has failed." After this scene, the film immediately cuts to a large luxury yacht in the French Mediterranean where Prince Meshal says that a few years earlier, he was "just about to graduate from Oxford and my mother had a horse in the Royal Ascot race. The horse won that same day I was graduating and my trust fund matured. So that tops any birthday present any of you have brought for me tonight." After the *imam*'s speech in the *madrassa*, Meshal's words demonstrate the stark inequality of this Persian Gulf kingdom. The film is suggesting that, yes, the West has failed them, but it has clearly not failed the royal family. The US desire for stability and access to oil fosters and supports undemocratic regimes that limit economic opportunity and political expression.

In the post–Cold War landscape, America's energy dependence has hijacked our foreign policy. The US does far more than fund both sides of the War on Terror (US military forces through taxes and terrorists through the oil wealth created by our consumption); American companies' actions have produced the conditions that inspire terrorism. Although the oil industry's manipulation of the US government is not depicted heroically, the film does not dispute that their joint actions benefit the nation. Instead, *Syriana* only implies that this arrangement prioritizes America's interests over its values.

The film advances the idea that this is the price we must pay for our modern way of living. We are in a struggle, a great scramble for power. Speaking to Holiday, Pope explains, "We use one-quarter of the oil in the world. . . . Your house is light and warm and my house is light and warm, but what if it was that way half the week. Hell, China's economy ain't growing as fast as it could because they can't get all the oil they need. I'm damn proud of that fact." Pope, Dalton, Holiday, Whiting, and virtually any character that glimpses the bigger picture accept this logic. Only Barnes and Woodman maintain a degree of idealism, faith in democracy and non-crony capitalism, and for Barnes this comes only after a long career serving these corporate and national security interests. As Whiting tells him, "Your entire career you've been used and probably never even known what for."

The Context for Understanding *Syriana*

That a Hollywood film critical of American foreign policy might be interpreted as supporting the idea that US oil interests must take precedence over American values (e.g., democracy and capitalism) is remarkable and was the product of three conditions in the early 2000s. First, a taboo surrounding honestly confronting the consequences of domestic oil consumption characterized this period. The last national political leader who did so, President Jimmy Carter, paid an enormous political price. In his 1979 "Crisis of Confidence" speech, Carter attempted to create the political capital to make possible a future of lower oil consumption, as he believed the world's supply was dwindling. Later nicknamed the "malaise speech," many interpreted it as blaming the American people for the energy crisis of the 1970s, and it has gone down in history as one of the most disastrous presidential speeches in the post–World War II era. Thus, since the 1970s, addressing energy consumption has been a politically delicate task.[26]

The second condition that supports the film's suggestion is the idea of peak oil. Popularly understood as the belief that the world is running out of oil, peak oil is the inability to find enough new oil to meet both increasing consumption and declining production in existing fields. In the early 2000s, as oil prices were rising and large multinational companies spent billions on share buybacks instead of new production, peak oil acquired a growing chorus of supporters. Indeed, there have been many moments, beginning in the 1860s, in which arguments that the nation (and later the world) was running out of oil have surfaced. The last two iterations of this story (in the 1970s and the early to mid-2000s) have seen high prices incentivize new exploration and technology, which then significantly expanded oil reserves.[27] But *Syriana* assumes peak oil to be a fact, and one that explains and perhaps justifies the corruption and violence depicted in the film. As Woodman responds to a question about Whiting and his brother, "What are they thinking? They're thinking we're running out. We're running out and 90 percent of what's left is in the Middle East. . . . It's really shaping up as a fight to the death."

This support for the idea of peak oil stands in contrast to a market-centric, neoliberal, small-government vision that still held bipartisan support in the early 2000s. Initiated under President Carter, neoliberal reform remade Washington's relationship to the economy. The third condition that supports *Syriana*'s argument is the uncritical belief that a neoliberal political economy reflects American values.

Before setting off to Beirut to assassinate Nasir, Barnes seeks out his former mentor, Stan Goff (William Hurt), to ask if Lebanon is safe for him to visit (it is not clear how or why Goff would know this). Goff waxes poetic about life after the CIA, declaring, "I like consulting. No, I love it. And I'll say this for it, private business is efficient. There I said it. Fucking cliché." But the film's most forceful and articulate statements in support of laissez-faire economics come from Woodman and Nasir. The prince takes Woodman aside and explains his problem:

> I want to start a petroleum exchange in the Middle East, cut the speculators out of the business. Why are the major oil exchanges in London and New York anyway? I'll put all of our energy up for competitive bidding. I'll run pipe through Iran to Europe, like you

proposed. I'll ship to China. Anything that achieves efficiency and maximized profit. Profit, which I will then use to rebuild my country. . . . Except your president rings my father and says, "I've got unemployment in Texas, Kansas, Washington State." One phone call later, we are stealing out of our social programs to buy overpriced airplanes. . . . I accepted a Chinese bid, the highest bid, and suddenly I'm a terrorist, a godless Communist.

Syriana suggests that if the United States possessed the courage of conviction, it would not need foreign policy that worked hard to guarantee a security of supply. If the US would only allow a world governed by laissez-faire markets, it would not need a military policy designed to project influence in oil-rich regions. The film's view is clear: an imperialistic foreign policy that hinders democratic and neoliberal reform does not privilege our interests over our values; it fundamentally mistakes where our true interests lie. There is an irony in placing the most articulate expression of these values in the mouth of a foreigner—Prince Nasir, the heir to a Gulf kingdom.[28] The idea is that oil is just another commodity; the market will reward those nations willing to sell it and punish those who fail to do so. Of course, the problem with this view is that it ignores the historical lessons of the energy crisis of the 1970s, when major oil-producing countries planned an embargo designed to achieve a political purpose that ultimately brought economic and political chaos to the United States. Because it powers modernity like nothing else, oil is not just another commodity. It has always been, as Daniel Yergin describes it, a "prize."[29] As such, it will always be political, the subject of foreign and domestic policy.[30]

Yet the film is not satisfied with the idea that oil will never be just another commodity. What if further democracy and capitalism do not address the problem of US involvement in the Middle East? It is a deeply pessimistic film that sees beneath the Bush administration's idealism and superficial explanations for the invasion of Iraq. The film's very title, *Syriana*, is a contemptuous reference to a think-tank term by which Western powers could remake the Middle East to their advantage.[31] But without an honest examination of US oil consumption, or how the oil curse damages oil producing countries, *Syriana* envisions no means of escape.

Syriana bravely attempted to explore the conditions that inspired the attacks on 9/11. As the United States grows weary of never-ending military commitments in the region and begins to question the assumptions that launched these efforts, we can expect new critiques to emerge that examine the relationship between oil, terrorism, and American foreign policy in the Middle East.

For all its confusion and complexity, *Syriana* offers a useful, if pop cultural, critique of American foreign policy in the immediate aftermath of 9/11, and a powerful cinematic exposition of how the oil curse shapes the Middle East and our relationship to it.

Notes

1. Stephen Gaghan, dir., *Syriana* (Hollywood, CA: Warner Bros. Entertainment, 2005).
2. Oil was a prominent part of the debate over the wisdom of invading Kuwait in 1991. For a sampling of this debate, see Micah Sifry and Christopher Cerf, eds., *The Gulf War Reader: History, Documents, Opinions* (New York: Random House, 1991).
3. Alan Greenspan, *The Age of Turbulence* (New York: Penguin Press, 2007), 463; Hillary Rodham Clinton, *Hard Choices* (New York: Simon and Schuster, 2014), 520.
4. A sampling of this scholarship includes John M. Blair, *The Control of Oil* (New York: Vintage Books, 1976); Anthony Sampson, *The Seven Sisters: The Great Oil Companies and the World They Made* (New York: Viking Press, 1975); David Painter, *Private Power and Public Policy: Multinational Oil Corporations and U.S. Foreign Policy 1941–1954* (London: I. B. Taurus, 1986); Robert Vitalis, *America's Kingdom: Mythmaking on the Saudi Frontier* (Stanford, CA: Stanford University Press, 2007); Timothy Mitchell, *Carbon Democracy: Political Power in the Age of Oil* (New York: Verso, 2011).
5. Robert Baer, *See No Evil: The True Story of a Ground Soldier in the CIA's War on Terrorism* (New York: Crown Publishers, 2002), xvii.
6. The critic Temenuga Trifonova expresses concern for the decline of narrative causality in films like *Syriana*, wondering if similar conspiracy thrillers have worked to render paranoia our dominant structure of feeling. Temenuga Trifonova, "Agency in the Cinematic Conspiracy Thriller," *SubStance* 41, no. 3 (2012): 125.
7. There is a large and growing scholarship on the oil curse found in political science and economics. This essay draws on only select ideas from this scholarship and is indebted in particular to Terry Lynn Karl, *The Paradox of Plenty: Oil Booms and Petro-States* (Berkeley: University of California Press, 1997).
8. For an example of this confusion, see "Bad News for 'Syriana.' But at Least It Didn't Put Anyone to Sleep," *New York Times*, January 15, 2006, https://www.nytimes .com/2006/01/15/arts/red-carpet-the-awards-season-the-audience-bad-news-for -syriana-but-at.html.
9. Wallace Katz, "Hollywood Rarity: Imperialism Unmasked," *New Labor Forum* 15, no. 3 (Fall 2006): 107.
10. Alissa Quart, "Networked: Don Roos and 'Happy Endings,'" *Film Comment* 41, no. 4 (July–August 2005): 48–5.
11. Harlan Jacobson, "Syriana/Good Night, and Good Luck," *Film Comment* 42, no. 1 (January–February 2006): 42.
12. "About," *Syriana*, Warner Bros., accessed May 5, 2011, http://syrianamovie.warner bros.com/about.html.
13. "Syriana (2005)," IMDb, accessed December 22, 2019, https://www.imdb.com/title /tt0365737.
14. Participant has produced more than one hundred feature films and documentaries that have earned seventy-nine Academy Award nominations with eighteen wins.

See "About Us," Participant, accessed December 22, 2019, https://participant.com/about-us.

15. Since the late 1980s, the revenue generated by international audiences has risen sharply, which has made cinema that is critical of American foreign policy possible. This stands in stark contrast with the television of that era. See Larry May, "Teaching American Politics and Global Hollywood in the Age of 9/11," *OAH Magazine of History* 25, no. 3 (July 2011): 45–46.

16. Peter Bradshaw, "Syriana," *Guardian*, March 3, 2006, https://www.theguardian.com/culture/2006/mar/03/1; Charles Krauthammer, "Oscars for Osama," *Washington Post*, March 3, 2006, https://www.washingtonpost.com/wp-dyn/content/article/2006/03/02/AR2006030201209.html.

17. Rahul Hamid, "Review," *Cineaste* 31, no. 2 (Spring 2006): 53.

18. Caroline Levine, "Narrative Networked: Bleak House and the Affordances of Form," in "Theories of the Novel Now, Part II," special issue, *Novel: A Forum on Fiction* 42, no. 3 (Fall 2009): 520; on the decline of narrative in war films post-9/11, see Garrett Stewart, "Digital Fatigue: Imagining War in Recent American Film, *Film Quarterly* 62, no. 4 (Summer 2009): 45–55.

19. Responding to low oil prices, a large wave of mergers and acquisitions swept the international oil industry in the late 1990s and early 2000s, including British Petroleum and Amoco, British Petroleum and Atlantic Richfield, Petrofina and Elf, Conoco and Phillips, Chevron and Texaco, and Exxon and Mobil.

20. Michael Ross, "Does Oil Hinder Democracy?" *World Politics* 53, no. 3 (April 2001): 325–61.

21. Max Weber characterized a monopoly on the use of force as an essential component of a state. Max Weber, *Politics as a Vocation* (Munich: Munich University, 1918).

22. This was clearly modeled after the Committee for the Liberation of Iraq (CLI), an organization that suddenly appeared in 2002 comprised of prominent politicians, academics, and retired military officers. The CLI argued in favor of the invasion of Iraq and then quietly disbanded.

23. On Western oil companies' efforts to gain access to oil fields in Kazakhstan and Azerbaijan, see Steve Levine, *The Oil and the Glory: The Pursuit of Empire and Fortune on the Caspian* (New York: Random House, 2007).

24. This SEC requirement was twice struck down, first by a federal court in 2013 and then by the Senate in 2017 under the Congressional Review Act. The SEC announced a third version of the rule in December 2019. Dylan Tokar, "SEC's Latest Extractive Industry Rule Seeks to Lighten Compliance Burden," *Wall Street Journal*, December 19, 2019, https://www.wsj.com/articles/secs-latest-extractive-industry-rule-seeks-to-lighten-compliance-burden-11576801736.

25. This idea was likely inspired by Unocal's effort to build an oil and natural gas pipeline to take resources from Turkmenistan through Afghanistan and Pakistan to India and the Arabian Sea. Oil executives feted members of the Taliban in Houston in the late 1990s. See Steve Coll, *Ghost Wars: The Secret History of the CIA, Afghanistan, and Bin Laden, from the Soviet Invasion to Sept. 10, 2001* (New York: Penguin, 2004), 307. The documentary filmmaker Michael Moore advanced the idea that this pipeline was the real reason for the US invasion of Afghanistan in 2002. Michael Moore, dir., *Fahrenheit 9/11* (New York: Dog Eat Dog Films, 2004).

26. See Kevin Mattson, *"What the Heck Are You Up To, Mr. President?": Jimmy Carter, America's "Malaise," and the Speech That Should Have Changed the Country* (London:

Bloomsbury, 2009); Daniel Horowitz, *Jimmy Carter and the Energy Crisis of the 1970s: The "Crisis of Confidence" Speech of July 15, 1979* (New York: Bedford/St. Martin, 2004).

27. See Tyler Priest, "Hubbert's Peak: The Great Debate over the End of Oil," *Historical Studies in the Natural Sciences* 44, no. 1 (February 2014): 37–79.

28. On the depiction of Arabs in *Syriana*, see Khadija Fritsch-El Alaoui, "Review: Teaching the Meter of the Impossible in a Classroom: On Liberal Hollywood's Mission Impossible," *Transformations: The Journal of Inclusive Scholarship and Pedagogy* 20, no. 2 (Fall 2009–Winter 2010): 129–37.

29. See Daniel Yergin, *The Prize: The Epic Quest for Oil, Money, and Power* (New York: Free Press, 1991).

30. On the embargo initiated by OAPEC in 1973, see Fiona Venn, *The Oil Crisis* (London: Pearson, 2002); on some of the economic and political consequences, see Meg Jacobs, *Panic at the Pump: The Energy Crisis and the Transformation of American Politics in the 1970s* (New York: Hill and Wang, 2016).

31. The term *Syriana* alludes to the idea that the Middle East is comprised of countries with false national borders drawn by Western powers after World War I, which therefore could be redrawn. Robert Siegel, "Ex-CIA Agent Robert Baer, Inspiration for 'Syriana,'" *All Things Considered*, NPR, December 6, 2005, https://www.npr.org/templates/story/story.php?storyId=5041385.

Chapter 23

Hoover Dam in Hollywood: Energy Anxiety in *Superman* (1978), *Transformers* (2007), and *San Andreas* (2015)

Daniel Macfarlane

Hoover Dam is an iconic American structure, one that has been portrayed across visual media including numerous Hollywood features running the gamut from the artistic to the popcorn thriller to the slapstick. Regardless of the filmic genre, a common element of Hollywood representations of Hoover Dam is its potential failure. For example, in the 1990s, two comedic films released one year apart, *Beavis and Butt-Head Do America* (1996) and National Lampoon's *Vegas Vacation* (1997), employ the scenario of Hoover Dam breaking for laughs. In the former, an animated feature-length film based on the MTV television series, the slacker duo wander into an unoccupied control room at the dam. Pushing different buttons, they open the spillways, causing the generating station to malfunction and the reservoir to flood downstream. Las Vegas loses power as a result. In *Vegas Vacation*, bumbling everyman Clark Griswold gets separated from his family during a tour of Hoover Dam. Seeing a leak, he picks at rock walls in the bowels of the dam. This causes more leaks, which Clark tries to plug with gum. Soon after, he falls and swings onto the downstream face of the dam, where he clings precariously before climbing back up.[1]

Even these types of depictions—juvenile comedies made at the end of the twentieth century—suggest uncertainty about Hoover Dam, tapping into concerns about energy supplies that have been a persistent feature of American politics and society since the 1970s. While energy anxieties are often linked to fossil fuels and nuclear power, this essay explores hydroelectricity. More specifically, I consider representations of the most recognizable hydropower structure in the world, Hoover Dam, through the lens of Hollywood films. Focusing on three big-budget blockbuster movies released since the late 1970s—*Superman* (1978), *Transformers* (2007), and *San Andreas* (2015)—I argue that these cinematic portrayals of Hoover Dam reveal conflicted feelings about American reliance on large-scale energy systems, technology, and power over nature.[2]

In the three films I consider, the titular subjects—Superman, Transformers, and the San Andreas Fault—are all powered by energy forms that humanity doesn't fully possess or understand but that could potentially be harnessed for the greater good. The filmic juxtaposition of these subjects with Hoover Dam suggests that the same is true of the dam itself. Out of the three films, two (*Superman* and *San Andreas*) portray Hoover Dam breaking, and while the dam is not wrecked in *Transformers*, it too conveys doubts about large energy infrastructures. Thus, even though Hoover Dam is emblematic of American ingenuity, modernism, and stability, these three films indicate in different ways that this famous piece of the built environment is potentially fragile or unpredictable, and that its capriciousness can have disastrous consequences for humanity.

Projecting Hoover Dam

Hoover Dam (initially named the Boulder Dam) was built in the 1930s by the federal Bureau of Reclamation. When it first opened, the dam was representative of the brave new world enabled by mass electrification—a key ingredient for progress and high living standards—and was one of the first modern American efforts to earn the moniker *mega project*. Seventy stories high, the curving concrete dam holds back Lake Mead, the country's largest reservoir. As Anthony Arrigo explores in *Imaging Hoover Dam*, it is a visually iconic structure.[3] Its prominence stems from a variety of factors, including its graceful arch-gravity design, position astride the Colorado River, importance to the wider region, and role as initiator of the big dam era. Though Hoover Dam was actually already somewhat small in dam terms by the 1950s, its placement in a narrow gorge enhances its vertical lines when viewed through a camera, making it appear bigger on screen than other dams that are actually much taller and wider. Such aesthetic qualities have helped Hoover Dam retain its status as the continent's most recognizable water impoundment structure.

Hoover Dam hosts about seven million visitors annually, making it the second most popular hydropower site to visit in North America, far behind Niagara Falls and its thirty million visitors a year (granted, most visitors to Niagara Falls aren't there primarily for its hydropower features). According to Donald C. Jackson's study of dams on postcards, power stations were popular tourist attractions in North America throughout the first two-thirds of the twentieth century.[4] As part of a growing appreciation for *hydro tourism,* as I've previously termed it, governments were eager to show off the power of the state, literally and metaphorically.[5] Hydro tourism can be considered a type of industrial tourism, which attracts people to massive engineering projects such as bridges and buildings, but also a type of nature or landscape tourism. Hydropower represented engineering progress that heralded perceived cultural connections to specific natural features and landscapes, while simultaneously reshaping them to provide a heroic future. Tourists came to see sublime nature, but they equally came to see it controlled by sublime technology.[6] For instance, guided tours of the Niagara generating stations became a regular feature of "doing" Niagara Falls—a practice that was later incorporated at Hoover Dam. As governments realized that people were intrigued by the construction phase of hydropower projects, they began to design amenities, infrastructure, and services precisely to enable tourists to visit power stations during and after construction.

The public's familiarity with Hoover Dam as an iconic structure and landmark that many have visited themselves enhances its utility as a symbol in film. Out of all Hollywood representations of hydropower, it seems that Hoover is the dam most commonly featured. Post–World War II cinematic representations of Hoover Dam are spread across genres, chiefly action-adventure and science-fiction films, but also in romantic and slapstick comedies (see table 23.1 for a list of films that portray Hoover Dam). That said, when Hoover Dam appears on the silver screen, it is not in a major supporting or starring role in the same vein as, say, the Los Angeles water infrastructure in *Chinatown* (1974) or Tennessee Valley Authority dams in *Wild River* (1960) (see Donald C. Jackson's chapter in this volume). In these limited or cameo roles, which generally involve brief screen time, Hoover Dam is often used for pragmatic reasons: it is an easily recognizable structure close to Las Vegas as well as major earthquake fault lines. For an audience, it serves as comprehensible shorthand for the Southwest, Colorado River basin, Grand Canyon, and greater Las Vegas area. Several of the films listed in table 23.1 are comedies that satirize or parody Hoover Dam, but the humor is only effective if the dam and the consequences of its potential destruction are recognizable tropes.

Table 23.1. Post-1945 Films Featuring Hoover Dam

The Amazing Colossal Man (1957)

Superman (1978)

Lost in America (1985)

Universal Soldier (1992)

Beavis and Butt-Head Do America (1996)

Fools Rush In (1997)

Vegas Vacation (1997)

Transformers (2007)

San Andreas (2015)

Superman, *Transformers*, and *San Andreas* have several key features in common: as prominent big-budget action-adventure films with large box office takes, they each had a wide viewership; they all include relatively lengthy portrayals of Hoover Dam; and their plots foreground themes of energy, modernity, and technology.[7] In the following sections, I will consider each of these films on their own in the order in which they were released, focusing on their respective uses of Hoover Dam. I will then analyze what these films collectively connote about American dams, abundance, and power.

Superman

Superman, based on the DC comic book character and starring Christopher Reeve, is a notable film in the modern cinematic canon. With a budget of $55 million, it was the most expensive film ever made up until that point, and its $300 million box office haul made it the second-highest-grossing film of 1978. What attracts our attention here takes place late in the film. Jimmy Olsen and Lois Lane, two *Daily Planet* colleagues of Clark Kent, Superman's mild-mannered alter ego, are on assignment at Hoover Dam when a rocket commandeered by villain Lex Luthor strikes the San Andreas Fault. Luthor's plan is to knock the California coastline into the ocean, using the fault as the perforation point and leaving the land he owns on the east side of the fault as the valuable new coastline. The ensuing earthquake causes holes and cracks to form in Hoover Dam, on which Jimmy is standing with his trademark camera. As water begins to push through, Superman arrives at the nearby electric switchyard to shut off the juice and then rescues Jimmy just before the dam collapses. Earlier, Hoover Dam had been visually introduced with a flyover shot, while during its destruction we are treated to intercutting views of the dam breaking from several angles. According to a documentary on the making of *Superman*, the filmmakers created a 1:50 scale model of Hoover Dam; they then ran the camera at a high speed while the miniature ruptured, allowing them to slow down the action and make it look more realistic.[8]

On screen, water pulses down the gorge after the breach. The view switches from wide-angle shots to a camera placed right at the bottom of the gorge, offering a low-angle, head-on perspective of the surging water that makes the audience feel like they are part of the deluge. Superman flies downstream and creates a rock dam to stop the water before it reaches a canyon community. Granted, this part makes little sense since there would be far more water released than is portrayed, and those looking for logic will find little solace in the subsequent dramatic finale. Superman, overcome with grief at Lois's death—the car she was driving had been swallowed by an aftershock—flies into space to reverse the earth's rotation. This makes time go backward so that Superman can prevent Lois's demise, though the sequence of events here is still unclear. The fault lines zip back up, Hoover Dam returns to an intact state, and Lois's car never gets crushed. Superman takes Lex Luthor and his henchman to jail. John Williams's classic score kicks in, Superman flies off, and the movie ends.

Transformers

Michael Bay's *Transformers* was the fifth-highest-grossing release of 2007. The film dedicates more screen time to Hoover Dam than the other two, centering it within a substantial plot line. An alien cube, the AllSpark, was discovered by humans in 1913. It has a kind of powerful energy or radiation that can turn any type of human technology or machine into a shape-shifting, sentient robot—i.e., a Transformer. When Megatron, leader of the Decepticons, an evil group of Transformers, was later found frozen in the Arctic, President Hoover had the Hoover Dam built around both so that the US government could secretly study them (the dam's thick cement walls prevented other Transformers from detecting them). Fast-forward to the present, and the Decepticons have discovered the location of the AllSpark. They want to use it to extract the earth's resources, obliterating humanity and taking over the universe in the process. The Autobots, a benevolent race of Transformers, decide to thwart them.

This genesis of Hoover Dam isn't revealed until the latter half of the movie. The viewer is first introduced to the dam from the perspective of a helicopter flying over the mountains, after which a massive shoot-out ensues between the warring robot factions. The action starts on top of the dam and then moves to the inside, interspersed with dramatic panning shots of the structure from above and below to establish its enormity. The human protagonists are apprised of the AllSpark's radioactive energy contained inside the dam—energy so powerful that any energy form on earth pales in comparison. The Decepticons extinguish Hoover Dam's electricity and communications, shutting down the cryostasis unit that has kept Megatron frozen. Some of the good guys flee the dam with the AllSpark, and the action shifts elsewhere for an extended battle that eventually brings the movie to its conclusion.

Along the way, the audience learns more about how Hoover Dam was built to try to hide and harness a virtually infinite source of power. It turns out that Megatron and the AllSpark are the "source of the modern age"; reverse-engineering from both of them (deep inside Hoover Dam) led Americans to develop microchips, lasers, cars, space flight, and so on. The dam was thus integral to processes that revolutionized society's living standards through new modes of energy and technology. In this way, the filmmakers unequivocally link Hoover Dam with modern technology, abundance, and American exceptionalism. However, as I'll discuss below, they present these advances as double-edged swords.

San Andreas

San Andreas was a bit of a box office and critical flop; it was the twentieth-highest-grossing film of 2015, though that does not constitute a strong performance considering that it cost over $100 million to make. The film's main conceit is that the eponymous West Coast fault is causing massive earthquakes, and the protagonist, a rescue pilot played by Dwayne "The Rock" Johnson, must save his family.[9] The first big action sequence, which takes advantage of advances in computer-generated imagery (CGI) special effects, occurs at Hoover Dam. About fifteen minutes into the film, the viewer is treated to a sweeping fly-over shot with an on-screen subtitle announcing the location.

On top of the dam, prominent Caltech seismologist Dr. Lawrence Hayes, played by the affable Paul Giamatti, communicates with his colleague Dr. Kim Park (Will Yun Lee) inside the dam. They are there testing Hayes's predictive earthquake theories after sensing a series of mini-quakes in the vicinity. Suddenly, a 7.1 magnitude earthquake hits and the dam starts to rupture. Ominous music, shaky camerawork, and loads of special effects magnify the drama. Park manages to escape the bowels of the dam and save a little girl in the process, but just before getting to safety, he is washed away as the dam catastrophically collapses. Hayes is left staring in disbelief from the dam footings as water and rubble cascade downstream, an extended close-up displaying the shocked and bewildered look on his face, echoed by the soundtrack's disconcerting chords. American power and might, encapsulated in this hydraulic structure, have seemingly crumbled like so many matchsticks. The implication is that if Hoover Dam is vulnerable, the fragile structures in cities close to the San Andreas Fault won't stand a chance. Indeed, the focus shifts to San Francisco, where a 9.6 magnitude quake strikes, causing a tsunami. The latter half of the movie follows a fairly predictable story arc that need not concern us here.

San Andreas's filmic wrecking of Hoover Dam seizes upon a recognizable trope. If a screenwriter or producer creating a movie about the San Andreas Fault needs some built infrastructure to crumble, the Hoover Dam is an obvious choice (as is the Golden Gate Bridge, also affected by earthquakes in this movie). Nevertheless, the fact that Hoover Dam is one of the first structures to be destroyed in the film speaks to the perceived fragility of America's energy infrastructure and suggests that rather than controlling nature, Hoover Dam is still subject to its fury. The technological marvel that once held such promise has actually increased risk and made humanity more vulnerable. Although the protagonists in *San Andreas* ultimately survive, together and happy, San Francisco is left in ruins, now an isolated island.

Energy Anxiety

The early Cold War was the era of big dam building in North America. After Franklin D. Roosevelt and Harry Truman expanded public power, Dwight D. Eisenhower sought to curb and contain the government's role. Eisenhower's "partnership policy" involved cooperation between the federal government, states, other subfederal agencies, and private enterprise. There was a great deal of congressional debate in the 1950s about public versus private power developments, such as those at the St. Lawrence River, Niagara Falls, and Hells Canyon.[10] Hoover Dam offered an example of a public/private compromise.[11]

In the first decades of the Cold War, dams not only projected the strength, scientific ingenuity, and technological capabilities of capitalist and democratic North American society, but also represented the high standard of living on the continent—itself a major weapon in the Cold War. Of course, the hydropower created by dams also directly contributed to the production of armaments. Richard P. Tucker avers that "much of the world's dammed rivers reflect Cold War zones of competition, and the concentration of fiscal and industrial resources at many dam sites in remote locations cannot be fully explained outside the framework of Cold War rivalries."[12] The Soviets were equally busy building massive hydroelectric installations and rerouting water systems, such as the Volga River and Aral Sea, not to mention helping with Egypt's Aswan High Dam on the Nile River. Other nations, such as China and India, were also damming large rivers. The hubristic drive to dominate nature was thus apparent across communist, capitalist, and nonaligned nations.

However, by the time *Superman* was released in 1978, the era of big dam building in the US was over. Indeed, by *Transformers* and *San Andreas*, the country was starting to remove dams. Dams blocked the passage of spawning fish, such as salmon, which increasingly became a reason for their removal. There were concerns about other ecological impacts of dammed rivers, as well—reservations that have come into clearer focus in recent years. A number of studies, as well as the 2014 film *DamNation*, have pointed out that hydroelectricity is not nearly as environmentally benign as many claim. Scientists have shown that hydropower reservoirs slowly emit methane, a greenhouse gas much more potent than carbon dioxide, from the decomposing plants and trees submerged under the water. Given this data, perhaps it should no longer even be considered a "green" or environmentally friendly form of energy production.[13]

By the 1970s, dam failures were also on the public's radar. The Johnstown and Saint Frances dams, both of which predated Hoover Dam, were the most notorious, but the list of American dam failures that led to fatalities during that decade includes Teton Dam, Canyon Lake Dam, Buffalo Creek Dam, and the Kelly Barnes Dam. Dam ruptures called American energy abundance into question. The emergence of this anxiety coincided with shifting ideas about nature, energy security, large technological systems, and the role of technocrats in American society. This was part and parcel of the burgeoning environmental movement of the 1960s and 1970s, marked by the publication of Rachel Carson's *Silent Spring* (1962), the Santa Barbara oil spill, the purported death of Lake Erie, recurring fires on the Cuyahoga River, the first Earth Day, the creation of the US Environmental Protection Agency (EPA), and the passage of the Wilderness Act, Wild and Scenic Rivers Act, National Environmental Policy Act, and other clean air and water acts.

Yet even before 1970, Americans had begun to reconsider the wisdom of remaking charismatic waterscapes for hydroelectricity. In fact, public opposition halted or significantly modified development at Niagara Falls, the Grand Canyon, Snake River, Echo Park, and Storm King Mountain. Views of the engineering profession also began to shift around the mid-1960s, with technology taking on "ambiguous and ultimately sinister connotations in American thought and culture."[14] Many people were manifestly concerned about technology as it pertained to chemical production and nuclear weapons, and by the 1970s some expressed apprehension about large-scale technological solutions that altered nature. This unease was especially apparent in the energy crises of the 1970s, which came about due to a number of coalescing factors: oil insecurity, natural gas shortages, concerns about nuclear power, and electricity utility problems.[15] This all took place within the context of the fracturing of the Cold War political consensus that had prevailed in the United States since the end of World War II, furthered by the Watergate scandal. The result was, as President Jimmy Carter said in 1979, a crisis of American confidence.

Concerns about the loss of national self-assurance were apparent in contemporary pop culture. Max Haiven argues that pre–World War II cinematic portrayals of megadams tend to be celebratory and triumphalist, while post-1945 representations "are understood as part of an industrial modernity gone terribly wrong" and "betray deep anxieties about the world that has created megadams and that has been shaped in their shadow."[16] These generalizations are often the case with Hoover Dam, but not always. For starters, pre-1945 portrayals of dams are not uniformly positive about hydropower. We shouldn't overlook the fact that a central plotline in the well-known 1939 film *Mr. Smith Goes to Washington* involved corrupt politicians advocating for a pork-barrel dam project.[17] This certainly didn't cast the power dam in a positive light. There are also films produced after 1945 in which Hoover Dam is used to project power and stability, such as in the 1997 movie *Fools Rush In*.[18]

Moreover, Hoover Dam isn't just any megadam, but one with very ascribed associations. Hoover Dam is a structure that can easily be mobilized to create heightened drama, particularly considering how recognizable it is for American audiences. One motivation for using Hoover is its eye-catching setting that allows for cinematographic excess—e.g., panning vertical shots, aerial flybys, low-angle shots from downstream, swirling views from the crest—to situate the dam on screen. In turn, these techniques enhance the magnitude of the dam. All three films discussed in this essay are big-budget blockbusters falling within the action-adventure and/or science-fiction genres. Consequently, they all feature the prominent use of special effects. *Superman*'s special effects may seem basic, even campy, by today's standards, but they were groundbreaking (pun intended) in the late 1970s. Moreover, both *Transformers* and *San Andreas* were at their respective vanguards of digital special effects; indeed, they are the type of movies in which the opportunity to show off such special effects often drives plot points. As a result, Hoover Dam becomes even more grandiose and memorable for the average moviegoer.

Because of Hoover Dam's status as the aesthetic epitome of the dam sublime, and dams as modern temples more generally, it is perfect for scenes with high tension. Even though Hoover Dam is on screen for just a few minutes in both *Superman* and *San Andreas*, and only slightly longer in *Transformers*, it does a lot of metaphorical work in that short span. Hoover Dam generates drama because of the very nature of dams as contingent infrastructure that, if ruptured, causes considerable peril not only for those on site, but also large swaths of people in the flood path as well as those further afield who will lose power or drinking water. Collapse, or the threat of it, invokes the inverse of technological accomplishment, controllable nature, and energy abundance.

By 1978, when *Superman* was released, confidence in the technological sublime and high modernist faith were waning in the United States, as was Cold War optimism.[19] Superman's inability to stop Lex Luthor can be read as symbolic of the decline of American power, especially in the wake of the oil crises of the 1970s. Conversely, Superman spinning the earth back in time represents a yearning for the days of American ascendance.[20] In the end, the day—and the dam—are saved by that vital American characteristic: heroic, rugged individualism. Superman's physical abilities signify an unparalleled technology and new power source, one that is altruistic and benevolent, and that can make up for the weaknesses and limits of America's existing energy regime.

Both the Transformers and Superman are superheroes, deriving their abilities from energy sources that humanity doesn't understand or command. Ultimately, however, *Transformers* is apprehensive about industrial modernity and American energy. The filmmakers dangle the Promethean possibility that the AllSpark's energy can be harnessed for the betterment of humankind. However, they also associate unlimited energy, represented by the AllSpark, with evil and hubris; we learn that Transformer society fractured in the deep past because of the Decepticons' imperialist designs for this cube, which they now aim to turn against humanity. In the film's climax, human Sam Witwicky (Shia LaBeouf) uses the AllSpark to defeat Megatron, with the knowledge that doing so will destroy the AllSpark as well. Thus, the take-home message of *Transformers* is conflicted: new technologies and energy sources, like the AllSpark and Hoover Dam, can produce tremendous material advances; the probability of humanity being corrupted by them, however, likely outweighs the potential benefits.

San Andreas and *Superman* also offer conflicted portrayals of Hoover Dam. On the one hand, the dam symbolizes American power; on the other, it—and American energy systems more broadly—are vulnerable and potentially dangerous. As these three films demonstrate, this ambiguity has come to characterize Hoover Dam's use as a cinematic trope, transmitting a sense of discomfort and anxiety about large-scale energy systems, nature, and the direction of the nation itself.

Notes

1. Mike Judge, dir., *Beavis and Butt-Head Do America* (Los Angeles: Paramount, 1996); Stephen Kessler, dir., *Vegas Vacation* (Hollywood, CA: Warner Bros., 1997).

2. I utilize a semiotics approach in this essay. *Semiotics* is a general term that includes many specific approaches to the study of culture *as* language, rather than *through* language. In this case, I follow James Monaco in viewing film as a language itself, one that can be understood by using the codes of cinema and society, and that communicates in essentially two ways: denotatively and connotatively. As Monaco explains, *denotative* refers to something that "is what it is"—something easily recognizable to viewers—while *connotative* refers to deeper meanings that go beyond the denotative. James Monaco, *How to Read a Film: Movies, Media, Multimedia*, 3rd ed. (New York: Oxford University Press, 2000). I have previously employed semiotics to look at how Adolf Hitler was portrayed in post-1945 films and the ways these representations shaped public historiography: Daniel Macfarlane, "Projecting Hitler: Representations of Adolf Hitler in English-Language Film, 1968–1990" (MA thesis, University of Saskatchewan, 2004).

3. Anthony Arrigo, *Imaging Hoover Dam: The Making of a Cultural Icon* (Reno: University of Nevada Press, 2014).

4. Donald C. Jackson, *Pastoral and Monumental: Dams, Postcards, and the American Landscape* (Pittsburgh: University of Pittsburgh Press, 2013).

5. On *hydro tourism* see Daniel Macfarlane, "Fluid Meanings: Hydro Tourism and the St. Lawrence and Niagara Megaprojects," *Histoire Sociale/Social History* 49, no. 99 (June 2016): 327–46.

6. David Nye, *American Technological Sublime* (Cambridge, MA: MIT Press, 1996). This book even features Hoover Dam on the cover.

7. Richard Donner, dir., *Superman* (Hollywood, CA: Warner Bros., 1978); Michael Bay, dir., *Transformers* (Los Angeles: Paramount, 2007); Brad Peyton, dir., *San Andreas* (Hollywood, CA: Warner Bros., 2015).

8. "Superman: The Movie | The Magic behind the Cape," Warner Bros. Entertainment, November 19, 2012, YouTube video, 23:42, https://www.youtube.com/watch?v=tNFAFBhh1cU; Gary Bettinson, *Superman: The Movie—the 40th Anniversary Interviews* (Chicago: Intellect, 2018).

9. *San Andreas* could be considered an extension of a group of natural disaster films that engage concerns about planetary systems and climate change, such as *The Day after Tomorrow* (2004) and *2012* (2009).

10. Daniel Macfarlane, *Fixing Niagara Falls: Environment, Energy, and Engineers at the World's Most Famous Waterfall* (Vancouver: UBC Press, 2020).

11. Sarah Elkind, *How Local Politics Shape Federal Policy: Business, Power and the Environment in Twentieth-Century Los Angeles* (Chapel Hill: University of North Carolina Press, 2011), chap. 4.

12. Richard P. Tucker, "Containing Communism by Impounding Rivers: American Strategic Interests and the Global Spread of High Dams in the Early Cold War," in *Environmental Histories of the Cold War*, ed. J. R. McNeill and Corinna R. Unger (New York: Cambridge University Press, 2010), 139.

13. One study estimates that hydroelectric dams emit a billion tonnes of greenhouse gases a year. Bridget R. Deemer et al., "Greenhouse Gas Emissions from Reservoir Water Surfaces: A New Global Synthesis," *BioScience* 66, no. 11 (November 2016):

949–64; Travis Rummel and Ben Knight, dirs., *DamNation* (New York: Patagonia, 2014).

14. Matthew Wisnioski, *Engineers for Change: Competing Visions of Technology in 1960s America* (Cambridge, MA: MIT Press, 2012), 3.

15. Robert Lifset, ed., *American Energy Policy in the 1970s* (Norman: University of Oklahoma Press, 2014); Meg Jacobs, *Panic at the Pump: The Energy Crisis and the Transformation of American Politics in the 1970s* (New York: Hill and Wang, 2016).

16. Max Haiven "The Dammed of the Earth: Reading the Dam for the Flows of Globalization," in *Thinking with Water*, ed. Cecilia Chen, Janine MacLeod, and Astrida Neimanis (Montreal and Kingston: McGill-Queens University Press, 2013), 221, 224.

17. Frank Capra, dir., *Mr. Smith Goes to Washington* (Culver City, CA: Columbia, 1939).

18. Hoover Dam metaphorically plays a stabilizing role in *Fools Rush In* and is portrayed in a positive light, with an engagement and a birth both taking place there. In terms of total screen time, this 1997 movie has one of the most extended uses of Hoover Dam in postwar Hollywood. Andy Tennant, dir., *Fools Rush In* (Culver City, CA: Columbia, 1997).

19. James C. Scott, *Seeing Like a State: How Certain Schemes to Improve the Human Condition Have Failed* (New Haven, CT: Yale University Press, 1998); Nye, *American Technological Sublime*.

20. Haiven, "Dammed of the Earth," 224.

Acknowledgments

This book is the product of a post-panel dinner discussion at the American Society for Environmental History's 2018 Meeting in Riverside, California. It benefited from audiences at the following two *American Energy Cinema* panel sessions at ASEH in 2019. The editors are grateful for the audience comments and discussions at those conferences. We also thank editor Derek Krissoff at West Virginia University Press and Brian C. Black, editor of the press's series on energy, for approving the project and believing in its success. We also thank Alix Genter for her excellent copyediting work on the volume. Most significantly, the editors thank the authors of the essays in this volume. Their poignant and valuable thoughts made the dream of this book possible.

Robert: I would like to thank Marcia Chatelain for suggesting I should teach a cinema course in the summer, and I would like to thank all the students of Petroleum Cinema who helped shape my thinking about the relationship between Hollywood and oil. I would like to thank Raechel Lutz and Sarah Stanford-McIntyre for the idea of doing this book as an edited volume and then putting in the hard work of making it a reality. Finally, I would like to thank Olena, the love of my life, for her support and companionship.

Raechel: Many people helped me work on this book. Participants at "Energy and the Left" at New York University in March of 2019 offered valuable insights on an early draft. Robert Lifset and Sarah Stanford-McIntyre not only were cooperative and supportive coeditors but are now also friends. My parents, Greig and Kathy Lutz, have helped to instill in me the confidence and perseverance to do difficult things. My love and gratitude to Tom for all he contributes to the fulfilling and joyful life we share.

Sarah: I am grateful to Raechel Lutz for inviting me to participate in the 2018 ASEH panel that generated this project, and I would like to thank both Raechel Lutz and Robert Lifset for their camaraderie, intellectual rigor, and hard work throughout this process. My thoughts on midcentury Westerns and American culture were shaped by a decade of conversations in classrooms and libraries at William & Mary, the University of Wyoming, and the University of Colorado. My thanks to these students and colleagues. My love to John and to Nora, who make all this worth it.

Contributors

James R. Allison III is an associate professor of history at Christopher Newport University and was once an energy and environmental attorney. His scholarship focuses on the interplay of energy development and rural and indigenous communities and landscapes. His 2015 book *Sovereignty for Survival: American Energy Development and Indian Self-Determination* (Yale University Press) explored the impacts of energy development on American Indian communities and explained how tribal governments leveraged their energy resources to expand tribal sovereignty. Currently, his research focuses on the historical construction of energy infrastructure that brought Appalachian coal through eastern ports and on to global markets.

Brian C. Black is a distinguished professor of environmental studies and history at Penn State Altoona, where he also currently serves as head of the Division of Arts and Humanities. He is the author or editor of several books, including *Petrolia: The Landscape of America's First Oil Boom*, *Crude Reality: Petroleum in World History*, and *Gettysburg Contested: 150 Years of Preserving America's Most Cherished Landscape*. Black's articles have appeared in the *Journal of American History*, *Environmental History*, *USA Today*, and the *New York Times*. He is also the founding editor of the Energy and Society book series with West Virginia University Press.

Mark Boxell is a PhD candidate in history at the University of Oklahoma. His research focuses on environmental history, the history of race and settler colonialism, and the American West. His dissertation is tentatively titled "Red Soil, White Oil: Race, Environment, and the Birth of Petroleum Dependency, 1890–1940."

Kate Brown is the Thomas M. Siebel Distinguished Professor in the History of Science at the Massachusetts Institute of Technology. She is the author of several prize-winning histories, including *Plutopia: Nuclear Families, Atomic*

Cities, and the Great Soviet and American Plutonium Disasters (Oxford, 2013). Her latest book, *Manual for Survival: A Chernobyl Guide to the Future* (Norton, 2019), which has been translated into nine languages, was a finalist for the 2020 National Book Critics Circle Award, the Pushkin House Award, and the Ryszard Kapuściński Award for Literary Reportage.

Julie A. Cohn is a research historian in the Center for Public History at the University of Houston. Her work focuses on energy infrastructures, environmental history, technological change, and the relationships between government, business, and the public. Cohn's recently published book, *The Grid: Biography of an American Technology*, examines the history of electrification in North America, and especially the story of how and why power companies chose to interconnect. Cohn holds a PhD in history from the University of Houston and both a BA and an MA in anthropology from Stanford University.

Christopher R. W. Dietrich is an associate professor of history and director of American studies at Fordham University. He is the author of *Oil Revolution* and editor of *Wiley-Blackwell's Companion to the History of U.S. Foreign Relations: Colonial Era to the Present*.

Alexander Finkelstein is a doctoral candidate at the University of Oklahoma. His research focuses on the environmental history of infrastructure and state development in modern American history. Alex received his BA from the University of Southern California and his MA from the University of Oklahoma.

Donald C. Jackson is the Cornelia F. Hugel Professor of History at Lafayette College in Easton, Pennsylvania. He is the author of books on the history of dams and hydroelectricity, including *Building the Ultimate Dam: John S. Eastwood and the Control of Water in the West* (1995) and, with David P. Billington, *Big Dams of the New Deal Era: A Confluence of Engineering and Politics* (2006). In addition, his book *Pastoral and Monumental: Dams, Postcards, and the American Landscape* (2013) explores the complex relationship between water control imagery and American culture.

Robert Lifset is the Donald Keith Jones Associate Professor of History in the Honors College at the University of Oklahoma, where his work examines energy and environmental history with a focus on the United States. Lifset is the author of the award-winning *Power on the Hudson: Storm King Mountain and the Emergence of Modern American Environmentalism* and the editor of

American Energy Policy in the 1970s. His work has appeared in the *Journal of American History, Environmental History, Historical Social Research, Reviews in American History*, and the *Hudson River Valley Review*. He is currently researching and writing a history of the energy crisis of the 1970s.

Raechel Lutz is an environmental historian who teaches high school students at the Wardlaw + Hartridge School in New Jersey. Her scholarly work investigates the intersections of nature, energy, technology, and visual culture. In addition to co-editing *American Energy Cinema*, Lutz is writing *The Good Polluter*, which investigates the environmental history of ExxonMobil's oil refineries. The project won the Alfred E. Driscoll Award from the New Jersey Historical Commission in 2018. She is also working on another edited volume titled *New Jersey's Natures*, which analyzes New Jersey's environmental history. *Environmental History, Technology and Culture, Environmental History Now*, and *Contingent Magazine* feature her writing. To learn more, visit www.raechellutz. com.

Daniel Macfarlane is an associate professor in Western Michigan University's Institute of the Environment and Sustainability. He is also a senior fellow at the Bill Graham Center for Contemporary International History at the University of Toronto and the president of the International Water History Association. His research examines water and energy, and he is the author or co-editor of books on Niagara Falls, the St. Lawrence Seaway, US-Canada border waters, and the International Joint Commission. He has previously published on representations of history in popular culture and film.

Caroline Peyton is an instructor at the University of Memphis. She specializes in environmental history, history of technology, and the history of the American South. Her research interests include the South's nuclear history and environmental risk. Her published articles include "Kentucky's Atomic Graveyard: Maxey Flats and Environmental Inequity in Rural America" in the *Register of the Kentucky Historical Society* (2017).

Tyler Priest is an associate professor of history at the University of Iowa. He is a widely published scholar of energy and environmental history, with expertise in the history of offshore oil. He is the author of *The Offshore Imperative: Shell Oil's Search for Petroleum in the Postwar United States* (Texas A&M, 2007) and co-author of the forthcoming book *Deepwater Horizons: The Epic Struggles over Offshore Oil in the United States*. He also co-edited a June 2012 special issue of the *Journal of American History*, "Oil in American History."

Michaela Rife is a PhD candidate in art history at the University of Toronto. Her dissertation examines narratives of settler colonialism and extractive land use in New Deal post office murals on the Great Plains in the context of the Dust Bowl. She also researches and writes about the intersections between artists and resource extraction in the American West.

Sarah E. Robey is an assistant professor in the history of energy at Idaho State University. Her research focuses on the history of nuclear science and technology, Cold War citizenship and civic engagement, and the history of civil defense and emergency management. She has held positions at the National Museum of American History, the National Air and Space Museum, and the Miller Center for Public Affairs. Her forthcoming book, *Atomic Americans: Citizens in a Nuclear State*, will be published with Cornell University Press in 2022.

Emily Roehl is a cultural historian and artist who makes work about energy, media, and social justice. Roehl received her PhD in American studies from the University of Texas, and she is the co-founder of Mystery Spot Books, an artist book publisher that produces small-run artist books, zines, and other publications that trace the contours of place-based experience.

Teresa Sabol Spezio is a Redford Fellow in Applied Research at the Robert Redford Conservancy for Southern California Sustainability and an environmental consultant. She is the author of *Slick Policy: Environmental and Science Policy in the Aftermath of the Santa Barbara Oil Spill*. Her research explores the intersections between chemical pollution, containment, risk assessment, and environmental justice.

Sarah Stanford-McIntyre is an assistant professor in the Herbst Program for Engineering, Ethics & Society at the University of Colorado Boulder. Her work focuses on the social, political, and environmental history of energy infrastructures in the American Southwest. Her digital history work can be found at sstanfordmcintyre.com. Her writing has appeared in multiple edited volumes, and she has work published and forthcoming in *Technology and Culture*, *Environmental History*, *Labor: Studies in Working-Class History*, and *Agricultural History*. Her current book project examines the social and environmental impact of oil exploration on working-class Texas communities and on state politics.

Yuxun Willy Tan is a finance professional at Xcel Energy, an industry leader committed to building a carbon-free future. He previously worked in external audit at Deloitte and graduated with a BBA in accounting from the University of Iowa. As a certified public accountant, he continues to find ways to contextualize culturally significant historical events through the lens of accounting.

Ryan Driskell Tate is a climate and energy research analyst at Global Energy Monitor, where he oversees research on the coal industry. His research and commentary have appeared in the *Washington Post*, the *Economist*, the *Times of India*, the *Syndey Morning Herald*, and elsewhere. He holds a PhD in history from Rutgers University and previously held fellowships with the University of Wyoming and the University of Colorado Boulder.

Ila Tyagi is a writing lecturer at Yale-NUS College in Singapore. Her teaching and research interests include American cinema, the environmental humanities, and science and technology. She completed a PhD in film and media studies and American studies at Yale University in 2018. Her work has appeared in the media journal *Synoptique* and the edited collections *Ecocriticism and the Future of Southern Studies* (Louisiana State University Press, 2019) and *Make Waves: Water in Contemporary Literature and Film* (University of Nevada Press, 2019).

Conevery Bolton Valencius writes and teaches in the Boston College Department of History. She is the award-winning author of *The Lost History of the New Madrid Earthquakes* (2013) and *The Health of the Country: How American Settlers Understood Themselves and Their Land* (2002). Valencius is currently working with science journalist Anna Kuchment to write the history of how researchers in the past dozen years tried to figure out how contemporary energy extraction—especially fracking—is involved with the alarming rise of earthquakes in Oklahoma, Texas, Arkansas, and elsewhere in the American heartland.

Caleb Wellum is the Energy Futures Postdoctoral Fellow in the Department of Communication Arts, University of Waterloo, Canada. He is a historian of the twentieth century with particular interests in cultural, political, religious, and environmental history of the United States. Wellum is currently at work on a book linking the rise of neoliberalism to the 1970s energy crisis in the United States. He contributed to the collectively authored book *After Oil* and has published in *Environmental History* and *Enterprise and Society*.

Index

Page numbers in *italics* refer to figures and tables.

CPSIA information can be obtained
at www.ICGtesting.com
Printed in the USA
JSHW011548080123
35824JS00003B/12